American Sign Language:

a teacher's resource text on grammar and culture

by

Charlotte Baker
Dennis Cokely

Cover design by Eugene Orr
Drawings by Frank A. Paul
Photographs by Thomas Klagholz

T.J. PUBLISHERS, INC.
817 Silver Spring Avenue, 206
Silver Spring, Maryland 20910

First Printing   October 1980
Second Printing   September 1982
Third Printing   April 1986
Fourth Printing   July 1988

CONTENTS

PREFACE

This text is part of a total, multi-media package designed for the teacher and student of American Sign Language (ASL). Included in this package are two texts for teachers and three texts for students:

American Sign Language: a teacher's resource text on grammar and culture

American Sign Language: a teacher's resource text on curriculum, methods, and evaluation

American Sign Language: a student text (Units 1-9)

American Sign Language: a student text (Units 10-18)

American Sign Language: a student text (Units 19-27)

Also included in this package is a set of five one-hour videotapes which are especially designed to accompany these texts.

As a package, the texts and videotapes provide the teacher with information about the structure of ASL and an interactive approach to teaching the language. They provide the student with carefully prepared ASL dialogues and drills as well as information about the structure of ASL and the Deaf Community.

The videotapes are designed so that there is a one-hour tape for each text. The first tape illustrates all of the examples in the grammar and culture text. The second tape provides a 'live' demonstration of a number of the techniques described in the curriculum, methods, and evaluation text. Each of the final three tapes (one for each student text) not only illustrates the dialogues for a particular text but also provides several ASL stories, poems, and dramatic prose of varying lengths and difficulty for use in the classroom or language lab.

ACKNOWLEDGEMENTS

The thoughts, hard work, and creativity of many people have gone into the making of this text. Likewise, the endless support, patience, and encouragement of our colleagues, friends, and families have made it possible for us to stay with this project for the past two and a half years and see it through to completion.

Unfortunately, the list would be too long to meet "professional standards"(!) if we mentioned everyone here by name. But we would like to thank several of our colleagues for their invaluable assistance in preparing this text:

For their helpful and critical review of an early draft—Robbin Battison, Ursula Bellugi, Larry Berke, M. J. Bienvenu, Mel Carter Jr., Betty Colonomos, Larry Fleischer, Gus Johnson, Ella Mae Lentz, Marina McIntire, Carol Padden, Ken Rust, Bill Stokoe, "Woody" Woodward.

For their patience during long photo sessions and skill as models of ASL—two Deaf, native Signers: M. J. Bienvenu and Mel Carter, Jr.

For his unique artistic skills, beautiful illustrations, and willingness to change countless lines of brow raises, puffed cheeks, and 'mm' mouths—Frank A. Paul.

For her hard work and wonderfully expressive signing on the videotape of all the examples of ASL as well as her generous support in answering endless questions about her language—M. J. Bienvenu.

For their willingness to work long evening hours to verify the accuracy and common usage of more than 300 examples of ASL—five Deaf, native Signers: M. J. Bienvenu, Astrid Goodstein, Don Padden, Vance Rewolinski, Farley Warshaw.

For his "good eye" and many hours spent in producing all of the beautifully clear photographs of non-manual signals—Tom Klagholz.

For permission to use and adapt the Sign Language Bibliography—Larry Fleischer.

For permission to use the illustrations on pages 35 and 39—Ed Klima and Ursula Bellugi.

For her willingness to "pitch in" during the last minute chaos—Micky Cokely.

For service "above and beyond the call" and for his loving support—our *tech rep*, Bob Elwood.

Finally, for typing all of the many drafts and xeroxing countless pages, for life-giving back rubs and unfailing good cheer, and especially for putting up with our terrible sense of humor—Beverly Klayman.

Some of the information in this text comes from research done by one of the authors while working on a grant from the National Science Foundation. We are grateful for NSF's long-standing support for research on American Sign Language.

FOREWORD

These teacher texts—*American Sign Language: a teacher's resource text on grammar and culture* and *American Sign Language: a teacher's resource text on curriculum, methods, and evaluation*—are an outgrowth of the evolution of Sign Language instruction. The history of Sign Language instruction in the U.S. has been closely linked with the history of deaf education. In fact, there is reason to believe that Laurent Clerc began conducting Sign classes at the Hartford School in 1817. However, for the next 150 years the field remained fairly small and received little attention. Then in recent years, it experienced a spiraling growth and a rapid increase in the number of classes and students. Yet up till now the field of Sign Language instruction has been severely hampered by a lack of resource texts, videotapes, and other materials designed for the teachers of Sign Language. Especially lacking have been clear descriptions of the grammar of American Sign Language and appropriate methods for teaching it.

As Sign Language teachers, the two of us look back upon those days when we first began. We remember clearly that we were teaching simple sign equivalents for common English words. We remember noticing that our students could sign quite neatly but could hardly understand anything we signed. We also remember telling our students again and again to use their faces and bodies more; but much to our chagrin, they continued to sign like statues with movable arms. From time to time, we told ourselves, "Gee, there must be a better way than this. But this is all I know how to do and, besides, everyone else is doing the same thing I'm doing. (Sigh)" There were also times when our students battered us with questions about why a sign was formed in a particular way, or used in one context and not in another. We felt frustrated because we often were not confident in the answers that we gave them. And yet the students kept asking us more and more difficult questions.

Exercises developed in the field of drama gave us hope for helping our students become more flexible in using their bodies and faces. However, our hopes were shattered when the good results we obtained with these exercises were not carried over to the way the students communicated with signs. The activities were helpful, but not enough. Once again, we asked ourselves what was wrong.

Then, amazing and puzzling information on complicated phonological, morphological, and syntactic principles in our visual-gestural language began to pour out of linguistic research labs, shocking us. What had been referred to as "bad English", "true deaf signs" and "shortcut language" was actually a highly capable, complex, and independent language! These discoveries and linguistic descriptions instilled a strange feeling in us and in many other Deaf people. It stirred anew a confidence in ourselves as a people with dignity, viewing ourselves not as incapable but as *capable* people with a language and a culture that we can share proudly with speakers of other languages, as well as with future generations of deaf children.

Excited as we were about this information and reconfirmation in ourselves, we still had to proceed with the teaching of our classes. We wanted to share the information with our students, but how? We wanted the latest for our classes; we wanted the best for and from our students. We sat on the bleachers and rooted for the researchers, little comprehending their linguistic, psychological, and neurological theories or terminology. And as we began to understand, more questions haunted us: "How do we teach these new findings? Are the students ready? Are we ready? What do we teach first?"

We had to start somewhere—so we began by giving complicated grammatical explanations, followed by a few exercises to give the students a feel for Sign Language and then went on to more principles. The students, assuming from past exposure that Sign Language was "simple" and "fun", were amazed at the complexity and wealth of this visual-gestural language. However, as knowledgeable and respectful as they became about that language, they didn't become much better communicators. Instead, the students acted as quasi-linguists, attempting to analyze what we signed and what they signed—which created a slow and awkward communication process.

It soon became clear that our enthusiasm in accepting American Sign Language as a true language and our attempts to explain what we knew about its formal structure were not enough. Convinced that ASL is a language separate from English, it seemed logical to explore the methods that are used to teach foreign languages. There was a gold mine of established research, theories, and methods in the field of second/foreign language instruction. But we still needed more understandable descriptions of ASL. And we needed a way to successfully apply what we knew (and were learning) about second/foreign language instruction in order to help our students become competent communicators in ASL.

These problems highlighted the need for Sign Language teachers to exchange ideas and information with each other and to receive basic training in methods that could be used for teaching ASL. In late 1978, the Rehabilitation Services Administration contracted with the National Consortium of Programs for the Training of Sign Language Instructors. Two primary goals for the Consortium were to create better communication and exchange of ideas among instructors and to develop a standard basic training curriculum for current and prospective instructors.

Concurrently, two of the foremost experts in the areas of Sign Language research, instruction, and evaluation began work on this comprehensive set of teacher resource texts, videotapes, and student texts. The authors then dedicated more than two hard years toward preparing these materials. These authors, both hearing individuals, have been extremely careful and conscientious in attempting to verify and confirm their linguistic description of ASL and their interactive approach for teaching it. A group of 15 Sign Language teachers and linguists—both Deaf and hearing—were asked to review and comment on the manuscripts for these texts. This unusual step is a tribute to the authors' sensitivity and desire to provide the best possible materials to date for Sign Language teachers. They have made a new beginning in the history of Sign Language instruction. They have paved the road so we, instructors, can travel with more ease and confidence.

The Communicative Skills Program of the National Association of the Deaf is most enthusiastic about the long-awaited arrival of these materials for the teaching of Sign Language, because they are written with Sign Language instructors in mind. As a set, the two teacher texts offer the most thorough and clear description of

ASL currently available for Sign Language teachers as well as an effective method for teaching and evaluating ASL as a second/foreign language.

For the first time, Sign Language instructors have materials especially prepared for them which address the questions of what is ASL and how to teach it. "What is ASL?" is addressed in the teacher text on grammar and culture. Drawing upon available linguistic research and their own resources, the authors present a clear and detailed explanation of major grammatical features of ASL, accompanied by some of the finest and most accurate line drawings of signs we have seen. "How to teach ASL?" is addressed in the teacher text on methods, curriculum, and evaluation. Drawing upon theories and methods developed in the field of second/foreign language teaching as well as their own experience, the authors present an interactive approach to teaching and evaluating ASL, which is supported by numerous activities, techniques, and a well-thought-out, six-course curriculum. This interactive approach is based on an untraditional (in our field) but logical idea—the instructor should teach Sign without voice and without English equivalents, using only gestures and American Sign Language.

In our personal experience as Sign instructors searching for more successful ways to teach our classes, we have experimented with this untraditional approach. The results have been amazing. We could see the students *really* learning the language, and developing *real* confidence in their faces and bodies (often unconsciously). Every time we left the classroom, we felt delighted at the results. We were reaching our primary objective—producing *real* communicators.

As program developers and administrators concerned with the implementation of quality programs, we consider these texts and this approach as a significant step forward in the process of refining the instruction of ASL. We hope you will find this approach exciting and fruitful, too.

Through the National Consortium of Programs for the Training of Sign Language Instructors, we anticipate increased communication among Sign Language teachers and the development of quality teacher training programs. With the success of these programs and the widespread use of the comprehensive materials provided by the authors, Sign Language instructors will be better prepared to meet the challenge of instilling in their students a respect for the language and culture of Deaf people and an ability to successfully communicate with members of the Deaf community.

With great respect for signers who are the source of inspiration for Sign Language teaching and an appreciation for all those Sign Language teachers who have been a part of the evolution of Sign instruction, we recommend this set of teacher resource texts. We commend the authors for their vision, dedication, and love in bringing them to completion.

S. Melvin Carter, Jr.   Ella Mae Lentz

Director   Project Coordinator
Communicative Skills Program   National Consortium of Programs
National Association of the Deaf   for the Training of
                                                 Sign Language Instructors
                                             National Association of the Deaf

INTRODUCTION

Background Information

During the past decade, linguistic research on American Sign Language (ASL) has blossomed. There are now research labs at Gallaudet College, Northeastern University, and the Salk Institute for Biological Studies as well as numerous individuals across the country who are actively involved in studying the linguistic structure of ASL and how the language is used by members of the American Deaf Community.

However, much of this exciting new information about American Sign Language has been circulated in the form of conference papers and unpublished manuscripts. Researchers have regularly shared these papers with each other, but, in general, the information has not been readily available to teachers and other users of the language. In addition, a majority of these research papers and other materials have been written in a "jargon" that is unfamiliar and difficult for most non-researchers to understand. Thus, although many teachers and other users of American Sign Language have expressed a strong desire to learn about the results of linguistic research on ASL, they have often been unable to acquire this information in a form that they could understand and use.

With this in mind, in 1977, T. J. O'Rourke, then Director of the Communicative Skills Program at the National Association of the Deaf, approached one of the authors of this text and asked her to write a teacher's manual based on a two-week workshop that she had given with Ella Lentz for Sign Language teachers in California. This manual was supposed to provide teachers with information about the structure of American Sign Language and help them become familiar with some of the terminology used by linguists to describe the language. That way, teachers could "catch up" with what had been happening in linguistic research as well as be better prepared to read other published and unpublished materials.

As work progressed on that manual, the authors began to feel that it would also be helpful to include an explanation of how to use this information about the structure of American Sign Language in the classroom. This would involve an explanation of methods for teaching ASL as a language with its own grammatical structure (not just vocabulary), an explanation of how to evaluate students' progress in learning the language, and a description of how to design program and course curricula which would most effectively assist students in becoming successful communicators in ASL. Gradually, what began as a few "extra chapters" grew into the companion teacher text on *Curriculum, Methods, and Evaluation*.

Similarly, as work progressed on these texts, the authors began to feel that it would also be helpful to have materials designed especially for students—materials that teachers could use *interactively* with students in ways that were being described in the teacher text on *Curriculum, Methods, and Evaluation*. These materials would need to supply students with information about the grammatical structure of American Sign Language as well as provide ways for them to develop skills in using the language. Hence, the companion student texts were developed to complement the information provided in the teacher text on *Grammar and Culture* and the methods and curriculum described in the other teacher text.

However, with the excitement of preparing this comprehensive package of materials for teachers and students of ASL came the weighty responsibility of insuring their accuracy and usefulness. Thus, the authors sought out the help of 15 of the nation's leading Sign Language researchers and teachers (including 8 native ASL Signers). Over the past two years, these experts have critiqued the manuscripts of the teacher texts to make them clear and accurate. In addition, all of the examples of ASL (approximately 300) that appear in the *Grammar and Culture* text have been carefully examined and verified as grammatically correct ASL by a team of 5 Deaf native Signers of different ages (ranging from 25–59) and geographic backgrounds (from Louisiana, Pennsylvania, Illinois, Nebraska, and Oregon). This team of native Signers viewed a videotape of the examples and individually scored each of them for their accuracy, frequency of occurrence in ASL, and corresponding meaning in English. Thus, although new information from future research on ASL will undoubtedly necessitate revisions of these texts, they do at present represent the "state of the art" concerning what is known so far about the grammar of American Sign Language and how to teach it.

The Grammar and Culture Text: what it is

This text provides a summary of what is presently known about the structure of American Sign Language as well as a description of the people who use that language—the American Deaf Community. It is written specifically for Sign Language teachers who have little or no training in linguistics. As such, every attempt has been made to avoid unnecessary linguistic terminology or to clearly explain the meaning of any terms which *are* needed to describe the structure of ASL. The authors have also tried to be sensitive to the fact that many of the people who will read this text will not be native users of English.

This text begins with a detailed description of the symbols which are used in the text to transcribe examples of ASL sentences. This is a very important section and should be read very carefully. Most of the grammatical descriptions of ASL in this text are based on actual examples which are "written" with the transcription symbols. Thus, to fully understand the descriptions of various grammatical features, teachers will need to be able to "read" the examples—and then be able to sign them for themselves. (A videotape of all of the examples is also available to facilitate reading the transcriptions.)

The first three chapters in this text provide background information on things that are found in all spoken and signed languages, on the history of ASL and life in the Deaf Community, and on the relationship between ASL, English, and English-like forms of signing in the Deaf Community. Chapter IV describes how signs are made, how they change over time, and how Signers with different backgrounds may vary in the kinds of signs that they use. Chapter V focuses on several types of signs—nouns and verbs, compounds and contractions, fingerspelled loan signs—and explores the question of what *is* and *is not* an idiom in ASL.

The final nine chapters are the "grammatical chapters" which correspond to the nine units in each of the three student texts. These chapters provide an in-depth description of the major grammatical features of ASL with numerous illustrations and examples. Each of the examples is transcribed from the corresponding videotape of a Deaf, native ASL Signer.

At the end of each chapter, there are three dialogues which illustrate how the grammatical features that are described in that chapter may be used in a conversation. The first dialogue after each chapter also occurs in the first student text (Units 1-9). The second dialogue after each chapter also occurs in the second student text (Units 10-18); the third dialogue after each chapter also occurs in the third student text (Units 19-27). The transcriptions of the dialogues show how they are signed on the corresponding videotapes. These transcriptions are more detailed in this text (than in the student texts) to provide the teacher with more information which s/he may or may not decide to use as the students work with the dialogues.

The topic of each dialogue focuses on some aspect of the Deaf Community. These topics are explored in more depth in separate essays which follow the dialogues. The essays also appear in the corresponding student texts.

The bibliography which follows each of the grammatical chapters includes articles or books which the authors have read and used in writing these chapters. Other published materials on related topics can be found in the Sign Language Bibliography after the last grammatical chapter.

The Grammar and Culture Text: what it isn't

This text is intended to be a "resource" text, not a comprehensive book on "everything you ever wanted to know about ASL". There are some obvious things missing in this text. For example, it doesn't describe how to 'count' in ASL or how to 'tell time' (although this occurs in several examples which focus on other things). Teachers will need to fill in these gaps with their own knowledge or with other materials.

This text does not provide a description of the way all ASL Signers sign. In part, this is because most of the research on ASL has focused on how White, middle class Deaf Signers use ASL—and most of these people are students or graduates of Gallaudet College! Wherever possible, this text tries to include information about variations in the grammar and vocabulary of different groups of people, but it still primarily focuses on the form of ASL used by one particular group. (To be clear, this is *not* because the signing of Gallaudet students is in any way 'superior' to any other form of signing, but is simply because Gallaudet Signers have generally been more accessible to researchers who have been studying ASL.)

This text isn't always consistent in the way it describes the grammatical features of ASL. Some chapters are more detailed than others; some provide more clear 'generalizations' and 'rules' than others. Often, this is because more is known about one topic than another. Even the transcriptions of examples are not always consistent. Sometimes this is because the authors felt the examples would be too difficult to understand if written in a particular way; at other times, the authors weren't sure about how to best transcribe a particular sign or grammatical feature. This text "breaks a lot of ground". Many things in it are new and need to be tested over time.

Parting Comments

We feel it will be most helpful to read this book from beginning to end and not skip over certain chapters or read them in a different order. Often, information provided in one chapter is necessary to understand the next chapter.

We suggest that you try to sign each of the examples as you read them, perhaps signing them several times until you recognize how each example illustrates the particular grammatical feature that is being described.

You may also find it helpful to talk through each chapter with other teachers who are reading the book. The information in each chapter is often complex, and it helps to share your questions as well as your insights and understanding with other people who are thinking about the same things.

Sometimes you may find it helpful to come back to certain sections after you have read some of the other chapters. So much in a language is interrelated: to understand one thing, you have to understand another thing—but to understand that thing, you have to understand something else . . . And ASL is certainly no different! When you have a greater understanding of the "whole", then it is easier to understand each "piece" of that whole.

We hope this text will be a valuable resource to you as you teach American Sign Language. We hope it will help "crystallize" many of the things you have already thought about or felt about ASL. We also hope you will share with us any of the ways you feel this text can be improved to better serve your needs and the needs of other teachers.

In writing this text, we have been continually fascinated (and frustrated!) by the tremendous complexity of American Sign Language with its wonderfully creative use of space and movement. Our respect and awe of this language has increased daily as we have tried to understand its structure and the richly expressive ways that Deaf people communicate with each other. We hope that, like us, you and your students will come to feel that sense of awe and appreciation of the language of the Deaf Community.

August 1, 1980   Charlotte Baker
Washington, D.C.   Dennis Cokely

Transcription Symbols

In order to understand the information in this text, you will need to read through the following 29 pages very carefully. These pages describe and illustrate the *transcription symbols* that are used throughout this text.

You are probably well aware of the tremendous difficulties one faces when trying to "write ASL". To date, there is no standard way of *writing* sentences in a signed language. This lack of a standard transcription system (a system for writing or transcribing ASL) poses major problems when trying to write a book about ASL. In order to write about the grammatical structure of the language, it is necessary to provide many examples of sentences in ASL and then describe what's in them.

For this text, we have tried to develop a transcription system that clearly shows the reader just how much information is in an ASL sentence. We have used many of the symbols that are used by linguists who study ASL. We hope this will help the reader become more comfortable in the future when reading articles and books written by these linguists. However, none of the transcription systems that are currently used in linguistic research on ASL are complete. None of these systems 'capture' all of the linguistic information that is communicated in ASL sentences. This is because we still have much to learn about the language and we still either miss a lot of the information or don't know how to write it down.

At first, the transcription system developed for this text may seem very complex. Many of the symbols may be unfamiliar to you, and trying to learn and understand all of these symbols will require some real effort. However, as you see them again and again in different sentences in the text, they will become more familiar and easier to understand quickly. That's a promise! A group of Sign Language teachers have already successfully learned this system on their own by working with it. The first step is a bit of a struggle—and then it gets easier and easier.

In the following pages, you will see a chart which lists approximately 30 symbols and provides an example and explanation of each symbol. While reading the chart, you should look at the illustrations on the opposite page to see how the symbols describe what the sign is doing. These symbols are used to describe what the *hands* do. Then you will see a list of symbols that are used to describe what the *eyes, face, head,* and *body* do. These symbols for *non-manual signals* are illustrated with photographs.

After you have read through the brief explanations of all of these symbols, we will 'talk through' some actual ASL sentences. These sentences are written down with the *manual* and *non-manual* symbols, and are also illustrated in drawings—so you can compare the written form of the sentence with the actual signing of the sentence.

As you read through the chart and the explanation of each symbol, if you come across unfamiliar terms, check the glossary in the back of the text for definitions.

ILLUSTRATIONS

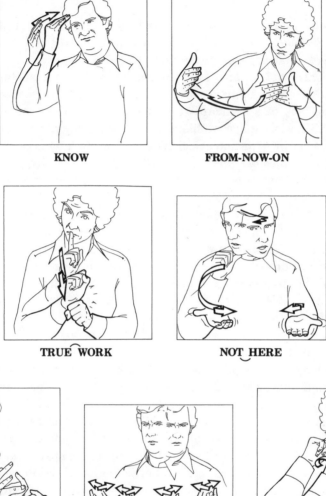

KNOW   FROM-NOW-ON

TRUE WORK   NOT HERE

#WHAT   DIFFERENT+++   BORED*

TRANSCRIPTION SYMBOLS

Symbol	Example	Explanation
CAPITAL LETTERS	KNOW	An English word in capital letters represents an ASL sign; this word is called a *gloss*.
-	FROM-NOW-ON	When more than one English word is needed to gloss an ASL sign, the English words are separated by a hyphen.
-	P-A-T	When an English word is fingerspelled, the letters in the word are separated by a hyphen.
⌢	TRUE⌢WORK	When two glosses are joined by this curved line, it indicates a *compound* sign. (See Chapter V)
⌣	NOT⌣HERE	When two glosses are joined by this curved line, it indicates a *contraction*. (See Chapter V)
#	#WHAT	When this symbol is written before a gloss, it indicates the sign is a fingerspelled loan sign. (See Chapter V)
+	DIFFERENT+++	When a plus sign follows a gloss, this indicates the sign is repeated. The number of plus signs following the gloss indicates the number of repetitions—e.g. DIFFERENT+++ indicates the sign was made four times (three repetitions).
*	BORED*	An asterisk after a gloss indicates the sign is stressed (emphasized).

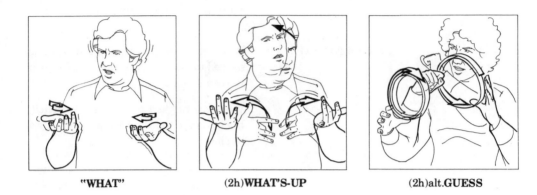

"WHAT"   (2h)WHAT'S-UP   (2h)alt.GUESS

BECOME-SICK*"regularly"*   LOOK-AT*"each other"*   CORRESPOND-WITH*"each other"*+*"regularly"*

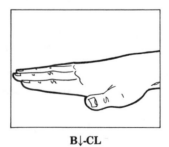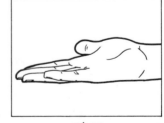

3-CL   B↓-CL   B↑-CL

Symbol	Example	Explanation
( )	**(ME)**	Parentheses around a gloss indicate that sign is optional in the sentence; one could sign that sentence without the sign written in parenthesis.
,	**YESTERDAY, ME**	A comma indicates a syntactic break, signaled by a body shift and/or a change in facial expression (and usually a pause). (See Chapter VI)
" "	**"WHAT"**	Double quotes around a gloss indicate a *gesture*.
(2h)	**(2h)WHAT'S-UP**	This symbol for 'two hands' is written before a gloss and means the sign is made with both hands.
alt.	**(2h)alt.GUESS**	The symbol 'alt.' means that the hands move in an 'alternating' manner.
" "	"open window"	Double quotes around a word or words in lower case indicate a mimed action.
" "	**BECOME-SICK***"regularly"* **LOOK-AT***"each other"*	Double quotes around an italicized word or words in lower case (after a gloss) indicate a specific modulation of that sign. The word or words inside the parentheses is the name for that specific modulation. (See Chapters IX, X, XIII, XIV)
" "+" "	**CORRESPOND-WITH** *"each other"+"regularly"*	When a plus sign joins two or more modulations, it means those modulations occur simultaneously with that sign.
-CL	3-CL	This symbol for *classifier* is written after the symbol for the handshape that is used in that classifier. (See Chapter X)
↓	**B↓-CL**	An arrow pointing downward indicates that the palm is facing downward.
↑	**B↑-CL**	An arrow pointing upward indicates that the palm is facing upward.

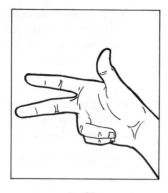

3→CL

L:-CL

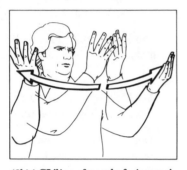

(2h)4-CL'line of people facing me'

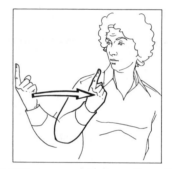

1-CL'person come up to me from rt'

1outline-CL'circular table'

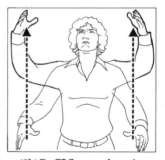

(2h)Ct-CL'huge column'

Symbol	Example	Explanation
→	3→CL	An arrow pointing to the right indicates that the fingers are not facing upwards. This is used to distinguish two sets of classifiers: **3-CL** and **3→CL**; **1-CL** and **1→CL**.
:	L:-CL	This symbol indicates that the hand-shape is 'bent'—as in a 'bent-L' hand-shape where the index finger is crooked, rather than straight.
' '	(2h)**4-CL**'line of people' **1-CL**'person come up to me'	Single quotes around a lower case word or words is used to help describe the meaning of a classifier in the context of a particular sentence.
outline	**1**_{outline}**-CL**'circular table'	This symbol indicates that the hand-shape is used to 'outline' a particular shape. (See Chapter X)
t	(2h)**C**_t**-CL**'huge column'	This symbol indicates that both hands in the classifier move or act 'together' to describe the referent—i.e. both hands have equal value and there is no 'dominant' hand. (See Chapter X)

*rt-**ASK-TO**-lf*

ASSEMBLE-TO-*cntr*

*pat-**ASK-TO**-lee*

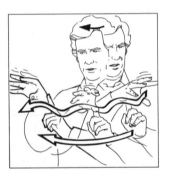

*me-**CAMERA-RECORD**-arc*

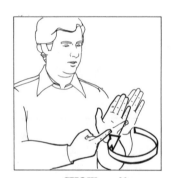

*me-**SHOW**-arc-lf*

Symbol	Example	Explanation
rt *lf* *cntr*	*rt*-**ASK-TO**-*lf* **ASSEMBLE-TO**-*cntr*	The symbol *'rt'* stands for 'right'; *'lf'* for 'left'; and *'cntr'* for 'center'. When a sign is made *in* or *toward* a particular location in space, that place or direction is indicated after the gloss. When a symbol like *'rt'* is written before a gloss, it indicates the location where the sign began. So *rt*-**GO-TO**-*lf* indicates that the sign moves from right to left. These symbols refer to the Signer's perspective—e.g. *'rt'* means to the Signer's right. The symbol *'cntr'* is only used when that space directly between the Signer and Addressee represents a particular referent (person, place, or thing). If none of these symbols appear, the sign is produced in neutral space. (See Chapter IX)
lower case words	*pat*-**ASK-TO**-*lee*	Italicized words that are connected (via hyphens) to the gloss for a verb can also indicate the location where the verb began or ended. For example, if 'Pat' has been given a spatial location on the right, and 'Lee' is on the left, then the sign *pat*-**ASK-TO**-*lee* will move from right to left. These specific words are not used until the things they represent have been given a spatial location. These specific words are used in place of directions like *'rt'* or *'lf'*.
___- -___	___-**GO-TO**-___ ___-**ASK-TO**-___	A blank line before and after a verb indicates that the verb is *directional*. These lines are only used in the text when discussing a particular verb and are not used in example sentences. In sentences, the blank lines are replaced by words, as shown above. (See Chapter IX)
arc	*me*-**CAMERA-RECORD**-*arc* *me*-**SHOW**-*arc*-*lf*	When a gloss is followed by the symbol *'arc'*, it means the sign moves in a horizontal arc from one side of the signing space to the other side. If another symbol like *'lf'* follows the symbol *'arc'*, it means the arc only includes that part of the signing space (See Chapters VIII, XII)

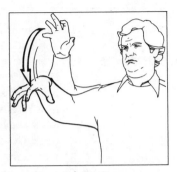

5:↓-CL@*rt*

COMMUTE-BETWEEN-*here* & *rt*↔

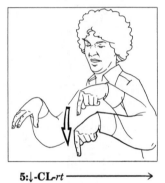

5:↓-**CL**-*rt* ⟶
INDEX-*down,lf*

Symbol	Example	Explanation
@	5:↓-CL@*rt*	This symbol indicates a particular type of movement that is often used when giving something a spatial location. It is characterized by a certain tenseness and a 'hold' at the end of the movement. In this example, the classifier for a large mass is given a spatial location to the Signer's right. (See Chapter X)
↔	**COMMUTE-BETWEEN-** *here* & *rt*↔ **INDEX-***lf* & *rt*↔	This symbol indicates a back-and-forth movement of the sign between two spatial locations. In the second example, the index finger points back and forth between a location on the left and a location on the right.
CAPITAL LETTERS	**RESTAURANT** *INDEX-lf*	When a sign is made with the non-dominant hand, it is written in italics. When an italicized gloss is written under another gloss, it means both hands make separate signs at the same time. In this example, the dominant hand makes the sign **RESTAURANT** while the non-dominant hand points to the left.
⟶	5:↓-CL-*rt* ⟶ *INDEX-down,lf*	An arrow proceeding from a gloss indicates the handshape of that sign is held in its location during the time period shown with the arrow. In this example, the dominant hand 'holds' the 5:↓ classifier in its location on the right while the non-dominant hand points down (on the left side) with the index finger.

In the next section, you will see a list of symbols that we use to describe various *non-manual* signals in ASL. These signals are made with specific movements of the eyes, face, head, and/or body. Some of the signals function as *grammatical* signals—for example, showing that a sentence is a question. These grammatical signals are described in Chapter VI. Other signals that function as *adverbs* and *adjectives* are described in this section.

We write the symbol for each non-manual signal on top of a line that is right above a gloss or series of glosses. This means that the signal occurs with all of the signs written below the line. The symbol for the non-manual signal is written above the line on the far right, as illustrated below. (The 'q' symbol stands for a particular type of 'question'.)

$$\overline{\text{WANT} \quad \text{LEAVE-TO-}rt}^{\text{q}}$$

'Do you want to leave?'

Sometimes you will also see lower case words or letters that are written inside parentheses above a gloss or series of glosses. These words indicate other non-manual behaviors that occur with that sign or group of signs. These words are frequently used to show the 'gaze' (direction of eye gaze), 'head', and 'body' behaviors of the Signer. For example, in the sentence below, the Signer turns his/her head to the right and looks to the right while signing **LEAVE-TO-**rt.

$$\overline{\text{WANT} \quad \text{LEAVE-TO-}rt}^{\text{(head, gaze rt)q}}$$

'Do you want to leave?'

If there is more than one non-manual signal that occurs with a sign or group of signs, the symbols (for these signals) are written together with a plus sign, as illustrated below. (The *'neg'* symbol stands for 'negation'.)

$$\overline{\text{WANT} \quad \text{LEAVE-TO-}rt}^{\text{neg+q}}$$

'Don't you want to leave?'

All of the symbols listed below represent non-manual grammatical signals that are described in Chapter VI. The symbols are listed on the left and their corresponding signals are illustrated in photos on the right. The gloss for each sign is written below the photograph of that sign. (Although the photographs do not adequately show the *movement* of the signs and non-manual signals, they are used here to give more detailed and exact information about what the eyes, face, head, and body 'look like' when making these signals.)

TRANSCRIPTION SYMBOLS   ILLUSTRATIONS

q (*'yes-no question'*)

(See Chapter VI, p. 122)

(These photos also illustrate what is meant by a 'brow raise', often written as *'br raise'* or simply, *'br'*.)

$$\overline{\text{YOU}}^{\text{q}} \qquad \overline{\text{YOU}}^{\text{q}}$$

wh-q (*'wh-word question'*)

(See Chapter VI, p. 128)

(These photos also illustrate what is meant by a 'brow squint', often written as *'br squint'*.)

$$\overline{\text{WHO}}^{\text{wh-q}} \qquad \overline{\text{WHICH}}^{\text{wh-q}}$$

$$\overline{\text{WHERE}}^{\text{wh-q}}$$

rhet.q *('rhetorical question')*
(See Chapter VI, p. 137)

rhet.q
WHO

rhet.q
WHY

rhet.q
HOW

neg (*'negation'*)
(See Chapter VI, p. 145)
(Signal includes head-shaking, not visible in photographs)

$$\frac{\text{neg}}{\textbf{NOT}}$$

$$\frac{\text{neg}}{\textbf{ME}}$$

$$\frac{\text{neg}}{\textbf{FEEL}}$$

$$\frac{\text{neg}}{\textbf{FEEL}}$$

nod+tight lips (*'assertion'*)
(See Chapter VI, p. 155)
(The 'nod' is more visible in drawings in the text.)

$$\frac{\text{nod+tight lips}}{\textbf{TRUE}}$$

t (*'topic'*)

   (See Chapter VI, p. 156)

$$\overline{\text{MORNING}}^{\;t} \qquad\qquad \overline{\text{PAPER}}^{\;t}$$

Notice the difference be-
tween the *'t'* signal and
the *'q'* signal in the two
photos on the right.

$$\overline{\text{PAPER}}^{\;t} \qquad\qquad \overline{\text{PAPER}}^{\;q}$$

cond (*'conditional'*)

   (See Chapter VI, p. 141)

   Conditionals have two
parts. The first part
is indicated with *'cond'*.
The sequence on the
right illustrates the
conditional sentence
'If it rains, I'll go'.

$$\overset{\text{cond}}{\overline{\text{RAIN}}} \qquad\qquad\qquad\qquad \textbf{GO-}\textit{lf}$$

rel.cl (*'relative clause'*)

(See Chapter VI, p. 163)

The sequence on the right illustrates the relative clause 'The woman who is off her rocker (crazy) . . .'

rel.cl
WOMAN

rel.cl
MIND WARPED[1]

In the next section, you will see a list of symbols that are used in this text to represent various non-manual adverbs and adjectives. Some of these non-manual signals have been studied more than some of the other signals, so their description is more detailed. This is by no means a full listing of all of the non-manual adverbs and adjectives in ASL, but this is a list of the signals found in sentences in this text. Next to the symbol for each non-manual signal, you will see a description of the approximate meaning of the signal, followed by one or more illustrations of what it looks like. At the end of this section, there are a few illustrations of *combinations* of the non-manual signals that are described here and in the preceding section.

---

[1]This sign could also be glossed as the compound **MIND AWRY**. However, we have chosen the other gloss because it is more familiar.

> **cs** 'very close to the present time'
>   'very close to a particular place'
>   (See Chapter VII, p. 177)

In the illustrations below, notice that the *'cs'* signal used by the male Signer in these photos is more intense than the *'cs'* signal used by the female Signer. (Also notice the variation in handshape on the sign **NOW**.) The *'cs'* signal can also be used with signs like **HERE** (meaning 'right here') or **INDEX**-*rt* (meaning 'right there; close by').

cs
NOW
'right now'

cs
ARRIVE-AT-*here*
'just arrived'

cs
NOW
'right now'

cs
ARRIVE-AT-*here*
'just arrived'

th 'without paying attention'
'carelessly'

th
DRIVE
'drive without attending to what's going on'

th
WRITE
'write carelessly'

mm 'normally; regularly'
'things going along fine, as expected'

mm
DRIVE
'drive along regularly'

mm
WRITE
'write at a regular pace'

puff.cheeks 'a lot; huge number of'
'large; huge'
'of great magnitude'

In the photos below, notice that the male's expression is more intense than the female's; he is indicating an even larger mass of things. (The sign glossed here as **SCADS-OF** is made with 'bent-5' classifiers that move outward.)

<u>puff.cheeks</u>
SCADS-OF
'very large mass of'

<u>puff.cheeks</u>
SCADS-OF
'very large mass of'

intense 'awfully large; surprisingly huge'
'of awfully great magnitude'
'to an unusually great degree'

As you can see, the meanings of the *puff.cheeks* and *intense* signals are similar. However, there seems to be a feeling that the amount, size, or degree is much greater than expected when the *intense* signal is used. For example, although it would be possible to use a combined *mm+puff.cheeks* signal with the sign shown below (meaning 'a very large mass whose size is what was expected or is normal'), the *'mm'* signal with the *intense* signal would be contradictory and does not occur in ASL. Some Signers say they have a negative feeling about the thing's size, etc., when they use the *intense* signal—like it's too large, too far, too many, etc.

<u>intense</u>
SCADS-OF
'awfully huge mass of'

<u>intense</u>
SCADS-OF
'awfully huge mass of'

intense
INDEX-*up,rt*
'incredibly far away'

pursed lips 'very small, thin, narrow'
'smooth'
'quickly; easily'

As you can see, there seem to be several different meanings of this signal. And its actual meaning seems to be determined by the context in which the *'pursed lips'* signal is used. However, as you study the photographs, notice that the lips are slightly different when referring to the 'thin (wire)' as opposed to the 'smooth (floor)' or the 'fast (runner)'. It is possible that there are actually two different signals here, but this needs to be studied more. (Also notice the variation in handshape used by the two Signers when referring to the 'thin wire'.) Finally, as we saw in the illustrations of the *'puff.cheeks'* signal, Signers can vary the intensity of these signals to show varying degrees of that adverb or adjective. This is seen again in the two photos of the male Signer ('thin wire')—where the signal shown on the right is more intense. These photos ('thin wire') also illustrate what is meant by an *'eye squint'*.

pursed lips
(2h)G_t-CL

'very thin wire'

pursed lips
(2h)G_t-CL

'*very* thin wire'

pursed lips
(2h)F$_t$-CL
'very thin wire'

pursed lips
(2h)B-CL
'smooth floor'

pursed lips
FAST
'very fast'

sta 'over and over again'
'too much; hard'

The tense mouth and head movement of the *'sta'* signal is repeated several times, as the sign is repeated. The two-part illustration here shows the *'sta'* signal with a modulation of the sign **WORK**.

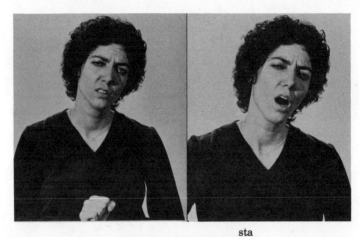

sta

WORK"*over & over again*"
'work hard again and again'

The next three signals (*'pah'*, *'pow'*, *'cha'*) have not been studied enough to be able to adequately describe their meanings. They are simply illustrated below so you will recognize what the symbols refer to. Each of these three signals involves a sudden, tense opening of the mouth.

pah

SUCCESS

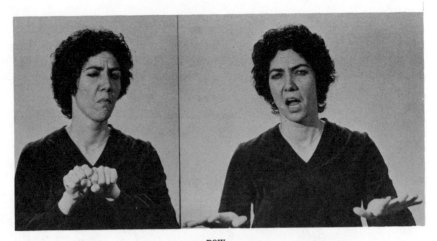

$$\overline{\text{SPLATTER}}^{\text{pow}}$$

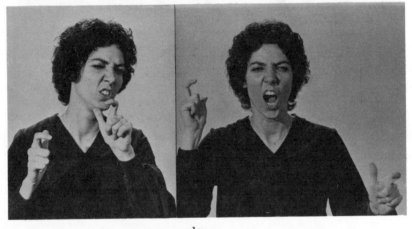

$$\overline{\text{HUGE}}^{\text{cha}}$$

As the next two sets of illustrations show, more than one non-manual signal can occur at a time. Sometimes when two or more signals occur at the same time, they change what each individual signal normally looks like. For example, as illustrated on the next page, the *'puff.cheeks'* signal normally includes a narrowing of the Signer's eyes. But the *'q'* signal involves a widening of the eyes. So when these two signals are combined, that part of the *'puff.cheeks'* signal is changed.

<u>puff.cheeks</u>
SCADS-OF

<u>puff.cheeks+q</u>
SCADS-OF

Similarly, the *'q'* signal involves a raising of the Signer's brows. But the *'neg'* signal lowers and draws the brows together (*brow squint*). So when these two signals occur together, the Signer's brows are both drawn together and raised. (Compare the Signer's brows during the *'neg+q'* signal illustrated below with her brows during the *'puff.cheeks+q'* signal illustrated above.)

<u>neg</u>
NOT

<u>neg+q</u>
NOT

One last symbol that is used frequently throughout the text is *'co'*—which stands for "conversation opener". Obviously, a Signer must get a person's visual attention before s/he can successfully begin a conversation with that person. There are a variety of ways to do this.[2] Some of these 'attention-getters' involve waving at the person, touching the person on the shoulder or arm, or beginning with an emotion-related sign—where the movement and affect of the sign will 'grab' the person's attention. Some of the signs often used like this are **THRILL, AWFUL, FINE,**

---

[2]These ways to get and 'hold' a person's attention are described in more detail in the companion teacher text on *Curriculum, Methods, and Evaluation* (Chapter VI).

BEAUTIFUL, CRAZY, and **DISGUST**. Once the Signer has that person's attention (and curiosity), s/he can then begin to describe what is 'awful', 'beautiful', or 'disgusting'. In the text, we show when signs or gestures are being used to get a person's attention by writing the symbol '*co*' above the gloss for that sign or gesture. Some of these conversation openers are illustrated below.

co
"SHOULDER-TAP"

co
AWFUL

co
"HEY"

co
FINE

Now that you have read through the list of symbols that we use to transcribe ASL sentences, let's try them out on a few sample sentences. As you will see in the text, each time sentences in ASL are transcribed, they are preceded by a *Context* and followed by what we call an approximate *structural equivalent* (written as *Struc*) and a *translation* (written as *Trans*).

The *context* is supposed to provide information about a situation in which those sentences might naturally occur. The approximate *structural equivalent* is an attempt to show in English the basic structure of each ASL sentence—to show the ordering of ideas and how much information is in each sentence. Because the approximate *structural equivalent* is written in English, it can not be an *exact* structural equivalent of each ASL sentence; the structures of the two languages do not match. However, it *is* an approximation—which we think will help show how ideas are organized in ASL sentences and how much information is conveyed with each sentence. The *translation* attempts to give an equivalent meaning of the ASL sentences and show how that meaning would naturally be expressed in English in a style that is appropriate for that context.

Sometimes the approximate *structural equivalent* and the *translation* are very similar because English would use a similar structure to convey that meaning. Sometimes they are quite different. Sometimes the approximate *structural equivalent* conveys more information than the *translation* because English speakers would not provide as much information in that context. Sometimes a particular English word or words are used in the *structural equivalent* and a different English word or words are used in the *translation*. Often this is done to show different alternative translations of a particular ASL sign or group of signs.

The signs used in the first sample sentence are illustrated below in the order in which they occur (left to right). In the same way, the transcription of those signs follows the order in which they occur (left to right). In this example, the Signer uses the conversation opener **"HEY"** to get the friend's attention and then asks a 'wh-word question'.

| "HEY" | WHAT'S-UP | (2h)"WHAT" |

Context   The Signer is walking in the hall and sees a friend angrily rush out of a meeting room. The Signer says:

(1)
$$\overline{\text{"HEY",}} \quad \overline{\text{WHAT'S-UP} \quad \text{(2h)"WHAT"}}$$
co . . . . wh-q

    Struc   'Hey! What's up? What is it?'

    Trans   'Hey! What's going on? Huh?'

The illustrations of signs in the next example are also shown in the order in which they occur (left to right in each row). (Sometimes the angle used to draw the illustrations varies in order to more clearly show what the hands are doing. As a result, sometimes it looks like the Signer's hands or eye gaze are doing something different than what is written down. But this is actually due to the angle at which the signs are drawn.)

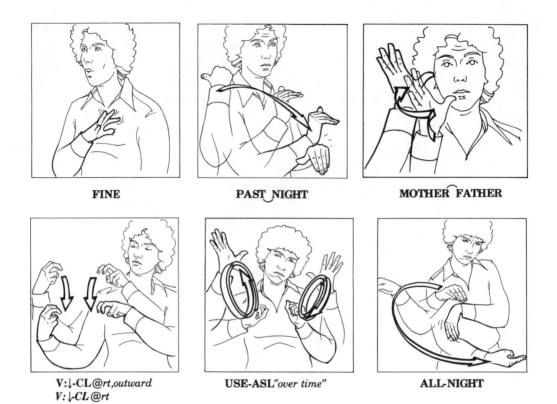

FINE   PAST NIGHT   MOTHER FATHER

V:↓-CL@rt,outward   USE-ASL"over time"   ALL-NIGHT
V:↓-CL@rt

Context   The Signer's parents have not been getting along very well and not communicating much with each other. Then one night they finally do some
real talking. So the Signer tells her girlfriend:

(2)
          co   t
      FINE, PAST NIGHT MOTHER FATHER,

      (gaze rt   )   puff.cheeks
      V:↓-CL@rt,outward }'sit facing each other'   USE-ASL"over time" ALL-NIGHT
      V:↓-CL@rt   }

    Struc   'It was great! Last night my parents, they sat down facing each
             other and did a lot of signing throughout the whole night long.'

    Trans   'It was terrific! Last night my parents sat down together and just
             talked and talked continuously all night long.'

In example (2), the 'topic' ('*t*') signal occurs while the contraction **PAST NIGHT**
and the compound **MOTHER FATHER** are signed. After that phrase, there is a
syntactic break—indicated by the comma. Then the Signer looks to the right and
uses two 'bent V' classifiers to represent the parents as they sit down facing each
other. The regular (two hands) alternating movement of the sign **USE-ASL** is made
in repeated, small circles—which adds the meaning 'continuously' and is indicated
with the modulation *"over time"*. The signal *puff.cheeks* occurs during the signs
USE-ASL"*over time*" and **ALL-NIGHT**.

Summary

Hopefully, by now you have a fair idea of how ASL signs and sentences are written down in this text. Of course, you will need to see and work with a variety of the examples in the text before you become really comfortable with all the symbols. It will probably help you to refer back to this section to remember the meaning of various symbols during your reading of the chapters.

One final note—as we said in the beginning of this section, our transcription system does not 'capture' everything that happens in the ASL sentences. At times, you may need to use your knowledge and intuitions about ASL to 'fill in the gaps'. Secondly, we do not always write down the sentences in a consistent manner. Sometimes there are parts of the sentences that we do not yet fully understand, so we write them down as best we can. Again, you will need to use your intuitions in those places where our knowledge is limited.[3]

---

[3]The videotape of all of the examples in this text is particularly helpful in demonstrating exactly what is meant with the written symbols.

Summary

Chapter I

What is a "Language"

In this chapter, we are going to examine some of the most important characteristics of the phenomenon called "Language". These major characteristics occur in every known ('living') language of the world. Put together, they give us the following definition of "Language":

> A language is a system of relatively arbitrary symbols and grammatical signals that change across time and that members of a community share and use for several purposes: to interact with each other, to communicate their ideas, emotions, and intentions, and to transmit their culture from generation to generation.

To understand this definition and how it applies to both spoken and signed languages, we will examine each of its components, one-by-one.

(a) A language has *symbols and grammatical signals*.

All languages have words or signs that stand for or represent something else. These words or signs are *symbols*. For example, the English word 'cat' is a symbol for a particular kind of furry, four-legged animal. In the same way, the ASL sign illustrated below is a symbol for that animal.

English symbol

(Drawing of a)
"furry four-legged animal"

(Drawing of) ASL symbol

All languages have *grammatical signals,* that is, ways of showing how the symbols are related to each other. For example, in the sentence 'John looked at Peter', which noun is the subject and which noun is the object? A speaker of English knows that John is the subject (i.e. John did the 'looking') and that Peter is the object (i.e. Peter was 'looked at') because in English, the subject noun normally occurs first in the sentence. *Word order* is an important grammatical signal in English that indicates the grammatical role (e.g. subject, object) of the symbols in English sentences. It is also important in Mandarin Chinese, Thai, and Vietnamese.

31

Many other languages like Russian, Swahili, Finnish, Latin, and Greek do not rely as much on word order to show the relationship between symbols. Instead, these languages rely more on a different type of grammatical signal called an *inflection*. Most of the time, inflections involve adding an affix to a word. That affix might mean 'subject' or 'object'. For example, in Latin (see example below), one can say either (a), (b), or (c), and all three sentences mean basically the same thing—i.e. 'John was looking at Peter'. Speakers of Latin know which noun is the subject because of the affix '-es'. ('Ioannes' means 'John' + 'subject'.) The affix '-um' indicates that Peter is the object in the sentence.

(1)   a. Ioannes aspiciebat Petrum.
      b. Ioannes Petrum aspiciebat.
      c. Petrum Ioannes aspiciebat.

Similarly, in Russian, the order of the symbols (the words) can vary since inflections can show the grammatical role of various words in the sentence. The three Russian sentences below also basically mean 'John was looking at Peter'. The addition of the affix '-a' indicates that Peter is the object in each sentence.[1]

(2)   a. Ivan smotrel na Petra.
      b. Ivan na Petra smotrel.
      c. Na Petra smotrel Ivan.

In this regard, ASL is more like Latin and Russian. ASL tends to change the form of the signs themselves to show grammatical relationships, rather than to rely on word/sign order to show those relationships. For example, the sentence 'John looks at Peter' could be signed in either of the two ways transcribed below.[2]

(3)   a. **J-O-H-N**-*rt*   *john*-**LOOK-AT**-*lf*   **P-E-T-E-R**-*lf*

$$\overline{\qquad\qquad\qquad}^{\;t}$$
      b. **P-E-T-E-R**-*lf*,   **J-O-H-N**-*rt*   *john*-**LOOK-AT**-*peter*

In these examples, the verb ____-**LOOK-AT**-____ moves from right to left and indicates that John is the subject and that Peter is the object. Whereas the inflections in the Latin and Russian examples were attached to certain nouns, the inflection that shows who is the subject and who is the object in the ASL sentence occurs on the verb ____-**LOOK-AT**-____. This inflection involves changing the direction of the verb so that it moves from the spatial location of the subject (i.e. on the right) to the spatial location of the object (i.e. on the left).

---

[1]The Russian word 'na' is a prepositional case marker which also indicates that what follows it (i.e. Petra) is an object.

[2]In example (3a), the name 'John' is fingerspelled on the right side, then the verb moves from the right (John's location) to the left, and the name 'Peter' is fingerspelled on the left side. In example (3b), the line with the small '*t*' above the fingerspelled name 'Peter' indicates that the non-manual signal for 'topicalization' occurs while that name is fingerspelled. The comma after the fingerspelled name 'Peter' represents a pause.

However, like many other languages with such inflections, not all orderings of the symbols are possible in ASL. For example, one cannot sign (4).[3]

(4)   **rt-**LOOK-AT-**lf**   **J-O-H-N-**rt   **P-E-T-E-R-**lf

Most languages use both word/sign order and inflections as grammatical signals. However, in general, languages tend to use one kind of signal more than the other. So, for example, English and Chinese are more dependent on word order to show how symbols are related, and ASL and Latin are more dependent on inflections to show how symbols are related.

(b) A language has symbols and grammatical signals that *members of a community share*.

A language doesn't work if its users mean different things when they use a symbol. For example, if you (the reader) use the imaginary word 'kerdit' to mean 'a place where people sleep', and someone else uses the word 'kerdit' to mean 'a place where people swim', then you and that person would not understand each other if you talked about 'kerdits'. Similarly, if someone thought that the *second* noun in an English sentence was the subject, then that person would not understand you correctly when you said 'John looked at Peter'. Members of a language community must agree about the meanings of symbols and how to use them in order for communication to take place through that language.

(c) A language is a *system* of symbols and grammatical signals that members of a community share.

All languages are composed of a limited number of units that are related or connected to each other in specific ways. For example, spoken languages use sound units as their basic building blocks. Each spoken language uses a particular set of these building blocks (i.e. sounds) and combines them in specific ways to form words. The words are then combined in specific ways to form sentences. Sentences, then, can be combined in specific ways to form speeches, stories, poems, conversations, and so on.

Similarly, the basic building blocks of a signed language are its handshapes, its palm orientations, its movements, and the locations where these occur. By combining a specific handshape, palm orientation, and movement in a particular location, one makes a sign. Combinations of signs form sentences, and combinations of these sentences can form speeches, stories, poems, conversations, and so on.

As such, languages are "hierarchical"—they are many-layered *systems*. At each layer, there are rules for determining what units can occur.

---

[3]A double asterisk indicates that something does not follow the rules of the language. The double asterisk preceding example (4) means that sentence is ungrammatical (i.e. it does not follow the rules of the language).

As stated earlier, each language has its own particular set of building blocks. For example, English has the 'th' sounds [Ө] as in 'thirty' and [ð] as in 'them'.[4] English does not have a uvular trill [ʁ], as in the French way of saying 'Paris', or the high, front vowel [ü], as in the French word for 'you' (familiar, singular)— [tü]. On the other hand, French doesn't have the [Ө] or [ð] sounds that are used in English.

Similarly, ASL has the handshape   which does not occur in French Sign Language. However, Taiwan Sign Language has handshapes which do not occur in ASL. For example, the handshapes illustrated below are used in the Taiwan signs for 'brother' and 'sister', respectively.

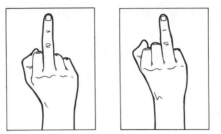

Handshapes in Taiwan Sign Language

The handshape with extended middle (third) finger also occurs in British Sign Language in such signs as those meaning 'holiday' and 'to trick/fool'.[5]

At each layer, there are also rules determining how these units can be combined with each other. These are called *"co-occurrence rules"*. For example, English uses the sounds [s] and [t], as in 'sew' and 'toe'. These two sounds can occur next to each other in words like 'stop', 'nest', and 'cats'. However, if they occur together as the first sounds in a word, the [t] cannot be the first sound. No regular English words begin with the sequence [ts], for example **tsin. Similarly, the sequence '-ng', transcribed as [ŋ], occurs at the end of many English words (e.g. song, rang, string), but cannot occur at the beginning of an English word—**ng____ . However, Bantu (a family of languages spoken in southern and central Africa) has words that begin with [ts]; Luiseño (a Uto-Aztecan language spoken in California) has words that begin with [ŋ]. Thus, each spoken language has a set of rules for determining *which* sounds can occur together and *where* they can co-occur in a word.

Similarly, ASL has rules determining which handshapes, movements, locations, and palm orientations can co-occur. For example, ASL (like Chinese Sign Language) has the handshape   that occurs in ASL signs like **CAT**, **IMPORTANT**, and

---

[4]Brackets are used in linguistics to denote actual sounds (which are often written differently from the way they are written in words). For example, the sounds in the English word 'cat' are written as [kæt].

[5]One could argue that the handshape with extended middle finger *does* occur in ASL in certain socially restricted signs. However, it is likely that this handshape derives from the pejorative gesture used by hearing and deaf members of the American population. All uses of this handshape in ASL have a related, pejorative meaning, whereas most of the regular handshapes in ASL freely occur in a wide variety of signs with non-related meanings. (It is interesting to note that this handshape does not commonly have a pejorative meaning among Britons, and thus, it is used more freely in British Sign Language.)

PREACH. ASL also has movements and locations which involve contacting the body. However, if signs with the above handshape contact a part of the body, that contact must be at the point where the thumb and index finger join (e.g. **CAT, INDIAN, TEA, VOTE, SENTENCE, INTERPRET, COUNT**) or on the side of the thumb and index finger (e.g. **BUTTON, HOLE, FLUNK**). In ASL, the three upright fingers in this handshape do not contact the body.[6] However, many signs with this handshape in Chinese Sign Language (CSL) operate in the opposite way. In CSL, the contact is made with the three upright fingers and *not* the thumb and index finger. This contact is seen in the following signs from Chinese Sign Language:

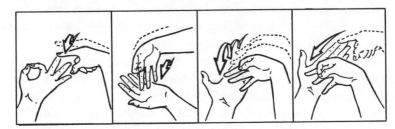

(Borrowed with permission from Klima & Bellugi 1979, pg. 157, Fig. 6.6)

Thus, ASL and CSL have different rules for that handshape when it contacts the body.

Other types of co-occurrence rules in ASL concern the use of two-handed signs. Linguistic research[7] has described two of these rules in some detail. One rule, called the rule of *Symmetry,* says that if both hands move, then they will have the same handshape and type of movement. This rule is illustrated in the signs **VISIT, FOOTBALL, DARK, PROCEED, EXCITED, MAYBE, TRY, CHAIN, HOPE, WALK, BOOK,** etc. The second rule, called the rule of *Dominance,* says that if each hand has a *different* handshape, then only one hand (the 'dominant' or 'active' hand)[8] will move. This rule is illustrated in the signs **ENOUGH, THAT, AMONG, SODA-POP, FIRST** (in a series), **WORD, CANDLE, WEAK, GROW, FLATTER,** etc. A second part of the Dominance rule says that the non-dominant hand will have one of the seven most *unmarked*[9] handshapes (illustrated on the next page).

FAIR

[6]An exception to this rule is the sign **FAIR** (used by some Signers) where contact is made on the side of the middle finger.

[7]cf. Battison 1978.

[8]The 'dominant' hand in a right-handed Signer is his/her right hand. The 'non-dominant' hand would then be the left hand.

[9]In linguistics, *unmarked* is an adjective used to describe language units which are easier to produce and are more frequently used. In the study of ASL, *marked* handshapes like those illustrated below are observed to be: (1) more difficult to produce, (2) learned later by deaf babies with deaf parents (Boyes-Braem 1973, McIntire 1974), and (3) occur less frequently in ASL as well as in other signed languages (Woodward 1978).

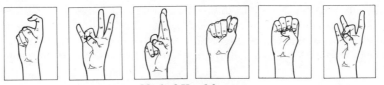

Marked Handshapes

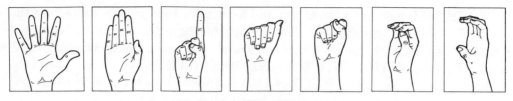

Unmarked Handshapes

So far, we have shown that there are rules in spoken languages which determine what sounds can occur and how they can be combined with each other. And we have shown that there are rules in signed languages which determine what handshapes, palm orientations, movements, and locations can occur and how they can be combined in a sign (with special rules for their combination in two-handed signs).

At the next layer, there are rules for determining how words or signs can be combined to form sentences (called *syntactic rules*). For example, 'Thelma has seen the man' is a grammatically correct sentence of English. The construction of that sentence follows the rules for forming sentences in English. The sentence '**Thelma has the man seen' does *not* follow the rules for combining words in English. However, that is exactly how the same sentence would be formed in German (which has different rules for the ordering of words in sentences).

(5)   Thelma hat den Mann gesehen.
      'Thelma has the man seen'   (English transliteration)

Looking at how signs are combined to form sentences in ASL, we see that sentence (6) is grammatically correct, and means 'Yesterday, after I finished my homework, I left'. However, re-arrangement of these same signs can yield ungrammatical sentences in ASL (i.e. sentences which do not follow the rules of the language), as seen in (7) and (8).

$$\overline{\text{brow raise}}$$
(6)   **YESTERDAY HOME WORK FINISH, ME GO**

$$\overline{\text{brow raise}}$$
(7)   ****YESTERDAY HOME WORK GO, ME FINISH**

$$\overline{\text{brow raise}}$$
(8)   ****HOME WORK YESTERDAY ME, FINISH GO**

Thus we see that languages (spoken or signed) are composed of a limited set of units which are combined with other units according to specific rules. As such, languages are "systems".

(d) A language is a system of *relatively arbitrary* symbols and grammatical signals that members of a community share.

The terms "arbitrary" and "iconic" are adjectives used to describe the relationship between the *form* of a symbol and the *meaning* of that symbol. If there is no resemblance between the form of a symbol and the thing it stands for (i.e. its meaning), then the relationship between the symbol and meaning is purely *arbitrary*. That is, there is no particular reason why that particular symbol is used to stand for that thing. For example, the English symbol 'pencil' does not look like or sound like the rectangular writing instrument that the word represents. The relationship between the word 'pencil' and the meaning 'thin, wooden writing instrument' is *arbitrary*. However, a drawing of a pencil (e.g. ⬤▬▬▬▷) *does* resemble the thing it represents. Therefore, the relationship between a drawing of a pencil and an actual pencil is *iconic*.

In addition, there are *degrees* of "arbitrariness" and "iconicity". Whenever a symbol is less than an exact physical replica of the thing it represents, the symbol is less iconic and more arbitrary. Thus, symbols can be iconic in some ways and arbitrary in other ways. For example, which of the symbols below most closely resembles the thing it stands for? In other words, which drawing is more iconic?

Clearly, drawing C is more *iconic* because it resembles an actual female more than do A and B. However, drawings A and B are also iconic because the circle resembles a 'head', and the other lines resemble, in proportion, the body, legs, and arms of a person. Speaking from the opposite perspective, we can say that A is clearly more *arbitrary* than C. Drawing A gives a minimal amount of visual information necessary for iconically representing a person whereas drawing C more closely resembles the thing it stands for.

We can represent these differences through the use of an arbitrariness-iconicity *continuum*, as seen below:

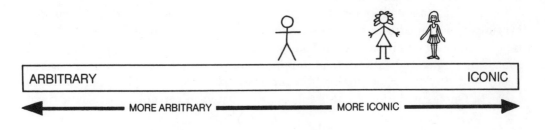

All of the drawings are located more to the right of the continuum because all of them resemble the thing they represent and are, therefore, iconic.

What kind of drawing would be located on the left side of the continuum? Suppose that a group of people decided to use ⋈ as a symbol for a girl. Does ⋈ resemble a girl? No, not at all. Therefore, the symbol ⋈ would be located on the far left side of the continuum.

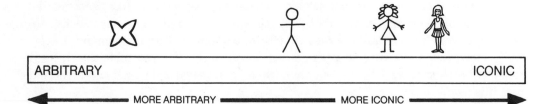

Returning to the definition of a language, stated above, we said that a language is a system of *relatively arbitrary* symbols and grammatical signals. Why is this arbitrariness important? If the symbols and/or signals of a language were completely iconic, then that language could only talk about (encode) a limited number of things. For example, if the symbols of our language were very iconic drawings, then we could only 'talk' about things that we could draw, like 🌲 and 🌼 and 📖 . We couldn't talk about abstract things like 'love' and 'beauty' and 'faith'. (What does 'love' look like?) However, if our symbols could be more arbitrary, then we could use ⊙⊙ for 'love', and ◇ for 'beauty', and ⊙ for 'faith'. Then, if we wanted to talk about something, but didn't have a symbol for it, we could either invent a new symbol or modify one we already had—for example, ⊘⊘ could mean 'not love'. Using this combination of some relatively iconic (and relatively arbitrary) symbols, we could say ◇ 👧 ⊘⊘ 📖 📖 (i.e. 'The beautiful girl does not love books.').

No languages that we know about are totally arbitrary. That is, all languages seem to have some symbols and/or signals which are iconic in some way. For example, the English words 'sneeze, snort, snoot, snout, sniff, snot, snarl, sneer, snicker, snob, snorkle, snub, and snuff' are somewhat iconic in that the nasalized sound in the sequence [sn] resembles the nose-related meaning of these words. Onomatopoeia (e.g. 'meow', 'bow-wow', 'moo') is also a clear instance of iconicity in spoken languages because the sounds in these symbols try to imitate the sounds made by the things they represent.

In addition, one well-known linguist[10] has reported that in at least 38 spoken languages, words with high front vowels (like the vowel sounds in 'bee' and 'tin') tend to refer to small things. Similarly, words with low vowels (like the vowel sounds in 'might' and 'father') tend to refer to larger things. Think about the words 'teeny' and 'tiny' (which is smaller?), or the nonsense words 'plib' and 'plab' (which is larger?). One explanation for this relationship between certain vowel sounds and

[10]Bolinger (1975).

the meanings 'largeness' and 'smallness' is that the tongue position for producing these vowels is quite different. One position (e.g. during the vowel in 'plib') results in a very small opening in the mouth cavity; the other (e.g. during the vowel in 'plab') results in a larger opening. Here the result of producing those sounds seems to resemble the meanings of the words in which these sounds occur. These are all examples of iconicity in a spoken language, which is often called *sound symbolism*.

Iconicity in a signed language refers to a *visual* resemblance between signs and the things they stand for. Many signs in ASL visually resemble their meaning; some do not. In all signs, there is a degree of arbitrariness. This is because there are always many possible ways to represent something in a signed language—just as there were several possible drawings to represent a 'girl' in the earlier discussion. For example, the sign **TREE** in Chinese Sign Language is symbolized by moving the Signer's thumbs and crooked index fingers upward along an imaginary trunk; **TREE** in Danish Sign Language is made by 'shaping the boughs' with the palms and then moving downward along the trunk; **TREE** in American Sign Language uses the upright arm and spread fingers of the signing (dominant) hand as the 'tree' which rests on the 'ground' provided by the non-dominant hand and arm.[11]

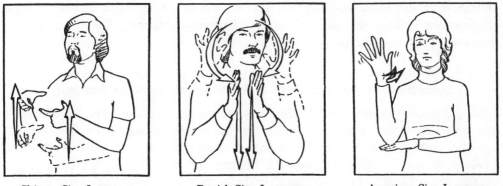

Chinese Sign Language   Danish Sign Language   American Sign Language

If the signs in a signed language were very iconic, then their meanings would be transparent and even people who have not studied that language would be able to understand it—just as a person could see the drawings of B and C on page 37 and know what they were symbols for. However, experiments with people who do not know ASL have shown that most signs in ASL are *not* iconic enough to be understood without being told their meanings.[12] On the other hand, if you tell someone the meaning of a sign, then that person can often see an iconic relationship between the form of the sign and its meaning. However, that relationship usually is not transparent enough for him/her to guess the meaning without being told. (Thus, signs are clearly different from "mime" or "pantomime" since mime and pantomime can be understood without prior explanation.)

---

[11]Illustrations below borrowed with permission from Klima & Bellugi (1979), pg. 21, Fig. 1.8.
[12]Hoemann (1975), Klima & Bellugi (1979).

Linguistic studies of ASL[13] have also shown that signs tend to become more arbitrary as time goes by. For example, the old ASL sign **HOME** was a compound of the signs **EAT** and **BED**. Now the sign is often made by touching the cheek (i.e. the location of the sign **BED**) twice with the handshape used in the sign **EAT**. Thus, the sign has changed and has become more arbitrary and less iconic. (Several more examples will be discussed in the next section on how languages change.)

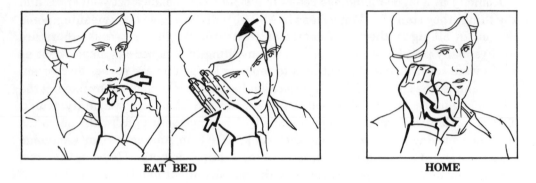

EAT BED   HOME

In conclusion, we see that the symbols and signals of a language must be arbitrary enough to be able to encode anything the user wants to talk about (and to allow for efficient use of the language), but can also be somewhat iconic. Thus, we say that language symbols and signals are *relatively arbitrary*.

(e) A language is a system of relatively arbitrary symbols and grammatical signals that *change across time* and that members of a community share.

Languages are as alive and changing as the people who use them. In the 1950's and 1960's came the 'beatniks' and the 'hippies' and their jargon 'hip', 'cool', 'neat', 'uptight', and 'groovy' (much of it borrowed from the 'rapping' and 'jiving' of the Black community). Teenagers started 'turning on' and 'digging it'. Then people became more 'mellow' and 'laid back' with the seventies, deciding to 'go with the flow' and 'keep on truckin'. Slang is one part of a language that changes especially rapidly.

Another type of vocabulary change reflects the growth and technological advances of a society. A hundred years ago, we didn't have words like 'television', 'videotape', 'microphone', and 'jet lag', or 'acrylon', 'dacron', and 'polyester', or 'astronaut', 'lunar module', and 'space capsule'. Languages change to meet the changing needs of the people who use them.

The ability of a language to coin or create new words like 'groovy' and 'dacron' and to combine old words or word parts in new ways like 'space capsule' and 'tele-vision' is one kind of language "productivity". Without this ability, a language could not grow and change with the expanding needs of the people who use that language.

Although languages frequently grow by using their own internal resources for expressing new meanings, sometimes languages "borrow" words or signs from other languages rather than invent their own words or signs. English, for example, has

---

[13]Woodward & Erting (1975), Frishberg (1975).

borrowed extensively from many languages: for example, 'boutique', 'detente', and 'discotheque' from French, 'igloo' from Eskimo, 'patio' from Spanish, 'cookie' from Dutch, 'moccasin' from an American Indian language, 'klutz' and 'chutzpah' from Yiddish, and 'algebra' from Arabic.

American Sign Language has several major ways of creating new signs.[14] One way is by *compounding*—a process also used in English, but not in all spoken languages. A compound is created by combining two words or two signs so that they become like one word or one sign with its own meaning—like the compounds 'cupboard' and 'blueprint' in English. Notice that you can put plates (not just cups) in a cupboard, and a blueprint doesn't have to be blue. Examples of ASL compounds are **EAT⌢NOON** (meaning 'lunch') and **GIRL⌢SERVE** (meaning 'waitress'). An example of a new compound created by ASL Signers is **1_{outline}-CL'rectangular⌢'ZAP'** for 'microwave oven', which is illustrated below.

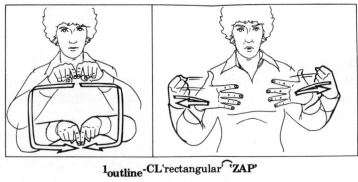

1_{outline}-CL'rectangular⌢'ZAP'

'microwave oven'

Another way of expressing new meanings in ASL involves changing the movement of an existing sign. For example, slightly changing the movement of the sign **QUIET** can change the meaning to 'acquiesce' or 'to give in to an argument'. (This derived sign can be made with one or both hands.)

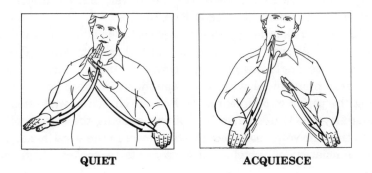

QUIET   **ACQUIESCE**

---

[14]Bellugi & Newkirk (in press), Klima & Bellugi (1979).

Similarly, nouns can be created by changing the movement associated with related verb signs. In this way, the movement that occurs during the sign **COMPARE**
can be changed to express the meaning 'comparison', and the movement of **GO-BY-
SKIS** can be changed to express the meaning 'skis'. Another familiar example is the
verb **SIT** and its related noun **CHAIR.**

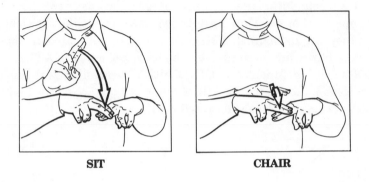

SIT   CHAIR

These are just some of the natural processes that ASL uses to express new meanings and create new signs. Linguists who are responsible for most of this research on
productivity in ASL have observed that only a small fraction of the vocabulary of
ASL is "borrowed" from other languages like English.[15]

Besides changes in vocabulary, changes in the grammar of a language also occur.
As an example, let's look at "Old English"—a form of the English language used
during the approximate period of 600-1100 AD. Old English was less dependent on
word order; it had many more inflections than are now present in Modern English.
For example, the form of an English noun used to be different depending on its
grammatical role in the sentence. Like the example from Latin described earlier, if
the English noun was the subject, it had a special ending attached to it. If it was the
direct object, it had a different ending attached to it. If it was the indirect object, it
had another ending attached to it. Now only nouns in the possessive case like
'John's' and 'the cat's' are inflected. For many older Signers of ASL, adjectives are
signed after nouns, as in **BALL RED**. Now, however, many younger Signers sign
the adjective before the noun (i.e. **RED BALL**).

Another way that spoken languages change concerns how words are pronounced.
For example, the first sound in the French word 'cherie' (meaning 'darling') is like
the 'sh' sound in the English word 'ship'. However, in the 14th century, the same
French word was pronounced with a 'ch' sound, as in the English word 'cheese'.
Thus, during the period of 600 years, the French 'ch' sound was replaced by a 'sh'
sound.[16] Similarly, the Old English way of pronouncing the word 'foot' was with a
'long o' [ō] so that the vowel sounded like the vowel in the word 'boat'. Thus, we see
that the pronunciation of vowels and consonants in spoken languages changes
across time.

---

[15]Bellugi & Newkirk (in press).
[16]Lockwood (1969).

Some of these changes in the pronunciation, vocabulary, and grammar of English can be seen in the following excerpts from the Lord's Prayer as they were written during four periods in the history of the English Language.[17]

1. Eornostlīce gebīddaþ eow þus Fæder ūre þū be eart on heofonum, sie bin nama gehālgod,
2. Tōcume þīn rīce. Gewur þe þin willa on eorþan swā swā on heofonum.
3. Ūrne daeghwæmlīcan hlāf syle ūs tōdæg.
4. And forgyf ūs ūre gyltas swā swā we forgyfaþ ūrum gyltendum.
5. And ne gelæd þū ūs on costnunge ac ālys us of yfele.

Old English (ca. 1000)

1. Forsothe thus ȝe shulen preyen, Oure fadir that art in heuenes, halwid be thi name;
2. Thy kyngdom cumme to; be thi wille don as in heuen and in erthe;
3. ȝif to vs this day oure breed ouer other substaunce;
4. And forȝeue to vs oure dettis, as we forȝeue to oure dettours;
5. And leede vs nat in to temptacioun, but delyuere vs fro yuel. Amen.

Middle English (Wycliffe, 1389)

1. After thys maner there fore praye ye, O oure father which arte in heven, halowed be thy name;
2. Let thy kingdom come; thy wyll be fulfilled as well in erth as hit ys in heven;
3. Geve vs this daye oure dayly breade;
4. And forgeve vs oure treaspases, even as we forgeve them which trespas vs;
5. Leede vs not into temptacion, but delyvre vs ffrom yvell. Amen.

Early Modern English (Tyndale, 1526)

1. Pray then like this:
   Our Father who art in heaven,
   Hallowed be thy name.
2. They kingdom come,
   Thy will be done,
      On Earth as it is in heaven.
3. Give us this day our daily bread;
4. And forgive us our debts,
      As we also have forgiven our debtors;
5. And lead us not into temptation,
      But deliver us from evil.

Modern English (1952)

During the past 150 years, ASL has also undergone major changes in the way that signs are made.[18] For example, many older signs which in the past were made by contacting the elbow are now made on the hand (e.g. **HELP, SUPPORT**). Some signs that were made at the waist are now made higher up the body (e.g. **YOUNG, FUTURE**). These are all examples of changes in the location parameter. Some handshapes have also changed. For example, **LAST** used to be made by striking the

---

[17]Excerpts from Clark *et al.* (1977) pp. 181–182.
[18]Woodward & Erting (1975), Frishberg (1975).

little finger of the non-dominant hand with the index finger of the moving hand. Now both handshapes tend to be the same (i.e. little fingers extended). Similarly, the handshapes in signs like **DEPEND, SHORT, INSTITUTE,** and **WHISKEY** have changed so that both hands have the same handshape. Many signs that used to be made with both hands on the face or head (e.g. **CAT, COW, HORSE, RABBIT, CHINESE**) are now often made with only one hand.[19] This change is also beginning to occur in French Sign Language.

Thus we see that the vocabulary, grammar, and 'pronunciation' of spoken and signed languages *change across time,* and that the vocabulary of these languages tends to change most rapidly.

(f) **A language is a system of relatively arbitrary symbols and grammatical signals that change across time and that members of a community share and *use* for several purposes: to interact with each other, to communicate their ideas, emotions, and intentions, and to transmit their culture from generation to generation.**

As "social animals", human beings tend to live in groups, or communities, and to seek out opportunities to interact and communicate with other human beings. To facilitate such communication, every human community has a language which has arisen and evolved to meet the needs of its users. Members of each community use their language to express themselves and to understand the expressions of other members. Adults use this language to teach their children about the world, in general, and about the culture of their own community.

Summary

During the preceding discussion, we have seen that languages are very complex systems. At each level within the system, there are rules that native users of a language must follow, often without being conscious of the rules. However, these rules are dynamic; they change across time just as all living things change. Languages grow and change because they are used by people who are continually growing and changing.

In the next chapter, we will begin to describe one of the world's approximately 4000 'living' languages—American Sign Language.

References

Battison, R. 1978. *Lexical Borrowing in American Sign Language.* Silver Spring, Md.: Linstok Press.

Bellugi, U. & D. Newkirk (in press). Formal devices for creating new signs in ASL. To appear in *National Symposium on Sign Language Research and Teaching: 1977 Proceedings.*

Bolinger, D. 1975. *Aspects of Language* (Second edition). New York: Harcourt, Brace, Jovanovich, Inc.

---

[19]Frishberg (1975), Woodward & De Santis (1977).

Boyes-Braem, P. 1973. A study of the acquisition of dez in American Sign Language. Working paper, Salk Institute, San Diego, California.

Clark, V., P. Eschholz & A. Rosa (Eds.) 1977. *Language: introductory readings* (Second edition). New York: St. Martin's Press.

Frishberg, N. 1975. Arbitrariness and iconicity: historical change in American Sign Language. *Language 51*, 3, 696–719.

Hoemann, H. 1975. The transparency of meaning of Sign Language gestures. *Sign Language Studies 7*, 151–161.

Klima, E. & U. Bellugi. 1979. *The Signs of Language*. Cambridge, Mass.: Harvard University Press.

Lockwood, W. B. 1969. *Indo-European Philology*. London: Hutchinson & Co.

McIntire, M. 1974. A modified model for the description of language acquisition in a deaf child. M.A. Thesis, California State University at Northridge.

Woodward, J. 1978. Sign marking: "stage" four handshapes. Paper presented at the Summer meeting of the Linguistic Society of America, July.

Woodward, J. & C. Erting. 1975. Synchronic variation and historical change in American Sign Language. *Language Sciences 37*, 9–12.

Woodward, J. & S. De Santis. 1977. Two to one it happens: dynamic phonology in two sign languages. *Sign Language Studies 17*, 329–346.

Chapter II

What is
American Sign Language?*

American Sign Language (also called ASL or Ameslan) is a *visual-gestural*[1] language created by Deaf people and used by approximately 250,000–500,000 Americans (and some Canadians) of all ages.[2]

What is meant by *gestural*? "Gestures" can be simply defined as any movements of the body that occur for the purpose of communication. In the past, people thought that the body movements of ASL were imprecise and irregular. Now we know that the gestures found in ASL are a special set of rule-governed behaviors, which are called *signs*. The concept of signs as a special subset of all possible gestures is illustrated in Figure 2.1.

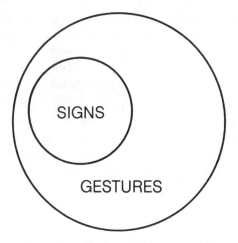

Figure 2.1 *Signs* as a subset of *gestures*

---

*Some of the information in this chapter is taken from the pamphlet *American Sign Language: a look at its history, structure, and community* (1978) by Baker and Padden.

[1]We have decided that another frequently-used term, *visual-manual,* is too narrow for describing ASL since the term *manual* focuses attention on the hands rather than on the whole body. The grammar of ASL makes use of the Signer's eyes, face, head, and body posture as well as his/her hands and arms. Therefore, we have chosen to use the term *gestural* since it is sufficiently broad to cover all of these expressive components of ASL.

[2]Actually, since there have been no careful surveys of ASL users to date, these figures should be interpreted loosely. The numbers quoted here are from O'Rourke (1975), Woodward (1978), and the 1974 (September) issue of the Journal of the American Speech and Hearing Association (p. 544).

The units of American Sign Language are composed of specific movements and shapes of the hands and arms, eyes, face, head, and body posture. These movements and shapes serve as the 'words' and 'intonation' of the language.

What is meant by *visual*? Since American Sign Language uses body movements instead of sound, 'listeners' (or 'receivers') use their eyes instead of their ears to understand what is being said. And because all linguistic information must be received through the eyes, the language is carefully structured to fit the needs and capabilities of the eyes.

A. History of American Sign Language

George W. Veditz, a Deaf teacher who became the president of the National Association of the Deaf in 1904, said "As long as we have Deaf people, we will have Sign Language".[3] Information collected from many different countries shows that Veditz was right. Throughout history, wherever there have been Deaf people, there have been signed languages that they or their ancestors have developed: Chinese Sign Language (Yau 1977), French Sign Language (Sallagoity 1975), Thai Sign Language (Reilly & Suwanarat 1980), and so on. Why do Deaf people develop and use signed languages? So they can effectively communicate with each other.

Languages do not have to be "vocal-auditory"; that is, they do not have to use sound. In fact, various scholars through the centuries have argued that the first languages used in pre-historic times were gestural languages.[4] There is even some evidence suggesting that the vocal apparatus necessary for speech did not develop until later on.[5] In any case, because Deaf people do not hear and therefore, cannot efficiently use a language composed of sounds, they use a different kind of language better suited to their communicative needs—a visual-gestural language.[6]

We do not have much information about the deaf people who lived in America before 1817. We assume that some came from Europe or the British Isles, and that others were born here. Some of those who came from other countries probably brought with them a knowledge of the signed language used in their country. So perhaps a few deaf people in a Spanish colony used Spanish Sign Language, and others in an English colony used British Sign Language and so on. When a signed language was not known—for example, deaf children born of hearing parents in America would not have known a foreign signed language—it is likely that the deaf individuals created their own signs, often called *home signs*. We do know that deaf people in different areas probably had very little contact with each other since there were no public transportation services and no schools or organizations for deaf

---

[3]A videotape of Veditz's very stirring 1913 speech, entitled *The Preservation of Sign Language,* is available through the Gallaudet College library.

[4]Condillac (1775), Valade (1866), Hewes (1974, 1975).

[5]Lieberman & Crelin (1971).

[6]Actually, a large percentage of Deaf people have some degree of residual hearing. That is, many Deaf people can hear some sounds with differing degrees of distortion. Hearing losses exist on a continuum. With the statement above, we are simply noting that a loss of hearing often means that a person is unable to use (i.e. send and receive) a spoken language efficiently or at all.

people to bring them together. So it makes sense to assume that several different signed languages or types of signing were used in America before 1817.

What happened in 1817? As the famous story[7] goes, a man named Thomas Hopkins Gallaudet, who was a graduate of Yale University, was training to become a minister. He met a young deaf girl named Alice, the daughter of his neighbor, Dr. Mason Cogswell, a well-known doctor in Hartford, Connecticut. Gallaudet tried to teach Alice to read and write a few words and had some success.

Cogswell was impressed by Gallaudet's initial efforts and encouraged him to become involved in establishing a school for deaf people in America. The clergymen's association of Connecticut had reported years earlier that there were approximately 89 deaf people in the state.[8] The need for a school was clear. So Cogswell and a group of concerned citizens raised funds to send Gallaudet to Europe to learn about methods for instructing deaf people.

Gallaudet first went to Great Britain to learn an "oral method" of instruction used by the Braidwood Schools in Scotland and near London. This method used speaking, reading, and writing, and was strongly against the use of signs. However, the directors of these schools refused to reveal their method. Similarly, the director of the London Asylum (also using oral methods) refused to give Gallaudet the information he wanted.

Fortunately, the director of a school for deaf students in Paris, a man named Sicard, was in London with two of his deaf pupils—who were also teachers at the Paris school, Jean Massieu and Laurent Clerc. They were giving demonstrations of the French method of instructing deaf students. This method used signs from French Sign Language (created by French Deaf people) with an added set of signs called *les signes méthodiques* (in English, *methodical signs*). These methodical signs were invented by Abbé Charles de l'Epée, the founder and first director of the school in Paris. Epée's methodical signs were used for certain grammatical words or parts of words that are found in spoken and written French (such as 'le' or 'la', meaning 'the') but that are not needed in French Sign Language. These signs were supposed to help deaf students translate from their signed language into written French.

Gallaudet was impressed by the presentations of Sicard, Massieu, and Clerc. He asked Sicard to teach him the French method of education using signs, and Sicard agreed. So Gallaudet went to Paris and there began to learn French signs from Massieu and Clerc, and the teaching method from Sicard.

After a short while, Gallaudet wanted to return to Hartford and convinced Clerc to go back with him to help establish a school there. During the 52-day voyage to America, Clerc continued teaching signs to Gallaudet, and Gallaudet taught Clerc the English language—Clerc's third language (after French Sign Language and French).

---

[7]Lane (1976, 1977).

[8]Based on the finding that the deaf population is usually about .1% of the whole American population, Lane (1977) estimates that there were about 2000 deaf people in America during the early 1800's. Schein & Delk (1974) report a total of 6,106 prelingually deaf people in America in 1830, according to the U.S. Bureau of the Census.

Then on April 15, 1817, with funds from the state of Connecticut, the U.S. Congress, and other sympathetic groups, Gallaudet and Clerc established the Institution for Deaf-Mutes—later renamed the American Asylum at Hartford for the Education and Instruction of the Deaf and Dumb, and presently called the American School for the Deaf. Clerc remained there as an instructor for over forty years. During that time, Clerc also trained some hearing people, who later became the directors of schools for deaf students in New York, Kentucky, Virginia, Indiana, Pennsylvania, Ohio, and Quebec.

Until recently, it was supposed that deaf people in America suddenly started learning and using French signs in 1817, and that they didn't have any language before that time. However, as discussed earlier, common sense tells us that possibly several different signed languages were used by the 2000 or more deaf people living in this country in the early 1800's. Certainly they were not all just waiting around for someone to give them an effective way of communicating![9]

In addition to this type of reasoning, there is also linguistic evidence which demonstrates that there must have been at least one other signed language used in America before Gallaudet and Clerc established the Hartford School. This evidence involves looking at *cognates* — words or signs in one language which are historically related to words or signs in another language. For example, we can look at words in German and English and see that many of them are similar, that they seem to have come from the same "language family".

Cognates

Modern German	*Modern English*
Haus	house
Fisch	fish
grune	green
helfen	to help

By studying a large number of these cognates, like 'Haus'—'house', linguists have found out that German and English are historically related, and that they both came from the same source language called "proto-Germanic".

---

[9]Right before publication of this text, an article was published in the magazine *Natural History* ("Everyone Spoke Sign Language Here" by N. Groce, Vol. 89, No. 6, pps. 10–16) which reported on an exciting discovery. It seems that a large number of deaf people lived on the island called Martha's Vineyard during the late 1600s up to the early 1900s. These people and the hearing people in their community used a signed language together—which was taught to their children (hearing and deaf) and quite comfortably incorporated into their community activities. Thus, this information confirms the claim that one or more signed languages were used in America before the arrival of Clerc and Gallaudet.

Similarly, linguists who study signed languages can look for sign cognates to see which signed languages are related to each other. If modern-day American Sign Language is related to French Sign Language (FSL), then there should be a large number of ASL-FSL cognates. And there is. For example, notice the structural similarity between the following signs in ASL and FSL.

Cognates

French Sign Language	*American Sign Language*

RIRE   **LAUGH**

AIDER   **HELP**

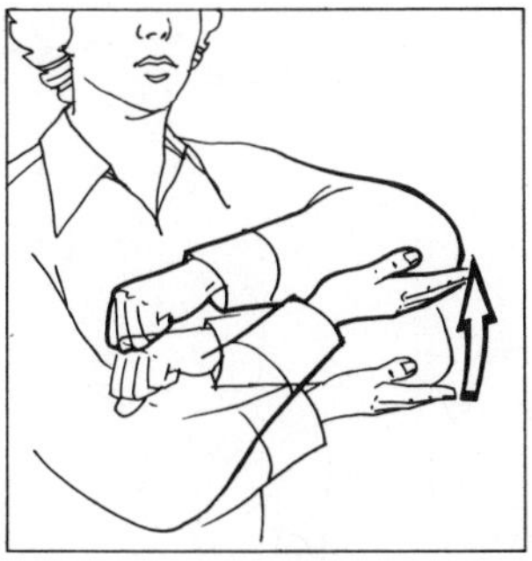

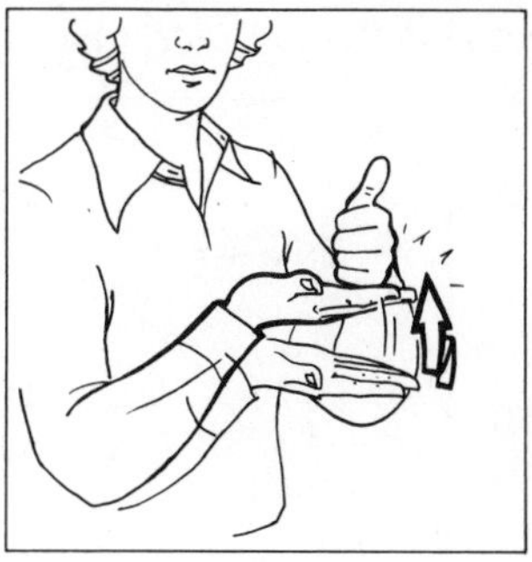

MENTEUR   **LIAR**

Note: As you can see, the French and English words used to gloss these signs are *not* cognates, but the signs themselves *are* cognates. This illustrates the independence of signed languages from spoken languages.

However, a linguist[10] in the Linguistics Research Laboratory at Gallaudet College studied these sign relationships and found that only approximately 60% of the signs in American Sign Language seem to be related to signs in French Sign Language. Although we know that languages change over time and that the last 150 years could account for some of these differences, there is still much more dissimilarity than can be accounted for by natural processes of language change. That remaining 40% must have come from somewhere else.

Below are some examples of ASL and FSL signs that are *not* cognates:

Non-cognates

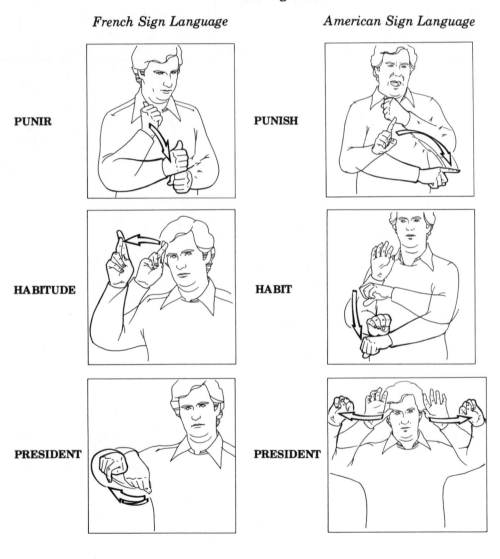

French Sign Language   *American Sign Language*

PUNIR   PUNISH

HABITUDE   HABIT

PRESIDENT   PRESIDENT

Note: As you can see, the French and English words *are* cognates, but the signs with these meanings **are** *not* cognates. This again shows the independence of signed languages from spoken languages.

---

[10]Woodward (1978).

Thus, we have evidence to believe that at least some deaf people had a knowledge of signs (from other signed language(s)) before Clerc began teaching French signs. Likely, these deaf people ended up combining some of the signs from their signed language(s) with French signs, and that combination became Old American Sign Language.[11] This explanation of the history of modern ASL is illustrated in Figure 2.2.

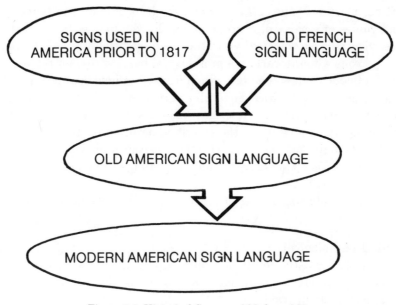

Figure 2.2 Historical Sources of Modern ASL

B. Who uses American Sign Language?

As said earlier, approximately 250,000–500,000 Americans and Canadians use American Sign Language. However, relatively few hearing people know this language. And there are deaf people who do not know ASL.

Why is ASL known and used by some deaf people and not by others? In general, deaf people who use ASL are those who see themselves as part of the *Deaf Community*, who are accepted as 'members' by the Community, and who share in the culture of Deaf people. Not all deaf people identify with or belong to the Deaf Community. Some, instead, prefer to identify with the larger 'hearing world' and try to belong to that group.

But what is this *Deaf Community* that uses American Sign Language?

---

[11]In fact, there are accounts of Clerc lamenting that his "graceful signs" were being changed, and that other signs which he did not teach were being used (Woodward 1978). (The collected writings of Laurent Clerc are available in Gallaudet College library.)

C. What is the Deaf Community?

Attempting to define the Deaf Community is not an easy task. Within the past ten years, several widely-varying definitions have been proposed. However, it appears that these definitions can be categorized into either of two general types: (1) the *clinical* or *pathological* view which takes the behaviors and values of the hearing majority as the "standard" or "norm" and then focuses on how deaf people deviate from that norm, and (2) the *cultural* view which focuses on the language, experiences, and values of a particular group of people who happen to be deaf.

The first view (the *pathological* view) has been traditionally held by the majority of hearing persons who interact on a professional basis with deaf people. In a sense, this is the "outsider's" view—a view which focuses on how deaf people are different from hearing people and which generally perceives these differences negatively. The second view (the *cultural* view) has been discussed and described only very recently, seemingly as a result of the recent recognition of ASL as a separate language (not a deviant code for English). This recognition has encouraged a new examination of the Deaf Community and its language in and of itself (an examination from the "inside").

Thus, we might categorize some of these specific definitions of the *Deaf Community* as follows:

(1) Clinical-Pathological
   (a) an audiologically definable group of persons whose hearing loss is sufficient to interfere with but does not preclude the normal reception of speech (Schein 1968)
   (b) a group of hearing-impaired persons who have learning and psychological problems due to their hearing loss and communication difficulties (Levine 1956, Davis & Silverman 1960, Myklebust 1960, Rainer *et al* 1963, Altschuler 1964, Rainer & Altschuler 1966)
   (c) a minority group composed of hearing-impaired persons who are treated in certain negative ways by the hearing majority (Vernon & Makowsky 1969)

(2) Cultural
   (d) a group of persons who share a common means of communication (signs) which provides the basis for group cohesion and identity (Schlesinger & Meadow 1972)
   (e) a group of persons who share a common language (ASL) and a common culture (Woodward & Markowicz 1975, Padden & Markowicz 1976, Markowicz & Woodward 1978)

The attitude of those who hold the first view is generally that there is something wrong with deaf people and that, as much as possible, society should help them become as "normal" as possible. The attitude of those who hold the second view is that the Deaf Community should be accepted and respected as a separate cultural group with its own values and language.

This latter view is based on linguistic and sociological research findings. However, these findings make defining the Deaf Community a complex task. For example, the Deaf Community is not like an ethnic or religious community where it is generally clear whether or not a person is a member—e.g. of the Black Community, Jewish Community, etc. That is, there does not seem to be a single distinguishing characteristic or trait that all members of the Deaf Community share. Rather, there is a complex set of factors which must be considered when trying to understand who are the members of the Deaf Community.

One factor which does seem very basic in understanding who is a member of the Deaf Community is called *attitudinal deafness*. This occurs when a person identifies him/herself as a member of the Deaf Community (which means supporting the values of that Community), and other members accept this person as part of the Community. Research has found that this factor is more important than the actual degree of hearing loss (*audiometric deafness*)—which does not actually seem to be very important in determining how a person relates to the Deaf Community.[12] Using the criterion of *attitudinal deafness* to understand who are the members of the Deaf Community has several important implications. First of all, it means that:

(a) not all individuals who have a hearing loss are members of the Deaf Community. Some individuals choose to function—or attempt to function—within the Hearing Community and do not become involved in matters affecting the Deaf Community.

Secondly, although the vast majority of members of the Deaf Community do, in fact, have a hearing loss,

(b) it may be possible for hearing individuals to be accepted as members if they display the appropriate *attitudinal deafness*.[13]

Thirdly, since attitudes can be expressed in many different ways and to differing degrees,

(c) there may be several potential avenues through which a person may gain acceptance by the Deaf Community, and

(d) there may be different levels of acceptance into the Deaf Community, depending on the person's skills and experience as well as attitudes.

The model we will present here is an attempt to describe the complex nature of the Deaf Community and to illustrate various membership stages within the Community. It is a tentative analysis based on available research and the descriptions of many members of the Deaf Community. This diagram shows four potential avenues to membership into the Community. Likely, there are more avenues than the four described and illustrated here. However, the model should serve to illustrate the complex interaction of factors which are important for understanding who are the members of the Community—in addition to the basic criterion of *attitude*.

The four avenues to membership described here are: audiological, political, linguistic, and social.

---

[12]Padden & Markowicz (1976).
[13]Meadow (1972), Furth (1973), Woodward & Markowicz (1975).

(a) *Audiological:* refers to actual loss of hearing ability. Thus, this avenue to membership is not available, by definition, to hearing people. It seems apparent that those individuals with a hearing loss are accepted by and identify with the Community at a much deeper level ("the core") and much more quickly than a hearing person with similar skills, experience, and attitudes.

(b) *Political:* refers to the potential ability to exert influence on matters which directly affect the Deaf Community on a local, state, or national level. For example, a person might hold an office in a state NAD chapter. Of course, the types of decisions and proposals which s/he makes will also influence how well other members of the Community accept that person.

(c) *Linguistic:* refers to the ability to understand and use American Sign Language. The level of fluency seems to be related to the level of acceptance into the Community. Since the values and goals of the Community are transmitted by its language, it is not surprising that fluency in ASL is very important.

(d) *Social:* refers to the ability to satisfactorily participate in social functions of the Deaf Community. This means being invited to such functions, feeling at ease while attending, and having friends who are themselves members of the Deaf Community. This ability may presuppose other factors, such as linguistic skills in ASL.

The complex way in which these avenues to membership may interact is illustrated in Figure 2.3.

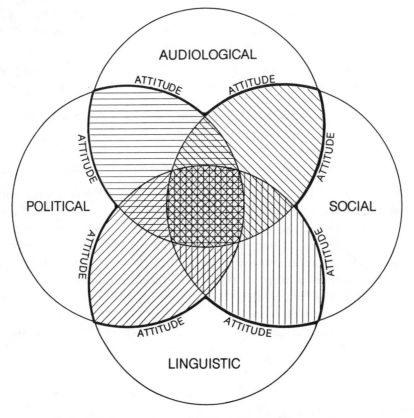

Figure 2.3 Avenues to membership in the Deaf Community

It should be apparent from this diagram that a person's attitude toward the Deaf Community is of utmost importance in being accepted into the Community. This diagram also shows that identifying with and being accepted by the Deaf Community is not simply a matter of linguistic skill in ASL or degree of hearing loss. Rather, it is a somewhat complex process in which certain skills (linguistic), activities (social, political), and realities (hearing loss) are weighed in relation to the individual's attitude toward the Community. The avenues of access depicted here are, from our point of view, channels through which an individual's attitudes and the Community's attitudes meet and are either compatible or incompatible. If they are compatible, and if the individual identifies with the Community, then s/he may be accepted as a member of the Community.

The most heavily shaded area in the center of the diagram represents the "core Deaf Community": those individuals who have a hearing loss and who share a common language, common values and experiences, and a common way of interacting with each other, with non-core members of the Deaf Community, and with the hearing community. The other shaded areas represent the wider Deaf Community.

With this diagram, we see that each member of the Community is *attitudinally deaf* and can be identified with at least two of the four factors described above—i.e. linguistic and social, audiological and social, or audiological and political. Thus, according to this model, it is possible for a person to have a hearing loss and not be a member of the Deaf Community (**AUDIOLOGICAL**), or for a person to be appointed to some political position in the government which influences the Deaf Community and not be a member of the Community (**POLITICAL**). It is also possible for a person to possess some degree of competence in ASL and not be a member of the Deaf Community (**LINGUISTIC**). Finally, it is possible for a person to attend or support social functions of the Community and not be a member of the Deaf Community (**SOCIAL**).

It is also clear from this model that hearing people are not considered "core members" of the Deaf Community since they do not have a hearing loss. It should also be clear that because of this fact, the avenues of access for hearing people are more limited (i.e. restricted to only three of the four avenues). In fact, the area which depicts a convergence of the political, linguistic, and social factors illustrates the highest level of acceptance into the Deaf Community that a hearing person can attain. Likewise, the area which depicts a convergence of political, audiological and social factors illustrates the highest level of acceptance in the Deaf Community which a hearing-impaired, non-ASL user can attain. In actual practice, the avenues of access for hearing people are even more limited than the diagram suggests since it is very difficult for a hearing person to have real political influence *within* the Deaf Community. This means that generally the avenues of acceptance for hearing people are the linguistic and the social avenues.

Finally, it should be pointed out that, within certain limits, over time people may move from possessing or using one combination of factors to another. This means that individuals within the Deaf Community relate to each other and are accepted by the Community in a dynamic, not a static, fashion. A person's role within the Community may change depending upon the development of, or change in, certain linguistic, political, and social skills. Of these skills, the most important seem to be social and linguistic. However, as was stated earlier, *attitudinal deafness* stands as the foundation for all such considerations and entails an understanding, acceptance, and identification with the culture of Deaf people.

D. The Role of ASL in the Deaf Community

To understand the role of ASL in the Deaf Community, we need to understand the context in which this Community has evolved. The single fact of being deaf usually entails a whole set of shared experiences. Until recently, the majority of deaf people attended special schools for deaf children.[14] A large number of these are residential schools where deaf students eat, study, sleep, and play together—apart from hearing students their age. After leaving school, deaf people tend to work together at the limited number of places that hire deaf people. At least 85–90% of deaf adults marry within the Deaf Community.[15]

Throughout their school and adult years, deaf people are also drawn together by numerous sports opportunities and events for deaf people, including regional tournaments and special olympics. Parties with captioned films, special tours, newsletters, and school reunions are other means of drawing deaf people together. A result of this continuous contact in academic, social, and job-related situations is that Deaf people have formed a cohesive and tight-knit Community.

Most deaf people (approximately 90%) have hearing parents. Since these parents use a language (usually spoken English) that their deaf child can neither hear nor use with any facility, communication with family members is limited. It is at the schools, with peers, that most personal and social information-sharing occurs and where close relationships are established—all through a language specially shaped for the eyes rather than the ears, and a language passed on by Deaf employees at the residential schools and by Deaf parents whose children then teach other deaf children how to use the language.

As history and experience shows us, at the heart of every community is its language.[16] This language embodies the thoughts and experiences of its users and they, in turn, learn about their culture and share in it together through their language. Thus, most Deaf people learn about their own culture and share their experiences with each other through American Sign Language.

In summary, we see that ASL is used for social communication within the Deaf Community. It is a language that Deaf people use with each other. However, with very few exceptions, it is not used in the area of education—which tends to be dominated by a majority of hearing people (approximately 90%)[17], most of whom do not know ASL. In fact, most educators have traditionally had very negative attitudes toward ASL (at least in part because they did not recognize it as a full and separate language) and have tried to discourage Deaf students from using ASL.[18]

---

[14]Schein & Delk (1974). However, this situation has been changing rapidly in the last few years as more and more deaf children are being "mainstreamed" into public schools.

[15]Rainer *et al* (1963), Schein & Delk (1974).

[16]Trybus (1980) provides an excellent review and discussion of the unifying role of a community's language.

[17]*American Annals of the Deaf* (1979), Vol. 124, No. 2, p. 184.

[18]Cokely (1980), Stevens (1980).

E. The Survival of American Sign Language

One may wonder how the Deaf Community has been able to maintain its own language despite strong attempts by many hearing people and "oral-deaf" people[19] to suppress ASL, and despite the fact that most of the Deaf child's education focuses on the learning of English.

One linguist who has studied this issue[20] suggests three reasons for the survival of ASL: First of all, the oppression confronting the Deaf Community may actually have caused its members to unite more strongly together. These strong bonds seem to be formed at a very early age among Deaf children. Ironically, one aspect of this oppression, namely the negative attitudes of most educators toward ASL, may actually have encouraged Deaf people to unite even more strongly in defense of their language and their communication rights. Secondly, because Deaf people have hearing losses, they naturally gravitate towards a language received through the eyes rather than the ears and a language which is structured for visual, rather than auditory, processing.

A third and fascinating reason for the survival of ASL centers on the fact that Deaf people rarely use ASL with a hearing person. Instead, Deaf people tend to use a variety of signing that is more like English when they talk with hearing people. This variety of signing has been called *Pidgin Sign English* and is discussed in Chapter III. As a result, very few hearing people know ASL.

At the 1977 National Symposium on Sign Language Research and Teaching, Barbara Kannapell shared a central reason behind Deaf people's tendency not to use ASL with hearing people.

> It is important to understand that ASL is the only thing we have that belongs to Deaf people completely. It is the only thing that has grown out of the Deaf group. Maybe we are afraid to share our language with hearing people. Maybe our group identity will disappear once hearing people know ASL. Also, will hearing people dominate Deaf people more than before if they learn ASL?

ASL is at the heart of the Deaf Community. If any changes in thinking or behavior were to happen within the Community, they would have to be proposed in the language of the people of the Community.[21] Thus, confining hearing people's knowledge to a more English-like type of signing effectively protects the Community from outside influence—which, in turn, protects the status of ASL in the Community.

In summary, because of (a) the strong cultural bonds between Deaf people, (b) Deaf people's general discomfort with English (see Chapter III for more explanation) but natural ease with ASL, and (c) the creation of a signing variety for use with hearing people that inhibits them from learning Deaf people's language (and, thus, from trying to "control" the Deaf Community), ASL has survived the onslaught of criticisms which range from calling it "ungrammatical" and "broken English" to the unfounded claim that it inhibits the learning of speech.

---

[19]Vernon & Makowsky (1969) provide some discussion of the attitude of "oral" deaf adults toward Sign Language.

[20]Woodward (1975).

[21]Markowicz & Woodward (1978).

This chapter began with a summary of what is known about the history of American Sign Language and its historical relationship with French Sign Language. We then described the people who presently use American Sign Language, factors relating to membership in the Deaf Community, the role of ASL within the Deaf Community, and some possible reasons for the 'survival' of ASL despite considerable efforts by many individuals and institutions to suppress Deaf people's continuing use of their language.

We would now like to briefly examine other types of signing that are frequently used for educational purposes and/or for interactions between deaf and hearing people. It is important to understand the forms and functions of these types of signing in order to distinguish them from ASL and to better understand the interaction of ASL and English in the Deaf Community.

References

Altschuler, K. 1964. Personality traits and depressive symptoms in the deaf. In J. Wortis (Ed.) *Recent Advances in Biological Psychiatry,* Vol. VI, New York: Plenum Press.

Baker, C. & C. Padden. 1978. *American Sign Language: a look at its history, structure, and community.* Silver Spring, Md.: T.J. Publishers, Inc.

Cokely, D. 1980. Sign Language: teaching, interpreting, and educational policy. In C. Baker & R. Battison (Eds.) *Sign Language and the Deaf Community.* Silver Spring, Md.: National Association of the Deaf.

Condillac, E. B. 1775. Essai sur l'origine des connaissances humaines. Published in 1947, in G. LeRoy (Ed.) *Oeuvres.* Paris, France.

Davis, H. & S. Silverman. 1960. *Hearing and Deafness* (Revised edition). New York: Holt, Rinehart and Winston, Inc.

Furth, H. 1973. *Deafness and Learning: A Psychosocial Approach.* Belmont, Ca.: Wadsworth Publishing Co., Inc.

Hewes, G. 1974. Language in early hominids. In R. Wescott (Ed.) *Language Origins.* Silver Spring, Md.: Linstok Press, 1–34.

Hewes, G. 1975. The current status of the gestural theory of language origin. In S. Harnad, H. Steklis & J. Lancaster (Eds.) *Origins and Evolution of Language and Speech.* New York: Annals of the New York Academy of Sciences, Volume 280, 482–504.

Lane, H. 1976. *The Wild Boy of Aveyron.* Cambridge, Mass.: Harvard University Press.

Lane, H. 1977. Notes for a psycho-history of American Sign Language. *Deaf American, 30,* 3–7.

Levine, E. 1956. *Youth in a Soundless World: a Search for Personality.* Washington Square, N.Y.: New York University Press.

Lieberman, P. & E. S. Crelin. 1971. On the speech of Neanderthal man. *Linguistic Inquiry, 2,* 203–222.

Markowicz, H. & J. Woodward. 1978. Language and the maintenance of ethnic boundaries in the Deaf community. *Communication and Cognition II,* No. 1, 29–38.

Meadow, K. 1972. Sociolinguistics, Sign Language and the deaf sub-culture. In T. O'Rourke (Ed.) *Psycholinguistics and Total Communication: The State of the Art.* Silver Spring, Md.: American Annals of the Deaf, 1–10.

Myklebust, H. 1960. *The Psychology of Deafness: Sensory Deprivation, Learning and Adjustment.* New York: Grune and Stratton.

O'Rourke, T. 1975. National Association of the Deaf: Communicative Skills Program. *Programs for the Handicapped*. Washington, D.C.: Department of Health, Education and Welfare, Office for Handicapped Individuals, April 15.

Padden, C. & H. Markowicz. 1976. Cultural conflicts between hearing and deaf communities. In *Proceedings of the Seventh World Congress of the World Federation of the Deaf*. Silver Spring, Md.: National Association of the Deaf.

Rainer, J. & K. Altschuler. 1966. *Comprehensive Mental Health Services for the Deaf*. New York State Psychiatric Institute, Columbia University.

Reilly, C. & M. Suwanarat. 1980. *Thai Sign Language: Model Dictionary by Handshape*. Bangkok, Thailand: Sebastian School for Children.

Sallagoity, P. 1975. The Sign Language of southern France. *Sign Language Studies, 7*, 181–202.

Schein, J. 1968. *The Deaf Community: Studies in the Social Psychology of Deafness*. Washington, D.C.: Gallaudet College Press.

Schein, J. & M. Delk. 1974. *The Deaf Population of the United States*. Silver Spring, Md.: National Association of the Deaf.

Schlesinger, H. & K. Meadow. 1972. *Sound and Sign: Childhood Deafness and Mental Health*. Berkeley, Ca.: University of California Press.

Stevens, R. 1980. Education in schools for deaf children. In C. Baker & R. Battison (Eds.) *Sign Language and the Deaf Community*. Silver Spring, Md.: National Association of the Deaf.

Trybus, R. 1980. Sign Language, power, and mental health. In C. Baker & R. Battison (Eds.) *Sign Language and the Deaf Community*. Silver Spring, Maryland: National Association of the Deaf.

Valade, Y-L. 1866. De l'origine du langage et de l'influence que les signes naturels ont exercée sur sa formation . . . Discours prononcé à la distribution solenelle des prix de l'Institution Impériale des Sourds-Muets de Paris. Paris, France: Imprimerie de Boucquin.

Vernon, M. & B. Makowsky. 1969. Deafness and minority group dynamics. *The Deaf American 21, 11,* 3–6.

Von der Lieth, L. 1967. *Dansk Døve-Tegnsprog*. Copenhagen: Akademisk Forlag.

Woodward, J. 1975. How you gonna get to heaven if you can't talk with Jesus: the educational establishment vs. the Deaf community. Paper presented at the Society for Applied Anthropology, Amsterdam, March.

Woodward, J. 1978. Some sociolinguistic problems in the implementation of bilingual education for deaf students. Paper presented at the second National Symposium on Sign Language Research and Teaching, San Diego, October.

Woodward, J. 1978. Historical bases of American Sign Language. In P. Siple (Ed.) *Understanding Language Through Sign Language Research*. New York: Academic Press, 333–348.

Woodward, J. & H. Markowicz. 1975. Some handy new ideas on pidgins and creole languages. Paper presented at the 1975 International Conference on Pidgin and Creole Languages, Honolulu, January.

Yau, S. C. 1977. *The Chinese Signs: lexicon of the standard sign language for the deaf in China*. Hong Kong: Chiu Ming Publishing Co., Ltd.

Chapter III

English in the Deaf Community

A. Introduction

In the preceding chapters, we examined how ASL is like all other languages of the world and then briefly traced its history and described some of the important functions of ASL in the Deaf Community. However, at this point, it is important to remember that ASL exists in a *bilingual* community. That is, another language, English, is also used in the Deaf Community and has impact on the Community and on its language—ASL.[1]

In fact, the main focus of educational programs for deaf children is the acquisition of English. Whereas some educators have recently argued that this rigid focus on English is unhealthy and that more attention should be given to learning history, science, math, etc.—through any available means of communication—it is still generally true that the majority of a deaf child's time and energy in school is spent on developing skills in English. Here what is meant by English is *spoken* English, *written* English, and a type of signing that has been called *manually coded English*.

In this chapter, we will examine what is meant by *manually coded English* and show how this form of signing is different from American Sign Language. However, we begin this discussion by talking more about what has happened historically in schools for deaf children in relation to the acquisition of English. This understanding of history (and the present-day situation) is important for understanding many peoples' attitudes toward ASL and how English has influenced ASL in certain ways.

B. English in Schools for Deaf Children

Just as hearing people have had difficulty in learning ASL for a variety of reasons, members of the Deaf Community have traditionally had difficulty in learning or acquiring native-like competence in English. There are several reasons why this has been true. First, those involved in educating deaf students have traditionally had very monolingual attitudes. That is, teachers and those in positions of power and decision-making have judged any and all student communication in terms of one language—English. This attitude is fostered, directly or indirectly, by teacher training programs which do not offer any courses in ASL (skill or structure) or which offer courses called "language development" that focus only on the development of English, but not on *language* development. Thus, it is no wonder that the

---

[1]In some cases there may be other languages which make the situation even more complex. For example, Deaf individuals with strong ethnic ties (Spanish, Puerto Rican, etc.) may exist in a *tri-lingual* situation.

deaf child's use of ASL or a variety of ASL that is used by his/her peers has been ignored.[2]

The predominant opinion seems to be that deaf students will learn less of the majority language (English) if they are in an ASL-English bilingual program than if they are confined to a monolingual (English) program. However, research done in other bilingual situations does not support this view.[3] In fact, monolingual attitudes in a bilingual situation can have serious negative results on the psychological, social, and academic success of students.[4] Thus, one major reason why some members of the Deaf Community may have difficulty in learning English is the monolingual attitude of educators in what is actually a bilingual situation.

Another reason concerns how language skills are normally developed and the unusual requirements placed on most deaf children. Most hearing children of hearing parents in the U.S. are involved in the process of acquiring English almost from the moment they are born. They are in a situation where they receive continuous auditory input and stimulation which fosters the development of their receptive skills which, in turn, foster the development of their expressive skills. The Deaf child of Deaf parents is generally in a similar situation except the input and stimulation is visual—ASL—not auditory. However, most deaf children in the U.S. have hearing parents. Generally these parents do not provide signed input and stimulation to their deaf children. Thus, these children enter school (generally at the age of 6 or 7) lacking full linguistic input and stimulation—either auditory or visual.

When a child enters school, s/he naturally wants to be accepted by the peer group. Generally the peer group has already begun to develop a signed means of communication which is considerably more like ASL than English. This means of communication develops because of the influence of older students or because of the influence of Deaf children of Deaf parents. The deaf child is then faced with the need to simultaneously learn both the means of communication that is necessary for satisfactory peer interaction and the different means of communication that is required by teachers—English.

A third reason why some members of the Deaf Community may have difficulty in learning English has to do with the nature of these two languages—ASL and English. English is an aural-oral language with its own vocabulary and syntax. The vocabulary and syntax of English have developed within a community of users who can speak and hear. ASL, however, is a visual-gestural language with its own vocabulary and syntax. The vocabulary and syntax of ASL have developed within a community of users who rely upon their bodies and eyes. The differences between these two languages in the areas of vocabulary and syntax are significant. If the classroom teacher is not sensitive to these differences, they may hinder the child's acquisition of English. Unfortunately these differences are rarely considered. In addition, the language that the child may be most comfortable with and that could be effectively used for teaching English is rarely recognized as valid or useful.

Finally, in the successful acquisition of any language by children, the development of receptive skills precedes the development of expressive skills. This means

---

[2]Cokely & Gawlik (1974).
[3]Cummins & Gulutson (1974), Lambert (1978).
[4]Diehold (1966), Saville-Troike (1973).

that a child receives considerable input and exposure to the target language in meaningful situations and begins to develop intuitions about the "rules" of a language before then expressing him/herself in that language. However, in many educational programs for deaf children (and perhaps most programs), the students are not given sufficient exposure to English in meaningful contexts to begin to develop their intuitions somewhat naturally. Rather, the students are often placed in a situation where they must express themselves in English without having developed the necessary receptive base.

These are a few of the reasons why some members of the Deaf Community have had difficulty in learning or acquiring native-like competence in English. Those members of the Deaf Community who do have native-like competence in English generally either have Deaf parents (and therefore acquired ASL before entering school), or have mild hearing losses, or lost their hearing after acquiring English. Educators have argued for years about the appropriate methods and techniques to use to help the majority of deaf students acquire competence in English. While most educators will agree that input and exposure must be visual, many of them have disagreed as to whether input should be limited to lipreading only or whether the use of signs should be allowed. Fortunately, in recent years, most educators have realized that the use of signs provides a more satisfying and effective visual means of communication than lipreading. However, the use of ASL is still considered inappropriate or wrong by the vast majority of educators since it does not represent English. Instead, these educators support the use of various codes designed to manually represent English.

C. The Use of Signs for Teaching English

One way of manually representing English is to fingerspell every word in an English sentence. Fingerspelling is the use of separate handshapes to represent letters of the alphabet of a spoken language. Thus, a word can be spelled out (e.g. **B-O-Y, G-I-R-L**). Not all Deaf communities use the same "manual alphabet". For example, American, British and Swedish Deaf people have different manual alphabets.

In educational situations, when a person uses speech and fingerspells every word in an English sentence, this is known as the Rochester Method or Visible English. Only about .5% of the educational programs for deaf students in the U.S. use this method.[5] One problem with the Rochester Method is that because fingerspelling is somewhat difficult to produce, the fingerspeller generally provides only approximations of English words. In one study, only 56% of the letters which should have been used to fingerspell an English message were clearly produced.[6] Because the fingerspellers in this study were teachers who were judged to be fluent users of the Rochester Method, the average teacher may have an even lower percentage. In addition, deaf people report that having to watch fingerspelling for prolonged periods of time is very tiring on the eyes.

---

[5]Jordan, Gustason & Rosen (1979).
[6]Reich & Bick (1976).

Another way to try to manually represent English is to use one of the invented manual *codes* for English. Used in this context, a *code* refers to an invented or artificially-developed means of representing a language. Thus, Morse code, Braille, SEE I, SEE II, L.O.V.E., Signed English and fingerspelling are all codes for English. A code which is invented relies upon the syntax and structure of a language which has naturally evolved over time. In this way, then, it is appropriate to refer to ASL as a signed *language*. However, SEE I, SEE II, L.O.V.E., Signed English, and fingerspelling are not signed *languages*; they are signed (or "manual") *codes* for English.

Some of the best known attempts to use signs for coding English are Seeing Essential English (Anthony 1971) or SEE I, Signing Exact English (Gustason, Pfetzing & Zawalkow 1972) or SEE II, and the lesser known Linguistics of Visual English (Wampler 1972), or L.(O.)V.E. These invented codes have been referred to as Manual English systems[7] or Manually Coded English (MCE). For the most part, attempts by schools or school systems to "standardize signs" are based upon the principles of these three invented codes.

Historically, the developers of these three codes worked together in 1969 in California. They developed guidelines and principles for inventing new signs or changing existing ASL signs to represent English words.

However, when David Anthony published SEE I, the other people in the group were dissatisfied with the results. They disagreed with his use of the system he invented to 'write' signs and with his application of some of the agreed upon principles. They began to develop their own book, still using the principles and guidelines they had developed together in 1969. This group decided to use drawings for signs in their book. Meanwhile, one member of this group, Dennis Wampler, felt that signs could not be adequately represented by drawings. Instead, he used a notation system based on the work of William Stokoe.[8] Wampler modified this notation system and published L.O.V.E. in 1972.[9] The rest of the group continued to develop drawings for signs, and SEE II was also published in 1972.

Before discussing some of the important principles of SEE I, SEE II, and L.O.V.E., it is again important to remember that they are *codes* for representing English. They are not separate languages since they all try to manually represent the same spoken language—English. Since these codes are visual-gestural in nature and since English is aural-oral in nature, linguists have said that these codes do not and cannot adequately and completely represent English.[10] They argue, in fact, that codes can never adequately and completely represent a language.

For example, a person can use the International Morse Code to represent the English word 'good' $\left[\overline{\overline{\text{G}}}\ \overset{\cdot}{\overline{\text{O}}}\ \overline{\overline{\text{O}}}\ \overset{\cdot\cdot}{\overline{\text{D}}}\right]$, but this array of dots and dashes cannot

---

[7]Cokely & Gawlik (1973), Charrow (1976).

[8]Stokoe had developed a symbol system designed to represent the handshape, position, and movement of a sign. For example, the sign glossed in English as **THURSDAY** was represented by the symbols H.ᵠ and the sign glossed as **CLOSE** or **SHUT** was represented by the symbols B⊥' B⊥ᴷˣ.

[9]At present, L.O.V.E. is not widely used for several reasons, one being a lack of adequate, readily accessible materials.

[10]Cokely & Gawlik (1973), Woodward (1973), Markowicz (1974, 1977–78), Stokoe (1975), Charrow (1976).

convey the spoken intonation used with that word in the following sentences: "Good boy, Timmy! I'm proud of you", "Good Morning! Can I help you?", "Good Morning? What's so good about it?". In the same way, signed codes are unable to express various aspects of the structure and forms of spoken languages. (The opposite is also true—that it is not possible to "vocalize" many of the structures and forms of signed languages.)

In any case, these codes do attempt to represent the vocabulary and structure of the English language. However, concerning the original purpose of these codes, there has not yet been any published research showing whether or not manual codes for English are useful for helping deaf children acquire competence in English.

Contrary to what is often stated,[11] these manual codes for English do not simply use ASL signs plus some invented signs. For example, often these codes will *initialize* the signs that are borrowed from ASL. This means that they will change the handshape of the ASL sign and replace it with a handshape from the manual alphabet that corresponds to the initial letter in a particular English word. For example, the flat open handshape that occurs in the ASL sign that means 'happy' or 'glad' is replaced with a 'G' handshape to represent the English word 'glad'. Thus, the natural *forms* of ASL signs are often changed.

In addition, these signs are then used in English grammatical patterns and are given a range of meanings which are unlike the grammatical patterns and associated meanings of ASL signs. For example, the sign glossed as **LOVE** is a verb in ASL, but is used as both a verb and a noun in manual codes for English (MCE). Similarly, the sign often mis-glossed as **ACROSS** and used as a preposition in MCE is actually a verb meaning 'go across something' in ASL. (The obvious ways that the *meanings* of ASL signs are changed is described in detail in the next section.)

Thus, these ASL signs are taken out of their naturally developed usage and are forced to function like English words. Because of these changes in form, grammatical function, and meaning, it is doubtful that these signs can be appropriately called "ASL signs".

What are the underlying principles of manual codes for English? One of the most basic principles that these codes follow is the "one sign–one word" principle. To understand this principle, it is helpful to consider multiple-meaning words in English, such as the word 'run' in the following sentences:

1. Pat can run home.
2. Pat left the water running.
3. Pat has a run in her stocking.
4. Pat will run for president.

In each of these sentences, the English word 'run' has a different meaning:

1. to move quickly by foot
2. to drip; to flow
3. a rip; a tear
4. to compete

---

[11]Gustason *et al* (1972), Anthony (1974), Bornstein *et al* (1975).

Other examples of multiple-meaning words in English are:

'play'   —which can mean recreational activity, or a dramatic production
'right'   —which can mean a direction, or correct, or a legal privilege
'pool'   —which can mean a game, or an area for swimming, or a collection of
           things
'fire'   —which can mean destructive burning, or to dismiss someone from a job,
           or to operate a gun
'check'   —which can mean a mark, or a paper substitute for money, or to investi-
           gate
'fall'   —which can mean a season, or to tumble suddenly, or a type of wig

In each of these examples, and hundreds of others, manual codes for English use
only one sign. In ASL, however, there usually are separate and distinct signs for
each meaning. Similarly, in many spoken languages (other than English), there
generally are separate and distinct words for each meaning. For example, let's look
again at the four meanings of the English word 'run' that were illustrated in sentences above. In ASL, French, and German, different symbols (signs or words) would
be used to refer to these meanings:

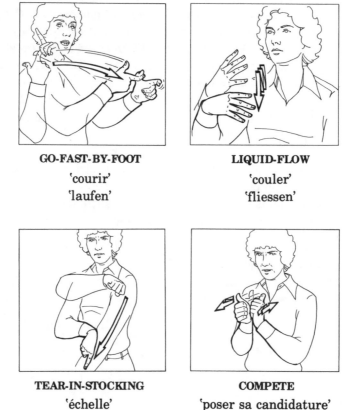

	GO-FAST-BY-FOOT	**LIQUID-FLOW**
French:	'courir'	'couler'
German:	'laufen'	'fliessen'

	TEAR-IN-STOCKING	**COMPETE**
French:	'échelle'	'poser sa candidature'
German:	'Laufmasche'	'kandibieren'

However, rather than using these four signs for the four different meanings, manual codes for English use only one sign (i.e. **GO-FAST-BY-FOOT**) to represent all of the meanings of the English word 'run'.

The criteria generally used by these codes in vocabulary selection are based on the *sound, spelling,* and *meaning* of English words. For a given English word, if two out of three of these factors are the same (sound and spelling, sound and meaning, or spelling and meaning), then only one sign will be used to represent that English word. Thus, although there are many different meanings of the English word 'run', they all have the same sound and spelling—hence, they are all represented by the same sign. Thus, the sign used to represent the English word 'run' (or 'play', 'right', etc.) may be identical in form to an ASL sign. But the way it is used in a sentence, and the meanings it is supposed to represent, is *very different* from the way that sign is used in ASL.

Another important principle of these codes is that English affixes must be manually represented. An affix is added to a word for a specific grammatical purpose. Affixes can occur at the beginning of a word (regain, unhappy) or at the end (walking, or punishment). Some affixes can also occur in the 'middle' of a word. ASL does not have the number nor the types of affixes that English has; so the developers of the manual codes for English felt they had to invent signs for these affixes in order to more closely represent English. However, because each manual affix is like a separate 'sign', this often means that a person using one of these codes must produce two, three, or four separate 'signs' for one English word (e.g. the English word 'unhappily' would be signed **UN+HAPPY+LY**). The following sentences may help to clarify this situation.[12]

(1) Written English: I gladly gave John $5.00.
     SEE I: I GLAD+LY GIVE+ED △ FIVE DOLLAR+S[13]
     SEE II: I GLAD+LY GIVE+ED J-O-H-N FIVE DOLLAR+S
     L.O.V.E.: I GLAD+LY GIVE+ED J-O-H-N FIVE DOLLAR+S

(2) Written English: Because I don't have a car, I can't go.
     SEE I: BE+CAUSE I DO+N'T HAVE A CAR I CAN+N'T GO.
     SEE II: BECAUSE I DO+N'T HAVE A CAR I CAN+N'T GO.
     L.O.V.E.: BE+CAUSE I DO+N'T HAVE A CAR I CAN+N'T GO.

Harry Bornstein and his associates at Gallaudet College developed a different manual code for English—called "Signed English". The Signed English project was originally developed to provide a manual system which could be used with spoken English for pre-school children. While this system claims to be different from the other manual codes for English, in practice, there are many similarities. For example, Signed English does not use the "sound-spelling-meaning" criteria for selecting signs. Instead, it uses dictionary entries. If a word has one entry in the dictionary,

---

[12]When one letter of a gloss is underlined, the sign is produced with that particular handshape from the manual alphabet.

[13]Note that SEE I requires name signs and does not encourage the use of fingerspelling. The symbol △ is used here to represent a name sign.

then Signed English will use one sign for that word. Therefore, in some cases (e.g. blind, brush, fall, and right), there are two signs because there are two dictionary entries. However, in most other cases, since there is usually only one entry, the result is the same as the other three codes. For example, Signed English still uses only one sign for 'run', 'play', 'fire', etc. Signed English has also borrowed some signs from the other manual codes for English and has invented others.

One major difference between Signed English and the other manual codes is the way that Signed English handles affixes. SEE I and SEE II have 'signs' for a large number of affixes—well over fifty. Signed English has limited the number of its signed affixes to twelve. Another difference between Signed English and the other manual codes is that Signed English has a set of teaching aids such as *Tommy's Day, The Three Little Pigs, Hansel and Gretel,* etc. These story books consist of drawings of signs used to represent the English words in the text or story. In 1973, a dictionary of Signed English was published and later revised in 1975.

Now adding the Signed English rendition to the sample sentences, the differences and similarities between Signed English and the other manual codes become more visible. Notice that unlike the other codes, Signed English uses a special "irregular past tense" marker for verbs like 'give' in example (1), and uses one sign **DON'T** in example (2) where the other codes use **DO+N'T**.

(1) Written English: I gladly gave John $5.00.
     SEE I: **I̲ G̲LAD+LY GIVE+ED △ FIVE DOLLAR+S**
     SEE II: **I̲ G̲LAD+LY GIVE+ED J-O-H-N FIVE DOLLAR+S**
     L.O.V.E.: **I̲ G̲LADLY GIVE+ED J-O-H-N FIVE DOLLAR+S**
     Signed English: **I̲ G̲LAD+LY GIVE+IRREGULAR-PAST-MARKER J-O-H-N FIVE DOLLAR+S**

(2) Written English: Because I don't have a car, I can't go.
     SEE I: **B̲E+CAUSE I̲ DO+N'T HA̲VE A C̲AR, I̲ CAN+N'T GO**
     SEE II: **BECAUSE I̲ DO+N'T HA̲VE A C̲AR, I̲ CAN+N'T GO**
     L.O.V.E.: **B̲E+CAUSE I̲ DO+N'T HA̲VE A C̲AR, I̲ CAN+N'T GO**
     Signed English: **BECAUSE I̲ DON'T HA̲VE A C̲AR, I̲ CAN'T GO**

Thus, we see that the invented manual codes for English attempt to model the vocabulary and structure of English sentences for the purpose of teaching English to deaf students. Many questions remain concerning how well these codes can and do model the English language and if they are useful in teaching English. The codes are very different from ASL in many ways: (1) they borrow only a small portion of the actual signs in ASL and invent other signs, (2) they often alter the form of ASL signs by changing the handshape (and by using only a highly restricted type of movement), (3) they often assign grammatical roles (e.g. noun *vs.* verb) to the signs which are different from the way they are used in ASL, (4) they often give the signs meanings which are very different from the meanings they have in ASL, and (5) they use the signs in the order in which words occur in English sentences, rather than the order in which signs occur in ASL sentences.

Because it is not possible in this space to examine any of these manual codes for English in greater detail, we refer the interested reader to several sources of additional information:

a. *Gallaudet Today*—Winter 1974/75, Volume 5, No. 2
  This issue of the quarterly journal published by Gallaudet College is devoted to "Communication" and contains articles on SEE I, SEE II, and Signed English.

b. "A Position Paper on the Relationship Between Manual English and Sign" by Dennis Cokely and Rudy Gawlik; *The Deaf American,* May, 1973.
  This article discusses the important principles which SEE I, SEE II, and L.O.V.E. have in common.

c. "A Linguist's View of Manual English" by Veda Charrow; Crammatte and Crammatte (Eds.) *Proceedings of the Seventh World Congress of the World Federation of the Deaf.* Silver Spring, Md.: National Association of the Deaf, 1976.
  This paper discusses some of the linguistic problems and difficulties with the manual codes for English.

d. *"Demonstration Stories in Various New Sign Systems"* Videotapes available from the Gallaudet College library (VTR #426).
  This tape provides examples of manual codes for English and Signed English. These are stories signed by the developers of these codes (or by people considered by the developers to be expert users of these codes). Also helpful may be the series of tapes #417-425. These tapes are lectures by Woodward, Anthony, Wampler, Bornstein, Gustason, and Schreiber who describe different types of signing.

e. *Recent Developments in Manual English*—Gerilee Gustason and James Woodward (Eds.), Department of Education, Gallaudet College, 1973.
  This booklet is a collection of papers presented at a special institute sponsored by the Department of Education at Gallaudet College.

D. Attitudes of the Deaf Community toward Manual Codes for English

How have members of the Deaf Community reacted to the invention and increasingly widespread use of these codes? To understand their reaction, it is important to remember that a language is an extremely important means of unifying a group of people and expressing who they are. When someone tries to change a community's language in an unnatural way, the community naturally becomes very defensive and possessive. Thus, it is not surprising that most Deaf adults have not accepted these codes for representing English. In fact, the attitude and reaction of most members of the Deaf Community toward these codes has been fairly negative. In an article in the *Gallaudet Today* issue on "Communication" (1974–75), Fred Schreiber, past Executive Secretary of the National Association of the Deaf (NAD), makes some very strong statements. For example, ". . . nothing could be worse than the horrendous proliferation of signs and the spectacle of professional educators not only condoning the activities of all those messiahs who believe they have been placed on earth for the sole purpose of leading us poor unfortunates to the promised land but who, in splendid isolation, actually join in the act."

There have also been many editorials and articles in the *Deaf American* by Deaf authors which show that the adult Deaf Community generally does not support these invented codes. Another clear comment about these codes is a play written by Gilbert Eastman, chairman of the Drama Department at Gallaudet College. This play, *Sign Me Alice* (1974), was one of the most popular plays ever shown at Gallaudet. It is based on *My Fair Lady* and shows how humorous and how tragic these "new signs" can be. The variety of "new signs" used in this play is U.S.E.—Using Signed English. Of course, no such system really exists. Eastman used the term U.S.E. to stand for all invented codes that represent English. The author's rejection of these codes and his perception of how their developers view ASL is obvious in lines such as:

Dr. Zeno: "A WOMAN WHO KEEPS SIGNING IN SUCH A DEPRESSING AND DISGUSTING MANNER (referring to Alice's use of ASL) HAS NO RIGHT TO BE ANYWHERE, NO RIGHT TO LIVE." (p. 9) "WHY CAN'T THE DEAF LEARN HOW TO SIGN ENGLISH?" (p. 11)

Vito: "U.S.E. FOR HEARINGS . . . TEACHERS WHO CAN'T UNDERSTAND OUR SIGN HAVE-TO USE NEW SIGNS. I UNDERSTAND ZERO. MINE BETTER." (p. 12)

Alice: "DO I HAVE-TO SIGN LIKE THAT FROM-NOW-ON? TO MY FRIENDS? NOBODY WOULD UNDERSTAND ME." (p. 31) "PEOPLE NEVER UNDERSTAND ME. I MUST FORCE MYSELF UNDERSTAND THEM." (p. 62) "I HAVE ALMOST FORGOTTEN MY-OWN LANGUAGE . . . AND TRY FOLLOW YOURS . . . YET YOURS NOT FOR ME." (p. 75) "YOU MUST REALIZE THAT U.S.E. HAS NOTHING TO DO WITH SIGN. U.S.E. ITSELF THAT ENGLISH. SIGN IS ANOTHER LANGUAGE." (p. 75)

Certainly the attitude expressed in these few lines is quite clear—attempts to use ASL signs to represent English in artificial ways are not accepted. These invented codes are not considered "real Sign". They are used by hearing people and some deaf people who can't understand or accept "real Sign".

Although these codes are not accepted or used by most members of the Deaf Community, they have had some influence on ASL in the area of vocabulary. However, if the Deaf Community accepts or adapts new lexical items (signs) from these codes, it is usually because these lexical items happen to follow certain natural rules of ASL sign production. Some of these principles will be discussed later.

In summary, it seems evident from the reaction of the Deaf Community that manual codes for English are viewed as intrusions on ASL. While it may be that these codes will have some influence on ASL (particularly in the area of vocabulary), it is unlikely that significant numbers of Deaf adults will use these codes to satisfy their needs for communication. Certainly the misuse of commonly accepted ASL signs (forcing them to function like English words) and the preference of most educators for manual codes that attempt to represent English (rather than for ASL) are indications to members of the Deaf Community that their own language— American Sign Language—is neither respected nor considered worthy of acquisition.

E. Pidgin Sign English in the Deaf Community

As is clear from the preceding discussions (see especially Chapter II), ASL plays a very important role in the Deaf Community. It enables effective and intimate person-to-person communication; it shows that a person is part of the Community; and it helps to identify the Deaf Community from the rest of society.

However, the vast majority of parents, teachers, doctors, speech therapists, counselors, psychologists, religious workers, and employers that contact and work with Deaf people are hearing speakers of English who do not know ASL. So what do these Deaf and hearing people use to communicate with each other? Most often, they interact with each other through the use of Pidgin Sign English—a combination of certain elements of both ASL and English.[14]

A *pidgin* is a language which develops naturally when people who do not know each other's language wish to communicate with each other. Normally, the pidgin is no one's native language. It typically combines certain vocabulary items and structures from the native languages of the people in contact with each other, and thus has a different grammar than either of the native languages. Pidgins are used all over the world. A linguist named David Decamp (1971) estimates that 2–3 million people use some form of pidgin every day in at least some language situations.

Pidgin Sign English (PSE) does not have one specific set of rules. Rather, there are many forms of PSE. The forms used by Deaf people tend to include more of the structures found in the grammar of ASL (e.g. verb directionality) and less of the grammatical forms of English (e.g. definite and indefinite articles: 'the' and 'a'). Conversely, the forms of PSE used by hearing people tend to include more English grammatical structures (e.g. use of the verb 'to be'), more transliterations of English idioms (e.g. 'to come across') and little of the structures found in ASL. As a person's signing skill moves from English to ASL, there are different stages which become less and less like English and more and more like ASL. The opposite is true as a person's signing moves from ASL to English. Thus, there exists a continuum of PSE varieties—some more like ASL, others more like English. This can be illustrated in the following way.

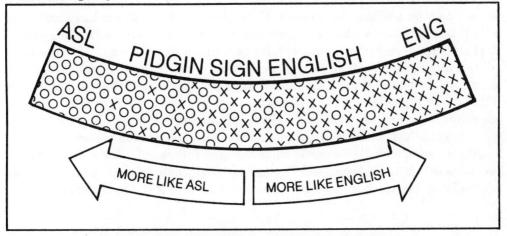

Fig. 3.1 Variation along the ASL-English continuum

---

[14]Woodward (1973b), Woodward & Markowicz (1975).

In Figure 3.1, the symbol 'o' represents features of ASL and the symbol 'x' represents features of English. Notice that in the middle of the continuum, there is a mixture of both symbols. However, as one moves toward ASL, there are fewer and fewer 'x's—indicating that fewer and fewer features of English are used. Likewise, as one moves toward English, there are fewer and fewer 'o's—indicating that fewer and fewer features of ASL are used.

The diagram above illustrates what has been called a *bilingual continuum*.[15] This continuum is a way of describing the interaction of the two languages (ASL and English) that are present in the Deaf Community. One result of the interaction of these two languages is the evolution of a pidgin which takes on several different forms depending on how much ASL or English the user knows.

PSE differs from the manual codes for English in several ways. First, it was not artificially invented, but evolved naturally because of the need for two groups of people (deaf and hearing) to communicate with each other. Second, unlike the manual codes for English, PSE is not intended to represent or model English. Because of this, the vocabulary used in PSE does not have a necessary relationship to the sound or spelling of English words. Signs are generally used because of the meaning they convey. Third, PSE may make use of some important features of both English (e.g. English word order, the verb 'to be') and ASL (e.g. number incorporation, verb directionality). How close to English or ASL people sign depends on their skills in ASL and in English, the topic of conversation, and who else is involved in the conversation.

Thus, the purpose of PSE—either more like ASL or more like English—is *communication*. For this reason, PSE has been generally accepted by the Deaf Community as a way to interact more comfortably with hearing people. The use of PSE by hearing people is acceptable to the Deaf Community because it does not represent an attempt to force unnatural changes on ASL.

In general, hearing people have used PSE because they have not had opportunities to acquire ASL. It is safe to say that the majority of Sign Language classes have *not* been ASL classes, but have been PSE classes—despite claims made in course titles. Typically these classes have had the following characteristics: first, they have focused only on teaching vocabulary. Consequently, the students have naturally used this vocabulary within the grammar or syntax of their native language— English; second, very often students have been encouraged or required to use their voices while signing—which simply reinforced the use of English grammar; third, the materials used in these classes have basically been lists of English words with illustrations or photographs of a sign which conveys only one of the many possible meanings of the English word, but make it appear that the meanings of the English word and the ASL sign are the same; fourth, materials which present ASL as a language were not available until rather recently; fifth, until a few years ago, most people viewed ASL as 'slang', 'bad English', or 'Deaf English'; sixth, a large number of Sign Language teachers have not been fluent users of ASL themselves and, thus,

---

[15]This continuum has actually been described as a bilingual, diglossic continuum. *Diglossia* refers to a situation in which two languages serve different functions within a given community and have different levels of status and recognition. For more detailed information, see Stokoe (1970) and Woodward (1973a).

were not able to model ASL for their students. Consequently, it is not surprising that most hearing people who learned signs in these classes have not used ASL, but instead have used a variety of signing that is more like English—PSE.

Because PSE represents a middle range of variation between ASL and a manual representation of English, it often serves as an intermediary through which English can influence ASL and ASL can influence manual representations of English. For example, in older ASL (and for many users of ASL today), it was common to find a 'noun-adjective' sign order—e.g. **BALL RED, GIRL INTELLIGENT, HOUSE WHITE**. Now, perhaps due to influence from English through PSE, some Signers sign—**RED BALL, INTELLIGENT GIRL, WHITE HOUSE**. English has also influenced ASL through certain English idioms which are signed quite literally— e.g. **ME CAN'T STAND YOU**. Here the sign for 'stand' is made with the index and middle fingers (literally, 'to stand'), rather than the ASL sign **PATIENCE** which would be more appropriate semantically.[16]

ASL has also had some influence on manual representations of English through PSE. For example, the use of single signs with *negative incorporation*[17] (e.g. **NOT-KNOW, NOT-WANT**) often occurs in PSE. Similarly, PSE Signers may make use of various modulations of *directional verbs*[18] (e.g. *you*-**GIVE**-*me*, *s/he*-**TELL**-*me*). And some users of manual codes for English have begun to use signs like this, even though more than one English word would be required to express the meaning that is expressed in each of these ASL signs.

The following sentences will show some of the differences and similarities between manual codes for English, PSE, and ASL. The examples of PSE on the next page are merely intended to show some of the possible varieties of PSE and are not exhaustive.[19]

---

[16]It is interesting to note that the sign **STAND** in ASL is produced with the palm of the left (non-dominant) hand facing up. However, in this borrowed phrase the palm faces to the right and the right hand is parallel to the ground, not perpendicular. Thus, there is a formational change in the sign **STAND** in this borrowed phrase which distinguishes it from the ASL sign for a 'person standing'.

[17]See Chapter VI.

[18]See Chapter IX.

[19]In these examples, we have more clearly identified the direction of the verb's movement as explained in the *Transcription Symbols*. For example, the sign *me*-**GIVE**-*you* (in the SEE I rendition) moves from the Signer to the Addressee. But the sign *pat*-**GIVE**-*secretary* (in the first ASL rendition) moves from the right to the left since 'Pat' has been given a spatial location on the right and 'secretary' has been given a spatial location on the left.

(1) Written English: Pat gave the books to the secretary yesterday.

SEE I: △ₚ *me*-GIVE-*you* +ED THE BOOK +S TO THE SECRET +ER +Y YESTER +DAY

SEE II: P-A-T *me*-GIVE-*you* +ED THE BOOK +S TO THE SECRETARY YESTERDAY

L.O.V.E.: P-A-T *me*-GIVE-*you* +ED THE BOOK +S TO THE SECRETARY YESTER +DAY

Signed English: P-A-T *me*-GIVE-*you* +IRREGULAR-PAST-MARKER THE BOOK +S TO
THE SECRETARY YESTERDAY

PSE: P-A-T G-A-V-E THE BOOK +S TO THE SECRETARY YESTERDAY

P-A-T *me*-GIVE-*you* THE BOOK +S TO THE SECRETARY YESTERDAY

P-A-T *me*-GIVE-*you* BOOK + TO SECRETARY YESTERDAY

P-A-T-*rt* *pat*-GIVE-*lf* BOOK + TO SECRETARY YESTERDAY

P-A-T-*rt* *pat*-GIVE-*lf* BOOK + SECRETARY YESTERDAY

```
                    (gaze,body rt        )t              (gaze lf            )
ASL:  YESTERDAY  P-A-T-rt   BOOK+-rt,  SECRETARY-lf  pat-GIVE-secretary
```

```
                    (gaze,body rt    )t   (gaze lf    )
      YESTERDAY  P-A-T-rt   BOOK+-rt,  pat-GIVE-lf  SECRETARY-lf
```

(2) Written English: Last week I went bowling with my friends.

SEE I: FINAL WEEK **I** GO +ED BOWL +ING WITH MY FRIEND +S

SEE II: FINAL WEEK **I** GO +ED BOWLING WITH MY FRIEND +S

L.O.V.E.: FINAL WEEK **I** GO +ED BOWL +ING WITH MY FRIEND +S

Signed English: FINAL WEEK **I** GO +IRREGULAR-PAST-MARKER BOWLING
WITH MY FRIEND +S

PSE: PAST WEEK **I** W-E-N-T BOWLING WITH MY FRIEND +S

PAST WEEK **I** FROM-*here*-GO-TO-*rt* BOWLING-*rt* WITH MY FRIEND +S

ONE-WEEK-PAST ME FROM-*here*-GO-TO-*rt* BOWLING WITH MY FRIEND +

```
                          t
ASL:  ONE-WEEK-PAST, ME FRIEND GROUP FROM-here-GROUP-GO-TO-rt BOWLING-rt
```

```
                      t
      ONE-WEEK-PAST, ME FRIEND GROUP FROM-here-GO-TO-rt BOWLING-rt
```

These examples help to show that PSE is not a single point on the continuum between ASL and English. Rather, PSE is actually a range of variations which will be more like English or more like ASL, depending upon such factors as the Signer's skill in ASL, the context, the participants, the topic, etc.

These examples also show how the varieties of PSE compare with the manual codes for English. Whereas some varieties of PSE may use one sign for each English word and follow English word order, still the selection of signs is more like ASL. For example, in these sentences, the PSE varieties began with the sign **PAST** and not the sign **FINAL** (used in the four codes)—which would be inappropriate in this context in ASL. If the manual codes for English were also placed on the ASL-English continuum that was seen earlier, they would be placed at the English end, with PSE stretching out across the broad middle area.

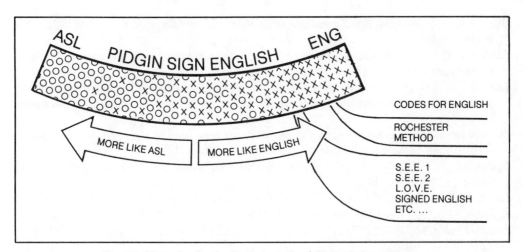

Fig. 3.2 Manual codes for English on the ASL-English continuum

In summary, PSE is not a static, easily identifiable point on the continuum. It is a blending of features of ASL and English which can have many different forms. It is not a system of manually coding English as are SEE I, SEE II, etc. It was not artificially developed for the purpose of representing English; rather, it evolved naturally from the bilingual situation in which users of ASL and users of English interact with each other. The "rules" of PSE are variable, depending upon the Signer's skills, the situation, the topic, etc. The primary goal of users of PSE is successful communication, not an exact representation of English. Because of this focus on meaning and communication, PSE has been a relatively comfortable way for users of ASL and users of English to interact—although the degree of mutual comfort depends on how much the interactants know each other's base language.

References

Anthony, D. 1974. *The Seeing Essential English Manual.* Greely, Colorado: University of Northern Colorado, The University Bookstore.

Bornstein, H., L. B. Hamilton, K. L. Saulnier & H. L. Roy. 1975. *The Signed English Dictionary.* Washington, D.C.: Gallaudet College Press.

Charrow, V. 1976. A linguist's view of Manual English. In Crammatte & Crammatte (Eds.) *Proceedings of the Seventh World Congress of the World Federation of the Deaf.* Silver Spring, Maryland: National Association of the Deaf, 78–82.

Cokely, D. & R. Gawlik. 1973. Option: A position paper on the relationship between Manual English and Sign. *The Deaf American,* May, 7–11.

Cokely, D. & R. Gawlik. 1974. Childrenese as pidgin. *Sign Language Studies, 5,* 72–82.

Cummins, J. & M. Gulutson. 1974. Some effects of bilingualism on cognitive functioning. In S. Carey (Ed.) *Bilingualism, Biculturalism and Education.* Edmonton, Canada: University of Alberta.

DeCamp, D. 1971. The study of pidgin and creole languages. In D. Hymes (Ed.) *Pidginization and Creolization of Languages.* London: Cambridge Univ. Press, 13–39.

Diehold, A. 1966. The consequences of early bilingualism in cognitive development and personality formation. ERIC No. ED 020 491.

Eastman, G. 1974. *Sign Me Alice.* Washington, D.C.: Gallaudet College.

Gustason, G., D. Pfetzing & E. Zawolkow. 1972. *Signing Exact English*. Rossmoor, California: Modern Signs Press.

Jordan, I., G. Gustason & R. Rosen. 1979. An update on communication trends at programs for the deaf. *American Annals of the Deaf,* June, 350–358.

Lambert, W. 1978. Some cognitive and socio-cultural consequences of being bilingual. Paper presented at the Georgetown Round Table on Languages and Linguistics, Washington, D.C.

Markowicz, H. 1974. Is Sign English English? Paper presented at the First Annual Conference on Sign Language, Gallaudet College, Washington, D.C.

Markowicz, H. 1977–78. Educational goals and the deaf image. *Teaching English to the Deaf,* Winter, *4,* No. 3, 11–15.

Reich, P. & M. Bick. 1976. An empirical investigation of some claims made in support of Visible English. *American Annals of the Deaf,* December, 573–577.

Saville-Troike, M. 1973. *Bilingual children: a resource document*. Arlington, Va.: Center for Applied Linguistics.

Schreiber, F. 1974–75. And the cons. *Gallaudet Today,* Winter, 5–6.

Stokoe, W. 1970. Sign Language diglossia. *Studies in Linguistics, 21,* 27–41.

Stokoe, W. 1975. The use of Sign Language in teaching English. *American Annals of the Deaf,* August, 417–421.

Woodward, J. 1973. Some characteristics of Pidgin Sign English. *Sign Language Studies, 3,* 39–46.

Woodward, J. 1973a. Implicational lects on the deaf diglossic continuum. Unpublished doctoral dissertation, Georgetown University, Washington, D.C.

Woodward, J. 1973b. Manual English: A problem in language planning and standardization. In G. Gustason & J. Woodward (Eds.) *Recent Developments in Manual English*. Washington, D.C.: Gallaudet College Press, 1–12.

Woodward, J. & H. Markowicz. 1975. Some handy new ideas on pidgins and creoles. Paper presented at the International Conference on Pidgin and Creole Languages, Honolulu, Hawaii, January 6–11.

Chapter IV

Sign Formation and Variation

This chapter begins with a description of how ASL signs are made to fit the needs and capabilities of the eyes and body. Then we examine several kinds of variations in signs that are influenced by such factors as the geographical and racial/ethnic background of the Signer, the Signer's age and sex, and the context in which the signs are used.

A. The Parts of a Sign

As presented in Chapter I, the "building blocks" of a sign are its handshape, palm orientation, movement, and location. That is, by combining a specific handshape, palm orientation, and movement in a particular location, one makes a sign. These four parts of a sign are called its *parameters*. Each parameter (e.g. the handshape parameter) has a set of members that are called *primes*. For example, the hand-shapes 'A', '5', and 'O'[1] (as in **GIRL, FATHER,** and **NONE**) are three primes within the handshape parameter. 'Palm up' and 'palm down' (as in **MAYBE** and **BALANCE**) are two primes within the palm orientation parameter. 'Circular' and 'back-and-forth' (as in **PLEASE** and **TRAIN**) are primes within the movement parameter. 'Head' and 'waist' (as in **RABBIT** and **RUSSIA**) are primes within the location parameter. The *Dictionary of American Sign Language* by Stokoe, Caster-line, and Croneberg lists 18–19 handshape primes, 24 movement primes, and 12 location primes.[2] Other linguists have used different ways of counting, and the question about exactly how many primes are within each parameter is still being studied.

---

[1]We think it is generally preferable to use a description or illustration to refer to a particular handshape—rather than a letter from the English alphabet or a number—so that students do not begin to 'see' English letters and numbers when they look at or produce ASL signs that have no relationship to English letters or numbers. That is why we used handshape illustrations in Chapter I. However, for reasons of space and convenience, we do occasionally use the letters and numbers here in this written text, but recommend that teachers avoid this in the classroom wherever possible. (See Chapter IV in the companion teacher text on *Curriculum, Methods, and Evaluation* for further explanation.)

[2]The dictionary did not list palm orientation primes. Some linguists have said there are about 6 such primes, although not all linguists agree that 'palm orientation' should be analyzed as a separate parameter.

Certain movements of the face, eyes, and/or head also seem to be a component of some signs. For example, the following signs usually include the non-manual behaviors that are written in parentheses: **READ**-*paper* (eyes look at the passive hand), **GROW-UP** (eyes follow the signing hand), **SHOCKED** (eyes are closed and then 'widened'), **SLEEP** (eyes close), **LOOK**-*up,* (eyes look up), **SNATCHED-UP** (mouth opens and closes, usually sucking in tongue sharply), **AIN'T-GOT-NONE** (lips are rounded and protruded, usually blowing out air), **LOUD-NOISE** (head is sharply jerked in side-to-side motion).

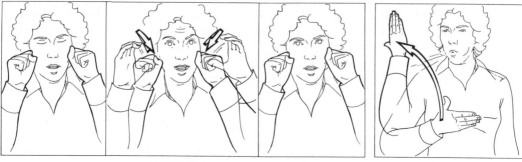

SHOCKED   **AIN'T-GOT-NONE**

In addition, there are a few signs that are made without any manual components, such as **YEAH-I-KNOW-THAT** which is made with a repeated 'twitching' on one side of the nose and **MENSTRUAL-PERIOD** which is made with a repeated puffing of one cheek. Research on the non-manual components of signs is still fairly new but has already shown that the components of many signs include more than a handshape, palm orientation, location, and movement of the hands.[3]

B. ASL Signs are Built to be "Seen"

An important characteristic of ASL signs is that they are constructed to fit the needs and capabilities of the perceiver's (the "see-er's") eyes. That is, the way that vision works has influenced how signs are made.[4]

For example, one obvious characteristic of human vision is that the thing we focus on is the thing we see most clearly — even though we are still able to see many other things in our peripheral vision. To illustrate this characteristic, look at the series of numbers below. If you focus on the number '1' in the middle of the series, that number is very clear and sharp. However, as the other numbers move away from number '1', they become less clear — although you can still see them in your peripheral vision. Similarly, if you focus on number '9' on the left side, the numbers farthest away become hard (or impossible) to recognize.

9   5   8   3   6   7   2   4   ⬚1   3   8   6   2   4   5   7   9

Thus, the thing we focus on is the thing we see best, but that sharpness and clarity of vision declines in our peripheral vision.

---

[3]Stokoe (1960), Woodward & Erting (1975), Baker (1976a, 1976b, 1979).

[4]A similar discussion may be found in Baker & Padden (1978).

How does the way we see affect the way that signs are made?

First of all, the person who is watching, the Addressee, looks at the face (eyes to mouth area) of the Signer during a conversation, *not* at the hands.[5] Thus, the face of the Signer and the area immediately around it is the area most clearly seen by the Addressee.

As might be anticipated from this fact, more signs in ASL are made in the face, head, and neck area than are made in the chest and waist area. As evidence of this, one researcher randomly chose 606 signs from the *Dictionary of American Sign Language* and found the following number of signs made in two major locations:[6]

	Signs
Head, Face, Neck Locations	465
Trunk Locations (shoulders to waist)	141
	606 total

As you can see, more than 75% of these signs were made in the area where the Addressee can see most clearly.

In addition, if we compare where certain signs were made in the early 1900's[7] with where these signs are made now, we can see that many of them have changed their location. That is, signs like **WILL, YOUNG, TIRED,** and **ANGRY** used to be made lower on the body (around the waist or lower chest) and are now made in the upper chest and neck area. (See Section D.4 on Historical Change in ASL signs.) Thus, some signs have changed their locations and are now made in areas which are more highly visible to the Addressee.

Another way in which our vision has influenced how signs are built concerns the fact that some signs are made with one hand, and some signs are made with two hands. By looking at where one-handed and two-handed signs are made, we can see that signs made on the chest and, especially, the waist (e.g. **BELT, RUSSIA, SKIRT, PREGNANT, SAILOR**) tend to be two-handed, whereas signs made on the face and head (e.g. **APPLE, BOY, MOTHER, WISE, DOLL**) tend to be one-handed.

How is this relationship between number of hands and location of signs influenced by the eyes? Notice that if two hands do the same thing, then the Addressee has more redundant visual information for identifying the sign. Since the Signer's waist area is less clear visually than the area around the face, ASL compensates for this lesser visual clarity around the waist by adding more visual information onto signs that are made there—by adding another hand that does the same thing.

Signs made around the face are already highly visible and do not need the additional information of a second hand. Indeed, many signs that used to be made with

---

[5]Siple (1978). An exception to this generalization occurs when the Signer fingerspells an uncommon or special word, and the Addressee may then look at the Signer's hand to clearly identify the word. Another more rare exception occurs when a sign is made outside of the normal signing space (e.g. **DRIBBLE-BALL**)—which also may require the Addressee to look at the sign in order to clearly identify it.

[6]Battison (1978), p. 42.

[7]This date refers to the old NAD films of several Deaf and hearing people signing about different subjects during the years 1910–1920.

two hands around the face have, through time, dropped one hand. For example, the signs **COW, MOUSE, HORSE, CAT, CHINA, DEVIL** and **GLASSES** were all made with two hands in the early 1900's, but many Signers now only use one hand to make these signs. (See Section D.4)

Thus, we can see several ways in which ASL signs are built to fit the needs and capabilities of the eyes. That is, ASL tends to locate signs in areas of greater visibility. It varies the number of hands used to make a sign according to the needs of the eyes for more information in areas of lesser visibility.

C. ASL Signs are Shaped by the Requirements of the Body

Besides being influenced by the visual needs of the Addressee, signs are also built to fit the dynamics of the Signer's body. Two general rules for forming two-handed signs will illustrate this point. (These rules were briefly described in Chapter I.)

Linguists[8] have observed that if the two hands in a sign move independently (e.g. **EXCITE, MAYBE, HOPE, PROGRESS, VISIT, PLAY**), they will usually have the same handshape, location, and type of movement. This is called the *Symmetry Condition*. Requiring that both hands move independently makes a sign harder to produce. However, this difficulty can be reduced by requiring that both hands then have the same handshape, location, and type of movement.

Similarly, if the two hands have different handshapes (e.g. **WORD, DRAW, NOT-LEGAL, ENOUGH, AMONG, SODA-POP**), then the dominant hand[9] will do the movement, and the other hand usually will not move. This is called the *Dominance Condition*. Thus, when the difficulty of the sign is increased by having two different handshapes, it is also reduced by generally allowing only one hand to move.[10] Another part of this rule reduces the difficulty of these signs even more. That is, the hand which does not move (called the *passive* or *base* hand) will usually have one of the following seven handshapes:

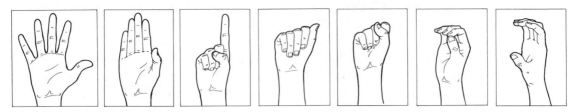

Unmarked Handshapes

These handshapes are considered to be the most natural, basic, and easy-to-make handshapes in ASL. They are called the most *unmarked* handshapes because they

---

[8]See Battison (1974, 1978).

[9]The right hand is the *dominant* hand if the Signer is right-handed; the left hand is *dominant* if the Signer is left-handed.

[10]Clearly, many of the newer, artificially invented signs break both of these rules. This may be one of the reasons why Deaf people often resist using many of the "new signs".

are the most common in ASL as well as in other signed languages.[11] More evidence of their simplicity is the fact that Deaf children of Deaf parents tend to learn these unmarked handshapes first.[12]

Just as there are handshapes which are easier to make, there are handshapes which are harder to make—called *marked* handshapes. The most "marked" hand-shapes in ASL are:

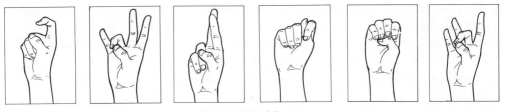

Marked Handshapes

As could be expected, because these handshapes are harder to make, they are used less frequently in the language. For example, Woodward (1978) found that fewer than 7% of the signs in ASL use these most marked handshapes. He also found that 8 other signed languages (French Sign Language, Finnish Sign Language, Swedish Sign Language, Australian Sign Language, British Sign Language, Japanese Sign Language, Providence Island Sign Language, and Rennell Island Sign Language) use them even less.[13] In addition, since the most marked handshapes are also harder to see or identify, they are more likely to occur in signs that are made around the face—another example of how ASL signs are built to be seen.

Thus, we can see several ways in which ASL signs are built to fit the needs and capabilities of the human body: ASL allows for complexity in one parameter by reducing complexity in the other parameters, and it uses only a minimum of the most complex handshapes.

D. Variation in ASL Signs

In all human languages, there are several types of variation that occur. For example, in spoken languages, words are often pronounced differently by speakers with different backgrounds, or speakers may use different words to represent the same thing. As an illustration, the English words 'sub', 'poorboy', 'hero', 'Italian sandwich', and 'hoagie' all may be used to refer to the same thing. However, one of these words is used more frequently in Philadelphia, whereas another word is used more frequently in the southern United States. This is an example of *regional* variation.

---

[11]Using the same 606 signs cited earlier, Battison found that 418 (or 67%) of them had one of these seven, most unmarked handshapes.

[12]Boyes-Braem (1973), McIntire (1977).

[13]These figures contrast greatly with the number of most marked handshapes in an artificial system like SEE II—which increases the number of 'R', 'E', and 'T' handshapes by more than 500% (Woodward, 1978a).

Variation can also be due to the *racial/ethnic* background of the language user. For example, 'shuckin', 'jivin', 'rappin', and 'the dozens' are common expressions in the U.S. Black Community, but are rare or non-existent in the vocabulary of most White speakers. Similarly, variation can be influenced by the *sex* of the language user. For example, few American males use the terms 'adorable', 'charming', and 'divine' when expressing admiration for something, whereas these words are fairly commonly used by many American women.

The *age* of a person can also influence his/her language. For example, older speakers of English may use the words 'frigidaire', 'osterizer', and 'victrola' to represent the things that younger speakers refer to as a 'refrigerator', 'blender', and 'record player'. Finally, the forms of a language frequently vary according to the *context* in which they are used. For example, in a formal lecture, one may use the terms 'children' and 'buttocks', but use the words 'kids' and 'butt' or 'behind' at home. Similarly, speakers may pronounce words in phrases differently in different contexts. For example, a speaker might say 'I don't know' in a lecture, but say 'I dunno' at home.

These and other types of variation occur naturally in any language and have been observed in languages all over the world. In the following sections, we will describe some types of variation that occur in ASL. At present, we know more about regional and historical (age-related) variation than we know about other types of variation in ASL. However, we do have examples of each of the types described above.

In some cases, linguists have noticed a type of patterned variation, but do not yet know what to attribute it to (e.g. to the regional or racial/ethnic background of the Signer). For example, in signs like **FUNNY, SWEET, SIT, BUTTER, NAME, HOSPITAL,** and **RABBIT**, some Signers use the handshape illustrated below on the left and some Signers use the handshape illustrated on the right.

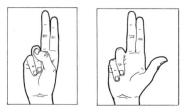

It is very important that ASL teachers be able to describe and illustrate the different types of variation in American Sign Language so that their students will have a healthy attitude about language differences and be better able to understand variations when they see them.

(D.1) Variation due to Region

People who are familiar with ASL know that there are some differences in how people from other parts of the country sign. Some of this regional variation in ASL can be attributed to the fact that the language has never been formally taught in schools. Since schools for Deaf students tend to be regional schools (i.e. children in one state tend to go to the residential school in that state), the signs used by these students often become generally accepted signs in a particular area. For example, there are several signed variations that express the meanings 'Halloween' and 'birthday'—although there are also more conventional signs which are generally recognized by Signers across the country. (The signs illustrated here may also be used in areas other than those indicated below the gloss.)

HALLOWEEN
(Louisiana)

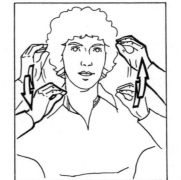

HALLOWEEN
(Virginia)

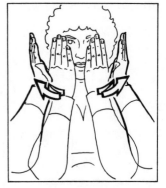

HALLOWEEN
(more conventional)

BIRTHDAY
(Philadelphia)

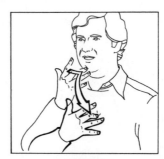

BIRTHDAY
(Indiana)

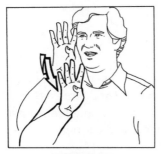

BIRTHDAY
(Virginia)

BIRTHDAY
(more conventional)

(D.2) Variation due to Racial/Ethnic Group

Another type of variation that exists in ASL is based on racial or ethnic factors. The history of racially segregated schools for Deaf children makes it easy to see how ASL variation based on race could develop. In general, Southern Black Deaf Signers tend to use older forms of signs. (See illustrations of the sign **YOUNG**.) In addition, they often use signs which are quite different from those of White Signers. (See illustrations of the signs that mean 'pregnant'.)[14]

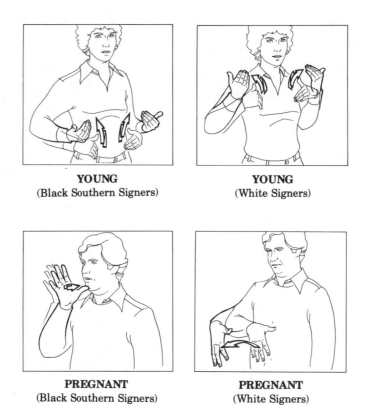

YOUNG
(Black Southern Signers)

YOUNG
(White Signers)

PREGNANT
(Black Southern Signers)

PREGNANT
(White Signers)

(D.3) Variation due to Sex

Although there is relatively little information on sex-based variation in ASL, one linguist[15] did find a major difference between male and female Signers for a particular type of historical change in signs (See D.4). This change concerns signs that were made on or near the elbow and now are often made on or near the hand, for example:

---

[14]Woodward & Erting (1975), Woodward (1979).
[15]De Santis (1977).

HELP, GUIDE, and **PUNISH.** In this study, the males were found to use many more of the newer, changed forms of the signs than were the females. (See illustrations of **HELP** below.)

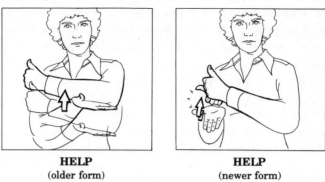

HELP
(older form)

HELP
(newer form)

We have also seen other male-female variations in signs, such as the different forms of the sign **TERRIFIC** used by males and females at Gallaudet College when talking about sports events.

TERRIFIC
(Gallaudet females)

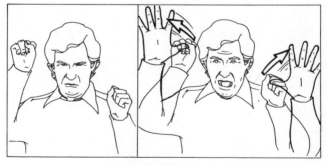

TERRIFIC
(Gallaudet males)

(D.4) Variation due to Age (Historical Change)

As discussed in Chapter I, all 'living' languages (languages that people use) change across time. In spoken languages, the sounds, vocabulary, meanings of words, and grammatical rules may change. For example, nine hundred years ago, the English line from the *Lord's Prayer* "Give us our daily bread" was "Urne gedaeghwamlican hlaf syle us"!

Some types of language change occur more rapidly than other types. For example, changes in the vocabulary of a language occur more rapidly than changes in the grammatical rules of that language. When changes occur more rapidly, one can see clear differences in the language of younger people (who use the newer forms) and the language of older people (who tend to continue using the forms they grew up with). Thus, language change creates another type of language variation—variation due to age.

Several linguists[16] have studied some of the changes that have occurred in ASL since its 'birth' around 1817. They have found several patterns which describe the kinds of changes that many ASL signs have undergone.[17]

For example, many two-handed signs in which each hand had a different hand-shape (e.g. **LAST, DEPEND, BRIEF, WORLD**) now have the same handshape for both hands. This change is also presently happening with the signs **INSTITUTE** and **WHISKEY** (which have a 'fist' handshape in the non-dominant hand, but are changing so that the non-dominant handshape is the same as the dominant hand-shape).

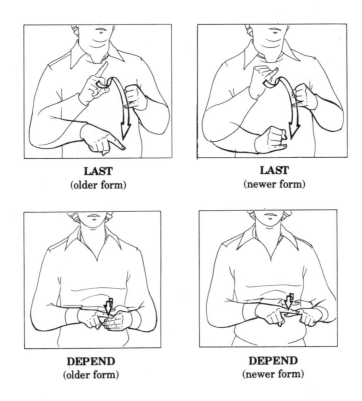

LAST
(older form)

LAST
(newer form)

DEPEND
(older form)

DEPEND
(newer form)

---

[16]Frishberg (1975), Woodward & Erting (1975), Erting & Oliver (1976), Woodward & De Santis (1977), Woodward (1978b).

[17]Probably the oldest actual examples of American signing are the collection of films (e.g. *Lorna Doone, The Preservation of Sign Language, Memories of Old Hartford*) made by the NAD during the early 1900's. These films (available from the Gallaudet College library) reveal many interesting lexical and structural variations as compared with present-day ASL.

This pattern of historical change is called *Symmetry* since the hands become symmetrical (the same). Another type of symmetrical change is seen in signs which previously were one-handed, but now have become two-handed, with the second hand having the same handshape and movement as the first hand. For example, the signs **ANGRY, DIE, HURRY,** and **JOURNEY** all were one-handed signs but are now generally made with two hands.

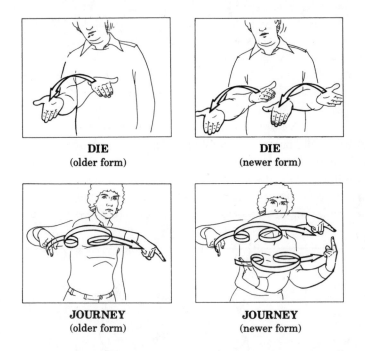

DIE
(older form)

DIE
(newer form)

JOURNEY
(older form)

JOURNEY
(newer form)

Another pattern of historical change is called *Displacement* since the place where the sign is made changes. There are two types of displacement: Head Displacement (referring to signs made in contact with the face) and Body Displacement (referring to signs made below the neck).

Signs made *on* the face have historically moved to locations *around* the face, so that the face is not 'blocked' during signing. For example, the signs **NOTHING, DENY,** and **WRONG** used to be made under the nose but are now generally made below the chin.

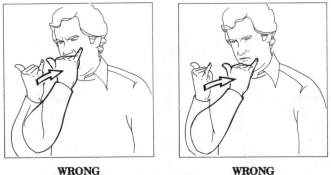

WRONG
(older form)

WRONG
(newer form)

As mentioned earlier, two-handed signs that are made in contact with the face have also tended to become one-handed. Since the sign is clearly visible in this area and since one-handed signs require less energy than two-handed signs, this change helps increase the efficiency of the language.

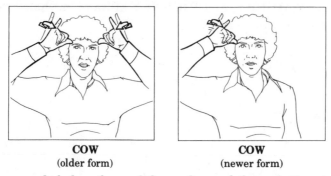

COW
(older form)

COW
(newer form)

Signs that are made below the neck have changed through time to become more *centralized*. That is, they have moved *inward* toward the "line of bilateral symmetry" (i.e. an imaginary line vertically dividing the body into two equal parts) and *upward* or *downward* toward the center of the signing space (i.e. the hollow of the throat). The arrows on the diagram below illustrate the direction of the location changes.

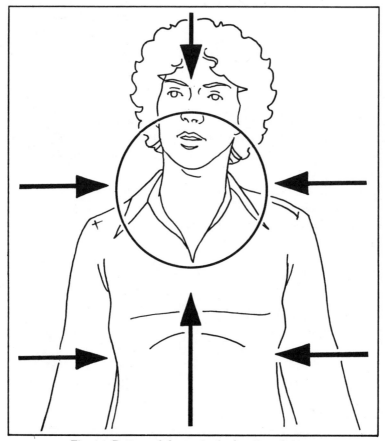

Fig. 4.1 Pattern of change in the location of signs

For example, the signs **LIKE, FEEL, PLEASE,** and **LOVE** were made to one side of the chest (supposedly over the heart) and now are usually made at the center of the chest.

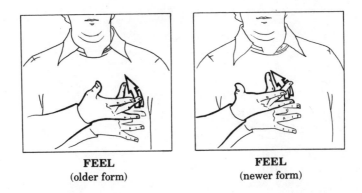

FEEL   FEEL
(older form)   (newer form)

Similarly, the signs **HELP** and **SUPPORT** were made under the non-dominant elbow or forearm; **GUIDE** was made on the arm; and **PROMISE** was made on the forearm. Now all of these signs are usually made on the non-dominant hand.

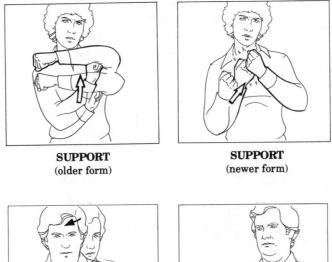

SUPPORT   SUPPORT
(older form)   (newer form)

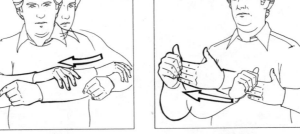

GUIDE   GUIDE
(older form)   (newer form)

The signs **YOUNG, WILL, TIRED,** and **BECOME-ANGRY** were made around the waist but are now generally made on the torso (sometimes as high up as the shoulders).

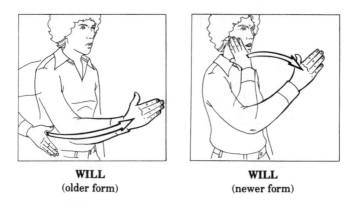

WILL	**WILL**
(older form)	(newer form)

Another pattern of historical change is called *Fluidity*. That is, if the older form of a sign had two parts (i.e. is or was a compound sign[18]), then the sign changed to make the parts more alike and to make the transition between the parts more smooth (or 'fluid').

For example, in the following two-part signs, the first part of the sign has become more like the second part: **WIFE** (from **FEMALE + MARRY**), **GOLD** (from **EARRING + YELLOW**), **REMEMBER** (from **KNOW + CONTINUE**). This is called *anticipatory assimilation* since the first part of the sign has 'anticipated' the second part's handshape and has copied it.

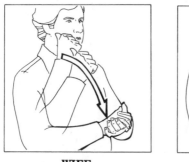

WIFE	**WIFE**
(older form)	(newer form)

---

[18]See Chapter V for a discussion of *compounds* in ASL.

In another, smaller group of two-part signs, the opposite type of assimilation (called *perseverative assimilation*) occurs. Here the first part of the sign influences and changes the second part of the sign, as seen in signs like **TOMATO** (from **RED + SLICE**) and **HOME** (from **EAT + BED**).

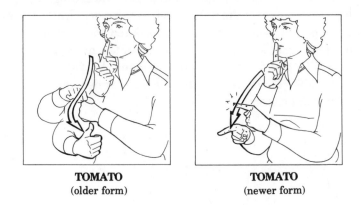

TOMATO
(older form)

TOMATO
(newer form)

As the two parts in a compound sign become increasingly like each other and the movement between them becomes more 'smooth', they begin to look like a sign with only one part. And when they have changed to the point where they are seen as single signs and are made like single signs, then these formerly two-part signs are, in a sense, no longer "compounds". Some examples of this are **WIFE, REMEMBER, HOME,** and **INFORM** (from **KNOW + BRING**). Some examples of ASL compounds that have not yet undergone this historical change are **EAT⌢MORNING** (meaning 'breakfast'), **GIRL⌢SERVE** (meaning 'waitress'), and **HOME⌢WORK**.

With another group of compound signs, one part has completely dropped off, leaving only the other part as the whole sign. For example, the old sign for 'bird' had a part showing the 'beak' and a part showing the 'wings'. Now only the 'beak' part is used as the sign **BIRD**. Similarly, the signs **SPRING** (from **SUMMER + GROW**) and **DARK** (from **BLACK + DARK**) have dropped the first part.[19]

These are just some of the ways in which ASL signs have changed during the past 150 years or so. Many of these changes are ongoing; that is, they are still in process today. For example, research[20] has shown that Deaf Signers in the South tend to use more older forms of signs and that the historical changes described here occur more slowly in the South. Similarly, the research described in Section D.3 suggests that females may also tend to use more of the older, less centralized signs. Thus, these historical changes occur gradually and are dynamic processes in the language.

(D.5) Variation due to Context (Conversational Change)

In this section, we will discuss signing differences in two general contexts: *formal* (e.g. academic lectures, business meetings) and *informal* (e.g. everyday conversations with friends and family). However, since most of the linguistic research on

---

[19]The sign **SPRING** is a noun made by restrained repetition of the verb **GROW**—following the pattern for forming nouns from related verbs, as described in Chapter V.

[20]Woodward & Erting (1975), Woodward & De Santis (1977).

ASL has dealt with signing in more informal contexts, our knowledge of ASL variation in formal contexts is very limited.

Formal signing in ASL seems to use more two-handed variants of signs (i.e. signs are made with both hands when they could be made with one hand—e.g. **ENJOY, ACCEPT, NOW**); signs are made larger than usual; and the signing speed is slower. There also seems to be less use of facial behaviors to express linguistic information.

As would be expected, some signs are considered more appropriate for formal contexts than other signs. For example, to express the meaning 'I don't know', the signs **DON'T** (or **NOT**) and **KNOW** would probably be used in a formal context, whereas the sign **NOT-KNOW** (especially the one-handed variant) would probably be used in an informal context.

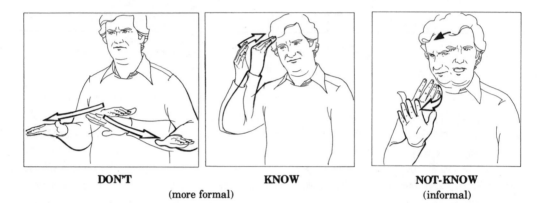

DON'T	KNOW	NOT-KNOW
(more formal)		(informal)

Similarly, the sign **DEAF** illustrated below on the left is considered to be more formal than the sign illustrated on the right. (The form on the left also seems to be an older variant of the sign and is seen in the old NAD films of Signers in the early 1900's.)

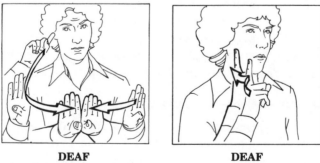

DEAF	DEAF
(more formal)	(informal)

In general, when a person is involved in a conversation, his/her language forms tend to be more informal. However, even within the context of a conversation, there can be considerable variation. For example, if a person is conversing with friends, s/he will probably use a more comfortable, informal style of communicating. However, if s/he is conversing with someone for the first time and wants to impress that person, then probably a more careful, formal style will be used.

We are now going to consider how the form of a sign often changes when it is used in an informal conversation. We call these changes *conversational changes* since they normally occur when people are comfortably using the language to converse together.

Conversational changes occur in every language; that is, people don't talk or sign the way that their language is usually written or drawn in vocabulary books. Written or pictured language is more rigid and exacting than spoken or signed language. When people use a language, the forms of the language become more efficient and smooth because the usual purpose of using the language is the effective communication of ideas and feelings.

For example, in English, a person might write 'I *don't know* what you mean', but, in a conversation, might say 'I *dunno* what you mean'. Similarly, people write 'te<u>n</u> percent', but, in rapid speech, may pronounce the phrase like 'te<u>m</u> percent'. These changes occur every day and are due to the process of *assimilation* whereby the sounds are changed to become more like each other.

How do these changes help the language become more smooth and efficient? In spoken languages, when the sounds are more like each other, it takes less energy and time to produce them. In the 'ten percent' example, the 'n' sound changes to an 'm' because the 'm' sound is made in the same place in the mouth as the 'p' in 'percent'. Contrary to what people sometimes think, these assimilatory changes do not occur because speakers are "lazy" (!) but because they help speakers to use their language in a comfortable way and to communicate more efficiently. Of course, there are limits on how much assimilation and other such changes can occur so that the words are still intelligible. Thus, there is a balance between the need for enough precision to be understandable and the need for 'smoothing out' the sounds in order to be efficient.

The same kinds of changes occur when Deaf Signers use American Sign Language in conversations. Students need to learn and understand these changes in order to be able to efficiently use the language and understand its use by Deaf Signers.

Several of the changes that occur in ASL conversations are also described as patterns of historical change (e.g. *Displacement* and *Fluidity*). This makes sense because the language is changing in ways that will make it more efficient. That is, after the conversationally changed forms occur repeatedly, they become natural forms in the language which Deaf children may learn from their Deaf parents.

Take, for example, the older sign for **SISTER** (from **FEMALE + SAME**). This sign is now taught to children in its assimilated form where the handshapes and palm orientations are the same. The same is true for signs like **BROTHER** (from **MALE + SAME**), **HUSBAND** (from **MALE + MARRY**), and **WIFE** (from **FEMALE + MARRY**).

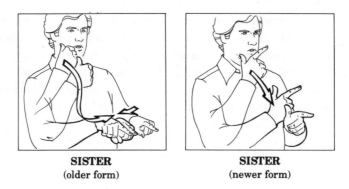

SISTER
(older form)

SISTER
(newer form)

Displacement is a type of conversational change that occurs very frequently. That is, the location of a sign is changed to become more centralized. If signs are made in more similar locations (i.e. closer to the hollow of the throat), then less energy is required in moving from one location to another. For example, signs that are often pictured in books as being made around or in contact with the forehead (e.g. **SUPPOSE, BECAUSE, THINK, STUPID, MISUNDERSTAND, KNOW, FOR-FOR, WHY, SUMMER, BLACK, DREAM, BOY, UNDERSTAND**) are frequently lowered during conversations to the cheek area or even the neck-chin area. Similarly, the signs **GOOD** and **NOT-GOOD** (often glossed as **BAD**) are pictured as starting from the mouth, but usually are lowered when used in conversations. The same is true for the signs **SEE, PICTURE,** and **GUESS** which are pictured as starting around the eyes but are usually lowered during conversations.

The more formal form of a sign is called its *citation form*. This form of a sign is often pictured in vocabulary books or is often shown in response to the question "What is the sign for ___?".

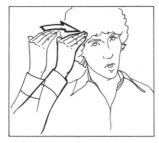

KNOW
(citation form)

KNOW
(a conversational form)[21]

---

[21]We are calling this and other examples "conversational forms" because they frequently occur during conversations. However, a Signer may use the citation form during a conversation, too.

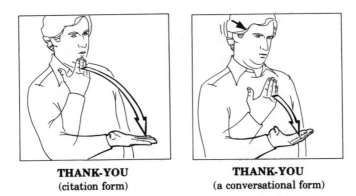

THANK-YOU
(citation form)

THANK-YOU
(a conversational form)

Since two-handed signs require more energy than one-handed signs, another way to increase one's efficiency while signing is to drop one hand when it is not necessary for understanding the meaning of a sign. For many two-handed signs, both hands are doing exactly the same thing. Thus, one hand can be omitted without losing any important information (e.g. **WANT, NOT-WANT, SUCCESS, ___-INFORM-___, NOW, HERE, COLD, FREEZE, RAIN, ___-OFFER-TO-___, LIVE, ADDRESS, UP-TILL-NOW, TRY, CAN, ACCEPT-FROM-___, SAD, NERVOUS, SCARED, LAUGH, CRY, ALLOW, WAIT, BASKETBALL, LEAVE-FROM-___, DRESS/CLOTHING, MELT/DISSOLVE, HAVE**).[22]

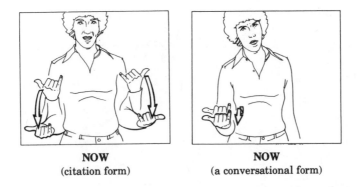

NOW
(citation form)

NOW
(a conversational form)

However, in general, when the hands contact or interact with each other, one hand usually is *not* omitted unless the meaning of the sign is obvious from the context (e.g. **PAPER, SHOE, SOCK, GLOVE, HAND, STAR, TEMPERATURE, AMONG, TRAIN, CHAIN, TOGETHER, BOTHER, GROW**).[23] Still, some of these

---

[22]Indeed, the older forms of several signs that used two hands (e.g. **GRANDMOTHER, GRANDFATHER, DEER, COW, HORSE, HONOR, RESPECT**) now tend to use only one.

[23]Exceptions sometimes occur when one hand is "encumbered" (e.g. holding something). Here signs which require contact with the non-dominant hand (e.g. **HARD, NEW, BROTHER**) are frequently altered so that they contact some other available surface (e.g. contact a table top or book, or the Signer's chest or thigh).

contact signs (e.g. **WRITE, READ, NAME, ALL-RIGHT, ___ -JOIN-TO- ___ ,
POSTPONE, DAY, MORNING, AFTERNOON, NIGHT**) do allow deletion of the
non-dominant hand during conversation because they are still easy to identify.

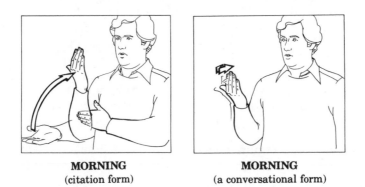

MORNING   MORNING
(citation form)   (a conversational form)

   Another type of conversational change that can increase one's efficiency involves
a reduction of a sign's movement. For example, the movement of one form of the sign
DEAF is usually pictured as starting at the ear and ending on the lips (or vice
versa). However, in conversations, this movement is usually much smaller, beginning on the side of the mouth and then contacting the cheek. The same occurs with
HOME, and sometimes the movement is reduced even more so that both contacts
are at the same place on the cheek.

DEAF   DEAF
(citation form)   (a conversational form)

The sign **YEAR** can be reduced so that the dominant hand does not circle the other hand, but instead does one quick rotation of the wrist (or forearm) and then contacts the top of the non-dominant hand. The sign **ONE-YEAR-PAST** is frequently reduced by keeping the two hands together and simply flicking the dominant index finger (pointing to the 'past'). (The signs **ONE-YEAR-FUTURE** and **ONE-YEAR-PAST**, illustrated in Chapter VII, are also reduced signs.)

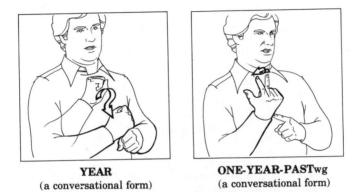

YEAR
(a conversational form)

ONE-YEAR-PASTwg
(a conversational form)

Signs that frequently occur together are often reduced and assimilated to each other. For example, when the signs **FOR** and **SURE** occur together, the outward movement of **FOR** is frequently reduced so that the sign moves from the temple down to the mouth. Similarly, the signs **WHY** and **NOT** are often so reduced together that they look like one sign.

FOR SURE

WHY NOT

When **THAT** and **#ALL** occur together, the extended pinky is often omitted on the sign **THAT**. So the sign has the 'A' handshape which begins the fingerspelled loan sign **#ALL**. (See Chapter V for a description of Fingerspelled Loan Signs.).

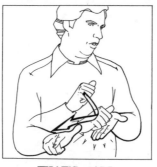

THAT'S ⁀ #ALL

In rapid discourse, other assimilations often occur just 'by chance'. For example, in the sentence below (taken from a videotape of a conversation), the Signer used a 'Y' handshape with the index finger extended (contacting his forehead) for the sign **THINK**—in anticipation of the sign **PLAY**. In addition, the movement of the sign **PLAY** was reduced to a slight twist of the wrist as it moved down to contact the base hand for the sign **NEW-YORK**.

Context   The Signer and his friend are talking about several football players. His friend asks about Joe Namath and the Signer responds:

(1)   (brow squint   )
          PAST THINK PLAY NEW-YORK J-E-T-S

       Struc   'In the past I think (he) played for the New York Jets.'

       Trans   'I think he used to play for the New York Jets.'

To achieve competence in ASL, students need to be able to recognize and understand these types of conversational changes. Teachers should supplement this partial list of examples with their own observations, since research and knowledge in this area is limited. Exposing the students to conversations between various Deaf Signers will help them become familiar with the difference between the way signs are pictured in books and the way signs are actually used.

E. Summary

We have described how ASL signs are built to be perceived with the eyes and how they are also shaped by the requirements of the body. In this way, we can see how ASL signs are specially constructed to be symbols in a visual-gestural language. We have also explored several types of variation in the production of ASL signs, which are influenced by such factors as the geographical and racial/ethnic background of the Signer, the Signer's age and sex, and the context in which signs are used. Again, we encourage teachers to instill in their students an appropriate understanding and acceptance of such variation in ASL, especially those variants commonly used in their geographic area.

References

Baker, C. 1976a. What's not on the other hand in American Sign Language. In *Papers from the Twelfth Regional Meeting of the Chicago Linguistic Society*. Chicago, Illinois: University of Chicago Press.

Baker, C. 1976b. Eye-openers in ASL. In *Sixth California Linguistics Association Conference: Proceedings*. San Diego State University, 1–13.

Baker, C. 1979. Non-manual components of the Sign Language signal. Paper presented at the NATO Advanced Study Institute, Copenhagen, August.

Baker, C. & C. Padden. 1978. *American Sign Language: a look at its history, structure, and community*. Silver Spring, Md.: T.J. Publishers.

Battison, R. 1974. Phonological deletion in American Sign Language. *Sign Language Studies 5*, 1–19.

Battison, R. 1978. *Lexical Borrowing in American Sign Language*. Silver Spring, Md.: Linstok Press.

Boyes-Braem, P. 1973. A study of the acquisition of dez in American Sign Language. MS, University of California, Berkeley.

De Santis, S. 1977. Elbow to hand shift in French and American Sign Language. Paper presented at the NWAVE conference, Georgetown University, October.

Frishberg, N. 1975. Arbitrariness and iconicity: historical change in American Sign Language. *Language 51*, 696–719.

McIntire, M. 1977. The acquisition of American Sign Language hand configurations. *Sign Language Studies 16*, 247–266.

Siple, P. 1978. Visual constraints for Sign Language communication. *Sign Language Studies 19*, 95–112.

Stokoe, W., D. Casterline & D. Croneberg. 1965. *A Dictionary of American Sign Language on Linguistic Principles*. Washington, D.C.: Gallaudet College Press. (Revised edition, Silver Spring, Md.: Linstok Press, 1976).

Woodward, J. 1978a. Sign Marking: "Stage" four handshapes. Paper presented at the Summer Meeting of the Linguistic Society of America, July.

Woodward, J. 1978b. Historical bases of American Sign Language. In P. Siple (Ed.) *Understanding Language Through Sign Language Research*. New York: Academic Press, 333–348.

Woodward, J. 1979. *Signs of Sexual Behavior*. Silver Spring, Md.: T.J. Publishers.

Woodward, J. & S. De Santis. 1977. Two-to-one it happens: dynamic phonology in two sign languages. *Sign Language Studies 17*, 329–346.

Woodward, J. & C. Erting. 1975. Synchronic variation and historical change in American Sign Language. *Language Sciences 37*, 9–12.

Woodward, J., C. Erting & S. Oliver. 1976. Facing & hand(l)ing variation in American Sign Language. *Sign Language Studies 10*, 43–51.

Chapter V

Selected Sign Types

In this chapter, we will briefly examine several types of signs which have received some attention in the linguistic literature on ASL. These linguistic studies have uncovered several 'interesting facts' about these signs which teachers need to be aware of. We feel such 'interesting facts' are important enough to include in this volume, but that longer treatment in separate chapters either would not be particularly useful, or, in other cases, would not be possible. Consequently, we have arbitrarily gathered this information together in one chapter.

In the following section, we will examine (a) some interesting differences in the formation of related nouns and verbs, (b) how compound signs are formed and used productively in ASL, (c) how certain frequently fingerspelled words have become adapted to and accepted into ASL as "loan signs", and (d) how some ASL signs have been frequently mislabeled as "idioms". In each of these sections, we will provide the reader with references for more in-depth explanations.

A. Nouns and Verbs

Until recently, most people thought that nouns and verbs in ASL like **CHAIR** and **SIT**, or **AIRPLANE** and **FROM-____-FLY-TO-____**, or **CAR** and **DRIVE**-*car* were signed the same way, that there was no difference in the formation of nouns and verbs that have related meanings. However, a closer look at the *movement* of these nouns and verbs has shown this assumption to be false. That is, many related[1] nouns and verbs are made differently—similar to the way English distinguishes some pairs like 'apologize-apology', 'erase-eraser', 'laugh-laughter', and 'sing-song'. ASL shows this difference through a change in the sign's movement.

While studying 100 such noun-verb pairs in which the *noun* denotes a concrete object (e.g. **CHAIR**) and the *verb* denotes the action performed with/on that object (e.g. **SIT**), some researchers[2] found that the movement of signs needed to be more carefully examined. They found that in order to 'see' and understand the difference in the movement of many nouns and verbs, the parameter of movement needed to be

---

[1]Here "related" means 'similar in form and in meaning'. Thus, the signs **SAILOR** and **FROM-____-SAIL-TO-____** do not fit this generalization since they do not have similar forms, although they do have similar meanings.

[2]Supalla & Newport (1978).

analyzed into 3 "dimensions": (1) *frequency*, (2) *directionality*, and (3) *manner*. Below are brief descriptions and illustrations of what is included within each dimension

(1) The *frequency* of a movement is either a 'single' movement or a 'repeated' movement.

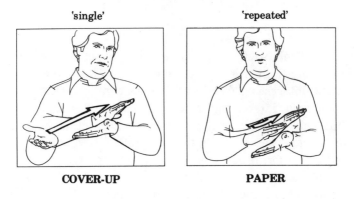

(2) The *directionality* of a movement is either 'uni-directional' (i.e. primary movement in only one direction) or 'bi-directional' (i.e. primary movement in two directions).

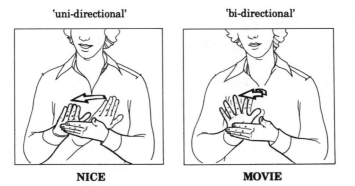

(3) The *manner* of a movement is either 'continuous' (i.e. movement is smooth and loose), or 'hold' (i.e. sign begins with a loose movement, but ends abruptly and stiffly, and is held for a short time), or 'restrained' (i.e. movement is small, quick, and stiff, and the hand may bounce back to its initial position).

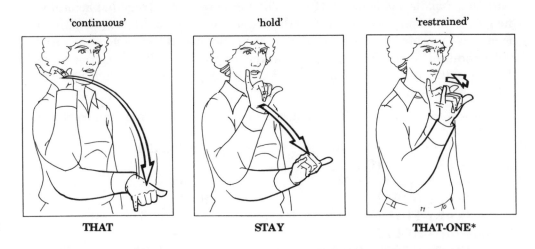

'continuous'	'hold'	'restrained'
THAT	STAY	THAT-ONE*

By describing each noun and verb in terms of these three dimensions (frequency, manner, directionality), the researchers were better able to see how their movements are different. For example, the movement of the verb **SIT** is 'single, uni-directional, and hold', but the movement of the noun **CHAIR** is 'repeated, uni-directional[3], and restrained'. The verb **PAINT** is 'repeated, bi-directional, and continuous', but the noun **PAINT** is 'repeated, bi-directional, and restrained'.

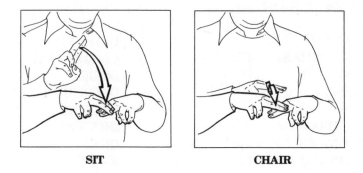

SIT	CHAIR

What the researchers found was that whereas the verbs in these pairs could have most of the different types of movement within each of the three dimensions (i.e. verbs could be found within each category), the movement of nouns was quite limited. With very few exceptions, *nouns* always have *repeated* and *restrained* move-

---

[3]In order to repeat the movement for the sign **CHAIR**, the dominant hand must return back to its original position. However, this 'preparatory' movement does not make the sign itself 'bi-directional' since the primary movement of the sign is one-way (i.e. downward). Notice how this differs from bi-directional signs like **MOVIE, TRAFFIC,** and **COMMUTE-BETWEEN-____-&-____** .

ment. (The directionality is usually the same as that of the related verb.) That is, regardless of the frequency and manner of the verb, the related noun always has the same type of movement: repeated and restrained.

Below are some of the related noun-verb pairs that were analyzed by the researchers, Supalla and Newport (1978). The signs are grouped together according to the movement dimensions of each verb.[4] Remember that in all of these pairs, the nouns have repeated and restrained movement. Because the movement is repeated and restrained, it becomes smaller, quicker, and tense. (While reading through these lists, the reader should be aware that some Signers differ in their production of these noun-verb pairs.)

(a) Verbs with 'single, uni-directional, continuous' movement and their corresponding nouns:

1.	FROM-___-FLY-TO-___[5]	AIRPLANE
2.	GO-BY-SKIS-TO-___	SKIS
3.	GO-BY-BOAT-TO-___	BOAT
4.	GO-BY-SHIP-TO-___	SHIP
5.	GO-BY-FLYING-SAUCER-TO-___	FLYING-SAUCER
6.	GO-BY-ROCKET-TO-___	ROCKET
7.	GO-BY-SUBMARINE-TO-___	SUBMARINE
8.	GO-BY-SURFBOARD-TO-___	SURFBOARD

(b) Verbs with 'single, uni-directional, hold' movement and their corresponding nouns:

1.	PUT-ON-BACKPACK	BACKPACK
2.	GO-TO-BED	BED
3.	OPEN-BOOK	BOOK
4.	PUT-BRACELET-ON-*wrist*	BRACELET
5.	PUT-BROOCH-ON-*chest*	BROOCH
6.	SIT	CHAIR
7.	CLIP-NAIL	CLIPPER
8.	PUT-CLOTHESPIN-ON-___	CLOTHESPIN
9.	OPEN-DOOR	DOOR
10.	PRESS-*doorbell*	DOORBELL
11.	TURN-*doorknob*	DOORKNOB
12.	PULL-DRAWER	DRAWER
13.	PUT-ON-DRESS	DRESS
14.	PUT-ON-EARPHONES	EARPHONES
15.	PUT-ON-EARRING	EARRING
16.	PUT-ON-GAS-MASK	GAS-MASK
17.	PUT-GASOLINE-IN-___	GASOLINE
18.	CLOSE-GATE	GATE
19.	PUT-ON-GIRDLE	GIRDLE

---

[4]We have adapted this list to fit our transcription conventions. In addition, we have included only the most common types of verb movements here.

[5]This verb could also be glossed as **FROM-___-GO-BY-PLANE-TO-___**. Indeed, probably most of the verbs in section (a) could be glossed as **FROM-___-GO-BY-___-TO-___**.

20. PUT-ON-GOGGLES	GOGGLES
21. SHOOT-GUN-AT-___	GUN
22. HANG-UP-___	HANGER
23. PUT-HEARING-AID-ON-*ear*	HEARING-AID
24. SCREW-ON-LID	LID
25. LOCK-UP-___	KEY
26. LATCH-UP-___	LATCH
27. FLICK-LIGHTER	LIGHTER
28. STRIKE-MATCH	MATCH
29. POP-*pill*-IN-*mouth*	PILL
30. SQUEEZE-*pliers*	PLIERS
31. PLUG-IN-AT-___	PLUG
32. PUT-RING-ON-*fourth finger*	RING
33. CUT-___-WITH-SCISSORS	SCISSORS
34. TURN-SCREW	SCREWDRIVER
35. PUT-ON-SUSPENDERS	SUSPENDERS
36. PUT-TAPE-ON-___	TAPE
37. USE-TELEPHONE	TELEPHONE
38. PUT-THONGS-ON	THONGS
39. OPEN-UMBRELLA	UMBRELLA
40. OPEN-WALLET	WALLET
41. BLOW-WHISTLE	WHISTLE
42. CLOSE-WINDOW	WINDOW
43. TURN-NUT	WRENCH

(c) Verbs with 'repeated, uni-directional, continuous' movement and their corresponding nouns:

1. USE-BROOM/(SWEEP)	BROOM
2. COMB-*hair*	COMB
3. PUT-*food*-IN-*mouth*[6]	FOOD
4. STRUM-*guitar*	GUITAR
5. LICK-*ice cream cone*	ICE-CREAM
6. USE-LAWNMOWER/(MOW-LAWN)	LAWNMOWER
7. USE-MOP	MOP
8. CRANK-*movie camera*	MOVIE-CAMERA
9. USE-RAKE	RAKE
10. USE-SEWING-MACHINE	SEWING-MACHINE
11. USE-SHOVEL/(DIG)	SHOVEL
12. USE-VACUUM-CLEANER/(VACUUM)	VACUUM-CLEANER

(d) Verbs with 'repeated, bi-directional, continuous' movement and their corresponding nouns:

1. ROCK-*baby*-IN-ARMS	BABY
2. RIDE-*bicycle*	BICYCLE
3. ERASE-*blackboard*	BLACKBOARD-ERASER
4. DRIVE-*car*	CAR

---

[6]This verb is usually glossed as EAT.

5. **FILE**-*fingernail*	**FINGERNAIL-FILE**
6. **SPRAY**-*hair*	**HAIRSPRAY**
7. **IRON**-*clothes*	**IRON**
8. **PUT-LIPSTICK-ON**-*lips*	**LIPSTICK**
9. **PAINT**-____	**PAINT**
10. **PLAY**-*piano*	**PIANO**
11. **CUT**-____-**WITH-SAW**	**SAW**
12. **ROLLERSKATE**	**ROLLERSKATES**
13. **ICESKATE**	**ICESKATES**
14. **SIT-ON**-*swing*	**SWING**
15. **BRUSH**-*teeth*	**TOOTHBRUSH**
16. **RUB**-*back*-**WITH**-*towel*	**TOWEL**
17. **PLAY**-*violin*	**VIOLIN**

When the noun is a *person* and there is a related verb, the noun is often made as a compound[7] sign, composed of a verb (usually in a shortened or reduced form) and the old sign for 'person', glossed as **AGENT** (made with two flat hands moving down the Signer's body). For example, the sign that means 'teacher' can be made by signing **TEACH** plus **AGENT**. The sign **AGENT** usually functions like the agentive affix '-er' ('worker') or '-or' ('actor') in English. Other compound nouns made in this way are:

PREACH⁀AGENT ('preacher')	**LEAD⁀AGENT** ('leader')
SERVE⁀AGENT ('waiter')	**DRIVE⁀AGENT** ('driver')
ACT⁀AGENT ('actor')	**PLAY⁀AGENT** ('player')
DANCE⁀AGENT ('dancer')	**SUPERVISE⁀AGENT** ('supervisor')
WRITE⁀AGENT ('writer')	**WORK⁀AGENT** ('worker')
READ⁀AGENT ('reader')	

Illustrated below is the verb **TEACH** and the noun **TEACH⁀AGENT**. Notice that the repeated movement of the verb is deleted when the verb occurs as part of the compound sign. This is an example of what we mean when we say the form of the verb is "shortened" or "reduced" in the compound sign.[8]

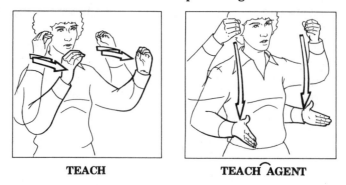

TEACH	**TEACH⁀AGENT**

---

[7]See next section (B) for a description of compounding in ASL.

[8]In everyday conversation, these joined verb and 'agent' signs are often blended together even more than illustrated here and often look like one sign. However, some Signers do not use the 'agent' sign to form certain nouns, but instead repeat the movement of the sign in a restrained manner—e.g. **TEACHER, PLAYER, ROBBER**.

Of course, not all ASL verbs have related nouns (e.g. **DESIRE, EXPECT/HOPE, FORGET, LIKE, MEAN, MISS, NOTICE-TO-___, REFUSE, SWALLOW, SCOLD**), nor do all ASL nouns have related verbs (e.g. **MOTHER, DOCTOR, DENTIST, NURSE, SERGEANT, BOSS, POLICEMAN, BOX, WOMAN, COW, PRINCIPAL, PRESIDENT, HORSE**). Similarly, not all nouns and verbs with related meanings have formationally-related signs in ASL. For example, the noun **FISH** and the verb **FISHING** are not similar in form.[9] Other examples of this are **PLANT** and **PLANTING, LIGHT** and **TURN-ON**-*light,* **COLOR** and **COLORING, SHOES** and **PUT-ON-SHOES, JAIL** and **PUT-IN-JAIL,** and **LETTERS** and ___-**SEND**-*letters*-**TO**-___.[10]

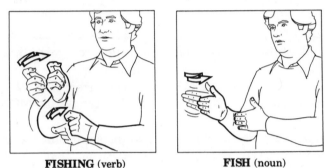

FISHING (verb)   FISH (noun)

PLANTING (verb)   PLANT (noun)

Thus, some of the ways that ASL Signers distinguish between verbs and nouns are: by using a different type of movement (e.g. **SIT** and **CHAIR**), by adding the 'agentive affix' to the verb (e.g. **TEACH** and **TEACH⌢AGENT**), or by having formationally unrelated signs (e.g. **FISHING** and **FISH**).

---

[9]However, the signs **FISH** (noun) and **FISH-SWIM** (verb) *are* formationally-related, but the noun has repeated and restrained movement. The same formational relationship is seen in the pair **PLANT** (noun) and **GROW** (verb)—which are also distinguished by their movements, following the pattern described earlier.

[10]In order to distinguish the glosses for related nouns and verbs that, in English, would be written with the same word (e.g. 'fish' can be both a noun and a verb) we have chosen here to add '-ing' to the gloss for the verb—e.g. **FISH** (noun) and **FISHING** (verb).

B. Compounds and Contractions

Like many other languages, ASL makes use of a process called *compounding* for creating new lexical items. This process, compounding, is often a very useful and productive means of enlarging the vocabulary of a language. For example, English frequently takes already existing words and joins them together as a compound to express new meanings like 'icebox', 'spaceship', 'printout' (as in 'computer _____'), 'input' or 'output', 'kickback' (as in to 'receive a _____ for services rendered'), and 'dishwasher'.

In a signed language, "compounds" are created from *two* (sometimes more) separate signs which then act together like *one* sign in a sentence. Often, when a compound is widely used for a long time, its form changes, and the two signs begin to look more and more like each other (through the process called assimilation—as discussed in Chapter IV), and eventually the two signs may look like only one sign. As this change takes place, Signers often no longer recognize that the sign (the compound) was originally created from two separate signs. For example, many ASL Signers do not know that the sign **REMEMBER** came from **KNOW + CONTINUE**, that **HOME** came from **EAT + BED**, or that **BUY** came from **MONEY + GIVE-TO**.

However, even from the beginning, when two signs are joined together as a compound, their form usually changes. For example, look at the compound **GIRL⌢SERVE**[11]—which means 'waitress'. Normally the sign **GIRL** has repeated movement at the cheek. However, when the sign **GIRL** is used in the compound **GIRL⌢SERVE**, it is 'reduced' so that it has only a single movement. This is a characteristic change in compound signs. That is, the first sign in the compound is 'reduced' in some way so that it is 'shorter' and takes less time to produce than it would if it were occurring as a separate sign.[12]

Compounds also tend to have a meaning that is different from their meaning as two separate signs or words. For example, when the separate signs **EAT** and **NOON** occur next to each other in a sentence, they usually mean 'eat at noon'. However,

---

[11]As described in the section on Transcription Symbols, the symbol ⌢ is used to indicate that the two signs joined by it form a compound. Through time, if the two signs become really merged together so that they usually are not recognized as two joined signs, but rather as one sign, then they are usually glossed as one sign—e.g. **REMEMBER, HOME, BUY.**

[12]Compounds in spoken languages also (usually) have a change in form. In English, the change is in vocal stress. For example, when the words 'black board' occur as two separate words (i.e. as a phrase), the vocal stress is on the second word 'board'. But when the words occur as a compound 'blackboard' (i.e. as a single lexical item), the stress is on the first word 'black'. Compounds in English are also sometimes written together as one word—e.g. 'blackboard', 'notebook', 'teacup', 'lipstick', 'firemen'.

when **EAT** and **NOON** occur as a compound (i.e. **EAT͡NOON**), together they mean 'lunch', as illustrated in the sentence below.

Context   A friend asks the Signer if he can attend a meeting at 2 p.m. tomorrow. The Signer replies:

(1) <u>neg</u>   <u>t</u>   (gaze rt   )
        STUCK   ME,   TOMORROW,   P-A-T   US-TWO-*rt*   GO-*rt*   EAT͡NOON   ONE-O'CLOCK

Trans   'Nope, I'm stuck. Tomorrow Pat and I are going to lunch at one o'clock.'

ASL has a large number of compounds that occur frequently in the language. Some of these are:

1. **EAT͡MORNING**—'breakfast'
2. **EAT͡NOON**—'lunch'
3. **EAT͡NIGHT**—'dinner'
4. **BLUE͡5:-CL'on body'**—'bruise'
5. **BED͡SOFT** (sign made near head)—'pillow'
6. **THINK͡SAME-AS**—'just as if; it's like; for example'
7. **FACE͡STRONG**—'closely resemble, bear a strong resemblance to'
8. **FACE͡SAME-AS**—'look like, resemble'
9. **THINK͡EASY**—'it's a snap/breeze/piece of cake, not tough'
10. **THINK͡TOUCH**"*over time*"—'to dwell on; be obsessed with'
11. **MONEY͡BEHIND**—'money in reserve'
12. **TRUE͡WORK**—'really mean it, (I'm) serious about it, (I) mean what (I) say, (I'm) not joking; it's really important'
13. **TALK͡NAME**—'to talk about, mention'
14. **FOOD͡BUY**—'to go food/grocery shopping'
15. **GOOD͡ENOUGH**—'just barely adequate'
16. **WRONG͡HAPPEN**—'accidentally; unexpectedly; coincidentally
17. **SLEEP͡CLOTHING**—'pajamas; nightgown'
18. **SLEEP͡SUNRISE**—'oversleep; sleep in'
19. **GIRL͡SERVE**—'waitress'
20. **MOTHER͡FATHER**—'parents'
21. **BROTHER͡SISTER**—'siblings'
22. **JESUS͡BOOK**—'Bible'
23. **TEACH͡AGENT**—'teacher'
24. **LEARN͡AGENT**—'student'

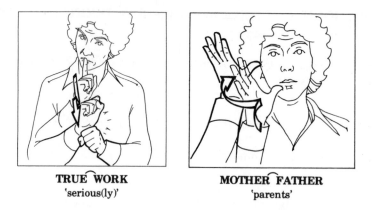

TRUE‿WORK   MOTHER‿FATHER
'serious(ly)'   'parents'

Compounds are created to express new meanings in the language. That is, if ASL Signers do not have a sign for something, they will often combine two existing signs into a compound to represent that meaning. For example, some Signers have used the compound **1**_{outline}**-CL**'rectangular'‿**'ZAP'** to mean 'microwave oven', **RED‿RECT-CL** to mean 'brick', and **NUDE‿1-CL**'go fast' to mean 'streaker'.

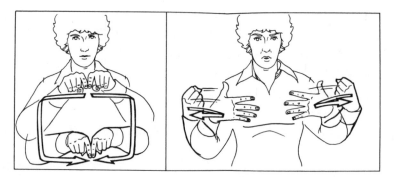

1_{outline}**-CL**'rectangular'‿**'ZAP'**
'microwave oven'

RED‿RECT-CL
'brick'

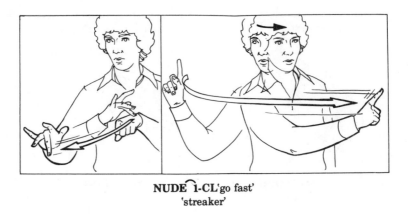

NUDE⌒1-CL'go fast'
'streaker'

Researchers[13] at the Salk Institute in San Diego have been collecting numerous examples of ASL compounds for several years to study this process of compounding in the language. Their work has shown that compounding is one of the major ways in which ASL expands its vocabulary.

However, very recent and ongoing research also at the Salk Institute has found that some of the joined signs that have been called *compounds* may actually be *contractions*. That is, some of the joined signs in ASL may actually be more like 'can't, won't, isn't, he's, and she's' (which are English contractions) than 'homework, blackboard, and teacup' (which are English compounds).

Contractions are a 'shortened' form of two words. For example, 'can' and 'not' can be shortened to form 'can't'; 'she' and 'is' can be shortened to form 'she's'. But the *meaning* of the contraction is *not* different than the meaning of the two separate words when they occur together—e.g. 'can't' means the same thing as 'can not' (although stylistically, 'can't' is considered to be more informal). In the same way, the signs **WHY** and **NOT** can be signed separately or can be contracted together as **WHY‿NOT**; the meaning is the same. This is also true of the signs **NOT** and **HERE** (**NOT‿HERE**), and **SEE** and **NONE** (**SEE‿NONE**).

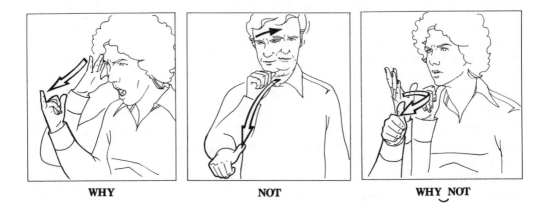

| WHY | NOT | WHY‿NOT |

[13]Newport & Bellugi (1977), Bellugi & Newkirk (1978), Klima & Bellugi (1979).

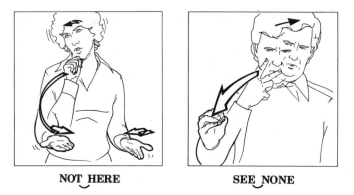

NOT HERE   SEE NONE

However, as we said earlier, *compounds* tend to have a meaning that is different than the meaning of the two words as a phrase—e.g. a 'black board' is black, but a 'blackboard' can be green; 'homework' can be done at school; people may frequently drink coffee in a 'teacup'. Compounds do not *always* have a different meaning like this, but they usually do since they are most often created to express new concepts.

In this text, we have tried to use this distinction between compounds and contractions in the glosses for signs. However, since this distinction is very new in research on ASL and since it is not always clear how to apply the criteria for distinguishing compounds and contractions to joined signs in ASL, we expect that some of our glosses may be in error. Teachers will need to keep informed about the results of future research in order to correct the possible transcription errors in this text.

C. Fingerspelled Loan Signs

Spoken languages of the world frequently "borrow" words from each other as a matter of convenience. That is, when a language doesn't have a word for a particular thing or concept, it can either invent its own word or use ("borrow") the word used to denote that thing or concept in another language. Or, sometimes the language already has a word for something, but chooses, through time, to use ("borrow") a word for the same thing or concept from another language. For example, when French became the language of the upper class in England for about 400 years (after the Norman Conquest in 1066), a 'well-bred' Englishman stopped saying that he was "abreast of things" and, instead, said he was "au courant".

This example illustrates two major generalizations about language borrowing: (1) *Language borrowing frequently occurs when two or more languages are "in contact" with each other.* This "contact" can mean actual physical proximity as occurred when French-speaking kings were ruling England, or contact through literature as when English people started reading and borrowing words from Latin and Greek during the English Renaissance, or contact through some other means like television and radio. (2) *Language borrowing tends to be more frequent in one direction than in the other; that is, the language with lower social status tends to borrow more frequently from the language with higher social status.* As such, between 1066 and 1700, English borrowed a great number of words from French, Latin, and Greek since these were considered the languages of 'high society' and 'culture'. Now many languages borrow words from English since speakers of English have gained considerable power and world-wide influence during the last 100 years or so. Below is a list of some words borrowed by English from a variety of different languages.[14]

From Norse:
sky, scowl, scant, scare, scatter, scrape, skirt, skin, sly, crawl, ugly, outlaw, leg, egg, law, give, they, their, them

From Celtic languages:
flannel, bin, ass, clan, slogan, whiskey

From French:
government, crown, prince, state, nation, parliament, jury, judge, crime, sue, attorney, property, court, society, majesty, treaty, alliance, tax, royal, money, valve, miracle, parson, sermon, baptism, incense, crucifix, veal, beef, mutton, bacon, jelly, peach, lemon, cream, boil, fry, broil, stew, roast, certain, chair, lamp, towel, blanket, parlor, dance, chess, music, leisure, conversation, story, romance, poet, literary, study, logic, grammar, noun, surgeon, stomach, nice, blue, second, very, age, bucket, gentle, final, fault, flower, cry, count, sure, move, surprise, plain, pray, saint, charity, mercy, religion, virgin, lechery

From Latin:
convention, animal, bonus, maximum, minimum, alumnus, quorum, exit, scientific, interrogatory, orthography, debt, describe, advantage, rape, violent, pedestrian, anniversary, contradict, climax, dictionary, benefit, multiply, exist, paragraph, initiate, scene, inspire, ex-, -ible/-able, poor, adequate, adduce, ad hoc, adjacent, adjunct, ad lib, admire, adolescent, advent, adventure, affiliate, afflict, agitate, alias, alibi, alien, allocution, altar, alternate, altitude, ambiguous, anticipate, apex, approximate, April, apt, arena, armament, arrest, articulate, ascend, asinine, aspire, assert, assimilate, associate, assume, attract, attrition, auction, audacious, audit, auxiliary, avert, avocation, axis

From Greek:
drama, comedy, tragedy, scene, botany, physics, zoology, atomic, thermos, phobia, aesthete, aero-, agape, ambrosia, amnesia, amnesty, amorphous, androgynous, anonymous, archaeology, ascetic, auto-, autocrat, autonomy, autopsy

From Dutch:
buoy, freight, leak, pump, yacht, (and place names like:) Brooklyn, Fishkills, Catskills, Amsterdam

From German:
cobalt, quartz, sauerkraut, lager, beer, blitzkrieg

From Italian:
opera, soprano, piano, allegro, virtuoso, balcony, corridor, mezzanine

From Arabic:
alcohol, algebra, cipher, sugar, zero

From North and South American Indian languages:
hominy, squash, chipmunk, moose, opossum, raccoon, skunk, moccasin, tom-

---

[14]Some of these languages have also borrowed from each other. For example, French borrowed the word for 'noun' from Latin. However, here we list this word under *From French* since English actually borrowed the word for 'noun' from French after French had borrowed it from Latin.

ahawk, wigwam, papoose, squaw, totem, powwow, hickory, potato, tobacco, chocolate, hammock, (and place names like:) Mississippi, Oklahoma, Topeka, Shawnees, Connecticut, Potomac, Ohio, Erie, Huron, Michigan, Alleghenies, Appalachians, Ozarks, Massachusetts, Kentucky, Wisconsin, Oregon, Texas, Chattanooga, Chicago, Milwaukee, Omaha, Hackensack

From Spanish:
alligator, barbecue, cigar, cockroach, guitar, key (meaning 'reef'), mosquito, Negro, adobe, canyon, cinch, mesa, patio, ranch, taco, tortilla, (and place names like:) Rio Grande, Colorado, Sierra Nevada, Santa Fe, San Francisco, Santa Barbara, Santa Cruz, San Jose, Los Angeles

From Yiddish:
yenta, lox, bagel, matzo, schmaltz, schlemiel, shmoe, kibbitz, schlepp

When a spoken language does borrow a word from another language, it often changes the pronunciation of the word to fit its own sound system. For example, in the early 1950's, the Russians sent the first 'satellite' into outer space—which they called a спутник , pronounced in Russian like 'spootneek'. Since English did not have a word for this thing (*Note:* the English word 'satellite' was not yet used with this meaning), it borrowed the Russian word and pronounced and spelled it as 'sputnik'. Similarly, when French borrowed the word 'picnic' from English, it changed both vowel sounds to a long 'ee', and changed the spelling of the last part of the word to fit the French writing system—'picnique'.

We still know very little about how signed languages borrow from other signed languages. However, we do have some information about words that ASL has borrowed from English. The existence of such English→ASL borrowing is natural since the users of ASL and English are in frequent "contact" with each other, and since the English language has generally been given higher prestige/status than American Sign Language.

How does a signed language "borrow" from a spoken language? One obvious way involves fingerspelling; that is, using the manual alphabet to represent the letters of a borrowed word. However, just as borrowed spoken words are often pronounced differently in another spoken language, fingerspelled English words that are frequently used in ASL are often changed so that they look more like ASL signs. That is, these fingerspelled words are modified so that they fit better with the structure of ASL signs. In fact, in many cases, the changes are so major that Signers often think of these "borrowings" as regular ASL signs and don't realize that they originally were fingerspelled words borrowed from English.

One researcher[15] has studied a large number of these frequently-used fingerspelled words and has described how they have changed through time to better fit the structure of ASL signs. He refers to these "restructured" fingerspellings as *loan signs* and writes them with the symbol '#' to distinguish them from regular fingerspelled words. Thus, **J-O-B** is a fingerspelled word, whereas **#JOB** is a loan sign.

Fingerspelled loan signs tend to keep the first and last letter of the word, but tend to delete the medial letters. For example, the loan signs **#TOY, #BUT, #DOG, #FIX, #ASK, #JOB,** and **#YES** delete the middle letter (e.g. **#TOY** looks like

[15]Battison (1978).

T-Y. Similarly, loan signs based on four-letter and five-letter English words tend to delete one or more of the middle letters. Some of these loan signs are **#HURT, #BANK, #EASY, #WHAT, #SOON, #BUSY, #CLUB, #COOL, #SURE, #WOULD,** and **#BREAD**.

#JOB   **#WHAT**

Many fingerspelled loan signs already only have two letters—e.g. **#IF, #NO** (as in 'say "NO" to someone'), **#OK, #KO** (for 'knockout'), **#DO, #BS** (for 'bullshit'), **#EX, #SO, #GO, #HA, #OR, #OH,** and **#NG** (for 'no good').

Thus, we see that loan signs are different from fingerspelled words in the number of handshapes that are used (corresponding to the English letters). However, loan signs are often different in several other ways. A movement may be added (as in **#EARLY**—which has a circular movement), the location may change (as in **#BS**—which is signed at or below the chin), or the orientation may change (as in **#JOB**—which ends with the palm facing the Signer). Some fingerspelled loan signs are also manipulated in space for grammatical purposes like regular signs (e.g. **#BACK, #ALL, #NO**). Some may be made with two hands (e.g. **#DO**), and some may have meanings different than the regular fingerspelled words (e.g. **#SO, #EX, #OFF, #ALL**).

In addition, there are often several variants of each loan sign. For example, the loan sign **#DO** has six different variants. All of them have an orientation that is different than the regular (i.e. palm *facing outward*) fingerspelled word. One variant is made with one or two hands, palm *up*, rapidly repeating the contact between the index finger and thumb and is often used with a questioning facial expression to mean 'Well, what can I do?' when someone is in a conflict situation or, with a different questioning expression, 'What are you going to do?'

#DO-DO

If both hands are used palm *down* with rapid repetition of the contact while moving the hands in tandem circles, the loan sign means 'chores' or 'many things to do'.

For a full description of the formation and meaning of each loan sign and its variants as well as a helpful discussion of the rules of ASL which influence such "restructuring" of fingerspelled loan signs, the reader is referred to the book *Lexical Borrowing in American Sign Language* by Robbin Battison (Silver Spring, Maryland: Linstok Press, 1978). The reader should also be aware that not all ASL Signers use all of these loan signs or their variants. In the text, Battison discusses some of the background characteristics of ASL Signers who do use many of these fingerspelled loan signs.

D. Idioms

An *idiom* is defined as "a group of words with a set meaning that cannot be calculated by adding up the separate meanings of its parts".[16] In other words, an idiom is a (a) *fixed phrase,* (b) *consisting of more than one word,* and (c) *its meaning cannot be inferred just by knowing the meanings of the individual words.*[17]

English has many idioms. Some are listed below.

Idiom	*Meaning*
1. kick the bucket	to die
2. hold (one's) horses	to slow down, wait, not be impatient
3. dead to the world	fast asleep
4. eat crow	to admit a mistake/defeat
5. let (one's) hair down	to act freely and naturally, to be informal, to relax
6. put (one's) foot in (one's) mouth	to say or do something inappropriate, causing embarrassment
7. throw (one's) weight around	to use one's status or authority in a showy or noisy manner
8. get wind of	to get news of, hear rumors about
9. cut it out	to stop doing something
10. hit it off	to get along well with someone
11. take (one) for a ride	to trick or fool someone
12. wind around (one's) little finger	to have total control or influence over another person
13. iron in the fire	one of the projects with which one is busy
14. make a clean breast of	to admit guilt, confess everything
15. give a piece of (one's) mind	to scold angrily

---

[16]Bolinger (1975), pg. 100.
[17]Fromkin & Rodman (1974), pg. 121.

Examining this list of English idioms in relation to the definition stated above, we see that they match the definition:

(a) all of these idioms are fixed phrases; that is, the parts of the idiom must occur in a specific order and form. For example, one can say 'Dan kicked the bucket yesterday', but *not* '**Dan kicked his bucket yesterday' or '**The bucket was kicked by Dan'. One can say 'Bill put his foot in his mouth', but *not* '**Bill put his foot in her mouth'.

(b) all of these idioms also consist of more than one word.

(c) the meaning of these idioms cannot be determined by looking at the meaning of the component words. The meaning cannot be understood 'literally'. One does not actually 'kick a bucket' or 'hold a horse'!

Most of the expressions which have been called "idioms" in descriptions of ASL are really not idioms. They do not fit the definition of an idiom. For example, the signs **FINISH, NONE/ZERO, AT-LAST/SUCCESS** are *not* idioms. They are simply frequently used signs which have several different uses. For example, **FINISH** can be used as a completive aspect marker (emphasizing the fact that something has been completed; see Chapters VII and XIII), or as an adverb meaning 'already', or as an exclamation meaning 'stop that!'. Similarly, the sign **NONE/ZERO** means 'not at all' or 'nothing' and is often used in contractions like **FUNNY⌣NONE** and **SEE⌣NONE**. The sign **AT-LAST/SUCCESS** means 'to succeed or accomplish something' or 'to finally do something'.

Often, the mistake in the past has been to assume that since these and other signs are used frequently in ASL, but do not have an easy "word for sign" equivalent— that they are "idioms". This is like saying that the English word 'run' is an idiom since it has so many different meanings and occurs so frequently in the language (English). However, by reviewing the three definitional criteria of idioms as stated above, we can see that such words and signs are *not* idioms, but rather, are frequently used, multiple-meaning words or signs.

An example of an idiom in ASL is **TRAIN FADE-OUT-OF-SIGHT** (usually glossed as **TRAIN ZOOM**[18]) meaning 'Sorry, you missed it and I'm not going to repeat it'. This is a fixed expression consisting of more than one sign, and its meaning is not based on the meanings of the two separate signs. However, it is interesting to note that ASL seems to have *very few* widely-used idioms, according to the standard definition of "idiom".

Bibliography

Battison, R. 1978. *Lexical Borrowing in American Sign Language.* Silver Spring, Md.: Linstok Press.

Bellugi, U. & D. Newkirk (in press). Formal devices for creating new signs in ASL. To appear in *National Symposium on Sign Language Research and Teaching: 1977 Proceedings.*

Bolinger, D. 1975. *Aspects of Language.* (Second Edition) New York: Harcourt, Brace, Jovanovich, Inc.

---

[18]This can occur as a compound sign or as two separate signs.

Fromkin, V. & R. Rodman. 1974. *An Introduction to Language*. New York: Holt, Rinehart, & Winston, Inc.

Klima, E. & U. Bellugi. 1979. *The Signs of Language*. Cambridge, Mass.: Harvard Univ. Press.

Newport, E. & U. Bellugi. 1977. Linguistic expression of category levels in a visual-gestural language: a flower is a flower is a flower. To appear in Rosch & Lloyd (Eds.) *Cognition and Categorization*. Hillsdale, N.J.: Lawrence Erlbaum Associates.

Suppala, T. & E. Newport. 1978. How many seats in a chair? The derivation of nouns and verbs in American Sign Language. In P. Siple (Ed.) *Understanding Language Through Sign Language Research*. New York: Academic Press, 91–132.

Chapter VI

Sentence Types

A. Introduction

The purpose of this chapter is to provide a general overview of several basic types of sentences in ASL and a general description of how ASL Signers show which type of sentence they are using. For example, how does one distinguish a declarative statement from a command? Or, distinguish a statement from a question?

In general, there are three basic types of sentences: statements, questions, and commands. In this chapter, we will describe these types of sentences in ASL, as well as other syntactic constructions that are built on these basic types—e.g. negated statements and questions, conditional statements and questions, and statements, questions, and commands in which a segment has been topicalized.

In all of these sentence types, the Signer's facial, eye, and head behaviors are very important for indicating which type is being used. We will provide illustrations of some of these behaviors that commonly occur, but warn the reader that research on these behaviors is still fairly new and far from complete. As such, the reader should use our descriptions and illustrations as general models, but be open to variations that may also occur among Signers in various contexts. In addition, available research has provided more information on some sentence types than on others; consequently, some of our descriptions are more detailed than others.

In ASL, certain facial, eye, and head behaviors function as grammatical signals that indicate which type of sentence is being used. For example, the grammatical signal that we write as 'q' involves specific facial, eye, and head behaviors which indicate that a sentence[1] is a *question*. As explained in the section on Transcription Symbols, the time period during which a non-manual grammatical signal occurs is indicated via a line drawn over the manual sign or signs that the signal accompanies. This is illustrated below:

$$\overline{\text{Signed Sentence A,} \quad \overline{\text{Signed Sentence B}}^{q}}$$

The line drawn over Sentence B with a superscript 'q' indicates that that sentence is a question. It also indicates that the non-manual behaviors which are used to signal a question occurred continuously during the production of all the signs below the line.

Most Signers use their eyes, face, head, and body fairly continuously while communicating in ASL. Some of these non-manual behaviors serve specific grammati-

---

[1]Actually, we are not only referring to full sentences as traditionally defined, consisting of a subject and verb, etc. Rather, the segment can consist of one sign or more which constitutes the question—e.g. 'Mary?', 'The blue pen?', 'Fell down?', 'It happened yesterday?'.

cal functions in the language; some are not grammatical, but serve other expressive functions (e.g. showing how one feels about what's being communicated). We use the superscript line and abbreviations like '*q*' to indicate when specific non-manual behaviors occur that serve a specific grammatical function. Research has not yet outlined all of the grammatical functions of non-manual behaviors, so our transcriptions here are limited by our knowledge. Often we write a description of other non-manual behaviors in parentheses above the manual signs. We are not always sure about the functions of these other behaviors, but try to include them to provide as full a 'picture' as we can of what the Signer is actually doing while communicating in ASL.

B. Statements

Although there are specific grammatical signals in ASL for questions, commands, negatives, conditionals, and topics, there does not seem to be any specific signal which accompanies all of the signs in a sentence to indicate that it is a declarative statement. Rather, the absence of any special signal (for question, command, or conditional) seems to indicate the sentence is a declarative statement. As such, it may be useful to think of the declarative statement as the most basic sentence in ASL—to which other signals are added or segments changed to indicate other types of sentences.

C. Questions

There are two basic types of questions in ASL: (1) *yes-no* questions—questions that can be answered by responding 'yes' or 'no' (e.g. 'Do you want to come?'; 'Is he happy?'), and (2) *wh-word* questions—questions that cannot be answered by responding 'yes' or 'no' and that use interrogative forms (question words or signs) which in English often begin with a 'wh' (e.g. 'What is her name?'; 'Who was that?'). ASL Signers also frequently use a third type of question called a *rhetorical* question—which is not a true question since the Addressee is not expected to respond; rather it is a way for the Signer to introduce information that s/he will then supply (e.g. 'Jim is unhappy. Why? Because he failed the test.'; 'I finally got into the cabinet. How? I broke the lock with a hammer.').

In the following pages, each of these three types of questions will be described and illustrated with examples and photographs that show the non-manual behaviors which frequently occur with each type.

(C.1) Yes-No Questions

'Yes-No' questions are accompanied by the grammatical signal that we write as '*q*'—composed of a brow raise, 'widened eyes', and frequently, a forward tilting of the head and/or body. Sometimes the shoulders are also raised. During the question (or at least by the end of the question), the Signer looks at the Addressee. This signal for 'yes-no' questions is illustrated below with the pronoun that means 'you' (see Chapter VIII on Pronominalization).

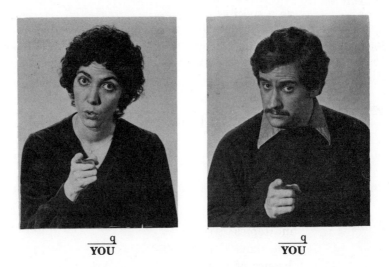

$$\overline{\text{YOU}}^{\,q} \qquad \qquad \overline{\text{YOU}}^{\,q}$$

This signal 'q' is frequently the only indication that the sentence is a 'yes-no' question. For example, compare the two sentences below. Notice that the manual signs are the same, but the non-manual behaviors differ—resulting in the difference between an assertion (1a) and a question (1b).

Context   At the end of a meeting, someone sees John storm out of the meeting room and then asks the Signer if John is upset. The Signer replies:[2]

(1a)   (frown_____)nodding
       J-O-H-N   BECOME-ANGRY

    Struc   'Yes, John has really become angry.'

    Trans   'Yes, John is really angry.'

Context   The Signer is surprised to see John storm out of the meeting and asks:

(1b)   _____q
       J-O-H-N   BECOME-ANGRY

    Struc   'John has become angry?'

    Trans   'Is John angry?'

However, the last sign in a question is often held longer than usual (as the Signer waits for the Addressee to respond), and sometimes the last sign is held while the Addressee is responding. In addition, sometimes the last sign is 'extended' by re-

---

[2]See Section F on Assertions for an explanation of the *'nodding'* signal in this example. Here the signal occurs with the manual signs—as opposed to example (2) where the Signer begins her response by nodding and then continues nodding during the first sentence.

peating the sign's movement, as illustrated in example (2). (Also see examples 18 and 19.) This repetition often looks like the fingers are 'wiggling', so we write this added movement as 'wg'.

Context   A week ago, a friend asked the Signer if she wanted to go fishing on Saturday, but the Signer said she would probably be out of town. Now it's Friday and the friend says, "You're still gonna be out of town, right?" The Signer replies:

(2)
```
nodding(gaze rt                          )
        TOMORROW   ME   GO-TO-rt   O-C,

                             q
WANT   GO-TO-rt   WANTwg
```

Struc   'Yeah, tomorrow I'm going to Ocean City. You want to go there, you want to?'

Trans   'Yeah, I'm goin' to Ocean City tomorrow. You wanna go?'

```
      q                          q
    WANT                       WANTwg
```

'Yes-no' questions also often end by pointing with the index finger to the Addressee—as illustrated in example (3). (Also see example 5.)

Context   The Signer has been planning to see the movie "Star Wars" with Pat. But, by chance, the Signer sees Pat telling another friend about the movie. So the Signer asks Pat:

(3)
```
                             q
FINISH   SEE   MOVIE   YOU
```

Struc   'Have you already seen the movie?'

Trans   'Did you already see that movie?'

Additionally, in a conversation, the Addressee often indicates that s/he wants to ask a 'yes-no' question by looking at and pointing to the Signer with the 'q' signal. When the Signer stops signing, the Addressee (now the "Signer") then asks the question.

Context   Signer B has been wanting to see "Star Wars". By chance, a friend (Signer A) starts talking about the movie.[3]

(4)   *Signer A:* ⎯⎯⎯⎯⎯⎯⎯⎯⎯⎯⎯⎯⎯⎯⎯⎯⎯ t
        KNOW+   MOVIE   S-T-A-R-W-A-R-S . . .

        Signer B: ⎯q⎯⎯⎯⎯⎯⎯⎯⎯⎯⎯⎯⎯⎯⎯⎯⎯q
                                             YOU . . . FINISH   SEE   YOU

        Struc   'You know the movie "Star Wars" . . .

                       'You . . . have you seen it?!'

        Trans   'You know that movie "Star Wars" . . .

                       'Oh? . . . Did you see it?!'

Notice that in example (4), Signer A began a longer statement, but was interrupted by Signer B's question. Signer B indicated that s/he wanted to ask something by looking at and pointing to Signer A with the '*q*' signal. Signer A then stopped, and Signer B asked the question.

Another way to indicate that one is going to ask a question is to use the sign *me*-**ASK-TO**-*you* as an 'opener'—as illustrated in example (5).

Context   The Signer is taking a course that has over 75 students in it so he knows he won't be missed if he cuts class and stays at the beach an extra day. But the students are all supposed to hand in their homework assignments that day. By chance, the Signer sees a fellow classmate and has the idea that maybe this classmate could turn in the homework for him. The Signer stops the classmate and says:

(5)   ⎯⎯⎯⎯⎯⎯⎯⎯co⎯⎯⎯⎯⎯   ⎯⎯⎯⎯⎯⎯⎯⎯⎯⎯⎯⎯⎯⎯⎯⎯⎯⎯⎯t
        me-**ASK-TO**-*you*,   ONE-WEEK-FUTURE   MONDAY,

        ⎯⎯⎯⎯⎯⎯⎯⎯⎯⎯⎯⎯⎯(nodding⎯⎯⎯)q
        you-**GO-TO**-*rt*   CLASS,   RIGHT   YOU . . .

        Struc   'Let me ask you something. Next Monday you're going to class, right?' . . .

        Trans   'Lemme ask you something. You're gonna go to class next Monday, right?' . . . (Well, could you hand in my homework?, etc.)

me-**ASK-TO**-*you*

[3]The '*t*' stands for 'topic' and is described in Section G.

ASL also has two related signs that can be used to indicate that a sentence is a question. (These signs as well as the *me*-**ASK-TO**-*you* opener can also be used with 'wh-word' questions.) One of the signs (that we gloss as **QM**—for 'question mark') seems to be used in more formal contexts, as illustrated in example (6). The other sign (that we gloss as **QM**wg—'wiggling question mark') seems to be more commonly used (see example 7) and often occurs as a response to someone else's statement, as illustrated in example (8).

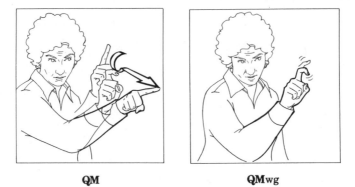

QM   **QM**wg

Context   At a faculty meeting, the teachers are discussing a proposed Evaluation Committee and who should serve on that committee. The Chairperson asks:[4]

(6)
```
             _____(gaze around room_____)q    _____q
             HAVE  VOLUNTEER  QM  "WELL",  (2h)NONE,
                            "WELL" —————————→ ,
```

```
             __nod___  __nodding___
             #OK,   SUSPEND
```

  Struc   'Do we have any volunteers, hmm? None? OK, then we'll hold it until later.'

  Trans   'Are there any volunteers? No volunteers? OK, then we'll hold off on that for awhile.'

Context   The Signer's report card shows an 'F' for "Cleanliness", so she unhappily leaves it on the living room table for her father to see it. Several hours later, she hesitantly asks her mother:

(7)
```
             _____q
             FATHER   BECOME-ANGRY  QMwg
```

  Struc   'Has Dad become angry?'

  Trans   'Is Dad angry?'

---

[4]The gesture that we gloss here as **"WELL"** is made with the open hand, palm facing upward.

In example (8a), Signer A makes a statement, and Signer B responds with the sign **QM**wg. In this context, with the accompanying *'q'* signal, the **QM**wg functions like a 'wide-eyed believing' exclamation as well as a question. In (8b), Signer B responds with the same sign, but this time with a furrowed brow and 'pinched' lip corners—giving the meaning of 'disbelief' or 'skepticism', as illustrated in the photographs below. These two uses of **QM**wg seem to be fairly frequent in ASL.

<table>
<tr><td align="center">**QM**wg
'Really?!'</td><td align="center">**QM**wg
'You gotta be kidding!'</td></tr>
</table>

Context   Signer A is a self-acclaimed expert on football. He tells his sister (Signer B):

(8a)   *Signer A:*   _____t   _____nod
                      WASHINGTON FOOTBALL TEAM, WILL CHAMPION

       Signer B: ____q
                      QMwg

      Struc   (A) 'Washington's football team will be the champion.'
              (B) 'Really?!'

      Trans   (A) 'Washington's football team is gonna win the championship.'
              (B) 'Oh, you really think so?!'

Context   (same as 8a)

(8b)   *Signer A:*   _____t   _____nod
                      WASHINGTON FOOTBALL TEAM, WILL CHAMPION

       Signer B: ('disbelieving')
                      QMwg

      Struc   (A) 'Washington's football team will be the champion.'
              (B) 'Is what you are saying really true? (I doubt it)'

      Trans   (A) 'Washington's football team is gonna win the championship.'
              (B) 'You gotta be kidding!'

(C.2) Wh-word Questions

'Wh-word' questions are accompanied by the non-manual behaviors that we write as *'wh-q'* — composed of a brow squint (although the brows are sometimes also raised as well as drawn together) and, frequently, a tilting of the head. Sometimes the body shifts forward, and sometimes the shoulders are raised. During the signing of the 'wh-word' question (or at least during the 'wh-word' sign), the Signer looks at the Addressee.

This non-manual signal for 'wh-word' questions is illustrated below with three of the 'wh-word' signs.

<u>wh-q</u>
WHERE

<u>wh-q</u>
WHICH

<u>wh-q</u>
WHO

As mentioned earlier, 'wh-word' questions are questions that cannot be answered by responding 'yes' or 'no' and that use an interrogative sign like **WHAT, WHO, WHEN, WHERE, WHICH, WHY, WHAT'S-UP, HOW, HOW-MANY, FOR-FOR,** etc. In general 'wh-word' signs occur at the end of the sentence, although they may also occur at the beginning. Sometimes the 'wh-word' sign and accompanying non-manual behaviors constitute the whole question.

ASL has a general interrogative form that has a range of meanings—such as 'what', 'where', 'who', 'why', 'when', etc. We gloss this general interrogative form as **"WHAT"**. Several examples that illustrate the use of **"WHAT"** are provided below.

wh-q
"WHAT"

Context   A girl just came into the Signer's office, put some papers on his desk, and went out the door on the right. The Signer asks an officemate:

(9)   co (gaze rt)   (cs)t
     "HEY",   **GIRL   RECENT   LEAVE-TO**-*rt*,

              wh-q
     NAME   (2h)"WHAT"

   Struc   'Hey! The girl that very recently left, what's her name?'

   Trans   'Say! That girl who just walked out—what's her name?'

Context   Someone asks the Signer if she could give him a ride home. He explains where he lives, but the Signer apparently doesn't understand the directions and asks:

(10)   wh-q
     LIVE   (2h)"WHAT"

   Struc   'Where do you live?'

   Trans   'Where do you live?'

Context   The Signer has just seen a man angrily rush into the room, yell at the Addressee, and then leave. The Signer asks:

(11)   (gaze to door where man exited)   wh-q
     (2h)"WHAT"   INDEX-*rt*   **(2h)"WHAT"**

   Struc   'What was that? That man—what was that about?'

   Trans   'What was that all about (with that guy who just left)?'

Context   Someone announces that Lee quit his job yesterday. The Signer is shocked
and exclaims:

(12)   (shocked)   _____wh-q
            QUIT,   (2h)**"WHAT"**

    Struc   'Quit?! What happened?'

    Trans   'He quit?! Why?' (or 'What's the story?')

  Notice that other, more specific interrogative signs could have been used in these
examples. (For example, **WHERE** could have been used in example 10; **WHY** or
FOR-FOR could have been used in example 12.) However, in context, the use of the
general interrogative sign was sufficient to elicit the desired information.

  Sometimes the general interrogative **"WHAT"** and a more specific interrogative
sign are used together. For example, in the context of (12), the Signer might have
used both the signs **WHY** and **"WHAT"**. In such cases, the Signer seems to be
asking for more details than the Addressee might normally provide if only a specific
interrogative sign is used.

Context   (same as 12)

(13)   (shocked)   _____wh-q
            QUIT,   **WHY,**   **"WHAT"**

    Struc   'Quit?! Why? What happened?'

    Trans   'Quit?! Why? What's the story?'

  Below are illustrations of some other 'wh-word' signs with some variations in how
they are made by different Signers or in different contexts.

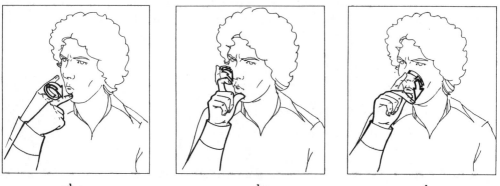

         wh-q   wh-q   wh-q
        WHO   **WHOwg**   **WHOwg**

wh-q	wh-q	wh-q
HOW-MANY	**WHAT'S-UP**	(2h)**WHAT'S-UP**

The following four examples illustrate several common types of 'wh-word' questions. In examples (14) and (15), the topic of the question occurs first, and then is followed by the interrogative sign. In example (14), both the pronoun (**THUMB-INDEX**-*rt*) and the interrogative sign (**WHO**) are repeated—a common occurrence in such questions.

Context   The Signer has seen a man come in, talk with the Addressee, and then leave. The Signer is curious.

(14)
```
       co   (gaze rt ) (                    cs)t
"HEY",       MAN  RECENT  LEAVE-TO-rt,
```
```
                                             wh-q
WHO  THUMB-INDEX-rt  WHO  THUMB-INDEX-rt
```

    Struc   'Hey! The man that very recently left, who is he? Who is he?'

    Trans   'Hey! Who's that guy that just left?'

Context   The Signer's sister stayed up late last night watching a baseball game on television. The Signer asks her:

(15)
```
                    t    wh-q          q
PAST NIGHT  GAME,  WHERE,  NEW-YORK
```

    Struc   'Last night's game, where was it? New York?'

    Trans   'Where was the game last night? New York?'

In example (16), the interrogative sign (**WHICH**) occurs at both the beginning and the end of the question.

Context   Two boys are arguing about the merits of different cars. One of the boys asks the other boy:

(16)

wh-q	(gaze,body lean lf)q	(head tilt rt)q	wh-q
WHICH FAVORITE,	**PONTIAC-*lf*,**	**CADILLAC,**	**WHICH**

    Struc   'Which is your favorite? Pontiac? Cadillac? Which one?'

    Trans   'Which do you like better—Pontiac or Cadillac?'

Example (17) shows how the interrogative sign alone can function as the question. It also illustrates how ASL Signers commonly 'act out' the question in a narrative (as if they were actually asking that question right now), rather than describe it. (Compare the structural equivalent and translation to see the difference.)

Context   The Signer is describing what happened to her this afternoon at Gallaudet College during a bomb threat.

(17)

cs	mm
AFTERNOON, ME	**ENTER H-M-B,**

(gaze rt)	(gaze lf & rt)	(gaze lf & rt) wh-q
PEOPLE	**(2h)alt. LEAVE, ME**	**(2h)WHAT'S-UP +**

    Struc   'Just this afternoon, I went into Hall Memorial Building as usual. I saw people quickly leaving left and right. I asked "What's happening? What's going on?" '

    Trans   'This afternoon when I entered Hall Memorial Building, people were rushing out left and right. So I asked what was going on.'

On page 124, we described how the last sign in a 'yes-no' question may be extended by repeating the sign's movement, and we gave an illustration of what this looks like with the sign **WANT**. When 'wh-word' signs occur at the end of questions (or as the question itself), they are also often extended by repeating the movement of the sign. Below are illustrations of this type of extension with the signs **HOW** and **WHY**, followed by sentences that show where such extension frequently occurs. Notice that **WHY** has more than one way to extend the sign, varying in the number of 'wiggling' fingers.

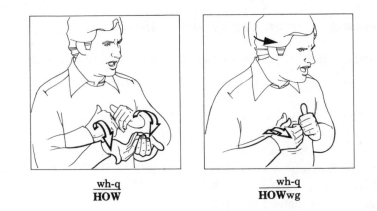

wh-q
HOW

wh-q
HOWwg

wh-q
WHY

wh-q
WHYwg

wh-q
WHYwg

Context   The Signer is shocked to see an old friend show up at a party since he lives 100 miles away and doesn't have a car or much money. She asks him:

(18)

                                                    wh-q
HOW   FROM-*rt*-COME-TO-*here*   HOWwg

    Struc   'How did you come here? How?'

    Trans   'How in the world did you get here?!'

Context   The Signer has heard some distressing news about a co-worker. He asks
            the co-worker:

(19)   <u>   co   </u> (gaze rt   )
            "HEY", **SOMEONE**-*rt*   *rt*-**INFORM**-*me,*

                                                           <u>wh-q</u>
            ONE-WEEK-FUTURE   FRIDAY   QUIT,   WHYwg

    Struc   'Hey? Someone told me that next Friday you're quitting. Why?'

    Trans   'Hey! I was told you're quitting next Friday. How come?'

However, Signers do not always extend the interrogative sign when it occurs at
the end of the question or as the question itself. Rather, such extension seems to be a
way of emphasizing the question (perhaps showing special interest in the topic).

Another sign that has a very similar meaning to **WHY** is the sign glossed as
FOR-FOR—meaning 'How come?', 'What for?', or 'Why?'. This sign could have been
used in example (19) instead of **WHY**.

<u>   wh-q   </u>
FOR-FOR

Two other interrogative signs are **WHAT** and **WHEN**.

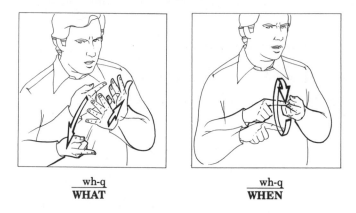

<u> wh-q </u>   <u> wh-q </u>
WHAT   **WHEN**

Although these are both ASL signs, native Signers seem to use them less frequently
now than in the past, and they are more often reserved for formal contexts. This is

especially true of the sign **WHAT**. Instead, many Signers now use the fingerspelled loan signs **#WHAT** and **#WHEN** (although **#WHEN** is less common). These signs require only one hand and are often viewed as more 'cool' or 'in-groupish' than the two-handed signs.

| <u>wh-q</u>
#WHAT | <u>wh-q</u>
#WHEN |

The following examples demonstrate several uses of these loan signs. As illustrated in (21), the sign **#WHAT** often serves as an exclamation as well as an interrogative sign.

Context   During a meeting, the Signer misses what the Chairperson says because someone has rudely walked over and stood in front of the Signer. The Signer asks her friend:

(20)   <u>(gaze rt to Chairperson)</u>
          #WHAT   **SAY**   **INDEX**-*rt*

      Struc   'What did s/he say?'

      Trans   'What did s/he say?'

Context   The Signer is shocked to hear about the way Pat has acted around the Addressee.

(21)   (grimace)wh-q
          #WHAT,

    <u>(gaze rt)   (eyes closed   )q</u>
    P-A-T   **REFUSE**   *pat*-**LOOK-AT**-*you*   *pat*-**LOOK-AWAY**-*rt,*   **AWFUL**

      Struc   'What?! Pat refused to look at you and he looked away?! That's awful!'

      Trans   'What?! Pat refused to look at you and just turned away?! That's awful!'

Context The Signer has just heard the surprising news that an old friend—Lee—
has just arrived in town.

(22)   (surprised) _____ q ___ wh-q
              L-E-E ARRIVE, #WHEN

    Struc 'Lee's arrived?! When?'

    Trans 'Lee's here?! When did he get here?'

ASL also has the fingerspelled loan signs **#WHY** and **#WHO**, which are occasionally used by some Signers. A loan sign that is frequently used is **#DO-DO**,
meaning something like 'What am I (you, s/he, we, they) gonna do?' or 'What can be
done?'—as illustrated in (23).

    ___ wh-q
    #DO-DO

Context The Addressee wants Lee to get a job, but the Signer knows that Lee likes
to stay home. The Signer is concerned about what will happen if Lee is
really opposed to getting a job and asks:[5]

(23)   _____ (gaze rt) _____ (_____ neg)cond
          SUPPOSE L-E-E-*rt* **NOT-WANT** **WORK**,

          ___ wh-q _____ q
          #DO-DO, *you*-**FORCE**-*lee*

    Struc 'Suppose Lee doesn't want to work—what will you do? Force her?'

    Trans 'What if Lee doesn't wanna work? What are you gonna do? Make
         her do it?'

---

[5]See Section E on Conditionals for an explanation of *'cond'*.

(C.3) Rhetorical Questions

Rhetorical questions (*'rhet.q'*) are accompanied by a brow raise and, frequently, a tilting of the head. A 'wh-word' sign usually occurs with this type of question. Rhetorical questions are not true questions since the Addressee is not expected to respond, but rather provide a way for the Signer to introduce and draw attention to the information that s/he will then supply. In effect, the Signer is posing a question and then responding to it him/herself. Rhetorical questions are frequently used in ASL conversations.

Below are a variety of rhetorical questions involving the 'wh-word' interrogatives **WHY, "WHAT", WHO,** and **HOW** as well as the sign **REASON**—which is often used in rhetorical questions and has a meaning very similar to the sign **WHY**.

Notice how the non-manual behaviors differ when 'wh-word' signs occur in rhetorical questions as opposed to when they appear in 'wh-word' questions.

rhet.q
WHO

rhet.q
HOW

rhet.q
WHY

Context   The Signer is telling his brother about something he just read in the newspaper.

(24)

```
          co                    rhet.q
STRANGE*, WOMAN  DIE,  WHYwg,  REFUSE  EAT
```

    Struc   'It's really strange! A woman died. Why? She refused to eat.'

    Trans   'Wow, it's wierd! This woman died because she refused to eat.'

Context   The Signer and another woman work at Gallaudet and are discussing where several of their co-workers live.[6]

(25)

```
       t                          small brow raise
P-A-T,  PEA-BRAIN*,  WORK  HERE  GALLAUDET,

       rhet.q            po
LIVE  "WHAT",  INDEX*-far rt  O-C
```

    Struc   'Pat, he's really dumb! He works here at Gallaudet, but lives where? Far away, in Ocean City.'

    Trans   'Pat is nuts! He works here at Gallaudet but lives way out in Ocean City.'

Context   The Signer and some friends are in a restaurant. The friends are joking about having the Signer 'pick up the tab', but the Signer replies:

(26)

```
     small br      rhet.q  (smile          )
EAT  FINISH,  WHO  PAY,     YOURSELVES*
```

    Struc   'When we're finished eating, who will pay? You all will!'

    Trans   'When we're done eating, you guys are gonna be the ones to pick up the tab!'

Context   Members at a club meeting are discussing ways to make more money for various projects. Someone suggests they seek "outside" assistance for ideas. The young Signer angrily responds:

(27)

```
            neg                        rhet.q
me-SAY-#NO-TO-you*,  MONEY  COLLECT  HOWwg,

                nod
OURSELVES  DECIDE  WILL*
```

    Struc   'No! How will we earn the money? We will decide for ourselves!'

    Trans   'No! We'll decide for ourselves how to raise the money!'

---

[6]On the accompanying videotape of this example, the Signer used a non-manual signal (*'po'*) that is not described or illustrated in this text. In the context of **INDEX***-*far rt* in this example, the *'po'* signal emphasizes how far away Pat lives.

Context   The Addressee sees a little boy, Lee, crying. The Signer explains:[7]

(28)   _____t   ____rhet.q   (gaze rt)
                        LEE   (2h)alt.CRY,   REASON,   POSS-*rt*   MOTHER   GO-*rt*

        Struc   'Lee's crying, what's the reason for it? His mother is gone.'

        Trans   'Lee's crying because his mother's gone.'

D. Commands

In general, commands are sentences that order the Addressee to do something. Although there has been little study of commands in ASL, we do know that they are usually indicated by stress (emphasis) on the verb and usually direct eye gaze on the Addressee. This stress usually involves making the sign faster and sharper. As explained in the section on Transcription Symbols, we indicate that a sign is stressed by writing an asterisk (*) after the sign.

There is another form of stress that sometimes occurs in commands when the Signer is being *very emphatic*. This form of stress involves a slower and very deliberate movement while looking very sharply at the Addressee. This type of slow, deliberate stress is stronger (more emphatic) than the fast, sharp stress. One context in which it may be used is when the Signer anticipates that the Addressee will not want to carry out the command; so the Signer makes the command more emphatic.

Below are a series of examples illustrating some types of commands in ASL. Notice that the verb that is stressed is the one which indicates what the Addressee is being ordered to do. (In examples (29) and (30), the sign **FINISH** is functioning as a verb.)

Context   A kid is pulling on the cat's tail and the cat is hollering. The Signer yells at the kid:

(29)   (gaze down,rt   )
          FINISH* YOU   TEASE-TO-*rt*   CAT,   FINISH* YOU

        Struc   'You stop teasing the cat! You stop it!'

        Trans   'Stop teasing the cat! Stop it!'

---

[7]The gloss **POSS-*rt*** refers to a 'possessive' pronominal reference to the right. (See Chapter VIII on Pronominalization.)

For readers who have the accompanying videotape: The Signer has used a name sign for the boy in this example.

Context   The Signer's new boyfriend is constantly nagging her about the way she dresses and talks. Finally, the Signer is fed up and yells:[8]

(30)   **ALL-MONTH** *you-*NAG*-me"long time",* **FINISH***

    Struc   'All month you've been nagging me—a long time. Stop it!'

    Trans   'You've been nagging me all month. Now stop it!'

Context   Standing with a group of people, the Addressee starts to say something very personal about the Signer. The Signer angrily yells:

(31)   **SHUT-UP*** **YOU**

    Struc   'You shut up!'

    Trans   'Shaddup!'

Context   The Signer is a school teacher. He tells a restless and playful child on his right:

(32)   (gaze down,rt)
       SIT*-*rt*

    Struc   'Sit down!'

    Trans   'Go sit down!'

Although the verbs in the next three examples would normally be signed with the fast, sharp form of stress, the reader should also try signing them with the slow, deliberate form of stress to see how it intensifies the stress on the verb. Notice that example (35) has two stressed verbs: *you-***INFORM***-"each other"** and the modal verb **MUST***. Usually, if two verbs are stressed, only the last one can have the slow, deliberate form. The reader may also want to try this out with example (29).

Context   A teacher tells an aide what to do with a "problem student" named Pat.

(33)   (gaze lf) (neg)   cond   tight lips
       SUPPOSE P-A-T   NOT-WANT   WORK, *you-***FORCE***-lf**

    Struc   'If Pat doesn't want to work, you force her to.'

    Trans   'If Pat doesn't wanna work, then make her.'

---

[8]The modulation of the verb that is written as *"long time"* is discussed in Chapter XIII on Temporal Aspect.

Context   (same as 33)

(34)   _____(_____neg)cond____ _____tight lips_____
       SUPPOSE   P-A-T   NOT-WANT   WORK,   YOU   PUNISH*   INDEX-*lf*

   Struc   'If Pat doesn't want to work, you punish her.'

   Trans   'If Pat doesn't wanna work, then punish her.'

Context   The referee of a tennis tournament reminds two young players about the
           time of their match on the last day of the tournament.[9]

(35)   (gaze downward at two boys, looking back 'n forth   )
       #OK-*rt*,   YOU-TWO   *you*-AGREE-WITH-*"each other"*,
       #OK-*lf*,

       _____q_____
       GAME   TOMORROW   TIME⌒TWO,   RIGHT,

       _____(___th)_____cond_____
       SUPPOSE   QUIT,   WITHDRAW-FROM-*game*,

       _____tight lips_____
       you-INFORM-*"each other"**   MUST*

   Struc   'OK. You two have agreed that the game tomorrow will be at two
             o'clock, right? If one of you quits or backs out, you tell each other.
             You must do that.'

   Trans   'OK. You guys have agreed that the game tomorrow's gonna be at
             two, right? Now if one of you decides to quit or back out, you gotta
             tell the other guy. That's a must.'

E. Conditionals

   Another type of sentence that has occurred in several examples in the preceding
sections is called a *conditional*. This type of sentence has two parts: a part that
states a 'condition' and a part that describes the result of that condition. This second
part can be a statement, question, or command. For example, the sentence 'If it rains
tomorrow, then I will cancel the picnic' is a conditional. The *condition* is 'If it rains
tomorrow', and the *result* is a statement—'I will cancel the picnic'. The result can
also be a question—'If it rains tomorrow, will you cancel the picnic?'—or a
command—'If it rains tomorrow, cancel the picnic'.
   Conditionals in ASL have two parts. In most cases, the condition is signed first
and is accompanied by the non-manual grammatical signal that we write as *'cond'*.
This signal is composed of a brow raise, usually with the head tilted in one direction
and, sometimes, the body slightly inclined in one direction. At the juncture (break)
between the condition and the result segment, there is a pause and a change in
several of the non-manual behaviors that accompanied the condition segment. If the
result segment is a statement or a command, the brows will be lowered and the

---

[9]The verb modulation that is written as *"each other"* is described in Chapter IX on Subjects and Objects.

head/body will usually shift in a different direction than that which occurred during
the first segment. If the result segment is a 'yes-no' question, the brows are usually
raised higher and the head is tilted toward the Addressee, with 'widened' eye gaze
on the Addressee. If the result segment is a 'wh-word' question, then the brows are
lowered and drawn into a 'squint', usually with a change in head/body position. So
we see that conditionals in ASL involve a brow raise during the condition, followed
by a pause—during which several types of changes occur in the non-manual behaviors of the Signer.

   The photographs shown below illustrate one 'condition' ('If it rains') and two
possible 'results'—a statement ('I'll go') and a 'yes-no' question ('will you go?').
Notice how the Signer's brows, head, and body position in the condition are different
from those non-manual behaviors in the two result segments.

GO-*lf*

cond
RAIN

q
GO-*lf*

Below are two examples of conditionals in ASL. In (36), the condition is followed by a 'yes-no' question. In (37), the condition is followed by a statement (actually, an assertion—See Section F.2).

Context   The Signer lives in New Hampshire and is trying to decide what to do during the weekend. He asks his friend:

(36)   <u>   cond   </u>   <u>   q</u>

          TOMORROW SNOW, YOU GO-TO-*rt* SKI YOU

        Struc   'If it snows tomorrow, will you go skiing?'

        Trans   'If it snows tomorrow, you gonna go skiing?'

Context   The Signer has decided on her weekend plans—if, of course, the weather cooperates!

(37)   <u>   cond   </u> <u>(gaze rt   )nodding</u>

          TOMORROW SNOW, ME GO-TO-*rt* SKI

        Struc   'If it snows tomorrow, I will go skiing.'

        Trans   'If it snows tomorrow, I'm gonna go skiing.'

Just as the presence of the non-manual behaviors in the grammatical signal '*q*' is often the only way of distinguishing a signed question from a signed statement, the behaviors denoted by the signal '*cond*' (which includes the behavioral change at the juncture between the two segments) is often the only way of distinguishing a conditional from two regular statements. This difference is illustrated in examples (38) and (39).

Context   The Signer is a baseball player. Someone asks about the tournament last weekend. The Signer responds:

(38)   <u>   t   </u>   ('regretfully'   )

          SATURDAY, RAIN, GAME CANCEL

        Struc   'Saturday, it rained and the game was cancelled.'

        Trans   'It rained on Saturday, so the game was cancelled.'

Context   The Signer is the baseball coach and warns his team:

(39)   <u>   cond   </u> <u>   nodding</u>

          SATURDAY RAIN, GAME CANCEL

        Struc   'If it rains Saturday, the game will certainly be cancelled.'

        Trans   'If it rains on Saturday, the game will be cancelled.'

However, ASL also has a few signs that can be used with the 'cond' signal to indicate that the sentence is a conditional. These signs—**SUPPOSE**, the finger-spelled loan **#IF**, and the 'wiggly F' (**#IFwg**) that is derived from the loan sign **#IF**—occur at the beginning of the condition segment.

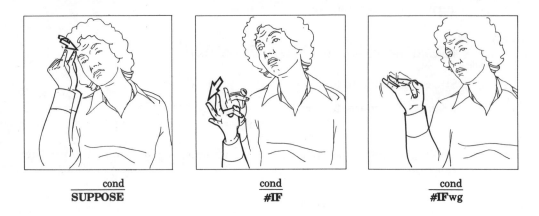

cond	cond	cond
SUPPOSE	**#IF**	**#IFwg**

Examples (23), (33), (34), and (35) in the preceding sections illustrate how the sign **SUPPOSE** is used in conditionals. Also see example (40) below.

Context   The Signer and a friend are discussing what might happen after the up-coming Eastern regional football play-offs:

(40)
```
                                    (gaze lf                     )
        SUPPOSE   WASHINGTON   washington-CHALLENGE-lf   NEW-YORK-lf,

        (gaze lf            )cond   (smiling          ) nodding
        washington-BEAT-new york,   FIRST-PLACE   "WELL"
```

> *Struc*   'If it's Washington versus New York and Washington beats New York, then Washington is in first place. It's as simple as that.'
>
> *Trans*   'If Washington plays New York and beats 'em, then they're in first place. That's all there is to it.'

In some cases, the signs **SUPPOSE** and **#IF** seem to be interchangeable. That is, in some cases, the choice of either **SUPPOSE** or **#IF** may be a matter of personal preference of the Signer. (However, there may be differences between these two signs that we do not yet have information about.)

The sign **#IF**wg is often used when the Signer wants to hold the sign while thinking or to emphasize the condition. Example (41) illustrates one use of this sign.

Context   A group is discussing going to Ocean City next week and who will be responsible for driving. The Signer doesn't want to drive, but will if necessary.

(41)

$$\frac{\text{(gaze rt)nodding}}{\text{\#OK, ONE-WEEK-FUTURE P-A-T DRIVE-TO-}rt}\text{ ,}$$

$$\frac{\quad\text{cond}\quad}{\text{\#IFwg ... CAN'T,}}\quad\text{"WELL"}\quad\frac{\text{nodding}}{\text{ME DRIVE-TO-}rt}$$

Struc   'OK. Next week Pat's going to drive there. If she just can't, then I'll drive there.'

Trans   'OK. Next week Pat's gonna drive. If she can't, then I guess I'll have to drive.'

F. Negation and Assertion

All human languages have ways to negate sentences—that is, ways to indicate that something 'is not true', 'did not happen', 'will not happen', etc. Conversely, languages have ways of asserting that something 'is true', 'did happen', 'will happen', etc. Both of these processes are illustrated in the following dialogue:

Speaker A: 'You didn't come to the party last night.'
Speaker B: 'I *did* come, but I left early.'

Speaker A says that something did not happen (using the contracted form of 'did not'). Speaker B then asserts that that thing *did* happen.

In the following pages, we will describe some of the vocabulary and grammatical signals that are used in ASL for negation and assertion.

(F.1) Negation

Like the '*q*' signal in 'yes-no' questions, ASL has a non-manual, grammatical signal that can negate sentences without the use of a manual, negating sign. We write this grammatical signal as '*neg*'. It is composed of a side-to-side headshake—frequently accompanied by a frown, and sometimes, a brow squint (brows drawn together and/or lowered), a wrinkling of the nose, and/or a raised upper lip. Two forms of this 'neg' signal are illustrated below. (The headshake movement is, of course, not visible in the photographs.) The female is illustrating a form that could be used in example (42); the male is illustrating a form that could be used in examples (43) and (44).

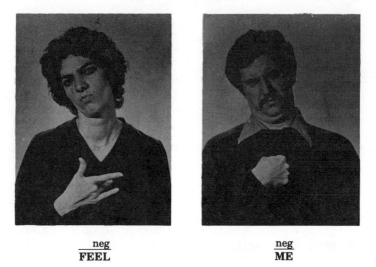

<table>
<tr><td align="center">neg
FEEL</td><td align="center">neg
ME</td></tr>
</table>

Context   A group of people are leaving for a picnic. They ask the Signer if she wants to join them. The Signer responds:

(42)
                             neg
ME   FEEL   GOOD   ME

    Struc   'No, I don't feel good.'

    Trans   'Nah, I don't feel so hot.'

Context   The teacher is picking "volunteers" for a project and mistakenly chooses the Signer. The Signer responds:

(43)
      co   neg   wh-q
"HEY",   ME   VOLUNTEER   ME,   "WHAT"

    Struc   'Hey! I didn't volunteer. What's going on?'

    Trans   'Hey! I didn't volunteer. Why did you pick me?'

Context A group of girls are playing in the living room near a broken vase. The Signer's mother comes in and asks her daughter if she broke the vase. The daughter responds:

(44)   ____q___   neg(gaze rt)
               ME————————→ **INDEX***-*rt*

        Struc 'Me? Uh-Uh. *Her.*'

        Trans 'Me? I didn't do it. *She* did it.'

In the examples above, the sentences were negated with the non-manual behaviors that comprise the signal *'neg'*. These behaviors basically mean 'not'. However, ASL also has two signs that basically mean 'not'—the sign glossed as **NOT** and the sign that we gloss as **DON'T**. The sign **DON'T** tends to be used in more formal contexts or in commands. Another sign, **NOT-YET**, also basically means 'not', but the negation is more 'momentary' (as in 'not now, but maybe later').

      NOT   **DON'T**   **NOT-YET**

When negation signs occur in sentences, they (and often, the whole sentence) are frequently accompanied by the *'neg'* signal. However, this is not always the case, and more research is required to understand why the *'neg'* signal occurs in some contexts and not in others. Uses of the negation signs **NOT, DON'T,** and **NOT-YET** are illustrated in examples (45)–(47).

Context Someone is telling a group of people that Lee is moving to Detroit, but the Signer knows that Lee has just accepted a new job here in Washington, D.C. The Signer exclaims:

(45)   ____co ('disbelieving')_____   ____(gaze rt____)____   ___neg__
           "HEY",   CRAZY,   L-E-E   NOT   MOVE-TO-*rt*   **DETROIT,   CRAZY͜YOU**

        Struc 'Hey! You're crazy! Lee's not moving to Detroit, You're crazy!'

        Trans 'Hey! You're nuts! Lee's not moving to Detroit. You're out of it!'

Context   The Signer is on a discussion panel with Pat who is seated on the Signer's left. Pat has just stated his views. Now it's the Signer's turn to talk.

(46)   <u>(gaze lf)</u>   <u>t</u>   <u>neg</u>   <u>rhet.q</u>
       P-A-T-*lf* POSS-*lf* LECTURE, ME DON'T SUPPORT, REASON . . .

       Struc 'Pat's talk, I don't support it. The reason? . . .'

       Trans 'I don't support what Pat said because . . .'

Context   A classmate asks the Signer if he has done all the class assignments— which include reading a book, writing a paper, and watching a videotape. The Signer forgot about the paper and responds:

(47)   <u>t</u>   <u>neg</u>
       WRITE PAPER, NOT-YET ME

       Struc 'Writing the paper, I haven't done that yet.'

       Trans 'I haven't written the paper yet.'

Negation signs often occur before the verb. However, they can occur at the end of the sentence. When they occur at the end, the effect seems to be that they are more emphasized.

Putting the negation sign at the end of a sentence is frequently seen in dramatic or artistic performances in ASL. This artistic device is illustrated in the two sentences below which occur in an ASL rendition of *Psalm 23* signed by Louie Fant. The negation signs in these sentences are **NEVER** and **NONE**.

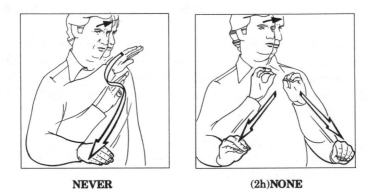

           NEVER   **(2h)NONE**

Context   "The Lord is my shepherd . . ."

(48)   <u>(lean rt</u>   )   <u>rhet.q</u>   <u>neg</u>
       ME WILL WANT-*lf*, NEED, (2h)HUNGER, WILL, NEVER

       Struc 'I will want (things), need (things), be hungry, will I? Never!'

       Trans (from Psalm 23) 'I shall not want.'

Context   "Yea, though I walk through the valley of the shadow of death . . ."

(49) (gaze rt)   rhet.q   neg
      FEAR-*rt*   AWFUL   HAPPEN+,   (2h)NONE

     Struc   'Fear of awful happenings? I have none.'

     Trans   (from Psalm 23) 'I will fear no evil.'

Another way to emphasize the negation is to repeat the negative sign. In such cases, the negative sign often occurs before the verb and then at the end of the sentence (and is often stressed at the end).

Context   (same as 45)

(50) ('disbelieving')   (tight lips)neg
      CRAZY,   L-E-E   NOT   MOVE-TO-*rt*   DETROIT   NOT*

     Struc   'You're crazy! Lee's not moving to Detroit. She's not!'

     Trans   'You're nuts! Lee's not moving to Detroit. No way!'

ASL has a wide variety of negation signs. Some of these are verbs—for example: **REFUSE** (made with an 'A' or 'S' handshape), **DENY, THUMBS-DOWN-ON-____ , CAN'T,** and ____-**SAY-#NO-TO-**____ .

REFUSE

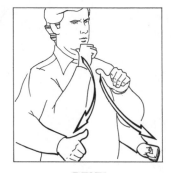
DENY

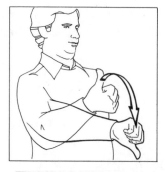
THUMBS-DOWN-ON-____

CAN'T

me-**SAY-#NO-TO**-*you*

Other negation signs function as adjectives or adverbs—for example: **NOT-POSSIBLE** (example 51), **NOT-FAIR** (which can also mean 'not cost much'), **NOT-MUCH** (example 52), **NOT-WORTHWHILE**, the fingerspelled loan sign **#NG** (from 'no good'—example 53), **AIN'T-GOT-NONE** (which has two colloquial forms—example 51), **IT'S-NOTHING, NOT-LEGAL/FORBID** (which can also be used as a verb), **NONE** (which has three forms—regular, emphatic, and colloquial) and **NEVER** (example 48). The sign **NOTHING** is also a negation sign that is used as a noun.

NOT-POSSIBLE

NOT-FAIR

NOT-MUCH

NOT-WORTHWHILE

(2h)#NG

NOT-LEGAL/FORBID

AIN'T-GOT-NONE

AIN'T-GOT-NONE

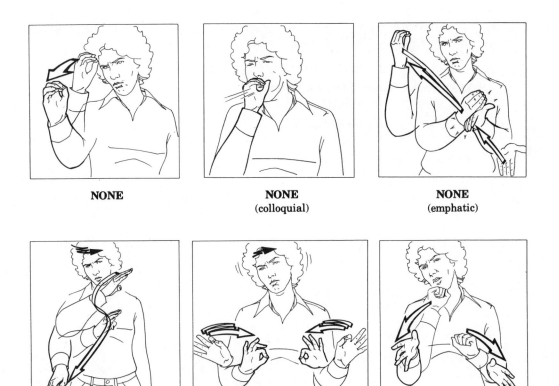

| NONE | NONE (colloquial) | NONE (emphatic) |
| NEVER | IT'S-NOTHING | NOTHING |

Context A friend asks the Signer if he is going to Europe this summer. The Signer responds:

(51)

$$\overline{\text{NOT-POSSIBLE,}}^{\text{neg}} \quad \overline{\text{MONEY,}}^{\text{t}} \quad \text{AIN'T-GOT-NONE}$$

> *Struc* 'Impossible! Money, I haven't got any.'

> *Trans* 'No way! I ain't got the bucks.'

Context The Signer is describing the proximity of major cities in the U.S. to a foreigner, and the foreigner asks about Baltimore. The Signer responds:

(52)

$$\text{YOU} \quad \text{KNOW} \quad \overline{\text{WASHINGTON D-C-}rt,}^{\text{(body lean rt \quad)t}} \quad \overline{\text{BALTIMORE-}lf,}^{\text{(body lean lf \quad)t}}$$

$$\overline{\text{NOT-MUCH}}^{\text{neg}} \quad \text{INDEX-washington \& baltimore}\leftrightarrow$$

> *Struc* 'You know Washington, D.C. is here. Well, Baltimore is here, and it's not far from Washington.'

> *Trans* 'You know where Washington, D.C. is. Well, Baltimore's not far from there.'

Context   The Signer is known for having problems with her car. A friend asks her
why she missed the club meeting last night. The Signer responds:

(53)
_____t
YESTERDAY,   #CAR   BREAK-DOWN,

___rhet.q
REASON,   CARBURETOR   (2h)**#NG**

    Struc   'Yesterday, my car broke down. The reason? The carburetor is no
good.'

    Trans   'My car broke down yesterday. The carburetor's all messed up.'

Context   A friend suggests that the Signer should sell her car since she's having so
many problems with it. The Signer exclaims:[10]

(54)
_____rhet.q _____neg
MY   #CAR   SELL,   NEVER*,   CHERISH*

    Struc   'Sell my car? Never! I cherish it!'

    Trans   'Sell my car? No way! I love that car!'

Some negation signs occur in contractions (see Chapter V, Section B on Compounds and Contractions)—for example: **NEVER HEAR, NOT HERE** (example
55), **WHY NOT** (example 56), and **NOT POLITE**. The sign **NONE** is also used in a
variety of contractions such as **FEEL NONE** (example 57), **FUNNY NONE**,
SEE NONE, and **HEAR NONE**.

    NEVER HEAR   **NOT HERE**   **WHY NOT**

---

[10]For readers who have the accompanying videotape: The stress on **NEVER*** is the sharp and fast
form, whereas the stress on **CHERISH*** is the slow, very deliberate form that was described in Section D.

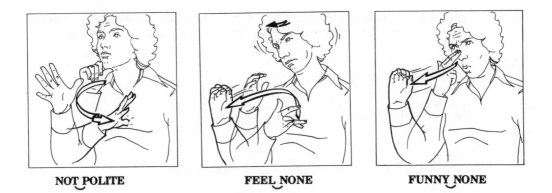

NOT POLITE   FEEL NONE   FUNNY NONE

Context   The secretary is taking roll at a meeting and calls out Pat's name. The
            Signer responds:

(55)
$$\overline{\text{P-A-T,}}^{\quad t\quad}\ \overline{\text{NOT HERE}}^{\quad neg\quad}$$

       Struc   'Pat, he's not here.'

       Trans   'Pat's not here.'

Context   The Signer and a friend are hiking in the woods and the Signer spots a
            river up ahead to his left.

(56)
$$\overline{\text{"HEY",}}^{\quad co\quad}\ \overset{\text{(gaze lf\ \ )}}{\text{INDEX-}lf}\ \ \text{WATER}\ \ \text{(2h)5↓wg-CL-}lf\text{'river',}$$

       WHY NOT   US-TWO   GO-ACROSS-*river*

       Struc   'Hey! There's a river over there. Why don't we go across it.'

       Trans   'Hey! There's a river over there. Let's go across.'

Context   A group of people are talking about a particular movie and how emotional
they became when they saw it. The Signer saw that movie, but says:[11]

(57)   (gaze lf)_____t
                  THAT-*lf* MOVIE-*lf*,

            (gaze rt)   (gaze lf)   (head back   )
            US-TWO-*rt*   FRIEND-*rt*   *we*-**GO-TO-*movie*,   LOOK-AT-*cntr*,**
                                                                   LOOK-AT-*cntr*,

            (gaze rt)_____t   ___t___
                  FRIEND-*rt*,   CRY"*over time*",   ME,   FEEL NONE

   Struc   'That movie, a friend and I went to it. We were watching it, and
            my friend, she cried continuously, but me, I felt nothing.'

   Trans   'A friend and I went to see that movie. She cried through the whole
            thing, but I wasn't moved at all.'

ASL also has a small set of signs that can be negated by adding an outward
twisting movement to the sign. This movement can be added to the signs **GOOD**,
KNOW, **WANT**, and **LIKE**—which then become **NOT-GOOD** (or **BAD**), **NOT-
KNOW**, **NOT-WANT** (example 23), and **NOT-LIKE**.

KNOW   NOT-KNOW

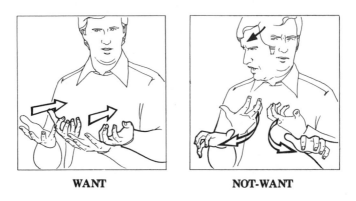

WANT   NOT-WANT

---

[11]The verb modulation "*over time*" is described in Chapter XIII on Temporal Aspect. Notice in this
example that the 'movie' is first located to the Signer's left. Then, when describing the experience of
watching the movie screen, the Signer moves that location to right in front of the Signer (*cntr*).

(F.2) Assertion

The study of assertions in ASL is another area that needs considerably more attention. However, we do know that Signers often use a head nod ('*nod*') or repeated nodding ('*nodding*') to emphasize that something 'is true', 'did happen', 'will happen', etc. Often, this nod or nodding is accompanied by a tightening of the closed lips ('*tight lips*').

Notice how the nod on the sign **WILL** in example (58) emphasizes (the truth of) the Signer's intention to attend the meeting.

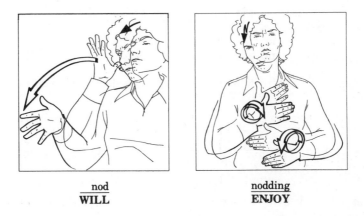

<u>nod</u> **WILL**	<u>nodding</u> **ENJOY**

Context   The Signer has a very busy schedule and can't attend all the meetings she is supposed to attend, but promises:[12]

(58)
```
                           t      (gaze rt )   nod
TIME THREE MEETING,    ME  GO-TO-rt  WILL
```

     Struc   'The meeting at three o'clock, I *will* go to it.'

     Trans   'I *will* go to the three o'clock meeting.'

Sometimes the nodding occurs throughout the whole sentence, insisting that the content of the sentence is true—as seen in (59).

Context   Someone says that the Signer's watchdog is no good because it doesn't even chase cats away. The Signer says he's wrong and that:

(59)
```
        rapid nodding
DOG   CHASE   CAT
```

     Struc   'Yes, the dog *does* chase cats.'

     Trans   'The dog does *too* chase cats.'

---

[12]For readers who have the accompanying videotape: The Signer makes a large forward nod during the sign **WILL** and then continues nodding.

Another way to emphasize that something is true is to use the sign **TRUE** (usually with some form of head nodding). This is illustrated in (60) where the sign is also stressed to emphasize the truth of Pat's claim.

Context   Someone claims that Pat has lied about being a doctor. The Signer angrily responds:

(60)   (head back, grimace   )
          WRONG   YOU,

                       nod   nod   nodding
          P-A-T   DOCTOR,   TRUE*

          Struc   'No, you're wrong. Pat *is* a doctor. It's true.'

          Trans   'No, you're wrong. Pat really is a doctor. She *is*.'

However, sometimes the Signer uses lip tightening (*'tight lips'*) to emphasize that his/her statement is true—without the use of some form of nodding. This occurs in (61)—where the Signer shakes his head as part of the *'neg'* signal, and the *'tight lips'* emphasizes the truth of the (negative) statement.

Context   Some friends at a party are insisting that Lee will show up soon. But the Signer tells them:

(61)   t   tight lips+neg
          L-E-E,   **COME**-*here*

          Struc   'Lee, he's *not* coming here.'

          Trans   'Lee's *not* gonna show up.'

G. Topicalization

Since it is not humanly possible to communicate everything one wants to say during the same moment in time, users of a language must organize their speaking or signing into 'chunks'. That is, say one thing, then another thing, then another, and so on. People make choices about the order in which they will communicate their ideas. To some extent, this order seems to be influenced by the particular language they are using.

For example, ASL Signers (like speakers of Mandarin Chinese and Tagalog) tend to indicate first what is the thing they want to talk about (called the *topic*) and then to make some statement(s), question(s), etc., about that thing (called the *comment*). For this reason, ASL is described as having a "topic-comment structure".

Sentences can also have topic-comment structures. For example, suppose Mary is telling John what she thinks about a particular car (the 'topic' of the conversation). This car has been at the dealer's for a long time, and a friend named Pat has been wanting to buy it. Mary says that she drove past the dealer's yesterday and noticed that the car was no longer there. John might respond:

(a) 'Oh, Pat finally bought the car.'

or

(b) 'That car? Pat finally bought it.'

In the first example, the topic (car) occurs at the end of the sentence. In the second example, the topic is stated first, followed by the comment ('Pat finally bought it'). In this case, we say that the segment 'that car' has been *topicalized* (meaning that it has been put at the beginning of the utterance). The grammatical process by which a topic segment is put at or toward the beginning of an utterance is called *topicalization*.

This process of topicalization occurs frequently in ASL. That is, the topic is frequently signed first, followed by some kind of comment. To clearly indicate what constitutes the topic in the sentence, ASL uses a grammatical signal that we write as '*t*' (for 'topic').

This signal has several components: (a) during the signing of the 'topic', the brows are raised, the head is tilted, and the Signer maintains fairly constant eye gaze on the Addressee (except where directional gaze is needed for establishing or referring to referents in space—See Chapter VIII on Pronominalization); (b) the last sign in the topic is held slightly longer than usual, resulting in a pause; (c) then, when the 'comment' is signed, the head position, brows, and gaze direction are changed. How they change depends on the type of comment that follows (e.g. statement, 'yes-no' question, command).

Several of these different components are illustrated in the photographs below. Suppose the Signer wants to say that she wrote a particular paper rather carelessly. She might sign:

$$\overline{\text{PAPER,}}^{\text{t}} \quad \overline{\text{WRITE-}paper}^{\text{th}}$$

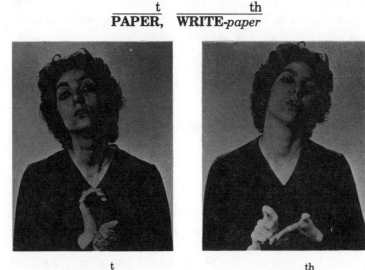

$$\overline{\text{PAPER}}^{\text{t}} \qquad\qquad \overline{\text{WRITE-}paper}^{\text{th}}$$

Many of the sentences in the preceding examples have topicalized segments. Looking at one of these examples (see example 62 below), notice how this process of topicalization, in effect, "sets the scene" with the topic and then gives more specific information about some aspect of that "scene".

Context   A group of people are talking about a particular movie and how emotional they became when they saw it. The Signer saw that movie, but says:

(62)
       (gaze lf) _____ t
         THAT-*lf* **MOVIE**-*lf,*

      (gaze rt   )   (gaze lf)   (head back   )
      US-TWO-*rt* **FRIEND**-*rt*   *we-***GO-TO**-*movie,* **LOOK-AT**-*cntr,*
                                                             LOOK-AT-*cntr,*

      (gaze rt) _____ t   ___ t
        FRIEND-*rt,* **CRY**"*over time*", **ME**, **FEEL‿NONE**

    Struc   'That movie, a friend and I went to it. We were watching it, and my friend, she cried continuously, but me, I felt nothing.'

    Trans   'A friend and I went to see that movie. She cried through the whole thing, but I wasn't moved at all.'

In example (62), the first "scene" is 'that movie' (the first topic) which the Signer and a friend went to see (the comment). The second "scene" is the friend (the second topic) who cried continuously (the comment). The third "scene" is the Signer (the third topic) who felt nothing (the comment). Using the analogy of film-making, this use of topicalization in ASL is like focusing with the camera on some "scene", then shooting some footage on what happens in that general scene. The film-maker may then choose to focus in on some smaller aspect of that scene and shoot some more footage which shows what happens in that smaller aspect of the scene.

In general, ASL Signers 'chunk' information in a "larger scene to smaller scene" fashion. In example (62), the larger scene involved two people going to a movie. Then the Signer focused in more narrowly on what happened to each person (two smaller scenes). Let's look at this again in example (63).

Context   A visitor is in a large, unfamiliar room and tells the Signer that she has been looking for her books, but can't find them. The Signer replies:

(63)
      _____ (gaze lf) ___ t _____ t
    KNOW   TABLE   INDEX-*lf,* **YOUR   BOOK**+,

    ON-*lf* **INDEX**-*lf*

    Struc   'You know the table over there—your books, they're on it.'

    Trans   'You see that table over there? Your books are on it.'

In example (63), the Signer instructs the Addressee to focus on the table (the larger scene), and then says that the books she is looking for (the smaller scene) are located on that table.

Many different kinds of things can be used to "set the scene" and function as the 'topic' in an ASL sentence. For example, the topic can be a person or object as seen in (62) and (63), a place (64), a time (65), or an event, etc. Or, the topic can be some combination of these—for example, a time and an event (66).

Context   The Signer is describing what she and Pat did on their vacation.

(64)
<u>   (gaze rt   )   t   </u>
WASHINGTON D-C-*rt* THEREABOUTS-*rt*,

   (gaze lf   ) (gaze rt   )mm
       P-A-T-*lf* US-TWO-*lf* TOUR+-*rt* SIGHTSEE+-*rt*

    Struc   'The Washington, D.C. area, Pat and I toured and went sightseeing around there.'

    Trans   'Pat and I went touring and sightseeing around the Washington, D.C. area.'

Context   The Signer is a baseball player. Someone asks about the tournament last weekend. The Signer responds:

(65)
<u>   t   </u>   ('regretfully'   )
SATURDAY, RAIN, GAME CANCEL

    Struc   'Saturday, it rained and the game was cancelled.'

    Trans   'It rained on Saturday, so the game was cancelled.'

Context   The Signer is on a committee that has weekly meetings. Someone asks how the committee work is going. The Signer responds:

(66)
<u>   t   </u>
YESTERDAY MEETING, BORING*

    Struc   'Yesterday the meeting, it was really boring.'

    Trans   'The meeting yesterday was really boring.'

So far we have talked about topicalization as a way of setting the scene (or "setting the stage") before making a comment(s) about particular characters, objects, events, etc., in that scene. Naturally, the Signer has a choice concerning what s/he is going to use to set the scene—i.e. a choice concerning what will occur in the topicalized segment. The Signer's decision about what s/he will topicalize depends on both the *context* in which the utterance occurs (e.g. the subject of the discussion, what was said immediately prior to the utterance, etc.) and *what the*

Signer wants to communicate. To understand how the context influences what will be topicalized, let's look at examples (67)–(69)—all of which basically mean 'Pat (already) bought a car'.[13]

Context Some people are talking about Pat, his new job, and how he's going to get to work. The Signer joins the conversation and says:

(67)   <u>   t   </u> <u>   nodding   </u>
          P-A-T, FINISH BUY CAR

    Struc 'Pat, he (already) bought a car.'

    Trans 'Oh, Pat's bought a car.'

Context A group of friends are trying to figure out how to get to the beach on weekends during the summer since none of them have a car. The Signer joins the conversation and says:

(68)   <u>   t   </u> <u>   nodding   </u>
          CAR, P-A-T FINISH BUY

    Struc 'A car, Pat's (already) bought one.'

    Trans 'Pat has bought a car.'

Context Someone is complaining about how hard it is to buy a car due to all the financing and insurance problems. The Signer suggests she should talk with Pat. She asks why. The Signer responds:

(69)   <u>   t   </u> <u>   nodding   </u>
          CAR BUY, FINISH P-A-T

    Struc 'Buying a car, Pat's (already) done it.'

    Trans 'Pat's already gone through buying a car.'

Notice that it would be inappropriate to sign example (69) in the context given for example (68). That is, the focus of the topic in (69) does not make sense in the context of (68) where the subject of the discussion concerns 'having a car'—not 'buying a car'.

---

[13]We have included the word 'already' in parentheses in the structural equivalents (*Struc*) because of the difficulty of translating the meaning of **FINISH** in different contexts. Sometimes the meaning is similar to the meaning of the English word 'already', but not always.

These examples illustrate one reason why it is so important that teachers of ASL—and of any language—teach the language "in context" so that students learn how to *appropriately* form and use sentences—as well as vocabulary, etc. These examples (and many others) also demonstrate the falsity of certain claims made in several books on ASL that say "the order of signs in short sentences does not make any difference". The exact meaning and appropriate use of sentences in ASL is often affected by the order of the signs (and how they are grouped into grammatical units).

Sometimes topicalized segments are preceded by the signs **KNOW-THAT, YOU KNOW,** or **KNOW** (which may have repeated movement).

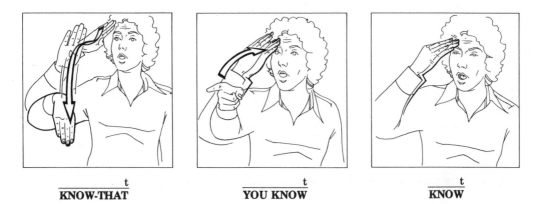

$$\overline{\text{KNOW-THAT}}^{\;t} \qquad \overline{\text{YOU KNOW}}^{\;t} \qquad \overline{\text{KNOW}}^{\;t}$$

In general, the introductory sequences **KNOW-THAT** or **YOU KNOW** are used when the Signer thinks the Addressee is familiar with the referent(s) that occur in the topic. The purpose of the introductory sequence **KNOW-THAT** or **YOU KNOW** is to help draw the Addressee's attention to those familiar referents. For example, in (70a) and (70b), the Signer assumes that the Addressee knows Pat (the referent).

Context   A club has had a long-standing bet concerning who would be the first person in the group to buy a car. The Signer tells one of the club members:

(70a)
$$\overline{\text{KNOW-THAT} \quad \text{P-A-T,}}^{\;t} \quad \overline{\text{RECENT}}^{\;cs} \quad \overline{\text{BUY} \quad \text{CAR}}^{\;nodding}$$

(70b)
$$\overline{\text{YOU} \quad \text{KNOW} \quad \text{P-A-T,}}^{\;t} \quad \overline{\text{RECENT}}^{\;cs} \quad \overline{\text{BUY} \quad \text{CAR}}^{\;nodding}$$

> *Struc*   'You know Pat, he just bought a car.'
>
> *Trans*   'Pat just bought a car.'

However, if the Signer is not sure if the Addressee is familiar with the referent, s/he may introduce the topic with the sign **KNOW+** and with a squinting of the eyes (see illustration of **KNOW**). In this case, the pause between the topic and comment is usually longer—while the Signer maintains eye gaze on the Addressee (holding the last sign in the topic) and waits for him/her to show some sign of recognition. If the Addressee responds positively (via head nodding, etc.), the Signer continues with the comment. If the Addressee is not familiar with the referent, the Signer will supply identifying information about the referent—and then continue with the comment. These two possibilities are illustrated in (71) and (72).

Context   (same as 70a—but the Signer isn't sure if that club member knows Pat.)

(71)
$$\overline{\hspace{3cm}}^{\text{qt}} \quad \overline{\hspace{1cm}}^{\text{cs}} \quad \overline{\hspace{1.5cm}}^{\text{nodding}}$$
KNOW+ P-A-T (Addressee nods 'Yes'), **RECENT BUY CAR**

    Struc   'You know Pat? ('Yes') He just bought a car.'

    Trans   'You know Pat? ('Yes') He just bought a car.'

Context   (same as 71)[14]

(72)
$$\overline{\hspace{5cm}}^{\text{qt}}$$
KNOW+ P-A-T (Addressee looks puzzled),

$$\overline{\text{rapid nodding}\hspace{2cm}}$$
         PAST NIGHT *you*-**MEET**-*pat* **#CLUB,**

$$\overline{\hspace{2cm}}^{\text{neg+q}} \qquad\qquad \overline{\hspace{1cm}}^{\text{cs}} \quad \overline{\hspace{1.5cm}}^{\text{nodding}}$$
REMEMBER YOU, (Addressee - 'Oh Yeah!') **RECENT BUY CAR**

    Struc   'You know Pat? ('Umm . . .') Yes you do, last night you met him at the club. Don't you remember? ('Oh Yeah!') He just bought a car.'

    Trans   'You know Pat - ('Umm . . .') Yeah, you met him at the club last night. Remember? ('Oh Yeah!') Well, he just bought a car.'

Notice that we have written a '*qt*' over the topic rather than simply a '*t*'. This is because the topic is also functioning as a question (and the Signer will wait for a response before continuing with a comment). The sign **KNOW**(+) often occurs in topics where the Signer is checking to see if the Addressee is familiar with the referent—i.e. in 'question-topics'. Another way to check to see if the Addressee is familiar with the referent is to use the sequence **KNOW+ YOU** or **KNOW YOU**—which tend to occur at the end of the topic, as seen in (73).

---

[14]For readers who have the accompanying videotape: Notice the Signer's raised upper lip and nose wrinkling during the '*rapid nodding*'. This is one form of the facial sign **UH-HUH** (meaning 'You know what I mean' or 'You know what/who I'm talking about'). (The eye squint during the topic is also clearer in this example than in example 71).

Context   The Signer and a friend are talking about several new books.[15]

(73)

<u>   t   </u>   <u>   qt </u>
BOOK   C-O-M-A,   KNOW   YOU   (Addressee nods),

<u>rapid nodding</u>
                       ME   SUCCESS   READ-*book*

> *Struc*   'The book "Coma"—you know the one? ('Yes') Yeah, you know it. I finally read it.'
>
> *Trans*   'That book "Coma"—you know the one? Yeah, well I finally read it.'

H. Relative Clauses

There is one more type of sentence that we need to consider in this chapter, although it does not seem to be used very often by ASL Signers and, in fact, appears only once in all the examples collected for this text. This grammatical structure is called a *restrictive relative clause*. Such relative clauses help identify the specific person or thing that the Signer wants to talk about. For example, in the English sentence 'The woman *who works in my office* got married yesterday', the words in italics form a restrictive relative clause that helps identify *which* woman got married yesterday.

In ASL, there is a grammatical signal (that we write as *'rel.cl'*) that occurs with all of the signs in the relative clause. This signal is composed of a brow raise, cheek and upper lip raise, and a backward tilt of the head. There is no pause between the relative clause and the rest of the sentence. Notice that in the example below, the noun **MAN** is part of the restrictive relative clause.

Context   The Signer is walking with a girlfriend and notices another good friend across the street on the right. The Signer tells her companion:

(74)   <u>(gaze rt   )</u>   <u>rel.cl</u>
         THAT-ONE*-*rt* **MAN   WITH   #DOG   MY   GOOD-FRIEND**

> *Struc*   'That man who is with the dog is my close friend.'
>
> *Trans*   'That guy with the dog is a real good friend of mine.'

I. Summary

In this chapter, we have described several basic types of sentences in ASL. These sentences include several kinds of questions ('yes-no', 'wh-word', rhetorical), commands, negative statements and questions, assertions, conditionals, sentences in which a segment has been topicalized, and sentences with relative clauses. The grammatical signals that are used to form these different types of sentences are very frequently composed of non-manual behaviors which co-occur with the manual

---

[15]The sign glossed as **SUCCESS** in this example could also be glossed as **AT-LAST**.

signs. Research on these grammatical signals is still fairly new. As such, Sign Language teachers will need to keep informed about future research findings in order to continue to better understand this important part of the syntactic structure of American Sign Language.

Bibliography: Sentence Types

Baker, C. 1980. Sentences in American Sign Language. In C. Baker and R. Battison (Eds.) *Sign Language and the Deaf Community*. Silver Spring, Md.: National Association of the Deaf, 75–86.

Baker, C. & C. Padden. 1978. Focusing on the non-manual components of American Sign Language. In P. Siple (Ed.) *Understanding Language Through Sign Language Research*. New York: Academic Press, 27–57.

Bellugi, U. & S. Fischer. 1972. A comparison of sign language and spoken language: rate and grammatical mechanisms. *Cognition 1,* 173–200.

Friedman, L. 1974. On the physical manifestation of stress in the American Sign Language. MS, University of California, Berkeley.

Friedman, L. 1976. The manifestation of subject, object, and topic in the American Sign Language. In C. Li (Ed.) *Subject and Topic*. New York: Academic Press.

Ingram, R. 1978. Theme, rheme, topic, and comment in the syntax of American Sign Language. *Sign Language Studies 20,* 193–213.

Liddell, S. 1977. An Investigation into the Syntactic Structure of American Sign Language. Unpublished Ph.D. dissertation, University of California, San Diego.

Liddell, S. 1978. Non-manual signals and relative clauses in American Sign Language. In P. Siple (Ed.) *Understanding Language Through Sign Language Research*. New York: Academic Press, 59–90.

Stokoe, W. 1960. *Sign Language Structure: An Outline of the Visual Communication Systems of the American Deaf*. Studies in Linguistics: in Occasional Papers 8, Buffalo: University of Buffalo Press. [Reprinted 1978, Silver Spring, Md.: Linstok Press]

Dialogues
and
Cultural Information

SENTENCE TYPES

The following three dialogues have been developed to illustrate various uses of the grammatical features described in this chapter. Each of these dialogues also appears in one of the three corresponding Student Texts. In the Student Texts, the transcription of each dialogue is less detailed than what is provided here for the teacher of ASL. Following the dialogues, in the sections called "Cultural Information", are brief discussions of the topic of each dialogue.

The following dialogues and cultural information correspond to:

Student Text: Unit 1
                Unit 10
                Unit 19

Dialogue: Sentence Types
(Student Text - Unit 1)

First Signer (Pat)

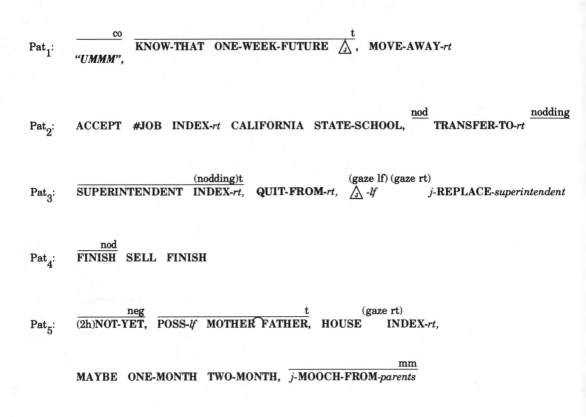

Pat₁:
$$\overset{\text{co}}{\text{"UMMM",}} \quad \overset{\rule{7cm}{0.4pt}\quad\text{t}}{\text{KNOW-THAT ONE-WEEK-FUTURE } \triangle, \text{ MOVE-AWAY-}rt}$$

Pat₂: ACCEPT #JOB INDEX-*rt* CALIFORNIA STATE-SCHOOL, $\overset{\text{nod}}{\text{TRANSFER-TO-}rt}$ $\overset{\text{nodding}}{}$

Pat₃: $\overset{\text{(nodding)t}}{\text{SUPERINTENDENT INDEX-}rt,}$ QUIT-FROM-*rt*, $\overset{\text{(gaze lf)}}{\triangle\text{-}lf}$ $\overset{\text{(gaze rt)}}{}$ *j*-REPLACE-*superintendent*

Pat₄: $\overset{\text{nod}}{\text{FINISH}}$ SELL FINISH

Pat₅: $\overset{\text{neg}}{\text{(2h)NOT-YET,}}$ POSS-*lf* $\overset{\rule{5cm}{0.4pt}\quad\text{t}}{\text{MOTHER FATHER,}}$ HOUSE $\overset{\text{(gaze rt)}}{\text{INDEX-}rt,}$

MAYBE ONE-MONTH TWO-MONTH, $\overset{\text{mm}}{j\text{-MOOCH-FROM-}parents}$

Note: In the Student Texts, the symbol $\triangle$ represents a name sign. The letter which appears inside the triangle corresponds to the first letter of that person's name. For example, $\triangle$ might be a name sign for Jan Smith. Further explanation of name signs is provided in the first Student Text.

Dialogue: Sentence Types
(Student Text - Unit 1)

Second Signer (Lee)

Lee₁:
$$\overset{\text{wh-q}}{\text{MOVE-AWAY-}\textit{lf}\ \ \text{FOR-FOR}}$$

Lee₂:
FINEwg, $\overset{\text{(head shaking\qquad\qquad)wh-q}}{\text{"WHAT"\ \ \#JOB\ \ "WHAT"}}$

Lee₃:
△ⱼ HOUSE #CAR $\overset{\text{puff.cheeks}}{\text{VARIOUS-THINGS}}$ $\overset{\text{wh-q}}{\text{\#DO-DO,}}$ $\overset{\text{q}}{\text{SELL}}$

Lee₄:
$$\overset{\text{q}}{\text{FINISH\ \ BUY\ \ HOUSE\ \ INDEX-}\textit{lf}\text{\ \ CALIFORNIA}}$$

Lee₅: SHOULD+ WHY NOT

Dialogue: Sentence Types
(Student Text - Unit 10)

First Signer (Pat)

      <u>co</u>   _____ t

Pat₁: "HEY", KNOW-THAT YOU SIGN LANGUAGE MEETING INDEX-*lf* CALIFORNIA,

    <u>_____ q</u>

YOU (2h)GO-TO-*meeting*

                            <u>_____ t</u>   <u>_____ br</u>

Pat₂: "THAT'S-RIGHT", CHICAGO INDEX-*lf*, FINEwg (2h)TERRIFIC, YOU MISS, BLAME YOURSELF

                         (gaze lf   )

Pat₃: "WELL", MANY* PEOPLE   FROM-*rt*-ASSEMBLE-TO-*chicago*,

        <u>(body lean rt)</u>   <u>t</u>   <u>nodding</u>

       DEAF, HEARING, INDEX-*arc-lf*, ENTHUSIASTIC EXCITED

      <u>neg</u> (gaze lf)   (gaze cntr   )   <u>puff.cheeks</u>

Pat₄: #NO+, CLASS-*lf* TEACH-*lf*, CLASS-*cntr* STUDY-*cntr* INVESTIGATE-*cntr*,

     (gaze rt)   (body lean rt)   <u>nodding</u>

     CLASS-*rt* "WELL" CURIOUS-*rt*, DIFFERENT+++-*arc*

                          <u>nodding</u>   <u>mm+nodding</u>

Pat₅: KNOW-THAT PLAN WILL PRINT BOOK, YOURSELF READ-*book*

         <u>nodding</u>

Pat₆: "THAT'S-RIGHT"

Dialogue: Sentence Types
(Student Text - 10)

Second Signer (Lee)

Lee₁:
$$\overline{\text{nodding}} \ (\text{gaze rt} \qquad)$$
YES+++,   CHICAGO-*rt*   MEETING,   ME   MISS

Lee₂: **KNOW-THAT, $\overline{\text{ME}}^{\text{t}}$,   STUCK   #JOB**

Lee₃: $\overline{\text{\#ALL-\textit{arc-rt}   TEACH   A-S-L}}^{\text{q}}$

Lee₄: **WISH*   ME   GO-TO-*chicago*   WISH**

Lee₅: **FINE*, $\overline{\text{BOOK}}^{\text{t}}$,   BUY   #WILL $\overline{\text{ME}}^{\text{nodding}}$**

Dialogue: Sentence Types
(Student Text - Unit 19)

First Signer (Pat)

```
                co                        (gaze at signing hand        )  _____q
Pat₁:   "HEY",  YOU  PAST+  GALLAUDET  NINETEEN  SEVEN  THREE,  RIGHT  YOU
```

```
        _____q  nod(gaze rt      )
Pat₂:   KNOW+  YOU  STATUE  GALLAUDET,      SOMEONE-rt  rt-TELL-me  MISSING
```

```
        _____wh-q
Pat₃:   BORROW-FROM-rt  FOR-FOR
```

```
                _____t                              _____neg
Pat₄:   "HEY"  GALLAUDET  INDEX-rt,  MANY*  CHANGE+,  "WOW"+,  CAN'T  BELIEVE
```

```
        ___nodding                 ___nod                            _____nod
Pat₅:           SAME-AS  MY  MOTHER,  GRADUATE  NINETEEN  FIVE  NINE  INDEX-rt,

        _____cs           (gaze rt)
        ONE-YEAR-PASTwg  GO-TO-rt  VISIT,  SHOCK*
```

```
Pat₆:   "THAT'S-RIGHT"  TRUE
```

Dialogue: Sentence Types
(Student Text - Unit 19)

Second Signer (Lee)

	nodding	(gaze lf, 'thinking')		neg	nod		wh-q

Lee₁: ME SOPHOMORE   "NO-NO", JUNIOR   RIGHT+, WHYwg

Lee₂: "HOLD-IT", MISSING ͞N͞O͞T, GOVERNMENT BORROW-FROM-*lf*
                                neg

Lee₃: (2h)"WELL" (2h)NOT-KNOW, SEEM REPLACE, ͞(͞2͞h͞)͞N͞O͞T͞-͞K͞N͞O͞W͞+
                                                                neg

Lee₄: nodding _____(gaze rt)_____ cond
         TRUE+, SUPPOSE   DEAF INDEX-*rt*,

         AGE++ GRADUATE GALLAUDET NINETEEN FIFTY THEREABOUTS,

                                        (gaze lf)
         FROM-*rt*-GO-TO-*lf* VISIT, INDEX-*rt*   STUNNED* "WHEW"

Lee₅: "PSHAW", SUPPOSE FIFTEEN YEAR FUTURE US-TWO GO-TO-*lf* VISIT,
                                                                        cond

         (gaze lf)
                 GALLAUDET AGAIN CHANGE

Lee₆: "PSHAW"

Note: Some people use the gloss **MIN͡D FROZEN** for the sign that we gloss as **STUNNED** in Lee₅. We are unsure if the second part of that gloss (**FROZEN**) is historically accurate, so we have chosen to just use the gloss **STUNNED**.

Student Text: Unit 1

Cultural Information: Educational Programs for Deaf Students

The first school for Deaf students in the U.S. was started by a Deaf Frenchman (Laurent Clerc) and a hearing minister (Thomas Gallaudet). The school was founded in Hartford, Connecticut in 1817. Since that time, the number of schools and classes for Deaf students has increased tremendously. Today, almost every state has a residential school for Deaf students. Some of these schools are located on the same campus as the state residential school for Blind students. Generally, students live at the residential school during the week and return home on weekends. While at the school, they attend classes during the daytime and then are supervised by dorm counselors or houseparents during the late afternoon and evening. (See Unit 8 for further information.)

For many students, the residential school is their first exposure to the Deaf Community: it is where they make life-long friends (often including the person they will marry); it is often the place where they first experience sustained contact with Deaf adults; and it is where they learn and refine their ASL skills. Because of this, the residential school plays a very important role in sustaining the Deaf Community.

According to a 1980 survey[1], there are approximately 62 public and 6 private residential schools in the United States. These schools serve approximately 17,000 students from pre-school through high school. Until recently, the majority of Deaf students attended residential schools. Now, according to the 1980 survey, approximately 7,500 students attend public or private day schools and 17,700 students attend public or private day classes.

The students in day schools or day classes are often "mainstreamed". (See Unit 7 for further information.) As a result, students now have less opportunities to become enculturated into the Deaf Community since they have fewer opportunities to interact with Deaf adults and Deaf peers. In fact, very few Deaf adults work in mainstreamed classes or schools. According to the 1980 survey, approximately 85% of all Deaf adults employed on the educational staffs of all educational programs work at residential schools, leaving only 15% in day programs.

However, the total number of Deaf adults in all educational programs is still very small. Educational programs for Deaf students in this country are, for the most part, dominated by hearing adults. The total number of educational personnel in programs cited in the 1980 survey is 13,362. The number of Deaf teachers is only 1,183 (11%). In addition, very few administrators or superintendents are Deaf.

---

[1]Craig, W. & H. Craig (Eds.) 1980. *American Annals of the Deaf,* Reference Issue, Vol. 125, No. 2, April.

Student Text: Unit 10

Cultural Information: The National Symposium on Sign Language Research and Teaching

In the Spring of 1977 (May 30– June 3), an historic meeting took place in Chicago, Illinois— the first National Symposium on Sign Language Research and Teaching (NSSLRT). Organized by the Communicative Skills Program of the National Association of the Deaf, the Symposium sought to bring together Sign Language teachers and researchers so that they could learn from each other and explore ways to help each other more in the future. Papers and workshops were divided into three major categories: Sign Language teaching, Sign Language research, and the utilization of Sign Language research. As the first national conference to focus solely on American Sign Language, this historic Symposium was a time of strong emotions for many people who, for the first time, were seeing Sign Language described as a "real language". Their enthusiasm and excitement led to a second NSSLRT the next year.

The second NSSLRT was held in Coronado, California on October 15– 19, 1978. Unlike the first NSSLRT, the second one had a central theme: *American Sign Language and English in a Bilingual and Bicultural Context*. This Symposium was attended by approximately 300 Sign Language teachers and researchers as well as teachers and administrators in schools for deaf children who tried to better understand each other's needs and problems and to share available information from research. A central concern of many of the participants was the widespread use of manual codes for English in schools and programs for deaf children and the exclusion of American Sign Language.

The third NSSLRT was held in Boston, Massachusetts (October 26– 30, 1980) with the theme *Teaching American Sign Language as a Second Language*. Workshops and papers at this Symposium were divided into five major categories: the language and culture of the Deaf Community, curriculum development, teaching methods, teacher and student materials, and evaluation. In addition to experts within the fields of Sign Language teaching and research, experts in the fields of teaching and evaluating spoken languages were invited to share their knowledge and experiences.

The NSSLRT meetings are co-sponsored by the National Association of the Deaf, California State University at Northridge, Gallaudet College, National Technical Institute for the Deaf, Northeastern University, and the Salk Institute for Biological Studies. For further information regarding the NSSLRT and NSSLRT proceedings, write: NAD/NSSLRT, 814 Thayer Avenue, Silver Spring, Md. 20910.

Student Text: Unit 19

Cultural Information: Gallaudet College

In 1856, a man named Amos Kendall donated some land in the northeast part of Washington, D.C. to establish a school for Deaf and Blind children. This school was incorporated in 1857 as The Columbia Institution for the Deaf and Dumb and Blind, and Edward Miner Gallaudet (the son of Thomas Hopkins Gallaudet) became its first superintendent. During the next several years, E. M. Gallaudet worked to establish a college division at the school. In April of 1864, the U.S. Congress passed a law, signed by President Abraham Lincoln, which established The National Deaf Mute College as part of the Columbia Institution. Congress then increased its support of the College over the following years and provided funds to purchase additional land, erect new buildings, and establish free scholarships. During this time, the Blind students were transferred from Kendall School to the Maryland School for the Blind.

In 1869, the first College class graduated — all males. Females were not permitted to enter the College until 1887. In 1891, a "Normal Department" was established to train hearing teachers. In 1894, the name of the College was changed to Gallaudet College in honor of Thomas Hopkins Gallaudet. Edward Miner Gallaudet served as President of the College until 1910 when he retired. Other important dates in the history of Gallaudet College are:

1937 — a Research Department was established
1957 — Gallaudet College became accredited
1969 — the Model Secondary School for the Deaf (MSSD) was established
1970 — the Kendall Demonstration Elementary School (KDES) was established

Gallaudet College, the world's only accredited liberal arts college for Deaf students, has an average enrollment of 1500 students from all over the United States, Canada, and several foreign countries. MSSD has approximately 350 students, and KDES has approximately 160 students. Several years ago, the college instituted a Ph.D. program in Administration, cooperated in establishing the National Center for Law and the Deaf on its campus, established a Center for Continuing Education, and now is continuing to increase the number of its graduate programs. More information on Gallaudet College can be obtained by writing: Office of Alumni & Public Relations, Gallaudet College, Kendall Green, Washington, D.C. 20002.

Chapter VII

Time

A. Introduction

In ASL, information about 'time' is communicated via "time signs" and modulations of these time signs, and with time-related modulations of verbs.[1] In this chapter, we will examine the set of time signs and their modulations as well as some of the non-manual behaviors that may occur with these signs to provide additional information about time. Later, in Chapter XIII on Temporal Aspect, we will discuss how ASL expresses information about time via modulations of verbs.

B. Relative Time—The "Time Line"

One way that ASL expresses information about time is with a specific set of signs that are produced in relation to what has been called the *time line,* illustrated on the following page.

As illustrated in Figure 7.1, this imaginary line runs through the Signer's body and into the areas in front of and in back of the body. In general, the Signer's body represents present time. Signs that refer to present time (**NOW, TODAY**), to the recent past (**ONE-DAY-PAST, FEW-DAY-PAST, RECENTLY**), and to the near future (**ONE-DAY-FUTURE, FEW-DAY-FUTURE**) are made close to the body.[2] Signs that refer to the more distant future (**WILL, FUTURE, LATER, DISTANT-FUTURE**) are made further in front of the Signer's body. Signs that refer to the more distant past (**PAST, LONG-TIME-AGO, ONCE-UPON-A-TIME**) are made further toward the area behind the Signer's body. Thus, time signs (often called "time indicators") have a relative *location* on the time line which agrees with their meaning.

---

[1]The term *modulation* refers to a change in the way a sign is made. A specific change in the form of a sign can result in a change in the meaning of that sign.

[2]The sign glossed as **ONE-DAY-PAST** can mean either 'yesterday' or 'the day before'. The sign glossed as **ONE-DAY-FUTURE** can mean either 'tomorrow' or 'the next day'.

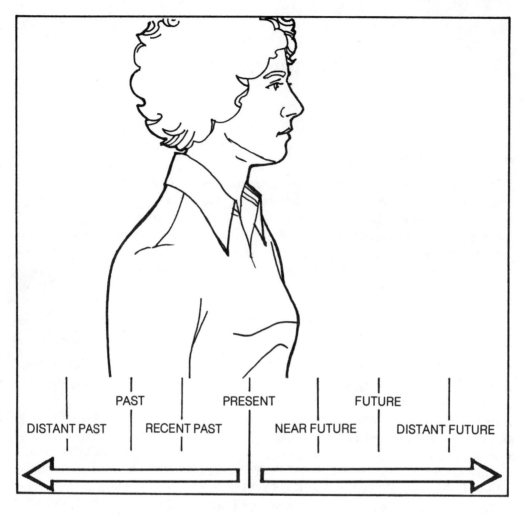

Fig. 7.1 "Time Line"

In addition, the *direction of movement* of each time sign indicates its relation to present time. For example, in the sign **FEW-DAY-FUTURE**, the thumb and fingers move forward (toward the 'future'); the sign **FEW-DAY-PAST** moves backward (toward the 'past'). In the sign **UP-TILL-NOW**, the index fingers move from the 'past' down into 'present' time; in the sign **FROM-NOW-ON**, the signing hand moves from the 'present' (represented by the passive hand—see Section E.1) forward into the 'future'.

FEW-DAY-FUTURE   **FEW-DAY-PAST**   **UP-TILL-NOW**

In conversational signing, the actual location of the time sign may differ from that of its *citation form* location. That is, the sign may be made closer to the area in front of the Signer's body called *neutral space*[3] where a majority of signs are made. For example, **ONE-DAY-FUTURE** may be signed in front of the body rather than at the cheek (and may be signed lower than the level of the cheek). This is a type of assimilatory change, like those discussed in Chapter IV. However, the direction of movement of the sign is not altered in conversational signing.

C. Non-manual Adverbs

Facial expression and other non-manual behaviors can also indicate time in ASL. For example, the concept of 'closeness to the present time/space' can be shown by raising and moving forward the shoulder, and raising the cheek and side of the mouth towards that shoulder. The combination of these behaviors has been called the *'cs'* signal. The larger or more intense these behaviors are, the closer the meaning is to present time.

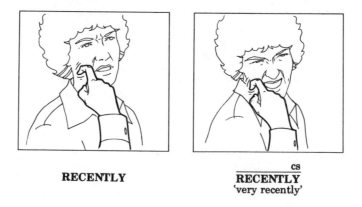

RECENTLY

$\overline{\text{RECENTLY}}^{\text{cs}}$
'very recently'

---

[3]This area is in the center of the signing space (See Figure 8.1 in the companion teacher's text on *Curriculum, Methods, and Evaluation*), comprising the area in front of the Signer's upper chest and lower face.

The 'cs' signal functions as an adverb and can occur with time signs like **NOW** (meaning 'just/right now'), **ONE-DAY-PAST** (meaning 'just/only yesterday'), and **ONE-YEAR-PAST** (meaning 'very recently last year') for the purpose of emphasizing their closeness to the present time.[4]

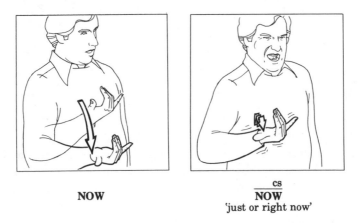

NOW

<u>cs</u>
NOW
'just or right now'

This 'cs' signal can also occur with verbs to indicate that something just happened or is about to happen (again, indicating an event very close to the present time). Notice that when the 'cs' signal occurs with a verb like **ARRIVE-AT**-*here,* the verb is also made closer to the body, indicating that the action occurred very close to the present time.

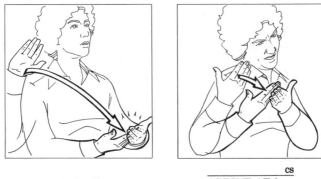

ARRIVE-AT-*here*

<u>cs</u>
ARRIVE-AT-*here*

---

[4]Similarly, the 'cs' signal can occur with signs like **NEW** (meaning 'brand new') and **FRONT** (meaning 'right in front').

Context The Signer and a friend are in the waiting room of a train station, waiting
for the Amtrak Express from New York. The Signer happens to look out
the window at the tracks and then turns to her friend and says:

(1) $\overline{\quad\text{t}\quad}$ $\overline{\qquad\qquad\text{cs}\qquad\qquad}$
             TRAIN, **ARRIVE-AT-***here*

       Struc 'The train, it just arrived.'

       Trans 'The train's here.'

Similarly, there are facial expressions that Signers frequently use to show that
something is 'far away' in time or space. We refer to one of these as *'puff.cheeks'*,
illustrated below with the signs **LONG-TIME-AGO** and **DISTANT-FUTURE**.
Another involves a very tense expression that we refer to as *'intense'*, illustrated
below with the sign **DISTANT-FUTURE**.[5] (In the illustration, the manual portion
of the sign is also stressed—indicated by the dotted lines which mean that the
movement was slower during that part of the sign.)

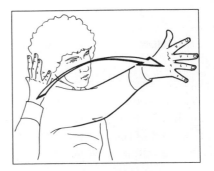

$\overline{\qquad\text{puff.cheeks}\qquad}$ $\qquad$ $\overline{\qquad\text{puff.cheeks}\qquad}$
LONG-TIME-AGO $\qquad\qquad\qquad$ **DISTANT-FUTURE**
'a very long time ago' $\qquad\qquad$ 'far into the future'

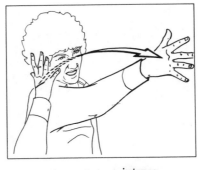

$\overline{\qquad\text{intense}\qquad}$
DISTANT-FUTURE*
'awfully far in the future'

---

[5]These two expressions have different, but related, meanings in other contexts and are described again
in later chapters. It may also be helpful for the reader to review the description of these behaviors in the
section on Transcription Symbols.

D. Incorporation of Number

Numbers in ASL are expressed with specific handshapes on one hand. By using a numeral handshape with the location, movement, and orientation of signs that quantify time (e.g. **ONE-HOUR, ONE-WEEK, ONE-MONTH**), a Signer can indicate a specific number of time units, such as 'two weeks' or 'three months'. In this way, the number is *incorporated* into the time sign. Some Signers can comfortably incorporate numbers up to '9' (e.g. **SIX-MONTH, EIGHT-WEEK**), whereas other Signers only incorporate numbers up to '4' or '5'.

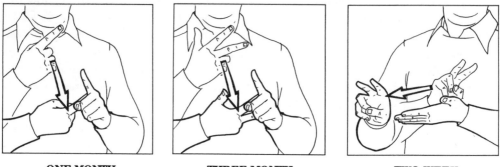

ONE-MONTH   THREE-MONTH   TWO-WEEK

These number handshapes are frequently assimilated into other types of signs as well, especially in joined signs—e.g. **CENT_FIVE** ('five cents'), **TIME_THREE** ('three o'clock'), **AGE_SEVEN** ('seven years old'). With these signs, the handshape of the first part of the sign frequently changes and becomes the same as the number handshape, as illustrated below.

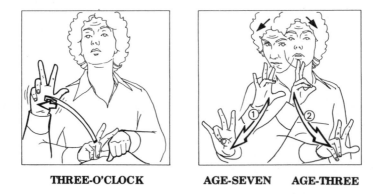

THREE-O'CLOCK   AGE-SEVEN   AGE-THREE

Number-incorporated time signs can also be moved in relation to the time line. That is, by changing or adding a movement to a number-incorporated sign which indicates its relationship to the time line, the Signer can signal if the time unit is occurring in the past or in the future. For example, to express the meaning 'two weeks ago', the Signer would incorporate the number '2' into the sign **ONE-WEEK** and then move the sign backward (toward the 'past'). To express the meaning 'in two weeks' or 'two weeks into the future', the Signer would use the '2' handshape and move the sign forward (into the 'future').

TWO-WEEK-PAST **TWO-WEEK-FUTURE** **TWO-WEEK-FUTURE**
(variant A) (variant B)

The sign **YEAR** is often abbreviated in movement, especially when it incorporates numbers. In this case, the active hand ('S' handshape) contacts the passive hand ('S' handshape) and then forms the number handshape while moving either forward or backward, depending on the intended meaning. A variant of the sign **ONE-YEAR-PAST** is made by maintaining contact with the passive hand and pointing the (active hand) index finger toward the 'past' while wiggling it up and down.

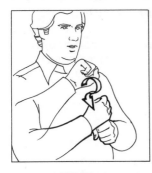  

YEAR **ONE-YEAR-FUTURE** **TWO-YEAR-FUTURE**
(conversational form)

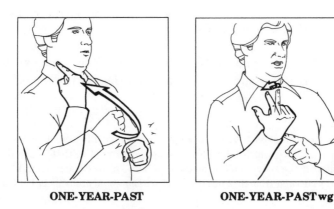

ONE-YEAR-PAST   **ONE-YEAR-PAST** wg

E. Passive Hand as Reference Point

(E.1) There is another set of signs which use the "time line", but which use the passive hand (rather than the body) as the point of reference. In this case, the passive hand can represent any time (e.g. present, two weeks ago, five years from now). The active hand then indicates time in relation to the time of the passive hand. Some signs that use the time line in this manner are **BEFORE, AFTER, NEXT, FROM-NOW-ON, UNTIL, POSTPONE,** and **PREPONE** ('move backward in time').[6]

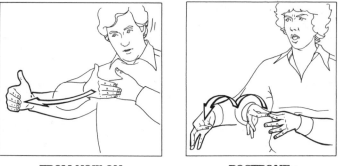

FROM-NOW-ON   POSTPONE +

Notice in example (2) that the passive hand in the sign **BEFORE** represents the time 'next September'. The active hand then repeatedly moves back from the passive hand to indicate a period of time *before* the time 'next September'.

Context   The Signer is a student who enjoys touring around. A friend happens to ask him if he has any upcoming travel plans. The Signer responds:

(2)
$$\overline{ \overset{(\qquad cs)t}{}}$$
ONE-YEAR-FUTURE   S-E-P-T   BEFORE+,

$$\overline{ \overset{nodding}{}}$$
ME   GO-*rt*   CALIFORNIA

   Struc   'Next year September—just before September, I'm going to California.'

   Trans   'Next year, right before September (or 'right at the end of August'), I'm going to California.'

(E.2) In ASL, different periods of the day are shown by signs which iconically represent the position of the 'sun' (active hand) on the 'horizon' (passive hand and

---

[6]We have chosen to use the gloss **FROM-NOW-ON** for the sign illustrated below since it is less awkward than **FROM-____-ON**, which might be more appropriate. Note that in the illustration, the passive hand is held close to the body—indicating the time 'now'. If the Signer was talking about a time in the future (e.g. 'next year') and 'from then on', the passive hand would probably be held further away in front of the body.

arm). Some of these signs are **EARLY-MORNING, MORNING, NOON, EARLY-AFTERNOON, AFTERNOON, LATE-AFTERNOON, EVENING, LATE-NIGHT, MIDNIGHT,** and **EARLY-MORNING** (the "wee hours"). Several of these signs and possible variations are illustrated below.

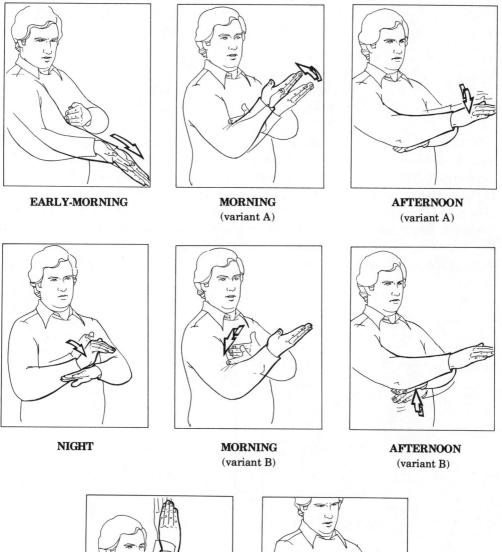

EARLY-MORNING

MORNING
(variant A)

AFTERNOON
(variant A)

NIGHT

MORNING
(variant B)

AFTERNOON
(variant B)

NOON
(variant A)

MIDNIGHT
(variant A)

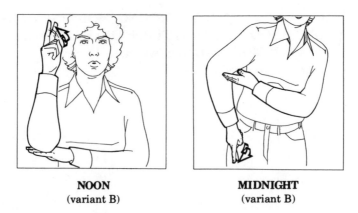

NOON
(variant B)

MIDNIGHT
(variant B)

(E.3) For some time signs, the flat palm of the passive hand represents the face of a clock, and the index finger of the active hand marks off units of time. The signs **ONE-SECOND** (often fingerspelled **S-E-C**), **ONE-MINUTE, FIFTEEN-MINUTE, HALF-HOUR,** and **ONE-HOUR** are signed using the passive hand in this way. (The sign **ONE-HOUR** has at least two variants—one in which the wrist twists as the index finger circles around the passive hand 'clock face', and another in which the index finger continues pointing upward while the whole hand makes a small, circular movement and then contacts the 'clock face'.)

ONE-SECOND

ONE-MINUTE

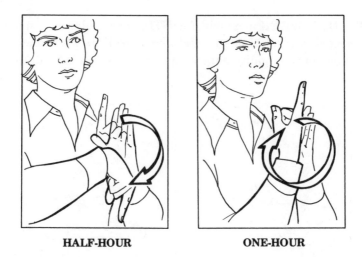

HALF-HOUR   ONE-HOUR

F. Time Signs—*Regularity*

The form of many time signs can be changed to express the concept of *regularity*. For example, the sign **MONDAY** can be changed to express the meaning 'every Monday'. For signs denoting days of the week (e.g. **MONDAY, THURSDAY**), this change (modulation) involves moving the sign down in a vertical line in front of the Signer's body while maintaining the same handshape and general orientation of the basic sign. (For the sign **EVERY-THURSDAY**, some Signers move from a 'T' to an 'H' handshape before moving the hand down vertically.) Or, to express the meaning 'every other Monday', the Signer adds a repeated 'hold' movement while moving the hand down in a vertical line.

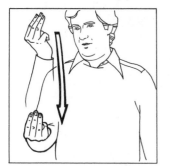
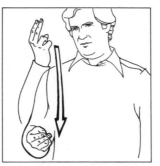
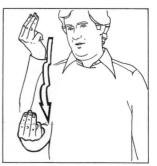

EVERY-MONDAY   EVERY-THURSDAY   EVERY-OTHER-MONDAY

The sign **HABIT** (meaning 'to do something regularly') also follows this pattern.

For signs like **ONE-WEEK** and **ONE-MONTH**, the regular movement of the sign is quickly repeated several times (indicating plurality) while moving the sign downwards. Numbers can again be incorporated into these 'modulated' signs.

EVERY-(ONE)-WEEK   EVERY-THREE-WEEK

The sign **REGULARLY** follows this pattern of fast repetition with downward movement.

Some Signers move the sign **EVERY-MONTH** to one side (i.e. to the right for right-handed Signers) rather than downward during the repetition. When a sign like **EVERY-WEEK** or **EVERY-MONTH** refers to an event in the future (e.g. 'From now on, we will have meetings every month'), the sign is often moved outward in agreement with the time line, as illustrated below. This type of outward repetition is also seen in the sign **FROM-TIME-TO-TIME**.

EVERY-(ONE)-MONTH-FUTURE   FROM-TIME-TO-TIME

Context A committee has had problems getting things done because it meets so infrequently. The Signer is chairperson of the committee and announces to the other members:

(3)

t

FROM-NOW-ON EVERY-MONTH-FUTURE, MEETING

Struc 'From now on every month, there will be a meeting.'

Trans 'We'll meet monthly from now on.'

The signs **EVERY-DAY** and **EVERY-YEAR** also use fast repetition to indicate regularity.

EVERY-DAY   EVERY-(ONE)-YEAR   EVERY-TWO-YEAR

For signs like those described in Section E.2, the concept of regularity is indicated a little differently. Instead of using downward movement and/or fast repetition, these signs use the 'horizon' provided by the passive hand and make a horizontal 'sweep' to indicate regular occurrence. Some signs which follow this pattern are **EVERY-MORNING, EVERY-AFTERNOON,** and **EVERY-NIGHT.**

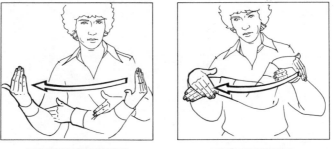

EVERY-MORNING   EVERY-NIGHT

G. Time Signs—*Duration*

The form of some time signs can be changed to express the concept of *duration*. For example, the sign **DAY** can be modulated to mean 'all day'; the sign **ONE-MONTH** can be modulated to mean 'all month long'. This concept of duration is expressed on time signs by using a much slower and tense movement. The Signer's facial behaviors (often the *'puff.cheeks'* or *'intense'* expressions) also indicate the length of time and/or the Signer's feelings about the duration. (For example, 'one day' can feel like a very long time if you are taking an exam 'all day long'.) Some signs which express duration in this manner are **ALL-DAY, ALL-WEEK, ALL-MONTH, ALL-YEAR, ALL-MORNING, ALL-AFTERNOON, ALL-EVENING,** and **ALL-NIGHT.** (In the illustrations, the dotted lines mean that part of the sign is very slow and tense.)

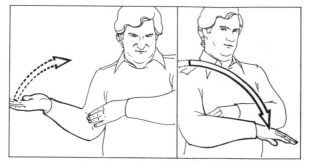

ALL-DAY

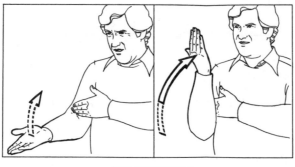

ALL-MORNING

Note that when the sign **ONE-DAY** is modulated to mean 'all day', the '1' handshape is replaced by a 'B' handshape.

H. Time Signs—*Approximate/Relative Time*

The concept of *approximate* or *relative time* is often expressed by first using time signs that indicate the boundaries of the time period and then using the sign

THEREABOUTS. For example, to say that someone will arrive 'around one or two o'clock', the Signer could sign **TIME⌢ONE   ONE⌣THIRTY TWO THERE-ABOUTS**. Or, to say that someone will probably call 'on Tuesday or Wednesday'—**TUESDAY WEDNESDAY THEREABOUTS**; or that someone will take a vacation in the spring—**A-P-R-I-L   M-A-Y   THEREABOUTS**.

THEREABOUTS

However, this concept of approximate time can be expressed with time signs like **MORNING** and **AFTERNOON** (and the other signs illustrated in Section E.2) by shaking the active hand up and down in a relaxed way. Sometimes the sign **THEREABOUTS** also follows these modulated signs.

SOMETIME-IN-THE-MORNING   SOMETIME-IN-THE-AFTERNOON

I. Time Signs—*Repetition and Duration*

The form of some signs like **ONE-WEEK, ONE-MONTH,** and **YEAR** can be changed to express the concept of a repeated and long period of time. For example, the sign **ONE-WEEK** can be modulated to express the meaning 'for weeks and weeks'. It is interesting that this modulation seems to use both the slow intense movement that is used to show *duration* and the repeated movement that is used to show *repetition* or *regularity*. As illustrated below, this modulation involves a straight movement toward the place of contact (the passive hand), followed by a slow, intense movement (indicated with the dotted lines) while the hand moves in an arc back to the place where the straight movement begins. This cycle is repeated (usually twice) and is often accompanied by a rocking movement of the head/body and an intense opening and closing of the mouth.

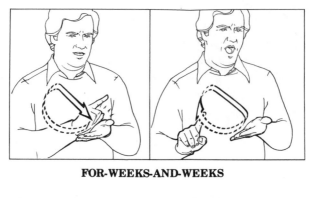

FOR-WEEKS-AND-WEEKS

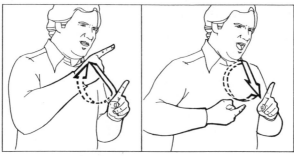

FOR-MONTHS-AND-MONTHS

Notice that the same type of modulation often occurs with the sign that we gloss as **SAME-OLD-THING**.

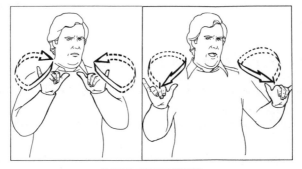

SAME-OLD-THING

J. Tense

Time signs which function as adverbs most frequently occur at the beginning (or close to the beginning) of the sentence in ASL. If a time is not specified in an ASL sentence, then it is assumed that the verb is in the present tense. If a time is specified (e.g. **ONE-DAY-PAST, TWO-WEEK-FUTURE**), then all the events the Signer describes are understood as occurring at that time. This holds true not only for that sentence but for all subsequent sentences—until a new time is specified, as illustrated in example (4). Thus, we see that *tense* in ASL is usually indicated with time adverbs (i.e. time signs that function as adverbs).

Context   A student who has taken many courses on ASL is telling her hearing friends about her increasing involvement in the activities of the Deaf Community.

(4)
```
                          t   (gaze lf)
TWO-MONTH  PAST,       ME  me-JOIN-TO-lf  N-A-D,

(gaze lf)
      ME  me-MAKE-PAYMENT-lf  FIFTEEN  DOLLAR,

(gaze rt                   )
      ME  me-GO-TO-rt  MEETING-rt  ROCHESTER-rt,

                          t   (gaze cntr           )
TWO-YEAR-FUTURE,  ME  me-GO-TO-cntr  MEETING  INDEX-cntr  C-I-N-N-cntr
```

Struc   'Two months ago, I *joined* the NAD. I *paid* them fifteen dollars, and I *went* to the meeting in Rochester. Two years from now, I *will* go to the meeting in Cincinnati.'

Trans   'Two months ago, I joined the NAD. I paid the fifteen dollar dues and went to the convention in Rochester. Two years from now, I plan to go to the meeting in Cincinnati.'

ASL has three other signs that give information about time: **WILL** (or the fingerspelled loan sign **#WILL**), **FINISH**, and **NOT-YET**. These signs tend to occur next to the verb.

WILL   **#WILL**

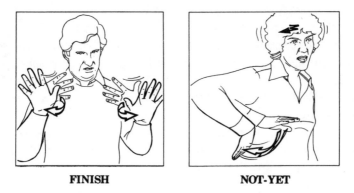

FINISH   NOT-YET

As seen in example (4), time adverbs like **TWO-YEAR-FUTURE** can be used to show that an event will occur in the future. Whereas the sign **WILL** also indicates future time, it tends to be used emphatically—e.g. in contexts where someone is questioning if an event will really occur and the Signer's response is an affirmation that it *will* occur, as seen in (5).

Context   The Signer is a "picky eater" and has just finished eating dinner. Her friend starts to throw out the rest of the chicken because he says she will never eat it and it will just go bad in the refrigerator. The Signer responds:

(5)   _____t_____   _____nodding_____
            CHICKEN, ME WILL* EAT, WILL* ME

   Struc   'The chicken, I *will* eat it! I *will*!'

   Trans   'I will too eat the chicken!'

In its most common form, the sign **FINISH** refers to the *completion* of an event, and thus, indicates that something occurred in the past.[7] The opposite of **FINISH** is **NOT-YET**—which indicates that something is *not completed,* but that the Signer plans to (or at least, is supposed to) complete it. These two signs are illustrated in examples (6) and (7).

Context   Someone asks the Signer if he is done with the report for class.

(6)   _____t_____   _____nodding_____
            WRITE PAPER, FINISH ME

   Struc   'Writing the paper, I finished it.'

   Trans   'I finished writing the paper.'
            ('I've already written the paper.')

_____

[7]The sign **FINISH** can also be made with a very tense movement or repeated tense movements, meaning 'That's enough!' or 'Stop it!'.

Context   (same as 6)

(7)
$$\frac{\qquad\qquad \text{t} \qquad\qquad \text{neg} \qquad}{\textbf{WRITE PAPER, NOT-YET ME}}$$

    Struc   'Writing the paper, I haven't yet done it.'

    Trans   'I haven't written the paper yet.'

The signs **FINISH** and **NOT-YET** are frequently used as one-sign responses to questions, as seen in (8) and (9).

Context   Two people are trying to decide which movie they should go see.

(8)   *Signer A:*
$$\frac{\qquad\qquad\qquad\qquad\qquad \text{t} \qquad\qquad \text{q} \qquad}{\textbf{FILM QUOTE S-T-A-R-W-A-R-S, SEE FINISH YOU}}$$

    Signer B:
$$\frac{\text{nodding}}{\textbf{FINISH}++}$$

    Struc   A. 'The movie "STAR WARS", have you seen it?'
                 B. 'Yes, already.'

    Trans   A. 'Have you seen the movie "STAR WARS"?'
                 B. 'Yeah, I saw it.'

Context   (same as 8)

(9)   *Signer A:*
$$\frac{\qquad\qquad\qquad\qquad\qquad \text{t} \qquad\qquad \text{q} \qquad}{\textbf{FILM QUOTE S-T-A-R-W-A-R-S, SEE FINISH YOU}}$$

    Signer B:
$$\frac{\text{neg}}{\textbf{NOT-YET}}$$

    Struc   A. 'The movie "STAR WARS", have you seen it?'
                 B. 'No, not yet.'

    Trans   A. 'Have you seen the movie "STAR WARS"?'
                 B. 'No, not yet.'

A more specific explanation of the grammatical role of the signs **FINISH** and **NOT-YET** is provided in Chapter XIII on Temporal Aspect.

K. Summary

In this chapter, we have looked at a wide variety of signs that are used to communicate information about 'time'. Many of these time signs are produced in relation to a conceptual *time line*—which uses the Signer's body as a reference for 'present' time and then marks off increasing degrees of 'past' or 'future' time as the Signer's hands move further away from the body in a backward or forward direction. Several non-manual signals also indicate degrees of 'closeness to' or 'distance from' the present time. Many signs use the passive hand (instead of the body) as the reference point for communicating information about time. A variety of time signs can "incorporate" numbers by changing the handshape of the sign. These signs can then indicate specific periods of time—like 'two weeks', 'three days', or 'four minutes'.

Some of the time signs can be modulated in certain ways to express time-related concepts like *regularity, duration, approximate/relative time,* and *long-continuing, repeated time.* To indicate the "tense" of an utterance, ASL Signers generally use time adverbs—which usually are signed at the beginning of the utterance.

As mentioned in the beginning of this chapter, another major way of communicating information about time is via specific modulations of verbs. Several of these verb modulations are described in Chapter XIII on Temporal Aspect. As you will see, some of them are very similar to the modulations that are used with time signs.

Bibliography: Time Signs

Cogen, C. 1977. On three aspects of time expression in American Sign Language. In L. Friedman (Ed.) *On the Other Hand: New Perspectives on American Sign Language.* New York: Academic Press, 197–214.

Fischer, S. & B. Gough. 1972. Some unfinished thoughts on *FINISH.* MS, Salk Institute, San Diego, California.

Friedman, L. 1975. Space, time, and person reference in the American Sign Language. *Language 51,* 940–961.

Frishberg, N. & B. Gough. 1973. Time on our hands. Paper presented at the Third Annual California Linguistics Association Meeting. Stanford, California.

Dialogues
and
Cultural Information

TIME

The following three dialogues have been developed to illustrate various uses of the grammatical features described in this chapter. Each of these dialogues also appears in one of the three corresponding Student Texts. In the Student Texts, the transcription of each dialogue is less detailed than what is provided here for the teacher of ASL. Following the dialogues, in the sections called "Cultural Information", are brief discussions of the topic of each dialogue.

The following dialogues and cultural information correspond to:

Student Text: Unit 2
Unit 11
Unit 20

Dialogue: Time
(Student Text - Unit 2)

First Signer (Pat)

Pat$_1$:
$$\overline{\quad}^{\text{co}} \quad \overline{\text{FINISH \quad READ-}paper \quad \text{DEAF \quad AMERICA \quad YOU}}^{\text{q}}$$
"HEY",   FINISH   READ-*paper*   DEAF   AMERICA   YOU

Pat$_2$:
$$\text{SHOULD, \quad \overline{NOW \quad DEAF \quad AMERICA \quad COVER}^{\text{t}}, \quad NEW+, \quad \overline{COLOR, \quad ART}^{\text{t}}, \quad DIFFERENT*}$$

Pat$_3$:
$$\overline{\text{LEAVE-IT-}rt}^{\text{neg}} \quad \text{HOME \quad INDEX-}rt,$$

MORNING   ME   READ-*paper*   HALF-HOUR, $\overline{\text{NOT-YET \quad FINISH}}^{\text{neg}}$

Pat$_4$:
$$\overline{\text{PARTICIPATE-IN-}nad}^{\text{nodding+brow raise}} \quad \text{FINISH,} \quad \overline{\text{CAN}}^{\text{nod}} \quad \overline{\text{GO-TO-}rt \quad \text{MEETING \quad EVERY-TWO-YEAR-FUTURE,}}^{\text{(gaze rt} \qquad \qquad \text{)}}$$

$$\overline{\text{RIGHT}}^{\text{nodding+q}}$$

Pat$_5$:
$$\overline{\text{TWO-YEAR-FUTURE, \quad WHYwg}}^{\text{wh-q}}$$

Pat$_6$:
$$\overline{\text{"THAT'S-RIGHT"}}^{\text{nod}}$$

Dialogue: Time
(Student Text - Unit 2)

Second Signer (Lee)

Lee₁:
    <u>neg</u>   <u>t</u>   <u>t</u>   <u>neg</u>

ONE-YEAR-PAST, ME RECEIVE-REGULARLY, STOP, ME *me*-PAY-TO-*rt,* AGAIN

Lee₂: SEE-SEE

Lee₃:
                            <u>t</u>   (gaze cntr   )

ONE-WEEK-FUTURE, MAYBE ME *me*-PARTICIPATE-IN-*cntr* N-A-D,

                          <u>br+nodding</u>

ME RECEIVE-REGULARLY D-A

Lee₄:
    <u>nodding</u>   <u>mm+nodding</u>   <u>t</u>

ME GO-TO-*lf* ONCE-IN-AWHILE, "UMMM" TWO-YEAR-FUTURE, ME GO-TO-*lf**

Lee₅:
                                    <u>t</u>

THAT-ONE-*lf* TWO-YEAR-FUTURE, N-A-D (2h)THRILL ONE‿HUNDRED YEAR CELEBRATE

Dialogue: Time
(Student Text - Unit 11)

First Signer (Pat)

Pat₁:
$$\overline{\overset{\text{co}}{}}\;\overline{\overset{\hphantom{xxxxxxxxxxxxxxxxxxxxxxxx}\text{t}}{\text{TWO-WEEK-PAST SATURDAY PARTY,}}}$$ #FUN* "WOW"++
"UMMM"

Pat₂:　YES+, WISH* EVERY-SATURDAY PARTY WISH* ME

Pat₃:　"WHY-NOT",　$\overline{\overset{\text{(eye squint}\hphantom{xx}\text{)puff.cheeks+cond}}{\text{PARTY}\textit{"regularly"}}}$ ALL-NIGHT, $\overline{\overset{\hphantom{xxxxxxxxxxxxxxxxx}\text{t}}{\text{ONE-DAY-FUTURE MORNING,}}}$

OVERSLEEP (2h)CAN (2h)"WELL"

Pat₄:　$\overline{\overset{\text{nod}}{\text{CAN}}}$ DIFFERENT++-*arc* VARIOUS-THINGS, CAN* $\overline{\overset{\text{nodding}}{}}$
"HOLD-IT"

Pat₅:　(2h)"WELL", IDEA SAME-AS AWHILE-AGO, $\overline{\overset{\hphantom{xxxxxxxxx}\text{t}}{\text{EVERY-FRIDAY,}}}$ $\overline{\overset{\text{(body lean lf)puff.cheeks}}{\text{#CF++-}\textit{downward,}}}$

$\overline{\overset{\text{(gaze rt}\hphantom{xxxxxxx}\text{)t}}{\text{EVERY-SATURDAY,}}}$ BOWLING, (2h)"WELL"

Note: In Pat₃, the combination of the non-manual behaviors and the *"regularly"* modulation with the sign **PARTY** seems to give the meaning 'party incessantly'.

Dialogue: Time
(Student Text - Unit 11)

Second Signer (Lee)

Lee₁:
$$\overline{}^{\text{puff.cheeks}}$$
       TRUE ++   USE-ASL*"regularly"*   ALL-NIGHT*

Lee₂:
     FINE +   ALL-WEEK   WORK*"long time"* $\overline{\text{FINISH,}}^{\text{br}}$ SATURDAY   PARTY

Lee₃:
    "HOLD-IT"   EVERY-WEEK   FROM-NOW-ON*   PARTY*"regularly"* $\overline{\text{SAME-OLD-THING}}^{\text{cond}}$*"regularly"*,

    "WELL",   PEOPLE   BORED*   *"WELL"*
                      "WELL"

Lee₄:
$$\overline{\text{DIFFERENT}++\text{-}arc \quad \text{(2h)}\#\text{WHAT}}^{\text{wh-q}}$$

Lee₅: RIGHT+   YOU, $\overline{\text{REMEMBER} \quad \text{ME} \quad \text{ONE-YEAR-PAST,}}^{\text{('trying to remember'}\text{)q}}$ $\overline{\text{TWO-YEAR-PAST,}}^{\text{('suddenly remembers')}}$ $\overline{\text{FINE}+++}^{\text{nodding}}$

Dialogue: Time
(Student Text - Unit 20)

First Signer (Pat)

Pat$_1$:
$$\overset{\text{co}}{\text{"HEY",}} \quad \overset{\rule{10cm}{0.4pt}\hspace{2cm}\text{q}}{\text{ONE-YEAR-FUTURE\ \ SUMMER\ \ EUROPE\ \ GO-}rt\text{\ \ YOU}}$$

Pat$_2$:
$$\overset{\rule{7cm}{0.4pt}\ \text{t}}{\text{KNOW-THAT\ \ MEETING\ \ W-F-D,}}\quad \text{EUROPE\ \ ONE-YEAR-FUTURE\ \ SUMMER}$$

Pat$_3$:
$$\overset{\ \ \text{t}}{\text{VACATION,}}\quad \overset{\text{wh-q}}{\underset{YOU}{\text{(2h)\#DO-DO}}}$$

Pat$_4$:
$$\text{JEALOUS\ \ ME,}\quad \overset{\rule{5cm}{0.4pt}\ \text{t}}{\text{UP-TIL-NOW*\ \ TWO-YEAR,}}\quad \text{VACATION}\ \overset{\text{neg}}{\text{(2h)NONE}}$$

Pat$_5$:
$$\text{RIGHT++,}\quad \overset{\rule{6cm}{0.4pt}\ \text{t}}{\text{ONE-YEAR-FUTURE\ \ SUMMER\ \ W-F-D,}}\quad \text{ME\ \ GO-}rt\ \text{DECIDE*}\ \overset{\text{nodding}}{\text{FINISH*}}$$

Pat$_6$:
$$\text{WANTwg,}\quad \overset{\ \ \text{t}}{\text{FEW-DAY-FUTURE,}}\quad \text{PLAN\ \ TICKET,\ \ TIME,\ \ SCHEDULE}\ \overset{\text{nodding}}{\text{ALL-INCLUSIVE}}$$

Dialogue: Time
(Student Text - Unit 20)

Second Signer (Lee)

$$\text{Lee}_1: \quad \overline{}^{\text{wh-q}}$$

Lee₁:
———————wh-q
EUROPE   FOR-FOR

Lee₂:
neg ———————————cs
MONEY   TWO-WEEK   VACATION   RECENT   (2h)BROKE   ME

Lee₃:
————t ————neg ——————————————t
EVERY-MORNING   SLEEP,   WORK,   (2h)NONE,   EARLY-AFTERNOON   (2h)#FIX,   HOUSE

Lee₄:
——————————————th
BLAME⌒YOURSELF*,   POSTPONE_"long time"_

Lee₅:
(————puff cheeks)———————q
TRAVEL-AROUND   #WILL   YOU

Student Text: Unit 2

Cultural Information: The Deaf American and the National Association of the Deaf

The *Deaf American* is a magazine that is published monthly (except for a joint July-August issue) by the NAD. This national magazine contains items of interest to the Deaf Community such as: interviews with Deaf persons, sports results, general interest articles, legislation-related projects and activities, etc. This publication, along with newsletters published by state NAD chapters or local clubs, helps members of the Deaf Community keep up with what is happening in the Community on a national and local level.

The National Association of the Deaf (NAD) began in 1880 at the First National Convention of Deaf-Mutes in Cincinnati, Ohio. The first president of the NAD was Robert P. McGregor of Ohio. In 1952, the NAD opened its first home office in Chicago. In 1960, the Junior NAD was established to provide young Deaf people with training in citizenship and leadership. In September 1964, the home office of the NAD was re-located to Washington, D.C. The name of the NAD publication was changed from the *Silent Worker* to the *Deaf American*. In 1964, the NAD decided to hire its first full-time Executive-Secretary, Frederick C. Schreiber. In 1969, the NAD began publishing books and articles on deafness, the education of deaf people, manual communication, and other related topics. In 1971, the NAD moved into its present location, the Halex House in Silver Spring, Maryland. Currently, the NAD has about 17,000 members. For more information about the NAD and its activities, please write: National Association of the Deaf, 814 Thayer Avenue, Silver Spring, Md. 20910.

Student Text: Unit 11

Cultural Information: Captioned Films

On September 2, 1958, a public law (PL 85-905) was signed into effect which authorized the Department of Health, Education, and Welfare to establish a free "lending library" of captioned films for all deaf persons. The primary purposes of this service were: to bring deaf people an understanding and appreciation of films which play an important part in the general and cultural advancement of hearing persons, to enrich the educational and cultural experiences of deaf persons, and to provide wholesome and rewarding experiences for deaf people to share with each other. This program was called the Media Services and Captioned Films Branch (MSCF) of the Bureau of Education for the Handicapped (BEH), U.S. Office of Education.

In April 1974, MSCF became a division within the Bureau of Education for the Handicapped and was renamed the Division of Media Services. The division was established with two branches: the Captioned Films and Telecommunications Branch and the Learning Resources Branch. The Captioned Films and Telecommunications Branch (CFT) is responsible for developing and maintaining the loan service of captioned films to groups which include at least one deaf person. Groups which receive and show captioned films are not allowed to charge an admission price to view the films.

The CFT Branch is not only responsible for acquiring, captioning, producing, and distributing captioned films but is also involved in research, production, and training activities in the area of instructional media. For further information about captioned films, contact: Division of Media Services, 400 Maryland Avenue, S.W., Donohoe Bldg., Corridor 4800, Washington, D.C. 20202.

Student Text: Unit 20

Cultural Information: The World Federation of the Deaf

The World Federation of the Deaf (WFD) was established in September 1951 at an international meeting in Rome, Italy. At that meeting, a constitution was adopted and officers of the international organization were elected. Among the purposes of the WFD is to provide an international forum for discussing various problems and advances in the lives of Deaf people on an international scale. The WFD also serves as a consulting body to the United Nations and has worked closely with such international organizations as UNESCO, the International Labour Organization, and the World Health Organization.

At the present time, there are 57 national organizations of Deaf people who are members of the WFD. The WFD has a number of commissions which focus on various aspects of deafness and the lives of Deaf people. Some of those commissions are: Art and Culture, Communications, Pedagogy, Psychology, and Social Aspects of Deafness.

The WFD has international meetings every four years in different countries throughout the world. For example, the VIIth World Congress of the WFD was held in Washington, D.C. in 1975. The theme of that Congress was "Full Citizenship for All Deaf People". In 1979, the VIIIth World Congress of the WFD was held in Varna, Bulgaria. The theme of that Congress was "The Deaf People in Modern Society". At the 1979 Congress, Dragojub Vukotic from Belgrade, Yugoslavia was elected President of the WFD. For further information about the WFD, contact: National Association of the Deaf, 814 Thayer Avenue, Silver Spring, Md. 20910.

Chapter VIII

Pronominalization

A. Introduction

Pronouns are words or signs that 'stand for' ('pro') a noun. For example, in English, the pronouns 'she', 'he', and 'it' can stand for 'Mary', 'John's brother', and 'the orange book', respectively. Pronouns increase the efficiency of a language because speakers do not have to continually repeat the whole noun or noun phrase. Instead, *they* can replace *it* with a simpler substitute. For example, instead of saying 'Mary stole the orange book and then Mary gave the orange book to John', a speaker of English can say 'Mary stole the orange book and then *she* gave *it* to John'. But notice that one cannot say** 'She stole it and then Mary gave the orange book to John'.[1] A speaker can't use a pronoun until its referent (the thing it refers to) is known. After it is clear that the subject is 'Mary', then the noun can be replaced by the pronoun 'she'. The same is true for 'it'.

In American Sign Language, pronouns are made by pointing (with one of several handshapes or non-manual behaviors) to a person or thing that is "present" in the area of the communication, or by pointing to a specific location in the signing space which has been chosen to represent a person or thing that is "not present" in the communication area.

There are about nine different handshapes that can be used for pronominal reference in ASL (i.e. for referring to a noun by using a pronoun). By far, the most common is the extended index finger, or '1' handshape (e.g. **YOU**). Others are the flat hand with fingers together (e.g. **YOUR**), the closed fist (e.g. **SELF**), the closed hand with thumb and pinky extended (e.g. **THAT-ONE**), the semi-open hand with fingers together (e.g. honorific **YOU**), and three handshapes that are used exclusively for plurals: '**2**' (or its variant   ), '**3**', '**4**', and '**5**'.[2] Certain head nods, eye gaze behaviors, and facial movements can also function as pronouns.

ASL pronouns are different from English pronouns in several ways. In ASL, like in spoken Chinese, the same pronoun can be used to refer to people or things or places and to males and females. In addition, the grammatical role (e.g. subject, object) of the pronoun in an ASL sentence also does not change the form of the pronoun. For example, the distinction that English makes between 'he' (subject) and 'him' (object) is not used in ASL. ASL will use the same pronoun in both cases.

---

[1]The double asterisk indicates the sentence is ungrammatical or inappropriate.

[2]In informal contexts, some Signers will also use a closed handshape with the thumb extended and will point with the thumb. We gloss this as **THUMB-INDEX**.

B. Pronouns Referring to "Present" People, Things, Places

(B.1) Indexing[3]

Singular: In general, when a Signer points with a '1' handshape to him/herself, it means 'I/me'. When a Signer points to the person s/he is talking with, the point means 'you'. When the Signer points to another person, it means 'he/him' or 'she/her'. Pointing to a thing means 'it'. Pointing to a place (e.g. the building behind the Addressee) means 'there'. Pointing down to the 'ground' means 'here'.

The direction of the Signer's eye gaze is also important for understanding the meaning of a pronominal reference (i.e. for understanding who or what the Signer is referring to). Looking at the diagram below, let's suppose that the Signer is *looking at* Addressee (Ad.) A and *points to* Ad. A. The meaning of the point is 'you'.

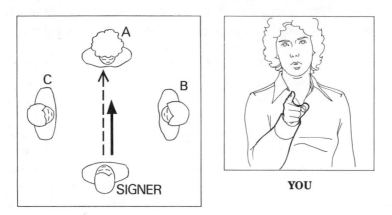

Fig. 8.1 'you'

Note: dotted line = eye gaze
full line = '1' handshape point

However, if the Signer is looking at Ad. B and then points to Ad. A, the meaning of the point is 'he/him' or 'she/her'.

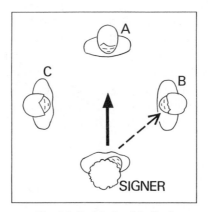

Fig. 8.2 'he/him' or 'she/her'

---

[3]*Indexing* usually refers to a type of pronominal reference in which the Signer points to someone or something with the index finger. Here, the term also includes pointing with any or all fingers.

Another way of referencing a person is with the open hand (fingers together, thumb out) where the fingers 'point' at the person. If the reference is to oneself, the palm faces toward the Signer and upward, and the fingers are bent at a right (90°) angle. If the reference is to another person ('you' or 'him/her'), the palm faces up. This type of "honorific" ('giving honor') reference is often used in formal contexts, such as during speeches and religious ceremonies, in artistic presentations such as poetry, songs, and drama, or as a sarcastic reference (accompanied by appropriate facial expression). The movement of this pronoun can either be a simple 'point', or can point and then move down the body line of the person it refers to. In a sense, the further the honorific pronoun is lowered (often with the Signer's eyes and head following the movement, resulting in a type of bow), the more honor is being given to that person.

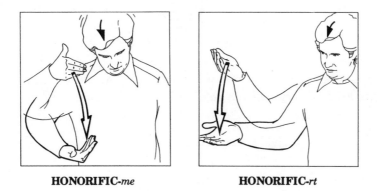

HONORIFIC-*me*   **HONORIFIC-*rt***

Plural: Pointing with the '1' handshape at Addressees C, A, and B can mean 'you and you and you'—something you might see a teacher use when selecting "volunteers".

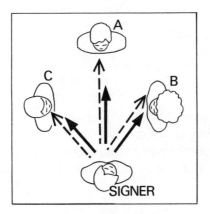

Fig. 8.3 'you and you and you'

Similarly, if the Signer is talking to Ad. C and points to A and B, the meaning is 'him/her' and 'him/her'.

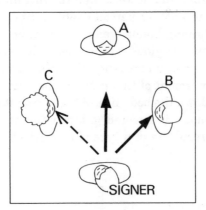

Fig. 8.4 'him/her' and 'him/her'

If the Signer is talking to Ad. C and points to C and A, the meaning is 'you and him/her'. This kind of very definite referencing can be done with any number of people.

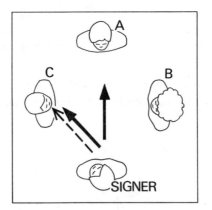

Fig. 8.5 'you and him/her'

However, if the Signer wants to refer to a group of people (three or more) without emphasizing each individual, the Signer can use the '1' handshape and 'draw' an arc which includes all the people the Signer wants to talk about.[4] If the Signer starts the arc by pointing to him/herself and stops with the last person on the other end, the

---

[4]The direction of this arc (right to left, or left to right) seems to vary according to the preference of the Signer and according to the actual locations of the people referred to in the *arc-point*.

arc-point means 'we' or 'all of us'. For example, if the Signer started the arc-point with him/herself and then moved from Ad. C to Ad. A to Ad. B, the meaning would be 'we/us'.

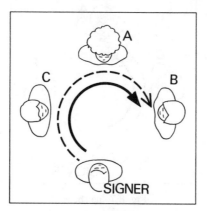

Fig. 8.6 'we/us' or 'all of us'

Some Signers return the point to themselves again at the end. If so, the last point will be on the opposite side of the chest from where the Signer started the arc-point. This seems to be an older form of the pronoun **WE**. Another form of this arc, meaning 'we', is very small and looks like the Signer is just pointing from one side of the chest to the other with a small arc in between contacts. This should not be confused with another pronoun that means 'we' but which has *no arc* and is used when the other referents are not present.

WE	**WE**
(other referents present)	(other referents not present)

If the Signer began the arc-point with him/herself and then moved from Ad. C to Ad. A, the meaning in this case would be 'the three of us' or 'us three'.

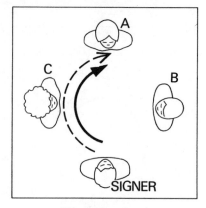

Fig. 8.7 'us three'

If the arc-point began with Ad. C and moved to A and B, the meaning would be 'the three of you' or 'you three'.

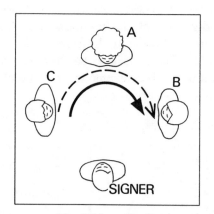

Fig. 8.8 'you three'

Another way to refer to two, three, four, or five people with one pronoun is to use the dual, trial, quadruple, or quintuple plural handshapes, as described below.

Plural: **Dual**

Dual pronominal reference uses a '2' handshape (or its variant) and moves it back and forth between the two people it refers to.[5] When the Signer looks at Ad. A and uses the dual handshape between A and the Signer, the meaning is 'us two'.

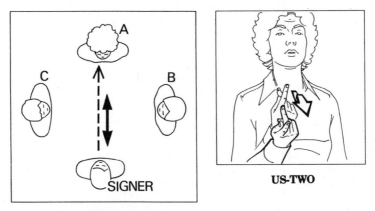

Fig. 8.9 'us two'

When the Signer is talking to Ad. A and uses the dual handshape between Ad. B and the Signer, the meaning is still 'us two', but refers to Ad. B and the Signer. (Usually the Signer will briefly look at Ad. B to clearly identify him/her as the other referent of the pronoun.) We gloss this use of the dual pronoun as **US-TWO-***rt* (since it includes the person to the Signer's right).

US-TWO-*rt*

---

[5]The dual pronoun can also be used to refer to two things—e.g. 'the two cabinets over there'. However, the dual pronoun cannot be used to refer to a person and a thing together.

When the Signer is talking to Ad. A and uses the dual handshape between A and B, the meaning is 'you two'. (Again, the Signer will usually glance at Ad. B briefly to clearly identify him/her as the other referent of the pronoun.) When talking to Ad. A and using the dual handshape between B and C, the meaning is 'those two' or 'them two'. (Again, this usually involves a brief glance at Addressees B and C.)

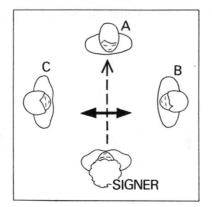

Fig. 8.10 'them two'

Plural: **Trial (meaning 'three')**

A Signer can use the '3' handshape to mean 'the three of us', 'the three of you', or 'the three of them'. This handshape is used like the dual handshape, but has a circular movement (palm facing up) and is made in close proximity to the three-person group it refers to. Figure 8.11 below shows three possible locations (1,2,3) of the signing hand.

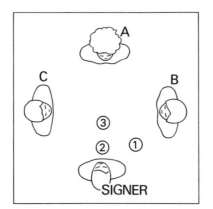

Fig. 8.11 Three possible locations
for trial pronominal reference

Looking at Figure 8.11, if the Signer uses the trial pronoun at Location #1, the meaning is 'us three' (Signer + Ad. B + Ad. A). At Location #2, the meaning is 'us three' (Signer + Ad. B + Ad. C). At Location #3, the meaning is 'you three' (Ad.

C + Ad. A + Ad. B). (In the illustrations below, the difference between **US-THREE** and **YOU-THREE** is shown by drawing the hand larger on the sign **YOU-THREE** —since this sign is made further away from the Signer and, hence, closer to the 'viewer'.)

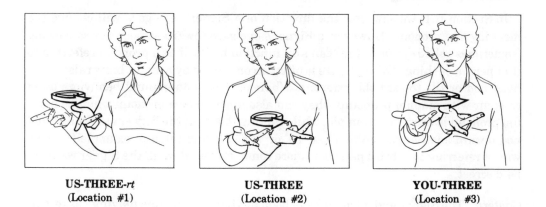

US-THREE-*rt*	US-THREE	YOU-THREE
(Location #1)	(Location #2)	(Location #3)

Suppose another person (D) is standing between A and B, and the Signer is talking with C. If the trial pronoun is used to the right of Location #3, the meaning would be 'those three' or 'them three'.

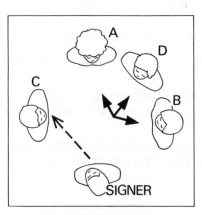

Fig. 8.12 'them three'

Plural: **Quadruple ('four') and Quintuple ('five')**

ASL also has pronouns which include four or five people and which follow the pattern of the other plural pronouns. These pronouns use a '4' handshape or a '5' handshape and have a circular movement (palm up) like the trial pronoun. When a Signer wants to talk about more than five people, s/he generally will not use a plural handshape, but will use the '1' handshape in either of the two ways previously described (i.e. individuating 'you and you and you . . .', or inclusive 'all of you'[6]).

---

[6]The honorific pronoun can also be used in this context (meaning 'all of you') with the palm up and the hand moving in an arc to formally include all of the people being referenced.

However, some Signers will also use the '1' handshape index when talking about five people since not all Signers are comfortable using the '5' handshape for pronominal reference.

(B.2) Eye-indexing

In Section B.1, we saw how the direction of a Signer's eye gaze will change the meaning of a pronoun. However, a Signer's eye gaze toward someone or something (sometimes called *eye-indexing*) can also function by itself as a pronoun referring to that person or thing. This eye gaze is often accompanied by a slight brow raise and a head nod or tilt toward the referent. Whereas these non-manual behaviors often co-occur with manual pronouns, they can also function as a pronoun when no manual pronoun is used. For example, while talking to Ad. A, the Signer can look at and nod toward another person to mean 'he' or 'she', as illustrated in example (1). This way of referring to a 'third person' is more commonly used when the Signer wants to be discreet.

Context   The Signer and a friend have been having a great time playing basketball together. Another man (who is standing to the Signer's right and is engaged in another conversation) has told the Signer that he wants to join them. The Signer says to his friend:

(1)   (gaze, head tilt to rt)   ____q
              WANT   PLAY,   #OK

     Struc   'He wants to play. O.K. with you?'

     Trans   'He wants to play, too. What do you say?'

As also illustrated above, when the Signer gazes and nods at the Addressee during a question, the meaning of the gaze and nod is 'you'.

Context   The Signer is playing basketball. A friend comes up and starts talking with the Signer. The Signer then asks her:

(2)   _____q
              WANT   PLAY

     Struc   'You want to play?'

     Trans   'Wanna play?'

Using gaze direction and head nodding as a 'second person'[7] pronominal reference (meaning 'you') in 'yes-no' questions is very common in ASL.

---

[7]Here 'second person' refers to the terms for 'person' reference in traditional grammars—e.g. in English (subject pronouns):

	Singular	*Plural*
First person	I	we
Second person	you	you
Third person	he, she, it	they

(B.3) Possessive reference

To indicate 'possession' or 'ownership', the Signer uses a flat hand, fingers together handshape (thumb apart or together with other fingers), and it is the *palm* of the hand (not the fingers) that 'points' to the person(s) who has ownership.

The possessive pronoun follows the same pattern as the indexic pronouns—i.e. the palm contacting the Signer's chest means 'my/mine'; the palm facing the Addressee means 'your/yours'; the palm facing another person means 'his/her/hers'. This pronoun is made plural by 'sweeping' (moving in an arc) the palm from one owner to the other owner(s), expressing the meanings 'your/yours' or 'their/theirs'. However, the meaning 'our/ours' is expressed by moving the palm (usually slightly cupped) in an arc across the Signer's chest, beginning on the right side[8] (side of thumb contacting chest) and ending on the left side (pinky contacting chest).

When the thing that is owned is present in the communication area, the Signer may choose to reference both the owner and owned thing with the possessive pronoun, as illustrated in examples (3) and (4).[9]

Context   At the end of the work day, the Signer walks to the company garage and happens to see an officemate standing next to a brand new car. The Signer asks her:

(3)
$$\overline{\text{YOUR} \leftrightarrow \text{POSS-}rt}^{\text{q}}$$

YOUR ↔ POSS-*rt*

Struc   'Yours?'

Trans   'Is that yours?'

Context   (same as 3)

(4)
$$\overset{\text{(gaze rt)}\qquad\qquad\qquad\text{q}}{\text{\#CAR-}rt \quad \text{YOUR}\leftrightarrow\text{POSS-}car}$$

Struc   'That car, is it yours?'

Trans   'Is that car yours?'

---

[8]If the Signer is left-handed, the contact will begin on the left side.

[9]In the following examples, the gloss **POSS** means 'possessive pronoun'. We use the gloss **MY** for the 'first person' possessive pronoun (**MINE** when the movement is repeated) and the gloss **YOUR** for the 'second person' possessive pronoun. However, since the location of the 'third person' pronoun can vary, we use the gloss **POSS**—followed by a directional symbol which indicates where the pronoun is made (e.g. **POSS-***lf*) or the name of the referent if it is already known in the context of that sentence (e.g. **POSS-***car*—see example 4).

Alternately, the meaning expressed in (4) could have been signed without referencing both the 'car' and the Addressee with the possessive handshape. Instead, the Signer could have indexed (pointed at) the 'car' and then used the possessive pronoun toward the Addressee alone, as seen in example (5).

Context   (same as 4—but the Addressee is standing a little further away from the car)

(5)   (br.squint)(gaze rt   ) _____q
           #CAR-*rt* INDEX-*rt,* YOUR+

     Struc   'That car there, is it yours?'

     Trans   'Is that car yours?'

When the possessive pronoun is repeated, it can also mean that something is a 'characteristic of' or a 'trait of' a particular person (or sometimes, an animal or thing). For example, in (6), the repetition of the possessive pronoun toward 'Lee' (on the right) indicates that he is 'characteristically clumsy'.[10]

Context   A group of people at a party are talking about the clumsy behavior of some of their friends.

(6)   _____t+th   _____nodding
           AWKWARD,   L-E-E-*rt* POSS-*lee*++

     Struc   'Being clumsy, Lee tends to be like that by nature.'

     Trans   'Clumsy! That's Lee (all over)!'

POSS-*rt*++
'characteristically'

---

[10]For readers who have the accompanying videotape: Notice the circular modulation of the sign AWKWARD—which also gives the meaning 'characteristically clumsy'. This modulation is described in Klima & Bellugi (1979), Chapter 11.

When talking about a character trait of a person, etc., the repeated possessive pronoun is sometimes preceded by the sign **TEND-TO** or the sign **THAT-ONE**, as illustrated in examples (7a) and (7b).[11]

Context   Several people are talking together. Pat joins them for a few minutes, makes some sarcastic, joking remarks to one of the people, and then leaves. The Signer turns to that person and says:

(7a)

——————————— t ——————————————————— nodding ————
KNOW-THAT P-A-T, TEASE"*over & over again*" **TEND-TO**-*rt* **POSS**-*pat*+

    Struc 'You know Pat, teasing again and again tends to be her nature.'

    Trans 'Pat's a real teaser.'

(7b)

——————————— t ——————————————————— nodding ————
KNOW-THAT P-A-T, TEASE"*over & over again*" **THAT-ONE**-*rt* **POSS**-*pat*+

    Struc 'You know Pat, teasing again and again—that's her nature.'

    Trans 'Pat's a real teaser.'

       TEND-TO-*rt*   **THAT-ONE-*rt***

---

[11]For readers who have the accompanying videotape: The repeated elliptical modulation ("*over & over again*") of the verb TEASE in (7a) and (7b) is more clearly visible in example (7b).

The signs **TEND-TO** and **THAT-ONE** may also be signed as contractions with the possessive pronoun, as illustrated below. When used in a contraction, the possessive pronoun is not repeated.

Context   (same as 7a and 7b)

(8a)

<u>   t   </u>   <u>   nod </u>
KNOW-THAT P-A-T, TEASE"*over & over again*" **TEND-TO POSS**-*rt*

Struc/Trans (same as 7a)

(8b)

<u>   t   </u>   <u>   nod </u>
KNOW-THAT P-A-T, TEASE"*over & over again*" **THAT-ONE POSS**-*rt*

Struc/Trans (same as 7b)

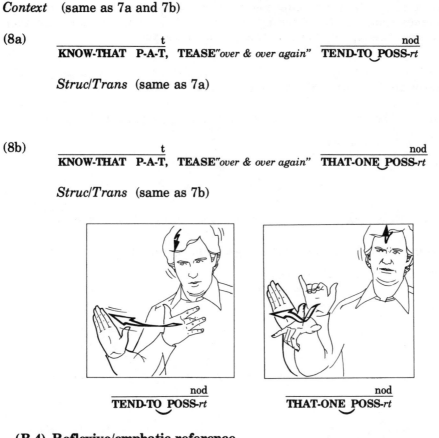

<u>nod</u>
TEND-TO POSS-*rt*

<u>nod</u>
THAT-ONE POSS-*rt*

(B.4) Reflexive/emphatic reference

The handshape with closed fist and thumb extended is used for reflexive reference (e.g. 'yourself'). Normally, this reference involves a loose, repeated movement. Reflexive pronouns basically follow the same pattern as the other pronouns.

The pronoun **MYSELF** has two common forms which are illustrated below.

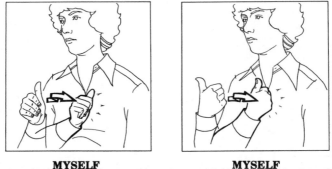

MYSELF
(variant A)

MYSELF
(variant B)

Second and third person singular reference (i.e. 'yourself', 'him/her/itself') is expressed by moving the fist toward the person with a repeated shaking of the hand ('pointing' with the area between the knuckles and the first finger joint). In the case of plurals (i.e. 'yourselves', 'themselves'), the pronoun will take the form of a sweeping arc across the locations of those persons, as illustrated in (9).

Context   A group of male insurance agents are having their annual company dinner at a very elegant and expensive restaurant. The wife of one of the insurance agents arrives a bit early to pick up her husband. She's concerned about the expense of the meal and asks the men:

(9)

brow raise		wh-q		q

EAT   FINISH,   WHO   PAY-TO-*arc*   WHOwg,   YOURSELVES

Struc   'When you've finished eating, who will pay for it? Yourselves?'

Trans   'When you're done eating, who's gonna take care of the bill? Are you?'

The sign **OURSELVES** is made with two contacts on the Signer's chest (from one side to the other). In rapid signing, this double contact is often made at the same place (on the side of the dominant, signing hand). If the people being referenced are present in the communication area, then the Signer may use the pronouns **YOURSELVES** and **MYSELF** to convey the meaning 'ourselves'.

OURSELVES   **YOURSELVES-AND-MYSELF**

Context   Members at a club meeting are discussing ways to make more money for various projects. Someone suggests they seek "outside" assistance for ideas. A young Signer angrily responds:

(10)

neg	rhet.q

me-SAY-#NO-TO-*you**,   MONEY   COLLECT   HOWwg,

nod

OURSELVES   DECIDE   WILL*

Struc   'No! How will we earn the money? We will decide for ourselves!'

Trans   'No! We'll decide for ourselves how to raise the money!'

Context   At that same meeting (see example 10), the club president decides it's time
to exercise his authority. He stands up and says:[12]

(11)
                              rhet.q
     COLLECT   MONEY   HOWwg,   #CLUB   TAKE-UP   #CAR   WASH-*car***,**

                     br
     UNDERSTAND+   YOURSELVES-AND-MYSELF   WASH-*car*

      Struc   'How to raise the money? The club will hold a carwash. Of course,
               that means we'll wash the cars ourselves.'

      Trans   'I'll tell you how we'll raise the money. The club will hold a car-
               wash and, of course, we'll do all the work ourselves.'

If the Signer uses the reflexive handshape with a sharp, single movement, the
reference is more emphatic, as illustrated in the examples below.

Context   The Signer's wife has been taking an Auto Mechanics course and has just
bought an old car that needs some work. The Signer wants to encourage
her to use her new skills and says:

(12)
                          cond   rhet.q
     SUPPOSE   #CAR   BREAK-DOWN,   #FIX   HOWwg,   YOURSELF*

      Struc   'Suppose the car breaks down, how will it get fixed? You'll do it
               yourself!'

      Trans   'If the car breaks down, you'll be the one who fixes it.'

This emphatic form of the pronoun frequently occurs in the compound sign that
means 'It's up to you' or 'That's his/her decision to make' (depending on the direction
of the pronoun).

Context   An overly dependent college student asks her mother what field she
should go into. Her mother responds:

(13)   **THINK͡ YOURSELF***

      Struc   'Think for yourself!'

      Trans   'That's up to you!'

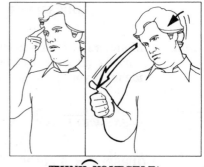

THINK͡ YOURSELF*

----

[12]For readers who have the accompanying videotape: Notice that the sign glossed here as
UNDERSTAND+ has a small, repeated movement and actually means something like 'of course', or
'that means', or in other contexts, 'provided that'.

Context A family with three teenagers are out at a restaurant having dinner. The teenagers are arguing that they want to be more independent from their parents. The father grins, looks at them, and says "OK . . .

(14)

<u> br.raise </u> <u> rhet.q </u>
EAT FINISH, WHO PAY, YOURSELVES*

    Struc 'When we're finished eating, who will pay? You will!'

    Trans 'When we're done eating, you guys can pick up the tab!'

(B.5) Demonstrative reference

ASL has several related pronouns that mean something like 'that thing' or 'that one'. These pronouns occur frequently in the language. However, we do not yet know how to clearly distinguish them and what are the appropriate contexts for using each form. For the purposes of this text, we use the glosses **THAT-ONE, THAT-ONE_INDEX, THAT-ONE***, and **THAT** to distinguish these related signs. Below are illustrations of each of these signs and examples that demonstrate a context in which each may be used.

      THAT-ONE   **THAT-ONE_INDEX**

Context The Signer and a friend are taking an art class and have been visiting several museums together. The Signer recalls one particular visit:[13]

(15)

                             (gaze lf)   t
REMEMBER ONE-WEEK-PAST US-TWO   GO-TO-*lf* A-R-T BUILDING,

                             t
PICTURE (2h)C-CL-*cntr to rt"in a row"*,

                 t
LAST-*rt* THAT-ONE-*rt*, ME YECCH-*rt*

    Struc 'Remember last week you and I went to the art building and there was that row of pictures. That last one on the right, I loathed it.'

    Trans 'Remember when we went to the art museum last week and saw that row of pictures? I really hated that one on the end.'

---

[13]For readers who have the accompanying videotape: Notice that the last sign in this example (glossed as **YECCH**) is a modulation of the sign **VOMIT**.

Context   At a clothes store, the Signer is standing near a coat rack and happens to
see a woman tell her son to go get the red coat on the chair so she can try it
on. The Signer exclaims:

(16)   (gaze right   )
        THAT-ONE͜ INDEX   MINE

     Struc   'That one there is mine!'

     Trans   'That's mine!'

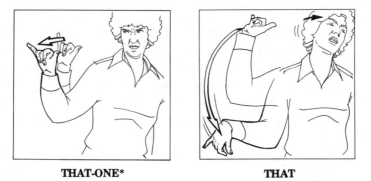

       THAT-ONE*   **THAT**

Context   The Signer is walking with a girlfriend and notices another good friend
across the street on the right. The Signer tells her companion:

(17)   (gaze rt   )   rel.cl
        THAT-ONE*-*rt*   MAN   WITH   #DOG   MY   GOOD-FRIEND

     Struc   'That man who is with the dog is my close friend.'

     Trans   'That guy with the dog is a real good friend of mine.'

Context   The Signer and a friend haven't seen each other for a long time and now
are reminiscing together about "old times". The Signer is talking about
the time he couldn't remember the name of a well-known actor.

(18)   qt
        REMEMBER   US-TWO   ARGUE   MOVIE   GENTLEMAN,

        (gaze rt)   (head lf, 'self disgust')
          FIND-*rt*   THAT-*rt*   DISGUST

     Struc   'Remember you and I argued about the man in the movie? When I
           found out it was *that* guy, I was disgusted with myself.'

     Trans   'Remember the time we were arguing about the movie actor's
           name and we found out who it was? I felt like a jerk because I
           should have known it all along.'

C. Pronouns Referring to "Non-Present" People, Things, Places

In Section B, we saw that Signers can refer to people or things in the communication area by 'pointing' to them with one of several possible handshapes. In this section, we will describe how Signers talk about people, things, and places that are *not* present in the communication area.

(C.1) Setting up referents in space: What, Where, and How

A crucial feature of ASL is its use of space—that is, its use of the area around the Signer's body. One way that a Signer takes advantage of the 3-dimensional nature of ASL is to "set up" or "establish" non-present referents (people, things, places) in specific locations around his/her body. Then the Signer can point to those locations (which 'stand for' the referents), and those points serve as pronouns—just like they did when the referents *were* present in the communication area.

1. *What* can be "set up" in space? Most nouns (e.g. 'Mary', 'my brother', 'New York', 'the river', 'a dog', 'a tree', 'an entrance', 'my class') can be and most often *are* given a location in space if: (a) the noun is not *body-anchored*[14] (and therefore can easily be signed in a specific location), or (b) the noun is body-anchored and the Signer wants to refer back to that noun. In some cases, even abstract ideas (e.g. 'Einstein's Theory of Relativity') are given a location in space for easy reference.[15]

2. *Where* are referents set up in space? There are several different strategies that Signers may use for deciding where to set up referents in space.

a. *Reality Principle:* If the Signer is recalling an event in the past in which persons or things were actually arranged in specific places, the Signer will set them up in the same arrangement. For example, if the Signer wants to describe a situation in which someone was seated to his/her left, the Signer will set that person up on the left. Similarly, if the Signer wants to talk about an event that involved four people seated in a circle, they will be set up in space following their actual arrangement in real life. Later, if the Signer wants to talk about the same four people in another situation where they were arranged differently, the Signer usually will re-establish their locations in space to match reality.

This principle is the same as the one discussed in Section B in which the Signer points to Addressee A (who is present in the communication area) when the Signer wants to refer to that person, or points to another person to refer to that person (rather than giving him/her a different location in space). Similarly, if the Signer wants to refer to a place that s/he can see (e.g. a building, a lake) or knows the

---

[14]Body-anchored signs (e.g. GIRL, HEART, MAN, HORSE, HOSPITAL, MEMBER, APPLE, RUSSIA, BODY, COAT) are made on some part of the body (other than the non-dominant hand) and, thus, usually cannot be given a location in space without using the special devices described later in Point 3 of Section C.1.

[15]Similarly, in English, one can say 'When the theory of Relativity was first presented, many people didn't believe *it*.'

direction one would take to arrive at that place (e.g. Baltimore, my house), the Signer will point to that place or point in the direction of that place.[16]

Thus, if the Signer is describing a past event and wants to talk about a particular place or thing, s/he will set that place or thing up in space according to where it was in relation to the participants at the time of the event. For example, if the building was in front of and to the right of the Signer during the event, then that's where the Signer will set up the building.

b. *Order of Referents with "Unknown" Locations:* If the Signer is talking about a past event (e.g. the Civil War) and doesn't know where the people or things were located, or is talking about some future event (e.g. the meeting next week), then obviously the "Reality Principle" can't be followed. An alternate strategy involves assigning locations to referents (Ref.) as they appear in a narrative, following a type of alternating pattern. See Figure 8.13.

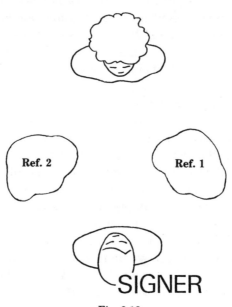

Fig. 8.13

Many right-handed Signers will set up the first-mentioned referent on their right (between the Signer and the Addressee). If another referent is set up, it will be located to the left of the Signer (between the Signer and Addressee).[17] However, if

---

[16]However, if the place is located behind the Signer, the Signer may give it a location just within the boundaries of the signing space in order to comply with the constraints of the language concerning where signs are made. For example, if the house is to the right and behind the Signer, s/he may turn around *or* may refer to it by pointing to the far right, but not behind the Signer (which is out of the normal signing space).

[17]However, if in the story about the Civil War, the two referents (e.g. two people) are supposed to be standing right next to each other, then they would probably be similarly placed next to each other in space.

the Addressee is standing or sitting more to one side (e.g. to the left) of the Signer, then both referents may be set up on the same side (e.g. to the right), as illustrated in Figure 8.14.

Fig. 8.14

There are several possible ways to set up three or more referents in space, depending on the relationships between the referents and when they occur in the narrative. Below are some possibilities:

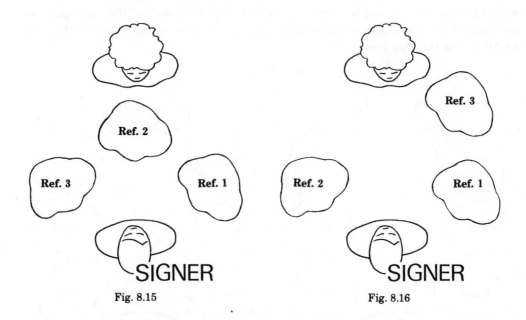

Fig. 8.15   Fig. 8.16

The order of referents shown in Figure 8.15 might be used when you know from the beginning that three people will be involved in the narrative. (In this case, to establish Referent 2, the Signer will point in a more downward orientation without looking at the Addressee, to make it clear that the Signer is not talking about the

Addressee.) Figure 8.16 might be used when the narrative is about two people, and then the Signer adds a third person (Ref. 3) to the narrative.

Fig. 8.17   Fig. 8.18

Figure 8.17 might be used to show that Ref. 1 and Ref. 2 have a special relationship with each other, as opposed to Ref. 3. For example, Ref. 1 and Ref. 2 might be students, and Ref. 3 is the teacher. Figure 8.18 might be used for the same purpose as Figure 8.17. For example, Referents 1, 2, and 3 might be the "three little pigs" and Ref. 4 is the "big bad wolf".

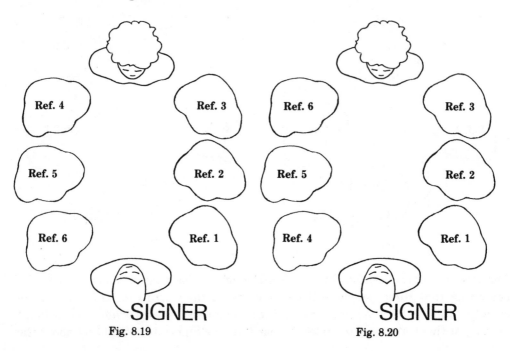

Fig. 8.19   Fig. 8.20

Fig. 8.21

Figure 8.19 might be used when talking about a meeting with six people seated around a table. Figure 8.20 might be used when talking about debating teams engaged in a panel discussion (three people per team). Figure 8.21 might be used when telling a narrative in which more and more characters are introduced. This scheme follows the pattern of Figure 8.16 and can be used for establishing 3,4,5, or 6 referents. As each referent is placed further and further away from the Signer, the angle of the point (from the floor) is increased. For example, in Figure 8.16, Ref. 1 is established to the right whereas Ref. 3 is to the right and up (in a slightly higher plane). In Figure 8.21, Ref. 5 is higher than Ref. 3, and Ref. 3 is higher than Ref. 1. Thus, locations can be distinguished by their horizontal plane, their distance from each other, and their distance from the Signer. These are just some of the possible locations and orders for establishing referents in space.

There is still very little known about the rules used by ASL Signers when setting up multiple referents in space and how these referents are moved into different spaces to reflect different "scenes" in a narrative. Clearly, this elaborate use of space is one of the most complex features of ASL.

At present, we can only report some of the most basic patterns for establishing referents in space (that are cited above with examples) and suggest the following principles:

(a) Once a Signer has established a person, thing, or place in space, all future references to it will be consistent with that initial location *unless* the referent has clearly been moved to another location or the topic has changed.

(b) Once a Signer has established a person, thing, or place in space, other Signers in the conversation will also make consistent use of that space when referring to the same person, thing or place. (*Exception:* Sometimes, when only one person has been given a spatial location and it is obvious that all 'third person' references are references to that person, then each Signer may choose to use a different location to represent that person. This variation seems to be influenced by what is the most physically comfortable place for each Signer to point to (depending on seating arrangement, etc.). Since the meaning of every 'third person' reference is clear, there is less need for all Signers to consistently use the same location.)

(c) When telling a story or describing a scene, it is helpful to formulate a "mental overview" of the various locations that will be used in the narrative (very much like an aerial photograph or a map), as illustrated below.

"Aerial view"   Signer's perspective

(d) In narratives, the location of the persons, things, and places may change—either because they have moved in the story, or because the Signer has shifted his/her 'perspective' (somewhat like the difference between a long-shot and a close-up in a film). The illustrations below and example (19) show how a Signer may change the location of a referent to indicate a change in perspective. In the example, notice how the location of the 'house' changes. First, it is to the Signer's right; but when she arrives at the house, the house moves to "center stage".

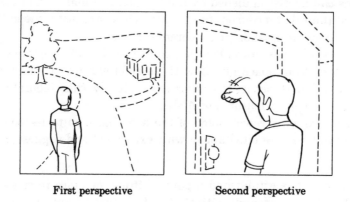

First perspective   Second perspective

Context   The Signer is telling a friend about what happened yesterday.

First perspective

(19)

<pre>
              ___t___ ___mm___ (gaze rt   )
YESTERDAY, ME WALK+ NOTICE-TO-<i>rt</i> HOUSE-<i>rt</i>,

___rhet.q___
WHO, MY GOOD-FRIEND,

(gaze rt   (br)   mm)   ___br___
        ME "WELL", ME WALK+-<i>rt</i> 1-CL'walk to house', ARRIVE-<i>rt</i>,
</pre>

Second perspective

<pre>
              ___mm___
ME KNOCK-ON-<i>door-cntr</i>, "waiting", OPEN-<i>door</i> INVITE-<i>me</i> ENTER-<i>house</i>,

HOUSE BEAUTIFUL*
</pre>

Struc   'Yesterday I was casually walking along and I noticed a house on my right. Whose house? My close friend's. So I thought "Why not?" and I walked on over to the house. When I got there, I knocked on the door, and then waited. The door opened, I was invited in, and I entered the house. The house was really beautiful.'

Trans   'Yesterday I was out for a walk and I saw this house. I realized it was my friend's house. So I walked over and knocked on the door. He opened the door and invited me in. So I went in and Wow! Was that house beautiful!'

3. *How* are referents established in space? ASL has a variety of ways to establish referents in space. These include (a) making the sign (for the referent) in a particular location, (b) fingerspelling the name of a referent in a particular location, (c) directing head and eye (and perhaps, body) movements toward a particular location while making the sign for a referent, or fingerspelling the name of a referent, (d) using a pronoun (e.g. **POSS-***rt*, **SELF-***rt*) right after the sign for a referent, (e) using a pronoun in a particular location later in the sentence or in another sentence when it is obvious who or what is the referent, (f) using a *classifier*[18] (that represents that referent) in a particular location, or (g) using a *directional verb*[19] when it is obvious who or what is the referent.

Each of these separate ways to establish referents in space will be described in this section with examples. However, in actual discourse, several of them may occur together. For example, a Signer may use (a), (c), and (d) together. The purpose for

---

[18]A *classifier* is a special type of sign that is described in Chapter X. Some classifiers are like pronouns because they can represent nouns, but they also can be moved in space like verbs.

[19]*Directional verbs* are signs that can vary their direction of movement according to the spatial location of the subject and/or object of the verb. (See Chapter IX)

separating them here is to help the reader understand them, not because they represent separate and/or 'equal' methods for establishing spatial referents.

(a) Signs which can be moved in space (i.e. signs that are not *body-anchored*— see Section C.1) and which represent people/things/places are often signed in specific locations. These locations then become the established locations for those referents. In the first example below, the place 'Washington, D.C.' is signed to the right, and the place 'Baltimore' is signed to the left. These locations become the established locations for the two cities. Then the verb **WORK** and the noun **HOUSE** are made in their appropriate locations, according to where they occur—i.e. in Washington, D.C. or in Baltimore.

Context   The Signer is visiting a friend in India (who learned ASL from a Deaf exchange student!). The Signer is trying to explain how some major U.S. cities are close to each other.

(20)
```
          _____(gaze,body lean rt_____)  (gaze,body lf )t
          YOU  KNOW  WASHINGTON D-C-rt ─────────→  NOT-FAR  INDEX-washington & baltimo
                                      BALTIMORE-lf─────────────────
```

```
               (gaze,body lean rt )   (gaze,body lean lf)
          ME  WORK-washington,    HOUSE-baltimore,
```

```
                                                        mm
          _____
          EVERY-DAY  COMMUTE-BETWEEN-washington & baltimore↔
```

Struc   'You know Washington, D.C. and Baltimore, they are not far from each other. I work in Washington, and my home is in Baltimore. Every day I commute between Baltimore and Washington.'

Trans   'You know Washington and Baltimore aren't far apart. I work in D.C. and live in Baltimore, and I commute every day.'

In example (21), the verb **NOTICE-TO**-*rt* and the Signer's gaze 'forewarns' that something will be set up to the right. Then the sign **WATER**⁀(2h)**5↓wg-CL** is made to the right and establishes the 'river' in that location. Then all of the other verbs are made in that same location.

Context   A family is on vacation and arrived at their campsite late last night. The Signer woke up very early this morning and is telling his father what he did.

(21)   <u>   cs+t   </u>   <u>   mm   </u>
      MORNING, ME WAKE-UP GET-OUT-OF-BED,

      (gaze rt   )   (gaze rt   )
      NOTICE-TO-*rt* **WATER** (2h)**5↓wg-CL**-*rt*'river',

      (gaze rt   )<u>puff.cheeks</u> ('smile')
      ME RUN-TO-*river* **JUMP-INTO**-*river*

      Struc   'This morning, I woke up and leisurely got out of bed. Then suddenly I noticed the river to my right. I ran straight over to it, and jumped into the water'

      Trans 'When I got up in the morning, I suddenly noticed the river over there. So I raced over and jumped in.'

(b) Setting up referents by fingerspelling in a particular location is also very common in ASL. In the first example below, 'San Francisco' (its abbreviation—S.F.) is fingerspelled to the Signer's right side. Then, 'people with warped minds' is signed to the left, and they move from their location on the left side to 'San Francisco' on the right.

Context   The Signer and friends are talking about what they like and don't like about different cities. The Signer jokingly says:

(22)   <u>   qt   </u>   <u>(th)t   </u>
      KNOW+ S-F-*rt,* **PEOPLE**-*lf* **MIND-WARPED**-*lf,*

                               <u>puff.cheeks</u>
      THAT-ONE-*lf* *people*-**ASSEMBLE-AT**-*sf*

      Struc   'You know San Francisco? People with warped minds, they're the ones who flock there.'

      Trans 'Well, you know San Francisco—that's where all the nutty people go.'

In the next example, the sign **NEW-YORK** is made to the right and the abbreviation for 'Los Angeles' is fingerspelled to the left. The verb then moves from the left to the right to show that 'Los Angeles beat New York'.

Context The Signer is a student and has been watching the World Series on television. She runs into another dorm room to tell a friend what happened.

(23)
<pre>
         co   t   (nod)qt
"HEY", AWFUL, BASEBALL WORLD S-E-R-I-E-S, KNOW+ YOU,

(gaze,body lean rt) (gaze lf)t
   NEW-YORK-rt ————————————————————→
                    L-A-lf,   la-BEAT-new york
</pre>

Struc 'Hey, Terrible! The baseball World Series, you know about it? New
York and Los Angeles—Los Angeles beat New York!'

Trans 'Hey, doggone it! You know the World Series—the Yankees and
Dodgers—the Dodgers won![20]

   (c) Head, eye, and body movements are very often used together with all of the
other ways for establishing referents in space. However, they can also serve this
function without any of the other devices. This 'solitary' use seems to occur more
frequently with body-anchored signs. In the example below, the Signer establishes
the 'woman' to the left by looking to the left and nodding his head in that direction
while making the sign **WOMAN** (which is body-anchored).

Context A friend just saw the Signer put a five dollar bill in his pocket. The friend
asks where the Signer got the money. The Signer explains:

(24)
<pre>
                                         t   q
ONE-WEEK-PAST CLASS PARTY, REMEMBER YOU,

(gaze,body lf)   th
   WOMAN HOLD-cup————————→ SPILL-DRINK-rt
                  CHAT+

(body lean rt,gaze at lf arm)   q
LIQUID-SPILL-ON-left arm,   REMEMBER YOU,

              cs
"WELL",   RECENT woman-GIVE-TO-me FIVE-DOLLARS
</pre>

Struc 'Last week's class party, you remember it? A woman on my left
was holding a cup and signing at the same time and spilled her
drink on my left arm. You remember? Well, she just gave me five
dollars.'

Trans 'You remember the class party we had last week, don't you? Remember the woman on my left who was drinking and signing and
then spilled her drink on my arm? Well, she just gave me five
bucks.'

---

   [20]In the context of sports, the sign for a particular city is often used to refer to that city's team since
most teams don't have name signs, or the signs are not known nationally. Thus, in the context of
BASEBALL WORLD S-E-R-I-E-S, the Addressee knows that **NEW-YORK** means the 'Yankees' and
L-A means the 'Dodgers'.

(d) Another way to establish a referent in a particular location is to use a pronoun (which 'points' to that location) right after the sign for that referent is made. This is illustrated in example (25) where the possessive pronoun (**POSS**-*rt*) establishes the referent 'Pat' to the right of the Signer.

Context   Someone asks the Signer why Pat didn't come to class. The Signer responds:

(25) $\underline{\phantom{\text{P-A-T, POSS-rt}}\overset{\text{(gaze rt)}}{}\overset{\text{t}}{}}$
       P-A-T,   **POSS**-*rt*   **MOTHER**,   **SICK**

      Struc   'Pat, her mother is sick.'

      Trans   'Pat's mother is sick.'

(e) A pronoun can also establish a referent in a specific location when it does *not* immediately follow the sign for that referent. That is, the pronoun can occur later in the sentence or in another sentence. This can happen when there is only one possible meaning of the pronoun (i.e. the referent is clear). In such cases, either only one person, thing, or place has been mentioned so far, *or* all of the other referents have already been established, and the Signer points to a new location. (However, when introducing a new referent after several other referents have been set up in space, usually the Signer will immediately assign a new location to that referent so that later pronominal references will be clear.)

In the following two examples, name signs are used for 'Lee' and 'Pat'. In both examples; the possessive pronoun occurs later in the sentence or in a separate sentence, but still establishes both referents to the right of the Signer.

Context   The Addressee sees a little boy, Lee, crying. The Signer explains:

(26) $\underline{\phantom{\text{LEE (2h)alt.CRY,}}\overset{\text{t}}{}}$ $\underline{\phantom{\text{REASON,}}\overset{\text{rhet.q}}{}\overset{\text{(gaze rt)}}{}}$
       LEE   (2h)alt.**CRY**,   **REASON**,   **POSS**-*rt*   **MOTHER**   **GO**-*rt*

      Struc   'Lee's crying, what's the reason for it? His mother is gone.'

      Trans   'Lee's crying because his mother's gone.'

Context   A young girl is telling her friends what happened to Pat yesterday.

(27) $\underline{\phantom{\text{PAT,}}\overset{\text{t}}{}}$ $\underline{\phantom{\text{YESTERDAY CUT-CLASS, POSS-rt MOTHER,}}\overset{\text{t}}{}}$ $\underline{\phantom{\text{BECOME-ANGRY}}\overset{\text{pow}}{}}$
       PAT,   **YESTERDAY**   **CUT-CLASS**,   **POSS**-*rt*   **MOTHER**,   **BECOME-ANGRY**

      Struc   'Pat, yesterday she cut class. Her mother, she became really angry.'

      Trans   'Pat cut class yesterday and her mother got really angry.'

(f) Another common way to establish a referent in space is to use a classifier (which represents that referent) in a particular location. This classifier can then be moved to show different actions of the referent and can change its spatial location.

In the next example, the classifier for a 'car' (**3→CL**) is signed to the right and establishes the 'car' in that location. Then the classifier for the referent 'boy' (**1-CL**) is signed to the left. These two classifiers are then moved in space to show what happened with the 'car' and the 'boy'. In the end, when the boy is knocked over, the **V-CL** is used to represent the boy's fall. (See Chapter X for illustrations and explanations of the symbols for these classifiers.)

Context   The Signer witnessed a terrible accident yesterday and tells his brother:

(28)
$$\overline{\text{YESTERDAY \quad HAPPEN,}}^{\text{t}} \quad \text{AWFUL,} \quad \text{\#CAR} \quad \text{3→CL}'\text{car move from rt to cntr}',$$

$$(\text{hold rt 3→CL}) \longrightarrow \overline{\text{VEHICLE-HIT-}boy}^{\text{pow}}$$
BOY **1-CL**-*lf* '*boy walk in front of car*'————————→ *V-CL*'*boy knocked up & over*'

       Struc   'What happened yesterday, it was awful. There was a car driving along from the right. A boy walked out in front of the car, the car hit him, and he was knocked up in the air and fell over.'

       Trans   'Yesterday something awful happened. This boy walked out in front of a moving car. It hit him and knocked him right up in the air.'

    Example (29) also shows how the locations of classifiers will establish the locations of different referents. In this example, the **1-CL** is used to locate the 'woman' on the right, and the two-handed **5:↓-CL** establishes the 'audience' on the left.

Context   The Signer is a teacher and attends weekly seminars on how to effectively teach large groups. A colleague asks her about the seminars and she responds:

(29)
$$\overline{\text{ONE-WEEK-PAST \quad MEETING,} \quad \text{BORING*,}}^{\text{t}}$$

(gaze rt)t   (body lean rt) (gaze lf) t   puff.cheeks
WOMAN,   **1-CL@***rt,*   **PEOPLE,**   (2h)5:↓**-CL-***lf*'audience',

(gaze rt)(body lean rt, gaze lf)
         LECTURE"*long time*",   **INDEX**-*arc-lf* **SOUND-ASLEEP**

       Struc   'Last week's meeting, it was really boring. This woman, she was here. The people, there was a huge audience. She lectured to them for a long time, and they were sound asleep.'

       Trans   'Last week's meeting was such a bore! This woman was lecturing on and on, but all the people in the audience were sound asleep.'

    (g) Many verbs in ASL can show who or what is the subject and object of the sentence via the direction of the verb's movement (see Chapter IX). The verb starts in one place (the location of the subject) and ends in another place (the location of the object). In general, these *directional verbs* cannot be used until the referents have been assigned spatial locations. However, in some cases, when it is obvious (from context) who or what is the referent, the directional verb can show who is the subject or object of the sentence and at the same time, give that subject/object a spatial location. For example, the 'doctor' in example (30) is given a location to the right by moving the verb 'give' from the right to the location of the Signer. (However, also notice that the Signer gazes to the right during the sign **ONE-DAY-PAST**.)

Context   The Signer has been sick for some time now and his friends know it. One friend asks if he has seen a doctor. The Signer responds:

(30)   t   rapid nodding   (gaze rt   )
               DOCTOR,   **FINISH ONE-DAY-PAST** *rt*-**GIVE-TO**-*me* **MEDICINE**

      Struc   'The doctor, oh yeah, I did yesterday and she gave me some medicine.'

      Trans   'Sure, I saw the doctor yesterday and she gave me some medicine.'

(C.2) Setting up referents on the non-dominant hand

In Section C.1, we talked about how ASL uses the space around the Signer's body to establish the location of various referents. Setting up things in space has several functions, one of which is pronominalization (i.e. so that the Signer can use pronouns rather than having to sign the noun over and over). ASL Signers also take advantage of the fact that they have two hands by using the fingers on one hand (the non-dominant hand) to represent different referents. These referents include persons, places, things, or events. This use of the fingers of the non-dominant hand is very common when *listing* things—e.g. the people invited to a party, the entrance requirements to a school, or the errands scheduled for a particular day.

Referents are established on the non-dominant hand either by (a) pointing with the dominant hand to a particular finger on the non-dominant hand (usually starting with the thumb) and then signing or fingerspelling the referent, or (b) raising the first non-dominant finger (with an emphatic outward movement) and then signing the referent with the dominant hand, successively adding one more finger on the non-dominant hand as each referent is named.

There are several variations of these two ways to establish referents on the non-dominant hand: (a) Signers may just point to each finger consecutively, that is, start with the thumb, then add the index finger and proceed through to the pinky, or (b) Signers may start with the thumb ('one'), add the index finger ('two'), add the middle finger ('three'), but then withdraw the thumb and instead, use the pinky as the fourth referent, or (c) if the Signer is only establishing two referents, s/he may use the index finger and third finger (as in the sign **TWO**). Up to ten referents can be established on the non-dominant hand by using the signs for numbers 1–5, by pointing to the point of contact (digit and thumb) for referents 6–9, and by shaking the thumb for the tenth referent to distinguish it from the first referent.

In the example that follows, 'Pat' is established to the right of the Signer with the possessive pronoun, and the three things that happened to 'Pat' are established on the non-dominant hand.

Context   The Signer is telling a friend about the problems which another friend, Pat, has.

(31)
<u>   t   </u>
YESTERDAY P-A-T, NARRATE AWFUL HAPPEN++,

<u>(gaze at thumb)   t </u>
INDEX-*left thumb* **HOUSE, BURN-DOWN*,**

<u>(gaze at finger)   (gaze rt)   t</u>
INDEX-*left index finger*   **POSS-***rt* **FRIEND L-E-E,**

MOVE-TO-*rt,outward* **CALIFORNIA,**

<u>(gaze at finger)   (gaze rt)   t </u><u> cs </u>
INDEX-*left middle finger*   **POSS-***rt* **MOTHER, RECENT DIE**

Struc   'Yesterday Pat, he told some awful things that have happened. First his house, it burned down; second his friend Lee, he moved away to California, third his mother, she just recently died.'

Trans   'Yesterday Pat told me some awful things that have happened to him. His house burned down; his friend, Lee, moved to California; and his mother just died.'

D. Summary

We began this chapter by describing handshapes that are used for pronominal reference. Pronouns in ASL are made by 'pointing' (with one of these handshapes) to a person or thing that is present in the communication area *or* to a location in space that represents that person, place, or thing. ASL has many different ways to "establish" or "set up" referents in locations around the Signer's body. There are also rules for determining *where* different referents will be located in space. Some of these rules are described in this chapter, but this is another area of ASL that needs more investigation.

Bibliography: Pronominalization

Baker, C. 1976. Eye-openers in ASL. *Sixth California Linguistics Association Conference Proceedings*. San Diego State University, 1–13.

Friedman, L. 1975. Space, time, and person reference in the American Sign Language. *Language 51*, 940–961.

Lacy, R. 1974. Putting some of the syntax back into semantics. MS, University of California, San Diego.

Liddell, S. 1977. An Investigation into the Syntactic Structure of American Sign Language. Unpublished Ph.D. dissertation, University of California, San Diego.

Dialogues
and
Cultural Information

PRONOMINALIZATION

The following three dialogues have been developed to illustrate various uses of the grammatical features described in this chapter. Each of these dialogues also appears in one of the three corresponding Student Texts. In the Student Texts, the transcription of each dialogue is less detailed than what is provided here for the teacher of ASL. Following the dialogues, in the sections called "Cultural Information", are brief discussions of the topic of each dialogue.

The following dialogues and cultural information correspond to:

Student Text: Unit 3
Unit 12
Unit 21

Dialogue: Pronominalization
(Student Text: Unit 3)

First Signer (Pat)

Pat$_1$:
$$\overline{\text{SEE FINISH N-T-D DRAMA}}^{\text{q}}$$
"UMMM" ——————————————→　　　　*YOU*

Pat$_2$:
$$\overline{\text{nodding}}$$
$$\overline{\text{SEE } \boxed{\text{B}} \text{ YOU}}^{\text{q}}$$

Pat$_3$:
$$\overline{\text{KNOW-THAT ONE-YEAR-PAST SUMMER, N-T-D SUMMER SCHOOL,}}^{\text{t}}$$
"UMMM" ——————————→

$$\overline{\hspace{3em}\text{nodding}\hspace{3em}}$$
ME　(2h)GO-TO-*rt*

Pat$_4$:
$$\overline{\text{nodding}}\quad \overline{\text{(gaze rt)mm}}\quad \overline{\text{(gaze rt}\hspace{2em}\text{)br}}$$
MYSELF　　**DRIVE+**　　**ARRIVE-AT-*rt***

$$\hspace{10em}\overline{\text{(gaze rt}\hspace{6em}\text{)}}$$
SEE-*rt*　INDEX-*arc-rt*　DEAF　SEVERAL　　INDEX-*arc-rt*　THEREABOUTS-*rt*

$$\hspace{4em}\overline{\text{(gaze rt}\hspace{2em}\text{)}}$$
ME　KNOW+　INDEX-*arc-rt*

Pat$_5$:
$$\overline{\hspace{2em}\text{neg}\hspace{2em}}\quad \overline{\text{(gaze rt)}\hspace{6em}}^{\text{t}}$$
"NO-NO",　**KNOW　CITY-*rt*　DRAMA　GROUP-*rt*,**

$$\hspace{9em}\overline{\text{nod}}\quad \overline{\text{nod}}\quad \overline{(\hspace{1em}\text{nod)}}\quad \overline{\text{nodding}}$$
SAME-AS　WASHINGTON　D-C,　CHICAGO,　THAT-*rt*　THEREABOUTS-*rt*

Dialogue: Pronominalization
(Student Text - Unit 3)

Second Signer (Lee)

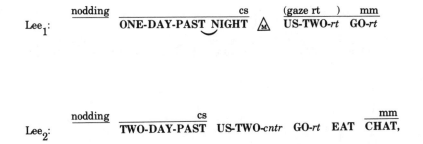

      <u>nodding</u>   <u>cs</u>   (gaze rt) <u>mm</u>

Lee₁: ONE-DAY-PAST NIGHT △ US-TWO-*rt* GO-*rt*

      <u>nodding</u>   <u>cs</u>   <u>mm</u>

Lee₂: TWO-DAY-PAST US-TWO-*cntr* GO-*rt* EAT CHAT,

     <u>(body lean rt)br</u>   (body lean lf,gaze lf)

       DRAMA,   SUMMER SCHOOL, VARIOUS-THINGS

                                                 <u>q</u>

Lee₃: YOURSELF ONLY-ONE-*you* GO-TO-*lf*

          (gaze lf   )   <u>q</u>

Lee₄: DEAF INDEX-*arc-lf* DRAMA SPECIALTY-FIELD

         <u>nodding</u>

Lee₅: *OH-I-SEE* + +

Dialogue: Pronominalization
(Student Text - Unit 12)

First Signer (Pat)

Pat$_1$:   ONE-DAY-FUTURE NIGHT $\overline{\text{MOVIE,}}^{\text{t}}$ $\overline{\text{YOU}\quad\text{GO-TO-}rt}^{\text{q}}$

Pat$_2$: $\overline{\text{INTERPRET}+,}^{\text{neg}}$ KNOW+ WOMAN $\overline{\text{SMALL-}rt\quad\text{BLACK}\quad\text{H-A-I-R}}^{\text{(gaze rt,pursed lips)}}$ $\overline{\text{THAT-ONE INDEX-}rt}^{\text{(rapid nodding)qt}}$

Pat$_3$: $\overline{\text{RIGHT}++,}^{\text{nodding}}$ $\overline{\text{US-TWO}\quad\text{GO-}rt}^{\text{(gaze rt)}}$ $\overline{\text{WHY NOT}}^{\text{wh-q}}$

Pat$_4$: THINK YOURSELF, $\triangle_{\text{A}}$, $\triangle_{\text{B}}$, $\overline{\text{US-THREE,}}^{\text{t}}$ $\overline{\text{GO-}rt}^{\text{nod}}$

Pat$_5$: $\overline{\text{DOESN'T-MATTER,}}^{\text{neg}}$ MOVIE IMPORTANT*, S-T-A-R-W-A-R-S

Dialogue: Pronominalization
(Student Text - Unit 12)

Second Signer (Lee)

                                                   q
Lee$_1$:   _____

       MOVIE   CAPTION   QMwg

        nodding   q
Lee$_2$:   _____   _____

       SAME-AS   EVERY-MORNING   #TV   THAT-ONE INDEX-_lf_

        neg   (gaze lf & rt↔   )t   neg
Lee$_3$:   ____   _____   _____

       ME   (2h)STAY-_here_,   MOVIE   INTERPRET   _me_-LOOK-AT-_lf_ & _rt_↔,   NOT-LIKE*   ME

                                                  q
Lee$_4$:   _____

       MOVIE   INTERPRET   DON'T-CARE   YOU

        ('happily surprised')
Lee$_5$:   S-T-A-R-W-A-R-S,   ME   _me_-JOIN-_you_*   GO-_lf_*

Dialogue: Pronominalization
(Student Text - Unit 21)

First Signer (Pat)

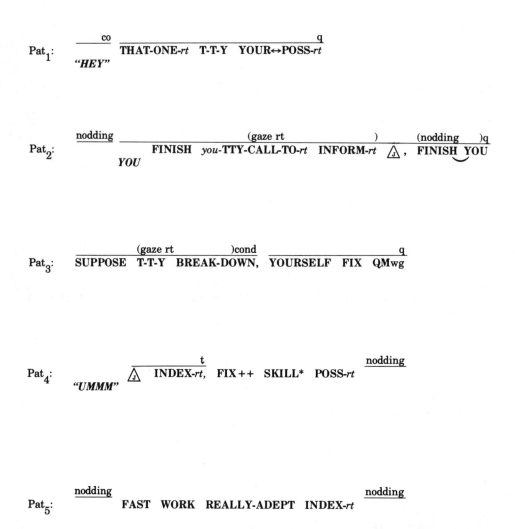

Pat₁:
```
                  co  _____q
                 THAT-ONE-rt   T-T-Y   YOUR↔POSS-rt
      "HEY"
```

Pat₂:
```
     nodding _____(gaze rt_____)____(nodding___)q
              FINISH  you-TTY-CALL-TO-rt  INFORM-rt  △ ,  FINISH YOU
              YOU
```

Pat₃:
```
     _____(gaze rt_____)cond  _____q
     SUPPOSE  T-T-Y  BREAK-DOWN,  YOURSELF  FIX  QMwg
```

Pat₄:
```
                  _____t____               nodding
                  △  INDEX-rt,  FIX++  SKILL*  POSS-rt
      "UMMM"
```

Pat₅:
```
     nodding                                 nodding
            FAST  WORK  REALLY-ADEPT  INDEX-rt
```

Dialogue: Pronominalization
(Student Text - Unit 21)

Second Signer (Lee)

Lee$_1$:
$$\overline{\text{nodding}} \qquad \qquad \overline{\text{ } \text{cs}}$$
NEW, RECENT ARRIVE-*here*

Lee$_2$:
$$\overline{\text{INFORM-}lf \triangle \text{,}}^{\text{t}} \quad \overline{\text{FOR-FOR}}^{\text{wh-q}}$$
"*WHAT*"

Lee$_3$: SILLY* YOU,

ME *me*-SUMMON-*rt* SOMEONE-*rt* (2h)FROM-*rt*-COME-TO-*here* (2h)#FIX* (2h)"WELL"

Lee$_4$: *OH-I-SEE*
$$\overline{\text{YOUR T-T-Y \#FIX FINISH INDEX-}lf \text{ QMwg}}^{\text{q}}$$

Lee$_5$: *OH-I-SEE FINE,*
$$\overline{\text{TOMORROW ME }me\text{-TTY-CALL-TO-}lf}^{\text{nodding}}$$

Student Text: Unit 3

Cultural Information: The National Theatre of the Deaf

The National Theatre of the Deaf (NTD) was started in 1966 at the Eugene
O'Neill Memorial Theatre in Waterford, Connecticut. Although comprised mostly of
Deaf professional actors and actresses, NTD does not perform solely for Deaf audiences. Rather, by also using professional, hearing actors and actresses, NTD per-
forms for mixed audiences of deaf and hearing people. NTD has toured all over the
world and has performed for hundreds of thousands of people. A Tony Award was
given to NTD for its outstanding contribution to the theatre, and several programs
have appeared on national television (e.g. "A Child's Christmas in Wales" and "My
Third Eye"). The company tours the U.S. every year in the Fall and Spring. In 1967,
a summer school program was initiated to provide professional training opportunities to aspiring Deaf actors and actresses. The NTD summer school has been held
annually ever since. In 1968, the Little Theatre of the Deaf (LTD) was formed. LTD
is composed of a few members of the NTD company who tour (between NTD tours)
with a special program aimed at children. Several notable individuals are former
members of NTD: Bernard Bragg, Gilbert Eastman, Louie Fant, and Jane Norman,
to name a few. For more information about NTD, contact: National Theatre of the
Deaf, 305 Great Neck Road, Waterford, Conn. 06385.

Student Text: Unit 12

Cultural Information: The Registry of Interpreters for the Deaf (RID)

The Registry of Interpreters for the Deaf, Inc. (RID) is a national organization of deaf and hearing individuals who help facilitate communication between deaf and hearing people. The RID was established in 1964 (although from 1964–1965, the name of the organization was The National Registry of Professional Interpreters and Translators for the Deaf). The original purpose of the organization was to maintain a list of qualified interpreters and to encourage the recruiting and training of more interpreters.

In 1964, the organization had only a few members compared with its present membership—over 4000. Most of these 4000 members also belong to one of the sixty (60) local chapter affiliates of the RID. These local chapter affiliates often publish newsletters, host workshops, and sponsor evaluations of individuals who wish to be certified by the RID. Each of these local chapter affiliates has its own president and other elected officers.

The evaluation and certification of interpreters by the RID began in 1972 in order to provide a certain level of quality control within the profession. Since that time, approximately 2000 individuals have been certified at varying levels of competence. Because of the growing demand for interpreting services in educational, legal, medical, and other settings and because of the specialized skills needed to effectively interpret in these settings, the RID has begun to certify individuals in specialty areas. In addition to evaluation and certification, the RID also publishes a variety of materials related to interpreting (e.g. *Regional Directory of Services for Deaf Persons, Resource Guide to Interpreter Training Programs, Introduction to Interpreting*). For further information, contact the RID Home Office: RID, Inc., 814 Thayer Avenue, Silver Spring, Md. 20910.

Student Text: Unit 21

Cultural Information: Telecommunication Devices

Just as wake-up alarms and other signaling devices have been adapted for use by members of the Deaf Community, it should not be surprising that devices have been developed which make it possible for deaf persons to use the telephone. These Tele-communication Devices for the Deaf (TDD) make it possible for individuals with such units to type messages back and forth to each other using regular telephone lines. Some of these devices provide paper printouts ("hard copy"); however, many of them use only a light display where the characters move from right to left and then disappear off the display ("soft copy"). Currently there are about ten different types of TDDs.

Because the first telecommunication devices were actually Western Union tele-typewriters (TTYs) with phone couplers, the acronym TTY has become a generic term used by deaf people to refer to telecommunication devices in general. Some people use the term "MCM" to refer to any portable device that gives "soft copy" since the MCM was among the first such units to be marketed. The advantage of a TTY is that it offers "hard copy" which can be filed for later use and which means the person does not have to constantly watch the display as the message is typed out. However, TTYs are generally not portable. MCMs, which provide "soft copy", are generally portable and can be taken on trips, to meetings, etc.

There are certain *rules* that people generally follow when using a TTY or an MCM: always identify yourself ("PAT JONES HERE" or "THIS IS PAT JONES") since you generally cannot tell who a person is by how s/he types; when you want the other person to respond, type GA ("THIS IS PAT JONES GA") so that the other person knows it is his/her turn to Go Ahead; when you are done with your conversation, type SK or GA ("SEE YOU TOMORROW SK or GA") so the person can decide to stop (SK = "Stop Key") or continue to respond (GA); conversations are ended by typing SKSK.

Obviously, it takes longer to type than to talk on the phone. For this reason, deaf people have been trying to obtain reduced phone rates, especially for long distance calls. Several states have, in fact, reduced phone rates for deaf people with TTYs.

Since not every deaf person has a TTY or an MCM, an International Telephone Directory of the Deaf is published periodically. In 1976, there were over 5,000 people listed in the directory. More and more hospitals, police and fire stations, banks, travel agencies, consumer agencies, etc., are also beginning to purchase and use TDDs. Generally, places and individuals who have TDDs will provide a phone number and some indication of this fact—e.g. #123-4567 (voice or TTY). For more information, contact: Telecom for the Deaf, 814 Thayer Avenue, Silver Spring, Md. 20910.

Chapter IX

Subjects and Objects

A. Introduction

As discussed in Chapter 1, all languages have ways of indicating the grammatical roles of nouns in sentences. That is, all languages have ways of signaling which noun (or noun phrase) is the subject of the sentence and what are the grammatical functions of other nouns (or noun phrases) which may also appear in the sentence. For example, consider the English sentence below.

'The girl gave the boy a kiss under the mistletoe.'

There are four nouns in this sentence—'girl', 'boy', 'kiss', and 'mistletoe'. Which noun is the subject of the sentence? That is, which noun represents the person or thing that did something? First of all, we know that *word order* is an important grammatical signal in English and is used to indicate the grammatical role of nouns. Thus, our knowledge of English word order tells us that the *first* noun in the sentence above (i.e. 'girl') is the subject. We also know that what was given was a 'kiss' (the direct object), and that the 'boy' (the indirect object) was the recipient of the action. Since the noun 'mistletoe' follows a preposition ('under'), it functions as the object (often called an "oblique object") of the prepositional phrase that indicates where the action occurred. So 'girl' is the *subject* of the sentence; 'kiss' is the *direct object*; 'boy' is the *indirect object* and 'mistletoe' is an *oblique object* in the locative phrase 'under the mistletoe'.[1]

Actually the rules for determining the grammatical role of nouns in English are complex and require considerably more explanation, but the example above should serve to illustrate the kinds of distinctions that are important and that one should look for in a language.

How are subjects and objects distinguished in ASL? ASL has at least three different ways to indicate who or what is the subject of the sentence and who or what is the object. These involve (a) specific changes in the way the verb is made (called *modulations*), (b) the use of certain sign orders, especially when the verbs are of a type which cannot be modulated, and (c) changes in the Signer's body position to represent different speakers (subjects) and addressees in "direct address" narratives. In each of these ways for indicating the subject and/or object, the direction of the Signer's eye gaze (and frequently, his/her head position) is also important for understanding the grammatical role of different referents in the sentence.

---

[1]The prepositional phrase 'under the mistletoe' tells the *location* of the event; thus, it can also be described as a "locative phrase". (See Chapter XI for a more detailed explanation of *locatives*.)

B. Verbs

Verbs in ASL can be modulated for a variety of purposes; that is, their form can be changed in specific ways to show different meanings. Some of these modulations are discussed later in the chapters on Locatives and Pluralization. In this section, we will examine how modulations of several types of verbs show who or what are the subjects and objects (direct, indirect, or oblique) in sentences.[2] All of these modulations use the space around the Signer's body (or the body itself) to illustrate these grammatical relationships, usually by varying the verb's direction of movement, and/or palm orientation, and/or location.

To understand how the signing space is used, it is important to remember that the spatial location of the Signer is *first person,* that the spatial location of the Addressee is *second person,* and that other (present or non-present) people, things, or places can occupy spatial locations referred to as *third person.* (See Chapter VIII on *Pronominalization*). Many verbs in ASL can use these spatial locations for first, second, and third person to show who is doing something (the subject), or to show who is receiving that action (the direct or indirect object), or to show where the action occurs (the oblique object).

For example, let's look at the verb ____-GIVE-TO-____ . By alternately changing the direction of movement of the sign, one can express the meanings 'I give you', 'I give him/her', 'You give me', 'You give him/her', 'S/he gives me', and 'S/he gives you', which are illustrated below in citation form.[3]

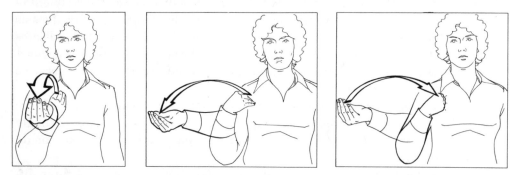

| *me*-**GIVE-TO**-*you* | *me*-**GIVE-TO**-*him/her* | *s/he*-**GIVE-TO**-*me* |

---

[2]As stated above, the term *modulation* has a very general meaning and simply refers to a modification or change in the form of the sign. Some of the modulations described in this chapter have also been referred to as *inflections* for the grammatical category called *person* (or *location*) in linguistic research on ASL. (You may wish to re-read the first section in Chapter 1 on inflections.)

[3]Note that, unlike English, this verb rarely means simply 'to give'. Instead, each form of the verb generally indicates a subject and object. Unfortunately, the glosses for such *directional verbs* in most Sign Language texts have given the false impression that these verbs are like the infinitive forms of English verbs (e.g. 'to give'). That is, these texts use glosses like **GIVE, TELL, SHOW,** etc., and then illustrate only one form of each verb—the one that means 'I give you', 'I tell you', or 'I show you', etc. By doing this, these texts give the false impression that the signs they have illustrated mean only 'give', 'tell', and 'show', when in actuality they also convey specific information about the subject and object of the verb. So students often mistakenly use the 'I ____ you' form of the verb to mean things like 'You ____ me' or 'I ____ him/her'. (See page 261 for examples of these common errors.) Clearly, such an approach to glossing misses important information that is communicated with many ASL verbs.

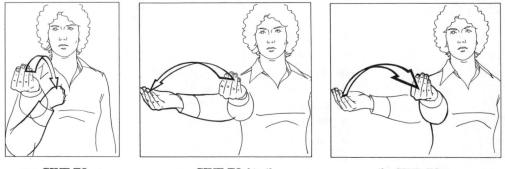

you-**GIVE-TO**-*me*	*you*-**GIVE-TO**-*him/her*	*s/he*-**GIVE-TO**-*you*

To express the meaning 'I give you', the verb moves *from* the Signer (i.e. the subject) *toward* the Addressee (i.e. the object). In general, this type of verb moves *from* the subject *toward* the object. Thus, since 's/he' is the subject in 's/he gives you', the verb moves from the *third person* location on the Signer's right to the *second person* location. In this way, the direction of the verb's movement indicates who is the subject and who is the object.

With some other directional verbs that are made with both hands, the non-dominant hand is held in a particular location, and the palm orientation of the moving dominant hand (i.e. the direction it faces) indicates the subject and object. For example, in the verb ____ -**FLATTER**-____ , the non-dominant hand is stationary while the dominant hand moves back and forth against it. The palm orientation of the dominant hand can then express the meanings 'I flatter you', 's/he flatters me', 'you flatter me', 's/he flatters you', etc., as illustrated below. (In the glosses of these illustrations, we have replaced the word 's/he' with the direction 'rt' to clearly show that the 'third person' is located to the right of the Signer.)

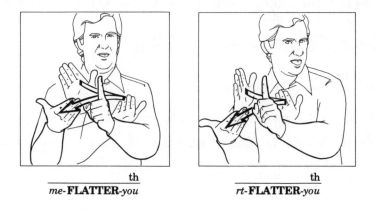

<u> th </u>	<u> th </u>
me-**FLATTER**-*you*	*rt*-**FLATTER**-*you*

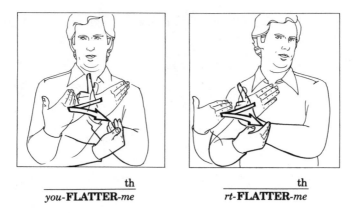

<table>
<tr><td>th</td><td>th</td></tr>
<tr><td>you-FLATTER-me</td><td>rt-FLATTER-me</td></tr>
</table>

Notice that the *location* of the verb (i.e. between first and second person, or between first and third person, or between second and third person) is also important for identifying the subject and object. For example, the location of the non-dominant index finger is crucial for distinguishing between 'you flatter me' and 's/he flatters me' as well as between 'I flatter you' and 'I flatter him/her' (not shown here). In addition, the head and body position of the verbs 'I flatter him/her' and 's/he flatters me' (*rt-***FLATTER-***me*) shows that there is a third person referent. That is, the head and/or body usually tilts *toward* the third person location when the Signer is the subject, and tilts *away from* that location when the Signer is the object.

The following four sentences use the directional verbs ____-**FORCE-**____ , ____-**TEASE-**____ , ____-**LOOK-AT-**____ , and ____-**SHOW-**____ . Notice how the specific modulation of each verb indicates who is the subject and who is the object (receiver of the action) in each sentence.[4]

Context   One of the Signer's friends is a teacher who is talking about the problems she feels she will have with a new student, Lee. The Signer asks:

(1)

```
           (gaze lf    )  (              neg)cond
    SUPPOSE   L-E-E-lf   NOT-WANT-lf   WORK-lf,
```

```
       wh-q                    q
    #DO-DO,   you-FORCE-lee
```

Struc   'If Lee doesn't want to work, what will you do? Will you force her?'

Trans   'What if Lee doesn't want to work? What are you gonna do? Force her?'

---

[4]In these examples, we are using the name of the 'third person' in the gloss of the verb to indicate the actual meaning of that verb in the context of that sentence. However, in the glosses for the illustrations, we are using the locations '*rt*', '*lf*', etc., to show where the third person referent in that sentence is located.

Context   A friend asks the Signer why he looks so "uptight". The Signer responds:

(2)   t   (body lean rt)rapid nodding
           ‾‾‾‾‾‾‾‾‾‾‾‾‾‾‾‾‾‾
           KNOW+ P-A-T,   BROTHER-*rt*,

                   (gaze rt   )   sta
                   ‾‾‾‾‾‾‾‾‾‾‾‾‾   ‾‾‾
           EVERY-DAY *pat*-TEASE-*me"over time"*

   Struc   'You know Pat, he's my brother—Every day he continually teases
            me over and over.'

   Trans   'You know my brother, Pat—Every day he keeps teasing me
            again and again and again.'

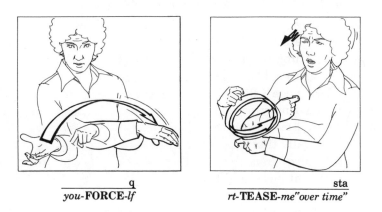

                        q   sta
                   ‾‾‾‾‾‾‾‾‾‾‾   ‾‾‾‾‾‾‾‾‾‾‾‾‾‾
                   you-FORCE-*lf*   *rt*-TEASE-*me"over time"*

Context   The Signer is shocked to hear about the way Pat has acted with the
           Addressee.

(3)   (grimace)   wh-q
                     ‾‾‾‾‾‾‾
                     #WHAT,

           (gaze rt)   (eyes closed   )q
           ‾‾‾
           P-A-T REFUSE *pat*-LOOK-AT-*you* *pat*-LOOK-AWAY-*rt*, AWFUL

   Struc   'What?! Pat refused to look at you and he looked away?! That's
            awful!'

   Trans   'What?! Pat refused to look at you and just turned away?! That's
            awful!'

Context A few weeks ago, the Signer received a gift (a picture of Laurent Clerc) and tells her aunt what she plans to do with it.

(4)

$$\overline{\text{KNOW+ \quad PICTURE \quad CLERC \quad OLD*,}}^{\;\;t} \quad \overline{\text{KNOW+ \quad YOU,}}^{\;\;q}$$

$$\overline{\text{TOMORROW \quad MY \quad FRIEND-}lf,}^{\;\;t} \quad \text{WILL} \quad \overset{\text{(gaze lf \qquad\qquad)}}{me\text{-SHOW-TO-}friend\text{-}arc}$$

Struc 'You know that really old picture of Laurent Clerc, you know the one I mean? Tomorrow my friends, I will show it to them together.'

Trans 'You know that really old picture of Laurent Clerc? Tomorrow I'm gonna show it to a group of my friends.'

$$\overline{rt\text{-LOOK-AT-}you}^{\;\;q}$$

$me\text{-SHOW-TO-}arc\text{-}lf$[5]

---

[5]In the context of example (4), moving the verb to a location on the left means that the object of the verb is **FRIEND**. The arc on the verb indicates that the referent of the sign **FRIEND** is plural and that the Signer is talking about a group of friends. This is explained more fully in Chapter XII on Pluralization. The 'arc' movement is a modulation called "all"—which is described in Chapter XIV.

A partial list of these kinds of directional verbs in ASL (i.e. those that indicate the subject and direct/indirect object) is given below. Most of these verbs can be found in the Stokoe *et al* dictionary (although some of the glosses are different).

____-ADVISE-____	____-#KILL-____
____-ANNOUNCE-TO-____†	____-KISS-____
____-APPROACH-____	____-LOOK-AT-____
____-ARREST-____	____-MAKE-CONTACT-WITH-____
____-ASK-TO-____	____-MAKE-FUN-OF-____
____-BAWL-OUT-____	____-MESH-WITH-____
____-BEAT-____	____-MOOCH-FROM-____
____-BEAT-UP-____	____-ORDER/COMMAND-____
____-BLAME-____	____-OVERCOME/DEFEAT-____
____-BORROW-FROM-____††	____-PARTICIPATE/JOIN-____
____-BOTHER-____	____-PAY-TO-____
____-BRIBE-____†	____-PICK-____
____-CHALLENGE-____	____-PICK-ON-____
____-COLLIDE-WITH-____	____-PITY-____
____-CONFRONT-____	____-PREACH-TO-____
____-COPY-____††	____-PUT-THUMB-DOWN-ON-____
____-CRITICIZE-____	____-QUIT-FROM-____
____-DECEIVE/FOOL-____	____-RESPECT-____†
____-DENIGRATE/PUT-DOWN-____	____-SAY-#NO-TO-____
____-FINGERSPELL-TO-____	____-SAY-#OK-TO-____
____-FINGERSPELL-NAME-TO-____	____-SAY-#YES-TO-____
____-FLATTER-____	____-SAY-YES-TO-____
____-FORCE-____	____-SCOLD-____
____-GET-EVEN-WITH-____	____-SELL-TO-____
____-GET-REVENGE-ON-____	____-SEND-TO-____
____-GIVE-ATTENTION-TO-____†	____-SHOOT-AT-____
____-GIVE-TO-____	____-SHOW-TO-____
____-HATE-____	____-STEAL-FROM-____††
____-HELP-____	____-SUMMON-____††
____-HIT-____	____-SUPPORT-____†
____-HONOR-____†	____-SUPPRESS-____†
____-INFLUENCE-____	____-TAKE-TURN-AFTER-____††
____-INFORM-____	____-TEACH-____
____-INSULT-____	____-TEASE-____
____-INTERROGATE-____	____-TELL-TO-____
____-INVITE-____	____-TOUCH-____
____-JOIN-TO-____	____-TOW-____
____-KICK-____	____-TTY-CALL-TO-____
____-KILL-____†	____-USE-BIG-WORDS-TO-____

†A cross after a verb means that there is some restriction(s) on its use. For example, the verb ____-SUPPRESS-____ cannot be modulated to indicate that the Signer is the object (i.e. ____-SUPPRESS-*me*). Often such restrictions occur because that modulation of the sign would be physically awkward to make. (The verb glossed as ____-ANNOUNCE-TO-____† could also be glossed as ____-TELL-TO-MANY-PEOPLE-____.)

††A double cross after a verb means that the usual direction of movement (i.e. Subject→Object) is reversed for that sign. For example, ____-COPY-____ moves from the object to the subject.

Some directional verbs are *reciprocal*; that is, by using both hands, these verbs can indicate that an action is jointly performed by two people or two things, or two groups. In a sense, each hand represents the action of one person or thing. So when both hands perform the verb simultaneously, they show that there are two "mutual" subjects. The location of the hands, their direction of movement, and/or their palm orientation then shows which people or things are the subjects of the verb.

For example, to express the meaning 'they look at each other', the hands simultaneously point toward each other from the two *third person* locations (usually with eye gaze back and forth between the two locations). To express the meaning 'we look at each other', the hands point toward each other from the *first person* and *second person* locations (with eye gaze toward the Addressee).[6] We gloss this reciprocal modulation as "*each other*".

they-**LOOK-AT**-*"each other"*

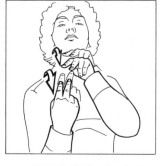

we-**LOOK-AT**-*"each other"*

Thus, verbs made with one hand like ____-**LOOK-AT**-____, ____-**INSULT**-____, and ____-**GIVE-TO**-____ become reciprocal by using both hands in the appropriate locations and orientations. Verbs normally made with two hands (e.g. ____-**INFORM**-____, ____-**STRUGGLE-WITH**-____, ____-**GET-REVENGE-ON**-____) become reciprocal by moving the hands from the two separate locations.

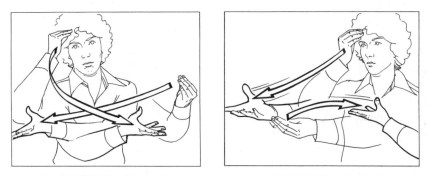

they-**INFORM**-*"each other"*   *we*-**INFORM**-*"each other"*

---

[6]Note that the actual location of the referents will determine the appropriate modulations of these verbs. For example, the two *third person* referents in the sign *they*-**LOOK-AT**-*"each other"* could both be located to the Signer's right.

Other two-handed verbs like ____-CORRESPOND-WITH-____, ____-QUARREL-WITH-____, and ____-CHANGE-PLACES-WITH-____ are always reciprocal and show who or what are the subjects of the verb.

The following three examples illustrate the use of reciprocal verbs in sentences. In example (5), the verb *you*-AGREE-WITH-*"each other"* is made between the two *second person* locations and further away from the Signer's body. Similarly, each hand in *you*-INFORM-*"each other"* moves from one of the *second person* locations toward the other location.

Context   The referee of a tennis tournament reminds two young players about the time of their match on the last day of the tournament.

(5)   (gaze downward at two boys, looking back 'n forth   )
             #OK-*rt*,   **YOU-TWO**   *you*-**AGREE-WITH**-*"each other"*,
             #OK-*lf*,

                                                         q
             GAME   TOMORROW   TIME TWO,   RIGHT,

                          (th)   cond
             SUPPOSE   QUIT,   WITHDRAW-FROM-*game*,

                                        tight lips
             you-**INFORM**-*"each other"**   **MUST***

        Struc   'OK. You two have agreed with each other that the game tomorrow will be at two o'clock, right? If you quit or back out, you tell each other. You must do that.'

        Trans   'OK. You guys have agreed that the game tomorrow's gonna be at two, right? Now if you decide to quit or back out, you gotta tell the other guy. That's a must.'

q	tight lips
you-**AGREE-WITH**-*"each other"*	*you*-**INFORM**-*"each other"**

In examples (6) and (7), the reciprocal modulation of each verb shows that the Signer is talking about himself and another person.

Context   The Signer and a friend have been disagreeing about everything for the past two weeks. After a lengthy discussion, they finally agree to see a particular movie together.

(6)   TWO-FULL-WEEK   UP-TILL-NOW   WE-TWO   *we*-DISAGREE-WITH-*"each other"*+*"over time"*,

        <u>   pah</u>
        SUCCESS   *we*-AGREE-WITH-*"each other"*

    Struc   'For two full weeks from then until now, the two of us have been disagreeing with each other continuously. At last we agree with each other!'

    Trans   'For the past two weeks, we've been continually disagreeing with each other, but finally we've agreed on something!'

Context   Someone asks the Signer why he still knows so much about a family that moved away several years ago. (Lee is one of the children in the family.) The Signer responds:

(7)   <u>(gaze rt)   t</u>   (gaze rt   )
    L-E-E   THAT-ONE-*rt*,   *we*-CORRESPOND-WITH-*"each other"*+*"regularly"*

    UP-TILL-NOW   MANY YEAR

    Struc   'Lee, that one—we have been corresponding with each other now for many years.'

    Trans   'You know Lee? Well, she and I have been corresponding for years.'

we-CORRESPOND-WITH-   MANY YEAR
"each other"+*"regularly"*

Listed below are some of the directional verbs which are or can be made reciprocal.

____-AGREE-WITH-____	____-INSULT-____
____-APPROACH-____	____-KISS-____
____-CHALLENGE-____	____-LOCK-HORNS-WITH-____
____-CHANGE-PLACES-WITH-____	____-LOOK-AT-____
____-CLASH-WITH-____	____-MAKE-FUN-OF-____
____-COLLIDE-WITH-____	____-MESH-WITH-____
____-CONFLICT-WITH-____	____-PITY-____
____-CONFRONT-____	____-PREACH-TO-____
____-CORRESPOND-WITH-____	____-QUARREL-WITH-____
____-DISAGREE-WITH-____	____-SAY-#NO-TO-____
____-FINGERSPELL-WORDS-TO-____	____-SAY-#OK-TO-____
____-GIVE-TO-____	____-SAY-#YES-TO-____
____-HATE-____	____-SHOOT-AT-____
____-HAVE-INSTANT-UNDERSTANDING-WITH-____	
____-INFORM-____	____-STRUGGLE-WITH-____
	____-TEACH-____

So far, all of the examples in this chapter have illustrated how directional verbs
indicate who is doing something (the subject) and who is receiving the action (the
object) by manipulating the direction of movement and/or palm orientation and the
location of the verb.[7] This manipulation of the verb is dependent upon knowing the
locations of *first person, second person,* and *third person* referents in space.

Similarly, since these locations in space can also represent actual locations (e.g.
'Chicago', 'my house', 'the lake'), some directional verbs (e.g. ____-FLY-TO-____ ,
____-DRIVE-TO-____ , ____-GO-TO-____) indicate actual movement from one *lo-*

---

[7]The section on "Verbs" in Chapter XII on Pluralization provides several examples of how directional
verbs can be modulated to show *plural* subjects and objects.

cation to another *location*. This is seen in example (8) below—where the *first person* location represents 'here'. In this example, the verb *rt*-FLY-TO-*here* moves from a *third person* location on the right to the *first person* location. This movement represents flying from an unspecified place to 'here'.

Context   The Signer's wife has been away on vacation for several weeks. A friend asks the Signer if he would like to get together for dinner next week. The Signer says he can't because:[8]

(8)
$$\underline{\hspace{5cm}}^{t} \qquad \text{(gaze rt} \quad)$$
ONE-WEEK-FUTURE,   WIFE   *rt*-FLY-TO-*here*

Struc   'Next week, my wife will fly from somewhere to here.'

Trans   'My wife's flying here next week.'

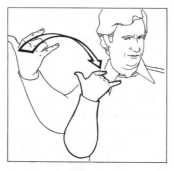

rt-FLY-TO-*here*

In example (9), the verb moves from the *first person* location (meaning 'here') to a *third person* location on the Signer's right (meaning 'San Francisco'). Then another verb moves from that location to another *third person* location on the Signer's left (meaning 'San Diego'). This last location is also lower because San Diego is 'south' of San Francisco.

---

[8]In most of the preceding examples, we have used the name of the referent in the gloss for each directional verb. However, in example (8), the Signer does not specify the meaning of the location on the right, so we simply describe the movement (*'rt'*). In example (9), we have used *'rt'* and *'lf'* instead of *'san francisco'* and *'san diego'*, respectively, since these names are not yet known at the time when the verb is made. However, in the gloss for the verb *san francisco*-DRIVE-TO-*lf,down,* we do use one name since, by this time, we know that the location on the right represents 'San Francisco'.

Context   Someone asks the Signer what she plans to do next summer. The Signer replies:

(9)

        <u>   </u>t   (gaze rt   )

ONE-YEAR-FUTURE SUMMER, ME   *here*-**FLY-TO**-*rt* S-F-*rt,*

(gaze rt   )mm <u>   </u>br (gaze lf,down   )

    SIGHT-SEE-*rt* **FINISH**-*rt,*   *san francisco*-**DRIVE-TO**-*lf,down* S-D

Struc   'Next year in the summer, I will fly from here to there—San Francisco, casually sightsee around in San Francisco, and then when I'm finished, I'll drive from San Francisco to there—San Diego.'

Trans   'Next summer I'm going to fly to San Francisco, do some sightseeing, and then drive to San Diego.'

here-**FLY-TO**-*rt*   *rt*-**DRIVE-TO**-*lf,down*

However, when the verb moves from the *first person* location to another location, it does not always mean that the verb has moved specifically from 'here' to that location. That is, sometimes the *first person* location has a more general, unspecified meaning, and the focus of the verb is on its end location, *not* where it started. This is also seen in the English sentence 'I'm going to drive to Chicago'. In this sentence, it is not clear if the person means s/he will drive specifically 'from here' to Chicago. Instead, the focus is on the end location (Chicago). However, the listener usually assumes that the speaker means 'from here' unless the speaker adds other information—like 'I'm going to drive from New York to Chicago'. In ASL, this 'unspecified' use of the *first person* location is only seen when the verb moves *from* the *first person* location to another location—not when the verb moves *to* the *first person* location. When the verb moves *to* the *first person* location, the meaning is clearly 'to here'.[9]

---

[9]This fact about ASL sometimes influences how a verb is glossed. That is, sometimes we include only the end location in the verb gloss when we think the initial *first person* location does not have a specific meaning—e.g. **GO-TO**-*school.*

A partial list of directional verbs that can indicate movement from and/or to a specific geographic location is given below. This list of verbs does not include many of the ways that classifiers can be used as verbs and move from one location to another (e.g. V-CL'walk from home to school'). (See Chapter X on Classifiers.)

____ -ARRIVE-AT-____†	____ -JUMP-TO-____
____ -ASSEMBLE-AT-____	____ -MOVE-TO-____
____ -BRING/CARRY-TO-____	____ -PLANE-CRASH-AT-____†
____ -COME/GO-TO-____	____ -PLANE-LAND-AT-____†
COMMUTE-BETWEEN-____ & ____↔	____ -PLANE-TAKE-OFF-TO-____
____ -DRIVE-TO-____†	____ -RIDE-IN-VEHICLE-TO-____
____ -ENTER/GO-INTO-____	____ -RIDE-ON-ANIMAL-TO-____†
____ -FLY-TO-____	____ -RUN-TO-____†
____ -FREQUENTLY-GO-TO-____	
____ -GO-____	

In all of the examples so far, we have seen that the direction of movement, location, and/or palm orientation of directional verbs 'agrees with' (is made in accordance with) the spatial locations of the subject and object (e.g. *me*-GIVE-*you*), with the spatial locations of mutual subjects (e.g. *they*-LOOK-AT-*"each other"*), or with spatial locations that represent actual locations (e.g. *san francisco*-DRIVE-TO-*san diego*). This is the same type of *agreement* that is described in the chapter on Locatives and is discussed in depth in the chapter on Pluralization. Here we see that there are *agreement rules* for the use of directional verbs in ASL. That is, there are rules which specify that the direction of movement, the location, and/or the palm orientation of directional verbs must 'agree with' the spatial locations of the persons, places, or things they refer to.

---

†A cross after a verb means that the form of the verb changes when it moves to 'here' (the *first person* location). With these verbs, often the sign will move from over the shoulder of the signing hand to the *first person* location.

Thus, sentences like (10) and (11) below are ungrammatical in ASL because they are not accurately modulated for *"person"* (or *"location"*). That is, they do not 'agree with' the spatial locations of the referents involved. These examples illustrate a common error made by students when they try to use ASL verbs as if they were English verbs and do not recognize that, in general, the way such directional verbs are made *always* supplies specific information about the subject and/or object.

Context   The Signer notices that a friend left her watch on the table and the Signer asks someone for it.

(10)
$$\overline{\phantom{**\text{L-E-E}}\quad^{\text{t}}}$$
**L-E-E   WATCH,   *me*-GIVE-TO-*you*   ME

     Struc   'Lee's watch? I give it to you me.' (Supposed to mean: 'Give me Lee's watch'.)

Context   The Signer meets a friend at a convention. The friend says he is going to a special teacher's meeting. However, another friend, Pat, has already informed the Signer that that meeting has been postponed and that she will tell the Signer the new time later. So the Signer says:

(11)
$$\overline{\quad^{\text{t}}\quad}\quad\overline{\quad^{\text{nod}}\quad}\;\text{(gaze rt)}$$
**MEETING,   POSTPONE,   P-A-T-*rt*   *me*-TELL-*you*   ME,

$$\overline{\quad^{\text{t}}\quad}\quad\overline{\qquad\qquad^{\text{nodding}}\qquad}$$
TIME   START,   WILL   *me*-INFORM-*you*   ME

     Struc   'The meeting, it's been postponed. Pat I tell you me. The time it starts, I will inform you me.' (Supposed to mean: 'The meeting is postponed. Pat told me. She will tell me the starting time.')

Example (12) is grammatical, but it doesn't mean what it's supposed to mean. Instead of showing that the Signer will also move to Chicago (located to the right), the second verb *here*-**MOVE-TO**-*lf* inappropriately indicates that the Signer is moving to a different place. Then the sign *me*-**SAME-AS**-*lee* refers to the fact that both Lee and the Signer will have 'moved'—but not that they both will have 'moved to Chicago'. Again, this example shows how directional verbs must 'agree with' the spatial locations of the persons, places, or things they refer to.

Context   The Signer's best friend, Lee, has moved to Chicago and the Signer plans to move there next summer.

(12)
$$\overline{\qquad^{\text{(gaze rt\;\;)t}}\qquad}\qquad\overline{\qquad^{\text{(gaze rt}\qquad\text{)}}}$$
**KNOW+   CHICAGO-*rt*,   L-E-E   FINISH   *here*-MOVE-TO-*chicago*,

$$\overline{\qquad\qquad^{\text{t}}\qquad\qquad}\quad\overline{\quad^{\text{(gaze lf}\qquad\text{)}}}\quad\overline{\quad^{\text{nodding}}}$$
ONE-YEAR-FUTURE   SUMMER,   ME   *here*-MOVE-TO-*lf*   *me*-SAME-AS-*lee*↔

     Struc   'You know Chicago? Lee has moved from here to Chicago. Next year in the summer I'm going to move from here to a different place just like Lee.' (Supposed to mean that the Signer will also move to Chicago 'just like Lee'.)

ASL has another set of verbs which are (or can be) made on the Signer's body and which indicate *where* some action occurred (e.g. push on the shoulder) or what body part is the recipient of some action (e.g. push shoulder).[10] As such, the location of these verbs varies depending on which area of the body is involved in the action. For example, by changing the location of the sign **SHAVE-___** , the Signer can show that the object of the verb is his/her head, face, armpit, etc.

SHAVE-*head*   **SHAVE**-*face*   **SHAVE**-*armpit*

Similarly, the verb **HAVE-OPERATION-ON-___** can be modulated to indicate where the operation occurred—e.g. on the head, shoulder, or heart. Notice that the location of the verb can also indicate quite exactly where the action occurred. For example, the Signer could have shown that the surgery occurred 'on the right forehead above the brow' or involved a 'large incision on the inside of the upper arm'.

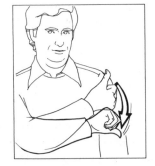
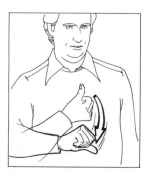

HAVE-OPERATION-ON-*head*   **HAVE-OPERATION-ON**-*shoulder*   **HAVE-OPERATION-ON**-*heart*

---

[10]We are unsure whether these objects should be analyzed as 'direct' or 'oblique'. One can argue that they should be considered 'oblique' objects since it is possible to modulate a verb like ___-**PUSH**-___ , or ___-**BITE**-___ to mean, for example, '*s/he* pushed *me* on the *shoulder*'—where the direct object would be 'me' and the location would act as the oblique object (i.e. 'on the shoulder').

The following three examples show how these kinds of verbs can be used in sentences to show where an action occurs.

Context   The Signer and her associate are talking about an employee named Pat who hasn't been getting his work done properly. The Signer says:

(13)
             ‾‾‾‾‾‾‾‾t‾‾‾‾‾‾
YESTERDAY, P-A-T (2h)TIRED* EYELIDS-DROOPING+,

(gaze rt, brow squint   )
ME "GO-AWAY"-*rt* WASH-*face* "GO-AWAY"-*rt*

    Struc   'Yesterday, Pat was really tired and his eyelids were closing with sleep. So I told Pat "Go wash your face. Go on." '

    Trans   'Yesterday Pat was so tired he was practically falling asleep so I told him to go wash his face.'

Context   Someone asks the Signer to go to a movie. The Signer replies that he has to go visit a girlfriend in the hospital who has just had an accident. The Signer explains what happened:

(14)
           ‾‾‾‾‾‾t‾‾‾‾‾‾   (gaze down at gun   )th
MY FRIEND, G-U-N L-CL'gun'⎰ 'turn gun and look at it from different angles',
                  'hold gun'⎱

         (gaze at lf shoulder   )
UNEXPECTEDLY   SHOOT-AT-*left shoulder*,   AWFUL

    Struc   'My friend, she was holding a gun and carelessly turning it around in her hand. Unexpectedly, it went off and shot her in the left shoulder. Awful!'

    Trans   'My friend was holding this gun and waving it around in her hand kind of carelessly and it accidentally went off and shot her in the left shoulder. It was awful!'

Context   Someone asks the Signer why he has a bandage on his head. The Signer explains:

(15)
           ‾‾‾‾‾‾t‾‾‾‾‾‾   ‾‾‾mm‾‾‾   ‾‾‾‾‾‾‾‾‾‾‾‾‾‾th‾‾‾‾‾‾‾‾‾‾‾
FEW-DAY-PAST, ME WALK+ V-CL⎰ 'trip and fall over something'
                        B-CL⎱

      ‾‾‾‾‾‾‾‾‾‾‾‾‾‾‾‾pow‾‾‾‾‾‾‾‾‾‾‾   ‾‾‾‾‾‾‾‾‾‾‾‾‾th‾‾‾‾‾‾‾‾‾‾
BANG-*rt forehead*-ON-*something*   LIQUID-SPILL-ON-*rt forehead*

    Struc   'A few days ago, I was just walking along when I carelessly tripped, fell over, and really banged my right forehead on something, and the blood came streaming out of my right forehead.'

    Trans   'A few days ago, I was just walking along when I tripped and bashed my forehead on something, and it started bleeding like crazy.'

A partial list of these verbs which can indicate an action (e.g. **BANG-ON-____**) or state of being (e.g. **HAVE-RASH-ON-____**) on a location of the body is given below. We have included a preposition (**ON, AT,** or **FROM**) in each of these glosses to emphasize that they can show *where* the action occurs. However, some of the verbs could be glossed without a preposition in some contexts (e.g. **BITE**-*lf wrist*); so some of the prepositions are in parentheses.

BANG-ON-____	**KISS-(ON)-____**
BITE-(ON)-____	**KNOCK-ON-____**
BLEED-FROM-____	**LIQUID-SPILL-ON-____**
BRUISE-ON-____	**PERSPIRE-FROM-____**
CUT-(AT)-____-WITH-KNIFE	**PUSH-(ON)-____**
CUT-(AT)-____-WITH-SCISSORS	**READ-(AT)-____** (e.g. **READ**-*lips*)
GRAB-(ON)-____	**SCRATCH-(ON)-____**
HAVE-FRECKLES-ON-____	**SHAVE-(AT)-____**
HAVE-OPERATION-____	**SHOOT-IN-____**
HAVE-RASH-____	**TAP-ON-____**
HIT-(ON)-____	**TATTOO-ON-____**
#HURT-(AT)-____	**WASH-(AT)-____**
KICK-(ON)-____	**WRAP-BANDAGE-ON-____**

Similarly, some of the verbs listed above can indicate actions that occur at other locations (not on the body). This is done by making the verb in a spatial location which represents something else. For example, the verbs **WASH-(AT)-____**, **KNOCK-ON-____**, **BANG-ON-____**, and **READ-(AT)-____** can be modulated to mean 'wash window', 'knock on door', 'bang on table', and 'read poster' when these objects have been previously given specific spatial locations. Example (16) illustrates how the location of the verb **BANG-ON-____** can indicate where that action occurred since the location of the 'table' is already established in space. (The verbs that refer to 'discussing things' and 'chatting' move in an arc across the area that represents the 'table'.)

Context   The Signer is telling a therapist about the troublesome behavior of her friend.

(16)
_____t   (gaze at table   )

FEW-DAY-PAST MEETING, TABLE 1$_{outline}$-CL'large round table',

           (gaze down at people   )
PEOPLE   (2h)4:-CL'people seated around table',

(gaze at people around table   )mm
people-DISCUSS-THINGS-*around table*   *people*-CHAT-*around table*

(gaze rt)t (body lean rt, gaze lf)
FRIEND,   *friend*-BANG-ON-*table*,

(body lean rt, gaze lf   )
(2h)MANY-LOOK-AT-*me** "HEY" MANY-LOOK-AT-*me**. . .

Struc   'A few days ago at a meeting, there was a large round table and people were seated around it. The people were all discussing things among themselves and chatting. My friend, he banged on the table, and said "All of you look at me! Hey! Look at me!". . .'

Trans   'At a meeting a few days ago, everyone was seated around this large table, and they were all chitchatting and talking among themselves. Then my friend banged on the table and repeatedly told everyone to look at him . . .'

In fact, a large number of verbs can be signed in specific locations to show that an action occurs at the place or thing represented by that location. For example, signing CLEAN in the location that represents a 'table' will indicate the 'table is clean'. Or, signing SIGHT-SEE in the location that represents a 'city' will mean 'sightseeing in that city'. Examples (17) and (18) illustrate how the location of the verb can indicate where an action occurs.

Context   Lee's parents have been criticizing him for having a messy room. So Lee goes upstairs to finally clean it up. Later he says the job is finished and goes out to play. After Lee's mother has "inspected" the room, she tells her husband:

(17)
    (gaze rt   )   t (gaze rt   )pah
L-E-E POSS-*rt* D-E-S-K, CLEAN+-*rt* PERFECT*-*rt*

        (gaze lf;   th)t (gaze lf   )
TABLE-*lf* FOULED-UP-*lf*, LEAVE-IT-*lf*

Struc   'Lee his desk, he really cleaned it up to perfection. The table that was all messed up, he left it.'

Trans   'Lee cleaned up his desk really well, but didn't touch that messy table.'

Context   A friend has been talking about how wonderful San Francisco is—the perfect place to live! She tells the Signer that he simply must go visit the city and see for himself. The Signer responds:

(18)   <u>nodding</u> (gaze rt   )   (gaze rt   )mm   <u>nodding</u>
        FINE+, **GO-TO**-*rt* **S-F** **SIGHT-SEE**-*rt,* **WANT**wg-*rt,*

        <u>   rhet.q</u>   <u>   neg</u>
        MOVE-TO-*rt,*   **NOT-WANT**

    Struc   'Fine, fine. Go to San Francisco and sightsee there, I really want to do that. But move to San Francisco? I don't want to do that.'

    Trans   'Sure, sounds fine. I do want to visit San Francisco and do some sightseeing, but I don't want to move there.'

Notice how, in example (17), the signs **POSS**-*rt,* **CLEAN**-*rt,* and **PERFECT**-*rt* all 'agree' in location; the signs **TABLE**-*lf,* **FOULED-UP**-*lf,* and **LEAVE-IT**-*lf* also 'agree'. The same kind of *agreement* is seen in example (18). The sign **SIGHT-SEE**-*rt* is made in the location assigned to 'San Francisco' and then **WANT**wg is signed in the same location to indicate that the Signer does want to do that action (sightseeing) in that place (San Francisco).

Sometimes it is not the *location* of the verb that identifies the object, but rather, a difference in the *handshape* and/or *movement* and/or *size* of the verb. For example, some verbs retain their basic movement but change their handshape to indicate what the object is. With these verbs, the handshape either will represent the object or will represent the handshape actually used when handling that object. Some of these verbs are **POUR-FROM**-___ (e.g. tea cup, pitcher, barrel), **THROW**-___ (e.g. baseball, football, shotput), **BREAK**-___ (e.g. twig, thick rod), **LIFT**-___ (e.g. rock, suitcase), **PICK-UP**-___ (e.g. cup, marble, rock), and **TAKE**-___ (e.g. ball, box, bag). The choice of appropriate handshape in these verbs is usually determined by the size and shape (or some other physical characteristics) of the object that is 'thrown', 'broken', 'lifted', etc. The three illustrations below show how the handshape of the verb **PICK-UP**-___ 'agrees with' the object.

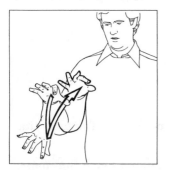  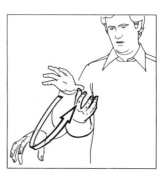

PICK-UP-___   **PICK-UP**-___   **PICK-UP**-___
(e.g. 'marble')   (e.g. 'cup')   (e.g. 'rock')

Several sentences with this type of verb can be found in the next chapter on Classifiers—e.g. **PICK-UP**-*rock*, **THROW**-*rock*, **PICK-UP**-*shoe*, **CARRY**-*shoe*, **THROW**-*shoe*, etc.

Whereas the verbs described above give information about the object via their handshape, the sign **DRIVE**-___ 'agrees with' the object by having a different type and size of movement. (Also notice the different facial expressions.)

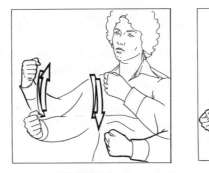

DRIVE-*car*

DRIVE-*truck/bus*

DRIVE-*racecar*
(Variant A)

DRIVE-*racecar*
(Variant B)

The following examples illustrate how two of these different modulations of the verb **DRIVE**-___ can be used in sentences.

Context   The Signer and a group of friends are talking about Pat's new job— driving a truck for a moving company.

(19)
$$\frac{\quad t \quad}{\text{P-A-T,}} \quad \frac{\text{puff.cheeks}}{\text{DRIVE-}truck/bus} \quad \frac{\qquad\qquad\qquad\text{nodding}}{\text{REALLY-ADEPT} \quad \text{INDEX-}rt}$$

Struc   'Pat, at driving a truck, she's really skilled.'

Trans   'Pat's really good at driving a truck.' (Note: The context of the sentence indicates that the meaning is 'truck' and not 'bus'.)

Context   The Signer is telling his younger brother about auto racing and racecar drivers.

(20)

<u>   t</u>
KNOW   INDIANAPOLIS   FIVE-HUNDRED   FAMOUS   COMPETITION,

<u>   (nodding)q</u>   (gaze rt)   <u>   neg</u>
KNOW+   YOU,   MAN   INDEX-*rt*   NAME   A-,   FINGERSPELL   NOT-KNOW,

<u>   nodding</u>
INDEX-*rt*   REALLY-ADEPT   DRIVE-*racecar*   REALLY-ADEPT   INDEX-*rt*

Struc   'You know the Indianapolis 500, the famous race, you know it? A man there named A . . ., I don't know the spelling. He's an expert at driving racecars, a real expert.'

Trans   'You know about the famous Indy 500, don't ya? There's a guy out there named A . . . somethin' or other who's a really dynamite driver.'

The preceding discussion of the many ways that verbs can be modulated to indicate the subject(s) and object(s) in sentences is far from complete, but does include some of the major types of modulations that have been studied to date. By now, the reader should have recognized that *if* the way a verb is made (i.e. its physical structure) allows it to be modulated for subject and/or object, then there is a strong tendency in ASL to take advantage of that 'movability' and to appropriately modulate the verb. That is, although not all verbs can be moved in space (because of the way they are made), if they *can* be moved in space, they probably *will* be and will 'agree with' the spatial locations of the persons, places, or things that the Signer is talking about. In this way, ASL Signers continually take advantage of the space around them for grammatical purposes.

However, many ASL verbs are not modulated in space for subject and/or object. Within this group of verbs, many are *body-anchored* —meaning that they contact the body during their production. This body contact tends to limit the 'movability' of the verb.

Below is a partial list of verbs which are not usually modulated for subject and/or object: (Some of them are not body-anchored.)

ACT/DRAMA	FAINT	PUNISH
ASK	FEEL-AFRAID	REFUSE
BE-DISAPPOINTED	FEEL-HURT	RELAX/REST
BE-FED-UP	FEEL-UPSET	SEARCH
BE-INDIGNANT	FORGET	SMILE
BOAST	GET-DRESSED	STARVE
BREATHE	GUESS	SUFFER
CELEBRATE	HEAR/LISTEN	SURPRISE
COMPLAIN	IMPROVE	SWALLOW
CONFESS	KNOW	TELL-LIE
CREATE/INVENT	LAUGH	TEMPT
DESIRE	LIKE	THINK
DISIMPROVE	LOOK-BACK-ON/RECALL	THREATEN
DISOBEY/REBEL	LOVE	UNDERSTAND
DRINK	MEAN	VOLUNTEER
ENJOY	MISS	WALK
EXPECT/HOPE	NOT-CARE	WORRY
EXPERIENCE	OVERLOOK	YELL/SCREAM

When verbs like these are used in sentences, the Signer usually needs to explicitly mention the subject and/or object[11] (by signing the noun or by using a pronoun) since the verb itself cannot convey that information. For example, notice the difference between the two sentences below. In example (21), a directional verb (____-FORCE-____) occurs in the sentence, so it is not necessary to use separate signs to show who the Signer is talking about and which is the subject and which is the object. However, in example (22), the verb PUNISH cannot itself include this information, so the subject and object are signed separately.

Context   A teacher tells an aide what to do with a "problem student" named Pat.

(21)
$$\frac{\qquad}{\text{SUPPOSE}} \quad \frac{\text{(gaze lf)}}{\text{P-A-T}} \quad \frac{(\qquad\quad \text{neg)}}{\text{NOT-WANT}} \quad \frac{\text{cond}}{\text{WORK,}} \quad \frac{\text{tight lips}}{\textit{you-}\text{FORCE-}\textit{lf*}}$$

> *Struc*   'If Pat doesn't want to work, you *force* her to.'
>
> *Trans*   'If Pat doesn't want to work, then make her work.'

---

[11]Exceptions to this include situations where the referents and their grammatical roles are clearly understood from context, or when other devices such as body shifting (see next section) are used.

Context   (same as 21)

(22)   _____(neg)   cond   _____ tight lips
       SUPPOSE P-A-T NOT-WANT WORK, YOU PUNISH* INDEX-*lf*

    Struc 'If Pat doesn't want to work, you punish her.'

    Trans 'If Pat doesn't want to work, then punish her.'

This difference is also illustrated in example (23) where the Signer uses the directional verb ____-LOOK-AT-____ with both hands, meaning 'Mary watched the interpreter' and 'I watched the interpreter' (consequently, 'We watched the interpreter') without needing to again sign **M-A-R-Y**, **ME**, or **INTERPRETER**. However, with the verb **UNDERSTAND**, the subjects need to be signed again.

Context   A friend asks the Signer if he and Lee have started going to the new series of lectures on landscaping. The Signer says they have, but doubts that Lee will go again. The friend asks why, and the Signer responds:

(23)   _____t (gaze rt)   (gaze lf,cntr)
       ONE-WEEK-PAST,   L-E-E US-TWO-*rt*   GO-TO-*lf,cntr* LECTURE,

                      (gaze lf,cntr)nodding
       HAVE   INTERPRET   INDEX-*lf,cntr,*

       (head back,gaze up at lf,cntr) _____ nodding
       lee-**LOOK-AT**-*interpreter* ———————————→
       me-**LOOK-AT**-*interpreter*   **ME + UNDERSTAND,**

       _____neg
       INDEX-*lee* UNDERSTAND NONE

    Struc 'Last week, Lee and I went to the lecture. They had an interpreter there. Lee and I both looked at the interpreter. I understood, but Lee understood none of it.'

    Trans 'Last week Lee and I went to one of the lectures, and there was an interpreter there. We watched for awhile and I understood alright, but Lee couldn't understand anything.'

However, there is another rule in ASL which helps to reduce this need to continually re-state the subject of non-directional verbs. This rule has sometimes been called *the rule of last-mentioned subject*. That is, if several non-directional (or directional) verbs follow a subject noun, then that noun will be understood as the subject of all those verbs (unless clearly indicated otherwise). For example, in (24), the noun **P-A-T** is understood as the subject of the non-directional verbs **HAPPY**, **COMPLAIN**, and **REFUSE** because it (**P-A-T**) is the last-mentioned subject. Then a new subject, **L-E-E**, is signed, and the verb **EXCITED** refers to that new subject because it (**L-E-E**) is now the last-mentioned subject.[12]

---

[12]The reader may be confused by our calling the signs **HAPPY** and **EXCITED** "verbs". However, there is reason to believe that these signs are stative verbs which function as *predicate adjectives* (i.e. 'be happy'; 'be excited'). See Chapter XIII.

Context   The Signer is talking with a friend who wasn't at the club meeting yesterday. (Pat and Lee were both running for president.)

(24)
<u>   t</u>   (body lean rt   )nod
YESTERDAY   #CLUB   ELECTION,   L-E-E   PRESIDENT,

<u>   neg   </u>   <u>   rhet.q   </u>   <u>   neg   </u>
P-A-T   HAPPY,   (2h)alt.COMPLAIN,   REFUSE,

(body lean rt   <u>   t   </u>   <u>   nodding</u>)
          L-E-E,   EXCITED

> *Struc*   'Yesterday at the club election, Lee became president. Pat wasn't
> happy. But complain about it? He refused. Lee, she was really
> excited.'
>
> *Trans*   'At the club yesterday, Lee was elected president. Pat wasn't too
> happy about it, but wouldn't complain. As for Lee, she was really
> thrilled.'

C. Sign Order and Topicalization

Sometimes other grammatical devices are used to clarify the grammatical role of
nouns when the verbs are non-directional.[13] Two of these devices are *sign order* (the
actual order of the signs) and *topicalization* (described in Chapter VI).

For example, in the sentence that means 'Lee really loves Pat', if neither of the
nouns are topicalized (signed first with the *'t'* signal), then the sign order will be
Subject-Verb-Object, as shown in example (25). (Notice how the direction of the
Signer's gaze during the verb **LOVE** also helps to show who is doing the 'loving'—
i.e. who is the subject.) When the Addressee sees a sentence like this with the order
Noun-Verb-Noun, s/he will know that the first noun is the subject of the sentence.

Context   Someone asks the Signer if Lee loves Pat. The Signer answers:

(25)   (gaze rt) (gaze lf) nodding
          L-E-E-*rt* LOVE P-A-T-*lf*

> *Struc*   'Lee loves Pat.'
>
> *Trans*   'Lee loves Pat.'

However, even when the verb is non-directional, the order of signs does not have
to be Noun-Verb-Noun. For example, the object of the sentence can be topicalized.
That is, the object noun can occur first in the sentence with the grammatical signal
that shows it is a 'topic', as seen in example (26). Here the order is Noun-Noun-Verb
(Object-Subject-Verb). (Again, notice how the Signer gazes to the left—Pat's
location—during the sign **LOVE**.)

---

[13]These devices also occur with directional verbs. However, the focus of this section is to show how they
are especially useful in sentences with non-directional verbs.

Context   Someone remarks that Lee has been giving Pat gifts every day and that Pat's office is overflowing with those gifts. The Signer replies:

(26)   (gaze lf)t   (gaze rt)(body lean rt, facing lf)nodding
          P-A-T-*lf*,   L-E-E-*rt*   LOVE

          Struc   'Pat, Lee loves him.'

          Trans   'Lee loves Pat.'

However, if the order is Noun-Verb-Noun and the first noun is topicalized, then the Addressee will understand that the first noun is the subject of the sentence, *not* the object.

Context   Someone remarks that Pat has been giving Lee gifts every day and that Pat must be really fond of Lee. The Signer replies:

(27)   (gaze lf)t   (gaze rt)   nodding
          P-A-T-*lf*,   LOVE   L-E-E-*rt*

          Struc   'Pat, he really loves Lee.'

          Trans   'Pat really loves Lee.'

Linguistic research on the relationship between sign order and topicalization still leaves us with many questions about how these two grammatical devices function together in ASL. However, at present, we can see that they provide another way to clarify the grammatical roles of nouns in sentences with non-directional verbs.

D. Body and Gaze Shifting—"Direct Address"

Another common device that is used in ASL to show 'who does what' is *body and gaze shifting*. For example, the Signer may move his/her body to the left or to the right 'into' a location that represents someone. While 'in' that location, everything the Signer says or does reflects what that person says or does. When this kind of body shifting into a location (and looking *from* that location) is used, the Signer also tends to take on other affective or characteristic traits of the person (e.g. smiling or sighing when signing **LOVE**). This is because the message has become "personalized". The Signer has essentially assumed the role of that person and is signing as if s/he were that person.

This kind of body shifting is often used in what is called *Direct Address*. That is, the body shift has the effect of putting what is said "in quotes", indicating *what* was said and *who* said it. A few examples will make this clearer. In example (28), a 'boy' comes up to the Signer from the right. By body shifting into the location on the Signer's right and looking left, the Signer indicates that the boy is speaking and what he said ("You wanna fight?", etc.). Then by shifting back into the Signer's own normal position and looking right, the Signer becomes herself and indicates her own response ("Hah?! You're not worth it. Get outta here."). This body shifting then continues back and forth to represent the dialogue of the boy and the Signer. Below are two illustrations from the dialogue in example (28).

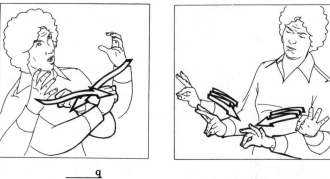

Boy says: $\overline{\text{FIGHT}}^{\text{q}}$ Signer replies: IT'S-NOTHING

Context   The Signer is describing an incident which happened to her when she was in school to a group of young children.

(28)

                                                       __t__ (gaze rt   )
REMEMBER   AWHILE-AGO   SCHOOL,   BOY,   1-CL'come up to me from rt',

(body shift rt;gaze up,lf   )q
WANT   FIGHT   WANT   FIGHT,

(body shift to cntr;gaze down,rt; frown   )
IT'S-NOTHING   "GO AWAY"   IT'S-NOTHING,

(body shift to rt;gaze up,lf;'angry'   )q (same   )
THINK   IT'S-NOTHING   ME   THINK   IT'S-NOTHING   ME,   OH-I-SEE,

(body shift to cntr; gaze down, rt; 'condescending')
IT'S-NOTHING   "GO AWAY",

(body shift to rt;gaze up,lf; 'glaring'   __t__   pow¡
FINE +   *me*-SAY-#OK-TO-*you*   IMPRESS-ON-MIND,   THREE-O'CLOCK,   *me*-HIT-*you**

Struc   'I remember awhile ago in school, this boy, he came up to me and said "You wanna fight? Wanna fight?" I said "You're nothing. Go away! You're nothing." He said "You think I'm nothing? Think I'm nothing? Oh, I get it." I said "You're nothing. Go away." He replied angrily, "Fine. Fine. O.K. I'll remember that. At three o'clock, I'm gonna really slug you." '

Trans   'I remember when I was in school, this kid came up to me and asked me if I wanted to fight. I said "Hah! You're not worth it. Get outta here." He started getting mad and said "So you think I ain't worth it, huh?" So I told him again to get outta here. Then he got really mad and said "All right! I'll remember that! At three o'clock I'm gonna punch yer lights out!" '

In example (28), notice that the Signer looked *up* as well as *left* when she was in the boy's location, and looked *down* as well as *right* when she was representing herself. This tells us that the boy was smaller than the Signer. It also illustrates how Signers can use the vertical plane (up-down) as well as the horizontal plane (left-right) to help identify who's talking. This vertical plane is often used when the people are at different heights or status—for example, when the dialogue is between an employer and employee, a teacher and student, a lecturer and audience, or a parent and child, as illustrated below in example (29).

Context   The Signer and a group of friends are discussing how funny some young Deaf children are. The Signer remembers a recent experience.

(29)

```
                           (gaze rt        )                    t (gaze rt)    mm
FUNNY*,  ONE-WEEK-PAST  INDEX-far,rt  CANDY  STORE,  ME  ENTER-rt,
```

```
(gaze rt,up          )  (gaze down,cntr                        )
INDEX-rt,up  MOTHER      INDEX-cntr  DAUGHTER  "WELL"  ABOUT-AGE-THREE,
```

```
              nod  (body shift to rt;gaze down,lf    )
THOSE-TWO-rt  DEAF,  MOTHER  (2h)"COME-ON"*++
```

```
(body shift to cntr;head back;eyes closed; 'pouting')
"hands on hips and shake head"
```

```
(gaze up,rt; 'pouting'                                        )
ME  MORE  INDEX-up  ME  MORE  INDEX-up  "hands on hips",
```

```
(body shift to rt;gaze down,lf; 'trying to be patient'                   )
MOTHER  (2h)"COME-ON"  HOME  TOMORROW+  "COME-ON"++  TOMORROW,
```

```
(body shift to cntr;head back;eyes closed; 'pouting'              )
"hands on hips and shake head"  ME  DECIDE  STAY  HERE  "hands on hips"
```

```
(body shift to rt;gaze down,lf)  (gaze at Addressee                   )
        "COME-ON",        FUNNY*  ABOUT-AGE-THREE  FUNNY*
```

Struc 'It was so funny! Last week there at the candy store, I casually went in, and there was a mother and her daughter, well, about three years old. The two of them were deaf. The mother said "Come on! Come on! Come on!" But the daughter put her hands on her hips, shook her head, closed her eyes, and pouted, saying "I want more of that. I want more of that" and put her hands back on her hips. The mother tried to be patient and said "Come on home. Tomorrow, tomorrow. Come on! Come on! Come on. Tomorrow." Again the daughter put her hands on her hips, shook her head, and said "I've decided to stay here" and put her hands back on her hips. The mother tried again—"Come on." It was so funny! About three years old! Funny!'

Trans 'This really funny thing happened last week at the candy store. I went in and saw this mother and her daughter, I'd say about three years old. Both were deaf. The mother tried to get her daughter to leave the store, but the little girl refused and kept saying that she wanted some more candy. The mother then said she could have some more tomorrow, but that she had to go home now. The little girl got real uppity and said "I've decided to stay here" and still refused to leave. Was that funny! A three year old kid! What a riot!'

Notice that by body shifting to the left and looking down and right, the Signer indicated that he was assuming the role of the mother talking to the child. By shifting back to the center and looking up and left, the Signer became the child talking to the mother. However, to indicate his *own* comments at the end, the Signer looked at the Addressee again.

This type of *Direct Address* narrative is used much more commonly in ASL than in English. (As shown in the translation of this example, English speakers tend to say things like 'The mother tried to get her daughter to leave the store, but the little girl refused' rather than give an exact quotation.) Again, we see that the use of gaze direction and body shifting for "role playing" is but one more way that ASL takes advantage of the space around the Signer's body for grammatical purposes.

E. Summary

This chapter has attempted to describe some of the ways that ASL indicates the grammatical role of nouns in sentences. These ways include the use of verb modulations, sign order, topicalization, and body shifting. This description is far from complete, and the teacher will need to use his/her intuitions for the types of examples not covered in this chapter. Hopefully, continuing linguistic research will clarify and increase our understanding of this important area in the grammar of ASL.

Bibliography: Subjects and Objects

Edge, V. & L. Herrman. 1977. Verbs and the determination of subject in American Sign Language. In L. Friedman (Ed.) *On the Other Hand: New Perspectives on American Sign Language.* New York: Academic Press, 137–179.

Fischer, S. 1973. Sign Language and linguistic universals. Paper presented at the Colloque franco-allemand sur la grammaire transformationelle du francais, Berlin, April.

Fischer, S. 1975. Influences on word order change in American Sign Language. In C. Li (Ed.) *Word Order and Word Order Change.* Austin, Texas: University of Texas Press, 1–25.

Fischer, S. & B. Gough. 1978. Verbs in American Sign Language. *Sign Language Studies 18,* 17–48.

Friedman, L. 1976. The manifestation of subject, object, and topic in American Sign Language. In C. Li (Ed.) *Subject and Topic.* New York: Academic Press, 125–148.

Klima, E. & U. Bellugi. 1979. *The Signs of Language.* Cambridge, Massachusetts: Harvard University Press.

Padden, C. 1979. A look at agreement and advancement in ASL. MS, Department of Linguistics, University of California, San Diego.

Woodward, J. 1973. Implicational Lects on the Deaf Diglossic Continuum. Unpublished Ph.D. dissertation, Georgetown University, Washington, D.C.

Dialogues
and
Cultural Information

SUBJECTS AND OBJECTS

The following three dialogues have been developed to illustrate various uses of the grammatical features described in this chapter. Each of these dialogues also appears in one of the three corresponding Student Texts. In the Student Texts, the transcription of each dialogue is less detailed than what is provided here for the teacher of ASL. Following the dialogues, in the sections called "Cultural Information", are brief discussions of the topic of each dialogue.

The following dialogues and cultural information correspond to:

Student Text: Unit 4
Unit 13
Unit 22

Dialogue: Subjects and Objects
(Student Text - Unit 4)

First Signer (Pat)

Pat₁: "UMMM"+, <u>MOTHER FATHER DEAF YOU</u> ^q

Pat₂: <u>neg</u>
     "NO-NO", HEARING, BROTHER SISTER SAME-AS HEARING   <u>nodding</u>

Pat₃: "WELL" <u>NOT-KNOW</u>, <u>MY MOTHER</u>, <u>NOT-KNOW</u> INDEX-*lf*,

with markers: neg over NOT-KNOW; t over MY MOTHER; neg over NOT-KNOW

ME *me*-ASK-TO-*mother*, <u>NOT-KNOW</u> INDEX-*mother*,

with markers: (gaze lf) over ME ... ; neg over NOT-KNOW

<u>SEEM MEDICINE INFLUENCE-*mother*</u> SEEM++

with marker: tight lips

Pat₄: <u>nodding</u> <u>PAST MOTHER</u>, BECOME-SICK,   INDEX-*mother* (2h)**FROM-*lf*-GO-TO-*rt* HOSPITAL**,

with markers: t over PAST MOTHER; (gaze lf) over INDEX-*mother*

                              ***INDEX-rt*,**

<u>DOCTOR</u> (2h)alt.SEARCH-*mother* INVESTIGATE-*mother*++, MEDICINE *doctor*-GIVE-TO-*mother*,

<u>FINISH</u>, FROM-*hospital*-GO-TO-*lf* HOME <u>FUTUREwg</u>, ME <u>BORN</u>, DEAF,

with markers: br over FINISH; (gaze lf) over FROM...; t over FUTUREwg; br over BORN

                     INDEX-lf,   ***"WELL"***

Pat₅: <u>SIGN</u>, <u>(2h)"NO-NO"</u>, <u>DOCTOR *doctor*-TELL-TO-*lf*</u>, <u>SIGN</u>, *doctor*-SAY-#NO-TO-*lf*,

with markers: br over SIGN; neg over (2h)"NO-NO"; rhet.q over DOCTOR ...; (gaze lf)t over SIGN

IMPORTANT ORAL+ BETTER*, "WELL"

Dialogue: Subjects and Objects
(Student Text - Unit 4)

Second Signer (Lee)

Lee₁:

nodding   (nod lf)t   (nod rt)t
MOTHER FATHER DEAF, BROTHER-*lf* TWO-*lf,* DEAF, SISTER-*rt* ONE-*rt,* DEAF,

puff.cheeks   q
#ALL-*arc* DEAF, YOUR MOTHER FATHER DEAF YOU

Lee₂:

wh-q
HOW HAPPEN DEAF HOWwg

Lee₃:

t   (nodding   )q
MEDICINE, DOCTOR *doctor*-GIVE-TO-*mother*

Lee₄:

q
YOUR MOTHER FATHER SIGN

Lee₅:

th   th neg
DOCTOR SILLY*, KNOW-NOTHING DEAF KNOW-NOTHING

Dialogue: Subjects and Objects
(Student Text - Unit 13)

First Signer (Pat)

Pat₁:
$$\overline{\phantom{YOU\ \ AWHILE\text{-}AGO\ \ SCHOOL\ \ ORAL\ \ RIGHT\ \ }}^{\text{q}}$$
YOU AWHILE-AGO SCHOOL ORAL RIGHT YOU

Pat₂:
$$\overline{\phantom{\#DO\text{-}DO\ \ ORAL\ \ SCHOOL\ \ }}^{\text{wh-q}}$$
#DO-DO ORAL SCHOOL #DO-DO

Pat₃:
              ('smile')q   wh-q
TEACH͡AGENT SIGN INEPT, RIGHT, HOWwg UNDERSTAND HOWwg

Pat₄:
                  cond   q
SUPPOSE WRONG, TEACH͡AGENT *teachers*-HELP-*you*

Pat₅:
               t
ORAL, READ-*lips*, (2h)#NG, BETTER SIGN BETTER

Pat₆: (2h)"WELL" (signed with Lee's "WELL")

Dialogue: Subjects and Objects
(Student Text - Unit 13)

Second Signer (Lee)

Lee₁:
<u>nodding</u>   (gaze rt)
RIGHT, INDEX-*rt* NEW-YORK, RIGHT YOU

Lee₂:
               <u>t</u>
"PSHAW" AWFUL, SIGN, NOT-LEGAL,

                         <u>t</u>
TEACH AGENT INDEX-*arc-rt*, *teachers*-FORCE-*me* ME SPEAK"*over & over again*",

                          <u>cond</u>   <u>pow</u>
SUPPOSE ME REFUSE ME *me*-SAY-#NO-TO-*teachers*, (2h)BECOME-ANGRY INDEX-*arc-rt*

Lee₃:
        <u>nodding</u>
"WELL" HARD+, ME READ-*lips*,

    (gaze up,rt; 'struggling to understand'   )
ME *me*-LOOK-AT-*teacher*"*over time*" READ-*lips* (2h)alt.GUESS,

               <u>cond</u> (gaze lf   )   <u>t</u>
SUPPOSE ME WRONG, CHILDREN-*lf* INDEX-*arc-lf*,

children-MAKE-FUN-OF-*me* *children*-TEASE-*me*, "WELL" HARD (2h)"PSHAW"

Lee₄:
           <u>t</u>   <u>puff.cheeks</u>
"WELL", SOMETIMES, *teachers*-BAWL-OUT-*me*"*regularly*",

         <u>t</u>   <u>puff.cheeks</u>
SOMETIMES, *teachers*-CRITICIZE-*me*"*regularly*",

EVERY-DAY TEACH AGENT *teachers*-TELL-*me*"*over & over again*"

    (gaze up,rt   )sta (gaze up,rt   )sta
MUST PRACTICE"*over & over again*" STUDY"*over & over again*"

Lee₅:
<u>nodding</u>
ME *me*-AGREE-WITH-*you* ME,

         (gaze lf & rt   )   <u>rhet.q</u>   <u>puff.cheeks</u>
EVERY-DAY CHILDREN SCHOOL FINISH, OUT-OF-*school*, USE-ASL "WELL"

Note: In Lee₅, the segment that is transcribed as a 'rhetorical question' might instead be analyzed as a 'topic'. We do not presently know which is correct.

Dialogue: Subjects and Objects
(Student Text: Unit 22)

First Signer (Pat)

Pat_1:
        co   wh-q
"HEY",   (2h)WHAT'S-UP   SAD,   (2h)WHAT'S-UP

Pat_2:
                         q
*me-**PITY**-you*,   *UNCLE OLD*

Pat_3:
            t   q
UNCLE DIE,   HAVE INSURANCE

Pat_4:
     t   (gaze lf   )   wh-q
DIE,   MONEY   C-CL-*lf→rt*'take money from Frat' ⟶
                                               "WHAT"

Pat_5:
TOUCHING "WOW",   TOUCHING "WOW"

Dialogue: Subjects and Objects
(Student Text - Unit 22)

Second Signer (Lee)

```
                              ____t____ (head tilt rt        )qt
Lee₁:   PAST  ONE-MONTH  UNCLE,  MOTHER  BROTHER,  DIE,  MOTHER  BREAK-DOWN*
```

```
        __neg__                  ____puff.cheeks____  _____rhet.q
Lee₂:     AGE-FIFTY  SIXTY  THEREABOUTS,  MOTHER  DEPRESSED  REASON
```

```
        (gaze rt                                    puff.cheeks)
        THOSE-TWO-rt  they-CLASH-WITH-"each other"+"regularly"  MANY*  YEAR  UP-TILL-NOW,
```

```
        (gaze rt          )nodding                                       ____t____            ____neg
        SEEM  they-HATE-"each other",  (2h)NOW  MOTHER  BAWL-EYES-OUT,  ME  UNDERSTAND  ME
```

```
        ____nodding____  _____q_____
Lee₃:   FINISH++,  KNOW+F-R-A-T,  UNCLE  JOIN-rt  LONG-TIME-PAST  NINETEEN  FIVE  ONE
```

```
Lee₄:   (gaze rt              )    (gaze rt              )
        MOTHER  TTY-CALL-TO-frat,  INFORM-frat  UNCLE  DIE,
```

```
        (gaze rt,cntr; body shift rt        )  (gaze rt                                )
        INDEX-rt   frat-SAY-#OK-TO-mother,  TWO-FULL-WEEK  they-CORRESPOND-WITH-"each other",
```

```
        _____cs+t  (gaze rt      )
        ONE-DAY-PAST,  MONEY-rt  frat-GIVE-TO-mother,
```

```
        (gaze rt look at money 'anguished'      )
        MOTHER                          BAWL-EYES-OUT
                C-CL-rt→lf 'take money from Frat',
```

```
                        (gaze rt          )
Lee₅:   MOTHER  CONSCIENCE,  (2h)HATE-rt  UNCLE,
```

```
        (look at money 'anguished'                    )
        TAKE-pile of money-FROM-frat  MONEY  PILE-OF-money,  BAWL-EYES-OUT-rt  CONSCIENCE++++
```

Student Text: Unit 4

Cultural Information: Causes of Deafness

When examining the factors that cause deafness (i.e. the etiology of deafness), it is useful to look at three general categories: factors prior to birth, factors during the time of birth, and factors during childhood, adolescence, and adulthood. Deafness prior to birth (*congenital deafness*) is generally due to one of two causes—heredity or rubella. Heredity, or genetic factors, has been the leading cause of deafness in the twentieth century, except during rubella epidemics. In fact, approximately 50–60% of all deafness can be attributed to genetic factors. There are approximately 55 known forms of genetic deafness; ten of these also involve both hearing loss and visual difficulties. The second cause of congenital deafness is rubella. The most recent epidemic of rubella in the U.S. was between 1963 and 1965. Rubella is usually responsible for 10% of the instances of congenital deafness. However, during this epidemic, the percentage increased to approximately 50%. In addition to deafness, rubella can also cause visual problems and heart defects.

Prematurity and blood type incompatibility are the most frequent causes of deafness during the time of birth (the perinatal period). Approximately four times more deaf children than non-deaf children are born prematurely. Factors such as loss of oxygen and cerebral hemorrhage (which can cause damage to the nervous system) are more common among premature babies than full-term babies. Rh blood type incompatibility is the second cause of *perinatal deafness*. In such cases, the newborn baby is severely jaundiced. In such a condition, death may result. Of those babies who survive, a high proportion are deaf.

After the perinatal period, there are several other potential causes of deafness. In later childhood, meningitis and encephalitis may cause deafness. About 10% of deafness in children is caused by meningitis—which is an inflammation of the protective coverings of the brain and spinal cord. Deafness can also occur if virus-causing mumps, measles, etc., infect the brain and cause encephalitis. Additionally, there are other adventitious causes of deafness, such as damage to the auditory nerve or eardrum caused by putting foreign objects in the ear, sudden loud noises, or blows to the skull.

A very common distinction which is used in discussing the onset of deafness is whether a person was prelingually or postlingually deafened. This refers to whether or not deafness occurred before or after the acquisition of a language. In the past, however, ASL was not recognized as a language and this distinction only referred to acquisition of spoken English. Thus, many Deaf children who were native users of ASL (i.e. they had Deaf parents and they knew ASL) were incorrectly categorized as prelingually deafened because they did not know English.

Student Text: Unit 13

Cultural Information: Oral Schools and Programs

Oralism can be defined as an approach to communicating with deaf individuals (students or adults) through the use of speech, speechreading (lipreading), and hearing aids. People who advocate such an approach are often called *oralists*. Schools and programs which support this approach and use it as the primary means of communicating with deaf students are referred to as oral schools or oral programs. In most oral programs, the use of Sign Language or signing of any type is generally forbidden, and graduates of such programs report that they were often punished if teachers caught them signing or gesturing.

In the past (and even now), discussions about how to teach deaf students have quite often focused on the "oral-manual controversy"—with one group supporting the use of oral methods of education and the other supporting the use of some form of manual communication. During the eighteenth century, the major points of this controversy were expressed in an exchange of letters between Samuel Heinicke (founder of an oral school in Leipzig, Germany) and Abbé Charles Michel de l'Epée (founder of a school which used signs in Paris, France). Interestingly enough, when Thomas Gallaudet went abroad in 1815 to learn about methods for educating deaf students, he went to oral schools in Great Britain (the Braidwood Schools) before he went to de l'Epée's school in Paris.

The first oral school for deaf students in the United States—the Clarke School—was opened in Massachusetts in 1867. By the 1880's, there were eleven strictly oral schools in America. This growth was due, in large part, to the work and efforts of Alexander Graham Bell—who was an avowed oralist. Bell, whose wife was deaf, not only opposed the use of Sign Language but he also opposed intermarriage among deaf people. Bell donated a substantial portion of his fortune to oral schools and programs.

In 1890, an organization was established for teachers of deaf students and others who support oral methods of teaching deaf children. This organization, the Alexander Graham Bell Association for the Deaf (AGB), has as one of its main goals to aid schools in their efforts to teach speech, speechreading, and the use of residual hearing. The *Volta Review* is a regular publication of the AGB. For more information, contact: The Alexander Graham Bell Association for the Deaf, Inc., The Volta Bureau, 1537 35th Street, N.W., Washington, D.C., 20007.

Student Text: Unit 22

Cultural Information: The Fraternal Society of the Deaf (FRAT)

In 1901 at a Michigan School for the Deaf alumni reunion, an idea took hold that led to the establishment of the Fraternal Society of the Deaf during that same year in Chicago, Illinois. At that time, deaf individuals were discriminated against by insurance companies that made them pay higher premiums than were paid by hearing people. Thus, this group of deaf individuals worked out a way to provide for their own insurance by establishing their own organization—the National Fraternal Society of the Deaf (NFSD or the "FRAT"). Initially, membership in the FRAT was limited to adult males only, who paid $5.00 per week for sickness and accident benefits.

In 1904, the organization began its own official publication—a magazine called *The Frat*. By 1929, membership had grown to 6800 and by the end of the Depression years, its treasury had approximately two million dollars. In 1936, the FRAT remodeled a building which it owned and had its first fully-owned Home Office in Oak Park, a suburb of Chicago. In 1955, a new Home Office was built in Oak Park and housed the Home Office until 1975 when the FRAT moved to Mt. Prospect, Illinois.

Today the FRAT has over 13,000 members, seven million dollars in assets, and over 17 million dollars worth of insurance in force. Women now make up 35% of the total membership since they were permitted to join in 1951. There are more than 100 trained field representatives in the FRAT who are qualified to sell insurance. For more information, write: NFSD, 1300 W. Northwest Highway, Mt. Prospect, Ill. 60056.

Chapter X

Classifiers

A. Information

ASL has a fairly large set of signs that are called *classifiers*. Linguists[1] have found that there are at least two types of classifiers: (a) classifiers in which a particular handshape (with a particular palm orientation) is used to represent a noun and can indicate the location of that noun and its actions, if any, and (b) classifiers that illustrate certain physical features of a noun as well as indicate its location in space. This second type of classifiers have been called *size and shape specifiers* or SASSes.

Although classifiers are very frequently used in ASL, the linguistic analysis of classifiers is still in its beginning stages. In this chapter, we will describe some of the important things that linguists have learned about these two types of classifiers to date. However, the teacher will need to supplement this description with the intuitions and knowledge of various native users of ASL until a more detailed linguistic analysis of classifiers is available. The first part of this chapter will focus on classifiers that represent the locations and/or actions of nouns; the second part will focus on classifiers that describe certain physical characteristics of nouns.

B. Classifiers that Represent Nouns: Functions

Some classifiers are like *pronouns* in that they stand for a particular group of nouns. For example, the English pronoun 'she' can stand for nouns like 'woman', 'waitress', and 'Queen Elizabeth', but not nouns like 'man', 'waiter', and 'Sir Henry Morgan'. Similarly, the ASL classifier that we gloss as 3→CL (CL = classifier) can represent an inanimate, land or water conveyance—e.g. a car, bus, truck, van, boat, or submarine—but not a person, animal, or plant. Thus, one reason these signs are called *classifiers* is because they stand for a particular group or "class" of nouns.

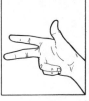

3→CL

Like pronouns, these classifiers generally cannot be used in a sentence until the Signer indicates which particular referent (e.g. my sister's car) the classifier stands for.[2] This is usually done by signing or fingerspelling the noun and then using the classifier that can represent that noun. For example, the Signer might sign **#CAR RED** and then use the classifier 3→CL in a particular location. Since classifiers that function as pronouns usually are made with only one hand, the other

---

[1]Klima & Bellugi (1979), Supalla (1978).

[2]There are a few exceptions to this general rule—for example, sometimes the A-CL is used in a general sense to mean a 'thing', as in having 'things all over the room', in which case the particular referents are not specified. This unspecified use of a classifier occurs more frequently when the referent is plural, as seen in the example of 'things all over the room'—(2h)alt.A-CL.

hand can be used to represent another noun. Then the Signer can illustrate the relative locations and/or actions of two referents. This is done by positioning the classifiers in particular locations in space and then moving them around in relation to each other. This is illustrated in the next two examples.

In the first example, each hand (3→CL) shows the location and actions of a particular car. The left hand represents the 'red car'; the right hand represents the 'orange car'. By moving these classifiers in space, the Signer shows how the orange car crashed into the side of the red car.

Context   A friend comes to visit the Signer and notices a red car parked up on the sidewalk in front of her house. The car is all banged up, and the friend asks what happened to the car. The Signer replies:

(1)
$$\overline{\hspace{6cm}}^{\,t}$$
MORNING,   #CAR   RED,

(gaze lf)   (gaze rt)t (eyes follow orange car _____)pow
                 ORANGE,   3→CL-*rt* 'move to lf and crash into rt side of red car'
         3→CL @lf ————————————————————————————→

Struc   'This morning, the red car, it was here on the left. An orange one, it came up from the right and crashed into the passenger side of the red car.'

Trans   'This morning an orange car smashed into it.'

3→CL-*rt* 'move to lf & crash into side of other car'
3→CL-*lf* ————————————————————————→

The '3→' classifier also appears in the next example and its meaning is understood from the sign **DRIVE**. That is, either the Addressee will know exactly what was driven (e.g. a car or van) because of acquaintance with the Signer's vehicle, *or* specific knowledge about what was driven is not considered to be important to understand the meaning of the sentence, and the Addressee will simply know that the Signer is talking about a motorized land vehicle. In this example, the classifier 1-CL is also used. This classifier represents a person, and in this case, represents a 'girl'.[3] By using the 1-CL on the left hand and the 3→CL on the right hand, the Signer illustrates an event in which his vehicle moved from the right toward the girl on the left and almost hit her, but swerved just in time to miss hitting her.

1-CL

Context   At work, the Signer seems distracted and upset. An officemate asks if anything is the matter. The Signer says "Well, sorta" and explains:

(2)
$$\overline{\text{MORNING,}} \quad \text{ME} \quad \overline{\text{DRIVE+,}} \quad \overline{\text{HAPPEN,}}$$
t   mm   rhet.q

(head rt,'unattentive')(look of 'shock')
GIRL   3→CL-*rt*'car almost hit girl, swerve around & move outward'
     1-CL-lf'walk outward' ⟶

BY-A-HAIR "WOW"

Struc. 'This morning, I was driving along as usual, and what happened? A girl walked right out in front of my car—(I didn't notice her). I suddenly saw her just in time and swerved around her. Missed her by a hair. Whew!'

Trans   'This morning I was just driving along and didn't see this girl walk right out in front of my car. When I suddenly saw her, I swerved around and just missed her. It was a real close call! Phew!'

Examples (1) and (2) illustrate several important things about classifiers. First, they illustrate how classifiers function as *pronouns*. But these pronouns are more specific than pronouns in English. For example, whereas English uses the pronoun 'it' to refer to a car, a stone, a tree, a book, etc., ASL uses a different classifier to represent each of these things.

Secondly, the examples above show how classifiers can function as *verbs*. For example, in (1), the 3→CL on the right hand 'crashed into' the 3→CL on the left hand. In example (2), the 1-CL on the left hand 'walked forward' and then the 3→CL on the right hand 'swerved around the girl'.

Thirdly, classifiers can convey information about the 'manner' of an action—information that would normally be expressed with an *adverb* in English. For example, in (1), the movement of the 3→CL on the right hand could have been 'fast'. And we saw that it hit 'hard' or 'crashed' into the left hand 3→CL. (This is also

---

[3]The 1-CL can also be used to represent an animal in situations where the animal assumes human-like characteristics—e.g. telling the story of *The Tortoise and the Hare*.

shown with the facial response 'pow'.) In example (2), the 3→CL could have 'abruptly swerved in a wide arc' around the girl.

Fourthly, classifiers give information about the *location* of the referents and their actions. (See Chapter XI on Locatives.) For example, in (1), the classifiers show that the red car is 'on the left', the orange car is 'on the right', and then the orange car hits the red car 'on the right side of the car'. Here the palm orientation of the classifiers is important for indicating exactly where the red car was hit. The fingertips represent the front of the car, and the palm side and the back (dorsal) side of the hand represent different sides of the car. On the right hand, the palm represents the driver's side; on the left hand, the palm represents the passenger's side of the car. So by moving the fingertips of the right 3→CL into the palm of the left 3→CL, the Signer shows that the front of the orange car hit the passenger side of the red car. Similarly, in the second example, the palm side of the 1-CL represents the front (face) side of the girl who walks out in front of the car that is moving toward her. She doesn't see the car; that is, the 1-CL faces outward, not right (toward the car). The driver suddenly sees her, and by moving the right hand 3→CL toward and then quickly around the left hand 1-CL, the Signer vividly illustrates the changing spatial relationship between the car and the girl.

In these ways, we see that classifiers enable the Signer to show the spatial relationship between different people or things. They also enable the Signer to use the signing space to illustrate the actions of people or things.

Some classifiers represent things that normally do not move by themselves. These classifiers are often used to show the location of something in relation to something else. For example, the classifier 1→CL is often used to represent things like a 'pencil, rifle, cigarette, closet rod, cannon, log, pole (on its side), hot dog, and needle'.[4] In example (3), the 1→CL represents a 'cigarette' that Lee found on his desk under some papers. Another classifier, B↓-CL, also appears in this example. This classifier can represent things like a 'sheet of paper, bed, kite, leaf, package of meat or shirts, or racing boat'. In example (3), the B↓-CL represents a 'piece of paper'. By using this handshape (B↓-CL) on both hands (with an alternating movement) in the location that represents the 'desk', the Signer shows that there were 'papers strewn atop the desk'.

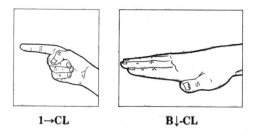

1→CL   B↓-CL

---

[4]Moveable variants of this classifier can also represent a leg, penis, or rocket.

Context   The Signer and a friend are talking about an officemate, Lee, who is a
chain smoker. The Signer says:

(3)

                                    t
     ONE-DAY-PAST L-E-E, THIRST* CIGARETTE,

     (gaze rt   )   (gaze down   )   t
            GO-TO-*rt* TABLE, (2h)alt.SEARCH, PAPER,

     (gaze down   )
     (2h)alt.B↓-CL'papers strewn atop desk',   (2h)alt.GRAB-*papers*-AND-TOSS-ASIDE

     (look of 'discovery')   pah
                             SUCCESS   1→CL@*cntr*'on desk'
     GRAB-paper-AND-HOLD────────────────────────────→

   Struc   'Yesterday Lee, he craved a cigarette. He went to his desk[5] and
             started looking all around. Papers, they were strewn all over the
             top of the desk. He grabbed the papers one after the other, tossing
             them aside, until he picked one up and saw something under it. At
             last, there was one on the middle of his desk.'

   Trans   'Yesterday Lee wanted a cigarette real bad. He rummaged
             through the papers that were scattered all over his desk and was
             throwing them left and right until he finally found one.'

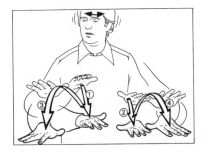

(2h)alt.B↓-CL

   The 'B' handshape with palm up (B↑-CL) can also represent things like a 'book,
piece of paper, or a pan'. Like the classifiers 3→CL and 1-CL, the orientation of the
palm is important for showing the orientation of the object. For example, if the
B↑-CL is used to represent a piece of paper on a desk, it usually indicates that the
'front side' of the paper is facing upwards. However, although the B↑-CL usually
indicates that the top/front side of something is facing 'up', the B↓-CL does not
always imply that the object is facing 'down'. For example, the use of the B↓-CL
in (3) did not mean that all of the papers were 'face down'. To specify
that some papers are 'face down', the Signer would need to add
some other indication of this. For example, if the Signer were a
teacher telling some students to turn their papers over 'face down'
after finishing an exam, the Signer would begin with the **'B'**
handshape with the palm up and rotate it to palm down.

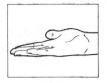

B↑-CL

───────────────
[5]From the context, we can assume that the sign TABLE refers to Lee's desk.

In example (4), the **B↑-CL** is used to represent a 'pie' that is put into the oven to bake. (If the Signer mistakenly used the 'palm down' (**B↓**) handshape, then the Addressee would naturally expect that the contents in the pie pan would spill out—since the palm represents the inside bottom of the pan.)

Context   Someone asks the Signer, a novice cook, what she did last night. The Signer replies by giving a step-by-step account.

(4)

```
                   t                          t    (gaze rt         )
PAST NIGHT,  MAKE  P-I-E,   FIRST,  EGG-rt,  MILK-rt,  VARIOUS-THINGS-rt,

(gaze rt                mm      )nod   (gaze lf)        t   (gaze lf      )
(2h)alt.DROP-things-IN-rt  FINISH,       O-V-E-N-lf,  "turn on oven",

                    nod+br    (gaze lf              )(gaze rt→lf        )
WAITwg"regularly",  TIME*,                          B↑-CL'put pie in oven'
                               "open oven door & hold"——————————→

                                  nod+br
             WAITwg"regularly"   FINISH*,
"close oven door",

(gaze lf                                      ) (look of 'satisfaction')
                  B↑-CL'take pie out of oven & hold'
"open oven door & hold"——————————→
```

Struc   'Last night, I made a pie. First, the eggs, milk, and other things, I dropped them into (the container) and finished (that part of the process). Then the oven, I turned it on and waited for awhile. When it was the right time, I opened the oven door, put in the pie, and then closed the oven door. I waited awhile until it was done, then opened the oven door, took the pie out, and proudly held it.'

Trans   'Last night I made a pie. First I put in the milk, eggs, and all the other ingredients. Then I turned on the oven and waited until it was the right temperature. Then I put the pie in, waited until it was done, and then proudly took out my pie.'

Another classifier is made with a 'bent-V' handshape (V:-CL). This classifier can represent a 'chair' or a 'person who is seated'. The classifier can also move in specific ways to represent the movements of various animals—for example, a 'cat, dog, mouse, snake, horse, or cow'.

In example (5), the classifier is used on both hands to represent the 'two chairs' and to illustrate the relationship between them and the 'window'.

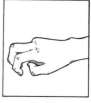

V:-CL

Context   Yesterday the Signer went to visit her brother's new apartment. She tells her roommate: (This is just the beginning of the description of his apartment.)

(5)

$$\overline{\quad\quad\quad t \quad\quad\quad}$$
BROTHER   A-P-T,   NICE*

$$\overline{\quad\quad\quad br \quad\quad\quad}$$ (gaze down)   (gaze down)   (gaze rt)
WINDOW-*cntr,outward,*   CHAIR   TWO   V:↓-CL@*rt,cntr* ⎫ 'facing window', #TV-*rt.* . . . .
                                    V:↓-*CL* @*lf,cntr* ⎭

> *Struc*   'My brother's apartment, it's really nice. There's a window, and there are two chairs that are positioned next to each other, facing the window. There's a T.V. . . .'
>
> *Trans*   'My brother's apartment is really nice. He's got two chairs facing a window, a T.V. . . .'

In the example above, the chairs are located in an area closer to the Signer's body than the area at which the window was signed. Similar to the 1-CL and the 3→CL, the orientation of the 'bent-V' handshape indicates the orientation of the object that is represented by the V:-CL. Thus, by having the bent fingers next to each other and facing toward the space in which the sign WINDOW was made, the Signer can indicate that the chairs are next to each other and facing the window. (In addition, the 'palm down' orientation of this classifier shows that the chairs are right-side-up, not turned over—which would be shown by using the classifier in a different orientation.) Again, we can see how classifiers very graphically illustrate the precise relationships between objects or persons by using the space around the Signer's body and varying their distance from each other and particular orientation.

To represent a 'person standing', the V-CL is used. When motion is added (alternately moving the fingers back and forth), the classifier can represent a 'person walking'. This is illustrated in example (6). Here the V-CL (with alternating index and middle fingers) moves from the right to the left to express the meaning 'she walks from her house to the school'.

V-CL

> *Context*   The Signer and some friends are talking about their problems with carpooling to school every day. The Signer remembers another friend's, Pat's, situation and says:

(6)

$$\overline{\quad t \quad}\quad\quad\overline{\quad\quad rhet.q \quad\quad}$$
P-A-T,   LUCKY,   WHYwg,

(gaze lf   )br   (gaze rt   )br   (gaze lf→rt   )
SCHOOL-*lf,cntr,*   HOUSE-*rt,cntr,*   NOT-MUCH   INDEX-*lf→rt,*

$$\overline{\quad\quad\quad\quad\quad t \quad}$$ (gaze rt→lf   )
EVERY-MORNING,   V-CL'walk from house to school'

> *Struc*   'Pat, he's lucky. Why? The school's here, and her house is here. They are not far from each other. Every morning, she walks from her house to the school.'
>
> *Trans*   'Pat's lucky because she doesn't live far from the school and walks there every morning.'

In example (6), the location of the 'school' was established at the left-center area by making the sign **SCHOOL** in that location; similarly, the 'house' was established at the right-center area by making the sign **HOUSE** in that location. These two things are positioned close to each other in the signing space to show that the actual 'school' and 'house' are close to each other. Then the **V-CL** (representing 'Pat') moves from one location to the other to show what Pat does.

Big things like a 'city, mansion, boulder, island, or large heap of something' can be given a location by using the classifier **5:↓-CL**. Example (7) illustrates how this classifier can be used to show the relative locations of two cities.[6]

5:↓-CL@rt

Context   The Signer is the manager of two shoe stores—one in Washington, D.C. and the other in Baltimore. He is visiting an uncle in Texas who asks him how he manages stores in different cities. The Signer explains:

(7)

```
                              t  (gaze rt    )nod                       t  (gaze lf)nod
KNOW   WASHINGTON_D-C,           5:↓-CL@rt
                                                        BALTIMORE-lf,   5:↓-CL@lf,———→

        (gaze back & forth between cities )
NOT-MUCH   INDEX-washington & baltimore↔,   EVERY-DAY
                                                          ↗

                                                  mm
ME   COMMUTE-BETWEEN-washington & baltimore↔
```

Struc   'You know Washington, D.C., it's here, and Baltimore, it's here. They are not far apart from each other. Every day I regularly commute between the two cities.'

Trans   'You know Washington, D.C. and Baltimore aren't far apart. I commute every day.'

---

[6]The last sign in this example has an 'A' handshape and is a "conventional" verb made from the A-CL (see Section F).

Note   In this example, **INDEX**@*rt* and *INDEX* @*lf* could be substituted
for 5:↓-CL@*rt* and *5:↓-CL* @*lf*.

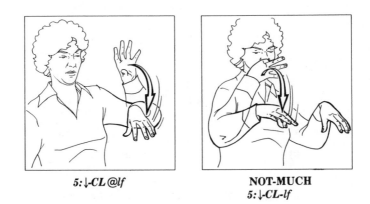

5:↓-CL @*lf*	**NOT-MUCH**
	5:↓-CL-lf

Most of the classifiers in ASL are singular; they represent *one* person (e.g. 1-CL),
one animal (e.g. V:-CL), *one* place (e.g. 5:↓-CL@*rt*), or *one* thing (e.g. 3→CL). But
suppose the Signer wants to represent more than one thing in space. How would this
be done?

C. Pluralization

(C.1) Singular Classifiers

As we saw in several of the preceding examples, one way to represent more than
one thing in space is to use classifiers on both hands. This enables the Signer to
represent the locations and actions of two referents.

However, there are also several ways to represent more than two things with a
singular classifier. Two of these ways involve some form of repetition. That is, the
Signer will repeat the movement of the classifier, each time giving it a different
location. (This is explained in greater detail in the chapter on Pluralization.) This
repetition can be done mainly with the dominant hand, or with alternating
movements of both hands (both having classifier handshapes).

However, these two types of repetition have different meanings. When both hands
are used in an alternating manner, it indicates that the referents are located in
several or many different places and *not* in a neat arrangement. That is, this 'two
hands alternating' movement indicates that the people or things are in a random
(unorganized) arrangement. The next example illustrates this way of indicating
many referents with a singular classifier handshape. In this example, the 'A' handshape classifier is used to represent the 'trophies' and 'statues' that are located in a

bar. Other things which the **A-CL** can stand for are a 'coffee mug, bottle, vase, can, thermos, lamp, and building' (located far away).[7]

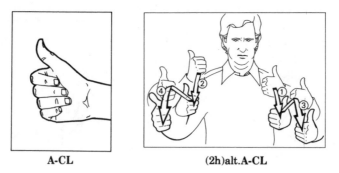

A-CL   (2h)alt.A-CL

Context   The Signer is trying to convince a group of friends to go to a particular bar.

(8)   (gaze rt   )   ___puff.cheeks
              FINEwg,   B-A-R   INDEX-*rt*,   DECORATED,

                              ___puff.cheeks
              TROPHY,   STATUE,   (2h)alt.A-CL

  Struc   'It's really nice. The bar over there, it's really well decorated. It has trophies and it has statues—lots of them all around.'

  Trans   'It's really a neat bar. It's fixed up with lots of trophies and statues all around the place.'

Below are two more illustrations of this 'two hands alternating' plural modulation with two other classifiers: 1→CL and C-CL. The illustration of '(2h)alt.1→CL' shows what a Signer might do when describing 'pencils strewn across a desk'. The illustration of '(2h)alt.C-CL' shows what a Signer might do when describing 'pictures on walls'. With this palm orientation, the classifier C-CL can represent things like a 'picture, card, or poster'. (With the palm orientation seen in the sign CUP, the C-CL can represent things like a 'bottle, jar, can, vase, ashtray, thermos, and glass'.)

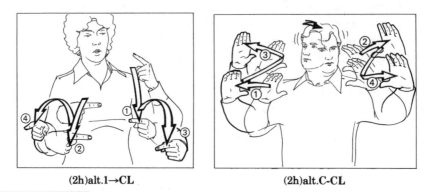

(2h)alt.1→CL   (2h)alt.C-CL

---

[7]See Section E on how the choice of which classifier to use often depends on the "perspective" of the Signer.

When the Signer wants to indicate that the referents are arranged in an *orderly* configuration, for example 'in a row', s/he will repeat the classifier in a straight line with the dominant hand. Often the non-dominant hand (with the classifier hand-shape) 'holds' the starting place of the line while the dominant hand makes each separate 'articulation' (production) of the classifier—each time moving to a slightly different location. This plural modulation (that we refer to as *"in a row"*) can be diagrammed as follows:

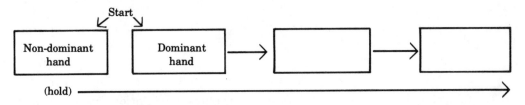

For example, to indicate that there are several pencils lined up in a row, the Signer can use the plural modulation illustrated below.

(2h)1→CL*"in a row"*

This process can be repeated to show, for example, 'several things in rows'. (The way that ASL distinguishes between 'three things in a row' and 'several things in a row' is explained in Chapter XII.)

To show that there is more than one row of things, the Signer can use repetition of the classifier in more than one row. This plural modulation (that we refer to as *"in rows"*) can be diagrammed as follows:

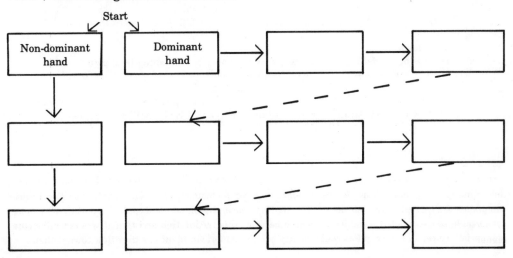

For example, to indicate that there are rows of statues on the wall, the Signer can use the plural modulation illustrated below.

(2h)A-CL*"in rows"*

The following example illustrates a use of this plural modulation (*"in rows"*) with the classifier ⼾-CL. This classifier can be used to represent a 'plane, glider, or jet'. In example (9), using the ⼾-CL with the *"in rows"* modulation expresses the meaning 'planes neatly lined up in rows'. Several other classifiers also appear in this example: 1→CL, 4→CL, and 5↓-CL. The classifier 1→CL represents a 'bomb' and is repeated to express the meaning 'several bombs (falling)'. The other two classifiers are plural classifiers and are described in Section (C.2). Here the plural classifier 4→CL represents 'many bombs'; the plural classifier (2h)5↓-CL represents 'many airplanes flying (overhead)'.[8]

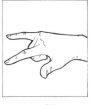

⼾-CL

Context   Some young children are talking about their favorite war films and the Signer remembers a recent T.V. show about Pearl Harbor.

(9)

<pre>
                        ___q___
REMEMBER   #TV +,

                        ___t___   (gaze down   )
JAPAN   AIRPLANE,   (2h)5↓-CL-*up,rt*'fly to up,cntr' (2h)LOOK-AT-*down,lf,*

              ___t__ (gaze down   )puff.cheeks   (gaze down   )
AMERICAN,   (2h) ⼾-CL-*lf,cntr"in rows"*,   (2h)5↓-CL'fly over American planes'

(gaze down   )
1→CL +'bombs falling from plane'   4→CL +'many bombs falling from plane'
⼾-CL'plane' ——→

(gaze down   ) ('grimace'   )('whew')
(2h)4→CL +'long strings of bombs falling from plane'   EXPLODE + + + +-*lf,cntr,*
</pre>

---

[8]For readers who have the accompanying videotape: Notice that the Signer uses her non-dominant (left) hand to 'locate' each plane ((2h)⼾-CL-*lf,cntr"in rows"*) instead of her right hand. Since the American planes are located in the left area of the signing space, the Signer said that it was *physically* more comfortable to use her left hand as the active hand in this modulation and that it was *visually* more appropriate so the Japanese pilots could clearly see the American planes as they flew toward them.

Struc 'Remember on the T.V.? The Japanese airplanes, a fleet of them was flying over from the right and the pilots looked down. The Americans, there were lots of[9] airplanes neatly lined up in rows on the ground. The fleet of Japanese airplanes flew over the American planes and dropped several bombs, then many bombs, then torrents of bombs, one right after the other and the American planes exploded in quick succession. Whew!'

Trans 'Remember that T.V. program where the Japanese air fleet flew over and saw the American planes lined up in rows down on the ground. So the Japanese started dropping all those bombs, tons of 'em, and blew them to smithereens! Wow!'

However, if the Signer wants to indicate that there are *many* things in a row, s/he would probably use what we call a "sweep". Here, instead of making several separate articulations of the classifier, the hand moves ('sweeps') straight across the row. This plural modulation (that we refer to as *"sweep in a row"*) is diagrammed below:

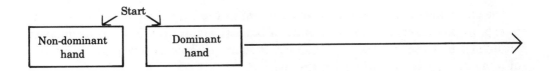

For example, to indicate that there are many vases lined up in a row on a shelf, the Signer could use the plural modulation illustrated below.

(2h)**A-CL**"*sweep in a row*"

To show 'many things in rows', the Signer would repeat this "sweep" more than once, each time in a different location in space. This plural modulation (that we refer to as *"sweep in rows"*) is diagrammed on the next page:

---

[9]The meaning 'lots of' is also expressed with the *'puffed cheeks'* signal.

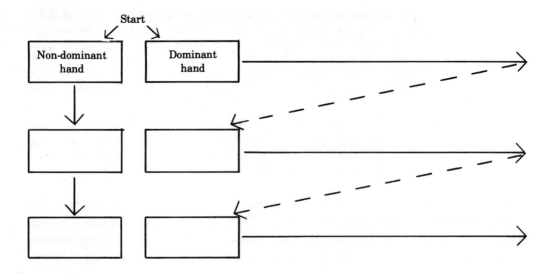

The plural modulation described above might be used, for example with the **A-CL**, to express the meaning 'rows and rows of bottles'. Using this "sweep" modulation would also indicate that there are many bottles in each row. Below is an illustration of what this would look like with the **A-CL**.[10]

(2h)**A-CL**"*sweep in rows*"

(C.2) Plural Classifiers

As we have just seen, ASL has several processes for pluralizing singular classifiers. However, ASL also has a small number of classifiers which are themselves plural; that is, they represent more than one thing. There are two types of plural classifiers: those which represent a specific number of referents, and those which represent 'many' things or people.

---

[10]Note the physical resemblance between the illustration of this modulation and the illustrations of **EVERY-ONE-WEEK** and **EVERY-THREE-WEEK** in Chapter VII.

The *specific-number classifiers* use the handshapes for numbers (e.g. '2', '3', '4', '5') and, like the 1-CL, represent a specific number of people (or animals). These specific-number classifiers are illustrated below.

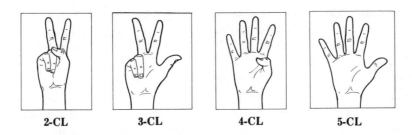

2-CL   3-CL   4-CL   5-CL

Example (10) illustrates how these specific-number classifiers can be used to indicate the location and actions of more than one person. Notice that because these classifiers 'incorporate' the number of referents, it is not necessary to use a separate number sign (e.g. **TWO**) to convey that information.[11] In this example, the 2-CL represents the 'two boys' that demand money from the Signer. This example also illustrates the use of eye gaze and body shifting to "role play" various people in a narrative (as described in the preceding chapter).

2-CL'come up to me from rt'

Context   A friend has heard that the Signer was almost robbed yesterday and asks the Signer about it. The Signer replies:

(10)

                <u>   mm   </u>   (gaze rt   )
YESTERDAY   ME   WALK*"regularly"*,   BOY   2-CL'come up to me from rt',

(body shift to rt;gaze up,lf   )   (gaze down rt;body shift to lf)
   "GIMME"   MONEY   "GIMME"   MONEY,   ME   "WHAT",

(body shift to rt;gaze up,lf   )   (gaze down rt;body shift to lf)
   "GIMME"   MONEY   "GIMME",   ME   "WHAT",

                  <u>   pow   </u>
BOY   (2h)BECOME-ANGRY

---

[11]However, if the Signer wants to emphasize the number because, in that context, the number has special significance, then s/he might use a separate number sign.

Struc   'Yesterday I was walking along as usual when two boys came up to me from the right. "Give us your money!", they said. I said "Huh?" (I didn't understand what was going on.) "Give us your money!" "Huh?", I said. The boys became really angry.'

Trans   'Yesterday I was walking along when these two boys came up to me and started telling me to give them my money. But I didn't understand what they wanted, and those guys got really mad.'

The next example also shows how these plural classifiers can be used to show the location and actions of specific numbers of people. For example, by using both hands, the Signer can then indicate the actions of two groups of people. In example (11), the right hand **3-CL** represents the Signer and her two friends while the left hand **3-CL** represents the Signer's younger brother and his two friends.

Context   The Signer's nephew is complaining about his younger brother. The Signer is sympathetic and laughingly remembers her own younger brother.

(11)   _____ nodding
       REMEMBER   AWHILE-AGO   ME   AGE͜TWELVE+,

                              _____ nod   ___ nod   (gaze rt   )t   ____ nod
       FRIEND   TWO   P-A-T-*rt,cntr***   L-E-E-***rt,***   US-THREE-***rt,***   GOOD-FRIEND-***rt,***
                 INDEX-rt —————————→

(body face lf,gaze lf   ) (body face lf   )
BROTHER-*lf***   INDEX-***lf***   TWO-***lf***   FRIEND-***lf***   THOSE-THREE-***lf***   AGE͜SEVEN-***lf***   THEREABOUTS,**

(body face lf   )
ALWAYS   *they-***BOTHER-***us"over time",***

_____ (gaze rt)   cond
SUPPOSE   US-THREE-*rt***   WALK   3-CL**'walk forward', ————————————→
                                                             _____ th
                   3-CL'closely follow us'   *they-***BOTHER-***us"over time"***

Struc   'Yeah, I remember awhile ago when I was twelve years old. I had two friends—Pat and Lee. The three of us, we were really good friends. My brother and his two friends—those three were about seven years old—were always bothering my friends and me. If the three of us went out walking, the three of them would follow us closely and bother us continuously.'

Trans   'I remember when I was twelve, I had two friends—Pat and Lee. The three of us were really close. My brother and his two friends were about seven and they were always bothering us. Like if the three of us were out walking around, those three would tag right along behind us and bother us constantly.'

So far we have said that from one to five specific individuals can be represented on each hand by using one or more of the classifiers in which each upright finger represents a person.[12] However, when both hands (with either the '4' or '5' hand-shape, fingers upright) are used *together*, they no longer represent a specific number of individuals, but represent a group of many individuals. That is, when both hands act together using a 4-CL or 5-CL, they represent the location and/or movements of a large group.[13] In addition, when the hands are used together like this, they indicate that the members of this group are in a particular, orderly arrangement—i.e. in some kind of row. For example, in (12), the '(2h)4-CL' represents a 'long line of people'.

Context   The Signer has been complaining about feeling bored. A friend asks him if he went out last night. The Signer shakes his head and explains:

(12)   _____t   (gaze rt   )
              PAST̰ NIGHT,   ME   GO-TO-*rt*   MOVIE,

              (gaze rt;look of 'surprise')br   puff.cheeks
                            ARRIVE,   PEOPLE-*rt*   (2h)4-CL-*rt*'long line',

              (gaze rt)
                    ME   "PSHAW"-*rt*   GO-*lf*   HOME

        Struc   'Last night, I went to the movies. When I got there, Wow! there were lots of people in this long line. I said, "Phooey!" and went home.'

        Trans   'Last night I went to the movies. But when I got there, there was a mob of people waiting in line. So I said, "The heck with that!" and went home.'

Whereas the (2h)4-CL and (2h)5-CL represent rows of people who are standing, the classifiers glossed as 4:-CL or 5:-CL can be used to represent people who are seated. The movement and palm orientation of the classifier will indicate the arrangement of the people and the direction they are facing. That is, as we saw in example (2) where the 1-CL represented a girl who faced outward and didn't see the oncoming car, the palm orientation of the plural classifiers will also indicate the direction that the people are facing (from the Signer's perspective). For example, if the people have their backs to the Signer, the palms of the classifiers will face outward. Or, if the people are seated in a semi-circle facing the Signer, the palms of

---

[12]Some native Signers also use the '6', '7', '8' handshapes as classifiers which represent that number of people.

[13]These two '4' and '5' handshape classifiers seem to be used in very similar contexts. The choice of which one to use may be influenced by the form of the referent, ease of production, or simply be a matter of individual variation.

the classifiers will initially face the Signer. These two possibilities are illustrated below.

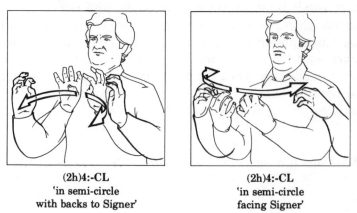

(2h)4:-CL
'in semi-circle
with backs to Signer'

(2h)4:-CL
'in semi-circle
facing Signer'

In addition, this (2h)4:-CL classifier can be used to describe an arrangement of many animals. For example, it could indicate that the dogs at a dog show are lined up in a circle, waiting for their turn to perform. Or, it could indicate a large row of birds perched on a telephone line, as illustrated below.

(2h)4:-CL
'birds on telephone line'

Another complex set of (non-specific number) plural classifiers is created by changing the palm orientation of the '4' and '5' handshapes so that the palm faces downward.[14] These are written as 4↓-CL or 5↓-CL when the fingers are straight, and 4:↓-CL or 5:↓-CL when the fingers are bent. In addition, the 4↓-CL and 5↓-CL can be changed so that the individual fingers 'wiggle' (bending at the first joint)— written as 4↓wg-CL or 5↓wg-CL. These plural classifiers are illustrated below.

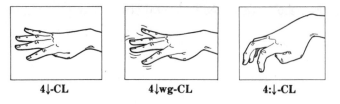

4↓-CL   4↓wg-CL   4:↓-CL

---

[14]Actually, the palm orientation may vary according to the location of the mass of things it is representing. For example, to represent 'stars in the sky', the palms would face upward with the hands above the Signer's head. Or, to represent a 'crowd in a stadium', the palms would follow the inside contours of the stadium.

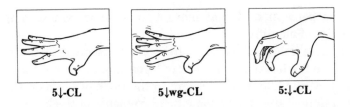

5↓-CL   5↓wg-CL   5:↓-CL

These plural classifiers can occur with either one or two hands; generally, the use of two hands means the group is *very* large. They can also represent a variety of things (e.g. cats, rocks, stars, chairs, shoes, insects), not just people. The particular choice of plural classifier (e.g. 4↓-CL, 4↓wg-CL, or 4:↓-CL) depends on (a) the perspective of the Signer, (b) if the group of things is moving or not, and (c) if the things are arranged in a particular order or not.

For example, if the Signer signed COW and then the classifier (2h)5:↓-CL, the meaning would be 'there is a huge herd of cattle'. This classifier does not indicate if the cattle are stationary or moving; it could be used in either case and only indicates that there is a 'huge herd'. If the Signer wants to specify that the cattle are 'milling around', s/he would use the classifier (2h)5↓wg-CL (perhaps with both hands overlapping each other repeatedly). If something happens that frightens the cattle, they would stampede away in an unorderly manner—(2h)5↓wg-CL 'moving outward'. As the herd drew back together and ran further away, the Signer is less able to see individual cows or steers, and they appear more like a huge moving mass—which would be indicated with (2h)5↓-CL.

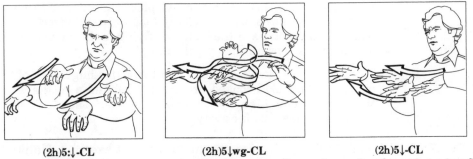

(2h)5:↓-CL   (2h)5↓wg-CL   (2h)5↓-CL
'huge herd of cattle'   'cattle milling around'   'mass of cattle moving outward'

Thus, we see that both the 5↓wg-CL (or 4↓wg-CL) and the 5↓-CL (or 4↓-CL) are used to show that a huge group of things is *moving* (and how or where it is moving). The decision concerning which of these classifiers is used depends on (1) if the group is moving in an orderly manner *or* is so far away that disorderly movement is not seen and instead appears more 'smooth' (use 4↓-CL or 5↓-CL), or (2) if the group is moving in a disorderly manner and the Signer can see that disorderly movement (use 4↓wg-CL or 5↓wg-CL).[15] Thus, the type of movement (if any) of the referents

---

[15]Returning to the example with the upright (2h)4-CL that represented many people: if this 'wiggling' motion is added to the classifiers (palms facing and touching each other), the meaning of 'many people milling around' (moving in an unorganized manner) is conveyed.

and the Signer's perception of that movement is important in determining the appropriate choice of classifier.

All three of these 'mass' plural classifiers are illustrated in the next example. Here they indicate the location of a 'flock of birds' and represent the actions of that flock.[16] Notice that the '(2h)5:↓-CL' refers to the flock of birds on the ground; the '(2h)5↓wg-CL' refers to the sudden, chaotic movements of the birds as they take to flight; and the '(2h)5↓-CL' refers to the huge mass of birds as they fly far away.

Context   The Signer is describing what he did in the park yesterday.

(13)   —————t—————   —————————————————mm—————————————————
         YESTERDAY, ME   WALK   1-CL'walking outward',

         ("double take" to rt)   ————(gaze rt——————————)intense
            LOOK-TO-*rt*+   BIRD   (2h)5:↓-CL-*rt*'huge flock of birds',

            (look around)   (look around)   (gaze lf   ) (gaze rt   )
         ME SEARCH ROCK ME SEARCH PICK-UP-*rock-lf* THROW-*rock*-AT-*birds*,

            ———t—— (gaze rt——————————)pow (gaze up,rt———————)puff.cheeks
         BIRD,   (2h)5↓wg-CL-*rt*'burst up into air' (2h)5↓-CL-*up,rt*'wings flapping'

         (gaze up,rt   )
         (2h)5↓-CL-*up,rt*'flying far away'

> *Struc*   'Yesterday, I was casually walking along when I suddenly saw, on the right, birds—a huge flock of them on the ground. I looked around for a rock, looked and looked, picked one up and threw it at the birds. The birds, they suddenly took off in all directions in a panic, then the mass of them started flying in the same direction, and the flock flew off into the distance.'

> *Trans*   'Yesterday I was walking along and I saw this huge flock of birds on the ground. So I looked around 'till I found a rock and then threw it at them. Man, did those birds scatter! They took off into the air and flew far, far away.'

The (2h)5:↓-CL and (2h)5↓wg-CL also appear in the next example. Unlike the example with the birds, the 5↓-CL is not used after the 'cats scatter away' since, logically, cats do not tend to run or move in groups, but as individuals. (As described in the chapter on Pronominalization, notice how the Signer changes her perspective. First the window is to the right; then the cats and the window are located in the center area as the Signer gives a "close up" account of what happened.)[17]

---

[16]The (2h)5↓-CL'flapping' means that the Signer added a bending movement at the wrists which seems to iconically represent the flapping of the birds' wings. We have only seen this variation used when talking about 'birds flying'. For readers who have the accompanying videotape: Notice that the (2h)5↓wg classifier that represents the birds 'bursting up into the air' is also sometimes glossed as SCATTER or SPLATTER (depending on the context).

[17]We apologize for the unkind actions towards birds and cats in these examples! Our intention is simply to illustrate the specific uses of these classifiers.

Context   Someone asks the Signer how she likes the new neighborhood. She says it's OK, except for a few minor problems—for example:

(14)
```
                              t   (close eyes)   ___rhet.q  (close eyes) (open eyes suddenly)
PAST  WEDNESDAY,  ME  SLEEP,  HAPPEN,      ME        "be jostled awake",
```

```
(close eyes) (open eyes) (gaze rt)                (gaze rt) (look of 'dismay'      )
   ME     WAKE-UP    GO-TO-rt  WINDOW-rt,     "push back curtains"-rt
```

```
                                    intense        (look around)
CRAZY,   CAT   (2h)5:↓-CL-cntr'horde of cats',  ME   "WELL"
```

```
(gaze lf)                          (gaze lf                        )
      NOTICE-TO-lf  SHOE-lf,      ME  me-PICK-UP-shoe,  (2h)"open window"-cntr,
```

```
('angrily'                )                                            pow
me-THROW-shoe-AT-cats,   CAT   (2h)5↓wg-CL-cntr'cats suddenly scatter away'
```

> *Struc*   'Last Wednesday, I was asleep. What happened? I was suddenly startled by something and I woke up. I went to the window and pushed back the curtains. Good Grief! There was a huge horde of cats out there! I looked around for what to do and saw a shoe on my left, so I picked it up, opened the window, and threw it at the horde of cats. The cats suddenly took off in all directions.'

> *Trans*   'Last Wednesday while I was asleep, something startled me. I woke up, went to the window, pushed back the curtains, and yikes! There were zillions of cats out there! So I looked around and saw a shoe, picked it up, opened the window, and threw it at those cats. And man! Did they scatter!"

Another classifier which can be used to represent a 'group' of people or things is made with both hands with 'C' handshapes—(2h)C-CL'group'. It is frequently used for setting up groups in different spatial locations and can also be moved as a verb. This classifier is frequently glossed as **CLASS**. In the following example, this classifier represents a group of 'senior-year students' and moves to show what they do ('go to New York')—which we gloss as **GROUP-GO-TO**-*lf*.

Context   The Signer and friends are discussing where they should go for their class trip. Someone asks where the Juniors and Seniors went last year. The Signer replies:

(15)
```
                                            t   ___puff.cheeks
ONE-YEAR-PAST  SENIOR-YEAR  (2h)C-CL'class',  GROUP-GO-TO-lf  NEW-YORK-lf
```

> *Struc*   'Last year's senior class, they went as a group to New York.'

> *Trans*   'Last year's senior class went to New York.'

This classifier can also be varied to show the relative size of the group. A relatively small group could be represented by having the fingers together (on each hand) and by having the two hands close together, perhaps even overlapping. A relatively larger group could be represented by having the fingers more spread apart (with '5' handshapes) and the hands more separated from each other—i.e. the further apart the hands, the larger the group.

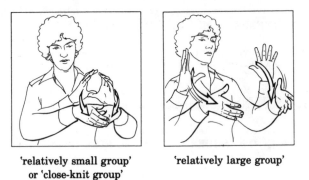

'relatively small group'
or 'close-knit group'

'relatively large group'

Summary: Singular and Plural Classifiers

As stated earlier, the majority of classifiers are singular—i.e. they represent the location and/or movements of one person or thing. These singular classifiers can be made plural by: (a) using both hands such that each hand represents one thing (meaning 'two things'), (b) using both hands with an alternating movement (meaning 'things in a disorderly arrangement'), or (c) using both hands with a repeated or 'sweeping' straight-line movement (meaning 'several' or 'many', 'things in a row' or 'things in rows').

Some classifiers are plural—i.e. they are used to represent the locations and/or movements of more than one thing. Some of these classifiers represent a specific number of people. Many of the plural classifiers use some form of the '4' or '5' handshapes and can represent large groups of people, animals, or things. The choice of which of these classifiers to use seems to depend on how the Signer perceives the movement and arrangement of the things they refer to.

D.   Size, Shape, Depth, and Texture: Descriptive Classifiers

In the preceding sections, we have presented a sample of classifiers which can represent a wide variety of nouns. For example, the A-CL can represent a coffee mug, trophy, statue, bottle, lamp, house, etc.—things that vary considerably in size and shape. Similarly, the 5:↓-CL can represent a huge mass of things including mice, birds, people, cattle, paper clips, rocks, trees, and houses. Other classifiers are more restricted in the things they can represent. For example, the 1→CL tends to represent things that are longer than wide and relatively slender—e.g. a pencil, rod, rifle, log, cigarette, and needle, but *not* a table, house or railroad car. However, most of the classifiers presented so far do not give much attention to the actual size, shape, etc., of the thing they represent. The 3→CL can represent a Volkswagen or a Cadillac. The 1-CL can represent a child or a Harlem Globetrotter. With these classifiers, the focus is on showing the relative locations and movements (if any) of the things they stand for.

However, ASL also has classifiers which can be used to describe the particular size, shape, depth, and/or texture of something as well as give it a relative location in space. In this way, these descriptive classifiers are often like adjectives. Like the other classifiers, they can represent or describe several different things, but all of these things must share certain features.

For example, something which is small, roundish, and does not have much depth (e.g. a coin, spot, piece of candy, eye, coke bottle top, poker chip, small cookie, or button) can be represented with the classifier F-CL. When the F-CL is used after a noun has been signed, it then gives more information about the size, shape, and relative depth of that noun. For example, using the F-CL after the sign CANDY would indicate that the Signer is talking about a 'small piece' of candy, *not* a box of candy or a candy bar. Similarly, using the F-CL after the sign PAPER would mean a 'small, round piece' of paper, *not* a sheet or strip of paper. (Each of these other things—e.g. 'candy bar' or 'sheet of paper'—would require a different classifier.)

Classifier handshapes like the F-CL can also be used in verbs like ____-PICK-UP-____, ____-TAKE-____, and ____-POUR-FROM-____. (See Chapter IX for more information on these verbs.) These verbs have the same basic movement. However, the handshape used with these verbs will vary according to certain physical characteristics of the referent (e.g. the thing that is 'picked up'). For example, when the referent of the verb ____-PICK-UP-____ is a marble, a coin, or a button—one of the things that can be represented with the F-CL—either the 'F' handshape or a variant of the 'F' handshape (i.e. no contact between thumb and index finger) will be used in the verb. We refer to this variant as the 'open-F' handshape. Both the F-CL and the verb *me*-PICK-UP-____ with the 'open-F' handshape are illustrated below. These are also used in example (16) to represent a 'quarter' (coin) and the actions of 'picking up the quarter' and 'putting it in the Signer's pocket'.

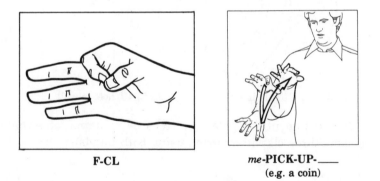

F-CL   *me*-PICK-UP-____
                                        (e.g. a coin)

Context   A friend sees the Signer buy a candy bar from the machine and says "Hey! I thought you told me you were broke!" The Signer says he "was", but this afternoon he was with some friends and . . .'

(16)

                <u>   mm   </u> (suddenly gaze down,rt   )

ME   CHAT*"regularly"*,   "do a double take"   NOTICE-TO-*rt*   F-CL-*rt*   SHINY-*rt*,

(gaze down,rt   )

    ME   *me*-LOOK-AT-*shiny thing*   *me*-PICK-UP-*shiny thing* ———————→

                                              TWENTY-FIVE-CENTS,

<u>   mm   </u>

me-PUT-*quarter*-IN-*rt pocket*

> *Struc*   'I was chatting as usual and then did a "double take" when I noticed to the right something small and round that was shiny. I looked over at it and picked it up. It was a quarter. So I casually put it in my right pocket.'
>
> *Trans*   'I was chatting away when suddenly a shiny thing on the ground caught my eye. When I picked it up, I found that it was a quarter. So I just put it in my pocket.'

Sometimes several different classifiers can represent the same kind of thing. However, other specific characteristics of that thing will determine which one of the classifiers will be used to represent it. For example, another thing the **F-CL** can represent is a 'hole'. However, two other classifiers—(2h)**L:ₜ-CL** and (2h)**Cₜ-CL**— can also represent a 'hole'.[18] What is different about the holes described by each of these classifiers? (Consider the size and depth of each hole.)

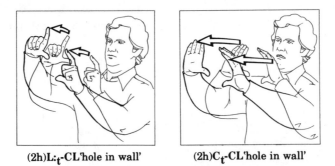

        (2h)L:ₜ-CL'hole in wall'   (2h)Cₜ-CL'hole in wall'

Or, what is different about the 'poles' (or 'trees' or 'columns', etc.) that are represented by the same three classifiers (each using both hands)?

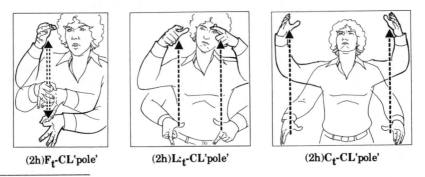

   (2h)Fₜ-CL'pole'   (2h)L:ₜ-CL'pole'   (2h)Cₜ-CL'pole'

---

[18]The 't' subscript means that the hands act 'together' to represent the same thing—as opposed to acting separately to describe two things.

The pole on the left is very slender—perhaps the width of a pencil or maybe a little bit wider. Notice that the non-dominant hand basically moves upward, indicating that the thing being described is 'straight' and 'tall'. This classifier (as well as the 'open-F' classifier and O-CL) does not require that the hands move together since each hand alone can encompass and 'hold' the thing.

However, the second and third poles are too wide to be encompassed by one hand, so both hands must move together to outline these poles. Although the (2h)L:$_t$-CL and (2h)C$_t$-CL are often used interchangeably for certain medium-size things, the pole with the (2h)C$_t$-CL is clearly seen as larger than the pole illustrated with the (2h)L:$_t$-CL.[19] Note that these classifiers are accompanied by different facial expressions which also illustrate the size (width) differences.

On the following pages each of these two-handed classifiers are used in sentences. In the first example, the Signer uses the (2h)F$_t$-CL several times above her head to describe the kind of light that has long, slender, cylindrical bulbs—i.e. fluorescent lights.

Context   Someone remarks that the Signer's eyes look really "glassy". The Signer responds:

(17)   nodding   th   rhet.q
           TRUE+, EYES VAGUE, REASON,

                 (gaze up,rt   )
           LIGHT   (2h)F$_t$-CL++-*up,rt*'bulbs'   *lights-*BOTHER-*me"regularly"*,

                                     t
           ONE   (2h)F$_t$-CL-*up,rt*'bulb',   BAD*

           (head turned away from lights   )
           *bad bulb-*FLICKER-AT-*me*++   *bad bulb-*BOTHER-*me"regularly"*

    Struc 'Yeah, that's true. My eyes are really blurry. The reason? The fluorescent lights keep bothering me. One of the bulbs, it's really bad. It flickers on and off repeatedly and keeps bothering me.'

    Trans 'Yeah, that's for sure. My eyes are really blurry because of the fluorescent lights. One of the bulbs is really bad and keeps flickering on and off and bothering me.'

In the next example, the (2h)F$_t$-CL describes a horizontal rod in a car—i.e. a clothes rack. The classifier X-CL (which often represents things like a 'hook' or a 'hanger') also appears in this example. First the X-CL is used on both hands simultaneously to indicate that the clothes rack hooks onto the sides of the car. Then the Signer switches from describing the clothes rack with the (2h)F$_t$-CL to representing it with the one-handed 1→CL—which can be moved in space. The X-CL then 'hooks onto' the 1-CL and represents a hanger. By moving both of these 'attached' classifiers from left to right, the Signer shows that the referent 'clothes' is plural (i.e. many hangers of clothes on the rack).

X-CL

---

[19]Some Signers also use the 'open-F' handshape in contexts where other Signers use the 'bent-L' (L:-CL) handshape.

Context   The Signer is planning to drive some expensive costumes up to Boston for
a new play. A friend asks how he's going to keep them from getting
wrinkled in his car. The Signer responds:

(18)
$$\overline{\text{MY} \quad \text{CAR,}}^{\text{t}}$$
MY   CAR,   HAVE   NEW   (2h)F$_t$-CL'horizontal rod'

X-CL-*rt*'hook onto right side of car',
X-CL-lf 'hook onto left side of car',

$$\overline{\text{KNOW+ \quad CLOTHES \quad X-CL-}\textit{lf}\text{'hook on rod'}}$$

KNOW+   CLOTHES   X-CL-*lf*'hook on rod' $\Big\}$ move lf→rt, $\overline{\text{KNOW}}^{\text{qt}}$ $\overline{\text{YOU}}^{\text{q}}$ ...
                1→CL-*lf 'clothes rod'*

> *Struc*   'My car, it has a new horizontal rod that hooks onto each side of
> the car. You know, clothes on hangers hang across the rod, you
> know what I mean?'...
>
> *Trans*   'My car's got a new rod that hooks onto each side. You know the
> kind for hanging clothes?'...

Since ASL does not have a specific sign that means 'clothes rack', the Signer in this
example described the object and then checked with the Addressee to see if s/he
understood the description. Classifiers that describe certain features of an object are
often used like this—when there is not one particular sign for that particular thing.

In the next example, the (2h)L:$_t$-CL represents a particular facial expression (like
putting a mask on one's face). It is round (as fitting the face) and does not have much
depth (as something on the surface of the face).

Context   The Signer and a group of friends have just seen a play. A friend of theirs,
Pat, was in the play.

(19)
$$\overline{\text{P-A-T,}}^{\text{t}} \quad \overline{\text{REALLY-ADEPT \quad DRAMA, \quad REALLY-ADEPT}}^{\text{(gaze rt)}} \quad \overline{\text{INDEX-}\textit{rt},}^{\text{nodding}}$$

ME   REMEMBER   PAST+   INDEX-*rt*   DRAMA,   P-A-T   (2h)BECOME-ANGRY,

$$(2h)\text{L:}_t\text{-CL@'on face'} \quad \text{CONTINUE} \quad \overline{\text{FOR-HOURS-AND-HOURS}}^{\text{nodding}}$$

> *Struc*   'Pat, he's really skilled at acting; he's really skilled. I remember
> awhile ago in a play, Pat became really angry and had that ex-
> pression on his face which lasted for hours and hours.'
>
> *Trans*   'Pat's a superb actor, really good. I remember him getting angry
> once in a play and holding that expression for hours and hours.'

In the next example, the (2h)C$_t$-CL indicates the width of a huge tree which is
pulled out of the ground and thrown. To represent the tree flying away into the
distance, the Signer uses the 1→CL (pointing outward)—which is smaller (as the
tree would seem to the eye at a distance) and only requires one hand (which makes it
more moveable in space).

Context   The Signer is a young girl who saw a great show on TV last night. She
asks her girlfriend:

(20)

                                                                    q
SEE   MOVIE   PAST NIGHT,   SIX   MILLION   DOLLAR   MAN,   (Girlfriend: "No")

(look of 'sheer delight')   t   (gaze rt)(gaze lf)
    FINEwg,   MAN,   (2h)BECOME-ANGRY,

         t (gaze lf   ) (gaze rt)pow
TREE-*lf*, (2h)C$_t$-CL-*lf* 'pull tree out of ground & heave it to rt'

(gaze rt   )
1→CL-*up,rt* 'tree sailing far away'

Struc   'Did you see the movie last night, the "Six Million Dollar Man"? It
was really great! The man, he became really angry. So he looked
around and saw this tree on the left. The tree, he pulled it out of
the ground and threw it far away and it sailed way out into the
distance!'

Trans   'Did you see the "Six Million Dollar Man" last night? It was terrific! He got really angry, ripped up this tree, and threw the whole
thing away! That tree went sailing way out there!'

Another descriptive classifier is used when referring to relatively small, rectangular things, such as 'checks, index cards, name cards, credit cards, Lego Blocks,
bricks, tiles, invitations', etc. This classifier, written as RECT-CL (for 'rectangular'), is usually made with both hands acting together to outline the rectangular
shape of the object. The Signer can vary the size of this 'outline' to indicate more
precisely the size of the rectangular thing—e.g. a smaller outline for a 'Lego Block'
and a larger outline for a 'check'.

RECT-CL

In the next example, the RECT-CL is used to refer to the Visa credit card.
However, when the Signer wants to move the 'card' in space to show what happened
(i.e. gave the card to the man), she switches to a one-handed classifier, the B↑-CL, to
represent the card. This is like the switch from the two-handed C$_t$-CL to the one-
handed 1→CL to represent the movement of the 'tree' in example (20).

This interaction of two-handed and one-handed classifiers is very common in ASL.
Two-handed classifiers are often used to more exactly describe something (e.g. huge
tree, Visa card). After that more specific description has been communicated, then a

less specific, one-handed classifier can be used to represent that thing (e.g. tree, card)—and can be more easily moved in the signing space to show the actions of the referent.

Context The Signer and a friend are talking. The Signer is worried that there's something wrong with her credit rating. For example . . .

(21)

                     t   nodding
ONE-WEEK-PAST, WANT BUY COLOR #TV, WANTwg ME,

                                nodding   q (Friend:"Yes") nod
HAVE V-I-S-A RECT-CL'card', KNOW+ YOU ————————→,

     (gaze lf   )   (gaze down   )
ME   *me*-GIVE-*card*-TO-*lf*, MAN USE-CHARGE-PLATE FINISH,

     (gaze lf;body lean lf   )
man-PICK-UP-*telephone*-*lf* "talk on phone" *man*-PUT-*telephone*-DOWN-*lf*,

     (gaze lf   ) (head jolt back, 'shocked')
man-SAY-#NO-TO-*me*   GULP

Struc 'Last week, I wanted to buy a color TV. I really wanted to. I have a Visa card—you know what that is? Yeah, well I gave the credit card to the man. The man put it through the charge machine. Then he picked up the phone, talked for awhile, hung up the phone and told me "NO". I was shocked and couldn't say anything.'

Trans 'Last week I really wanted to buy a color TV. I've got a Visa card (you know what that is, don't you?). So I gave it to the salesman and he wrote up the charge. When he was done, he called for verification. After talking on the phone for awhile, he hung up and told me I couldn't charge the TV. I was stunned and speechless.'

The '1', '5', and 'B' handshapes can also be used to describe the shape of something. When these handshapes are used in this way, they seem to 'trace' or 'outline' the shape of the referent. Thus, in this text, we sometimes write them as $1_{outline}$-CL, $5_{outline}$-CL, and $B_{outline}$-CL. The following two examples illustrate how the $1_{outline}$-CL can be used to describe the shape of a referent. In example (21), the classifier indicates that the referent (i.e. the table) is 'round'. It also gives information about the relative size of the table. That is, the size of the 'outline' (of the table) is neither small nor very large—relative to the Signer's body—and hence, we know that the table is 'medium' or 'regular' size.[20] In example (22), the classifier is made with both hands—which outline the 'rectangular' shape of the referent (i.e. a strip of paper) and indicate its relative size.

---

[20]Notice that the 'outline' also occurs in the horizontal plane where a table top would naturally be—as opposed to, for example, the vertical plane of a round mirror on a wall. Also notice the *'pursed lips'* signal with this classifier, indicating that the table is 'smooth'.

1_{outline}-CL'circular'   (2h)1_{outline}-CL'rectangular'

$1_{outline}$-CL'circular'   (2h)$1_{outline}$-CL'rectangular'

Context   The Signer and a friend both have new apartments. The friend has been describing the dining room in his apartment. Then the Signer says:

(22)
	t	(gaze at 'table')pursed lips

MY A-P-T, HAVE TABLE $1_{outline}$-CL-*cntr*'circular, medium size',

INDEX-*down,cntr* GLASS, FINEwg

    Struc 'My apartment, it has a table that is smooth, round, and medium size—it's glass. It's really nice.'

    Trans 'My apartment has a round, glass table. It's really neat.'

Context   The Signer and a friend are decorating a room for a party with strips of paper of different sizes, shapes, and colors. The Signer asks:

(23)
	co	(pursed lips)t

"HEY", PAPER GREEN (2h)$1_{outline}$-CL'rectangular, narrow',

you-GIVE-*me*

    Struc 'Hey! That piece of paper that is green, rectangular, and narrow, give it to me.'

    Trans 'Hey! Gimme that thin, rectangular piece of green paper.'

As we saw in examples (18) and (20), Signers frequently use two-handed classifiers to describe the size and shape of something and then switch to a one-handed classifier which represents that thing and can indicate its specific location in space and/or actions. The next example provides another illustration of how the Signer may switch from a more descriptive classifier to a more representative classifier. Here the Signer uses the $1_{outline}$-CL to show that the referent (i.e. picture) is 'small' and 'square', and then uses the one-handed L:-CL to indicate where it is located (i.e. on the wall on the right).

L:-CL

Context   The Signer and a friend are discussing how different co-workers decorate their offices.

(24)

<u>   (gaze rt)   </u>   t
L-E-E, POSS-*rt* O-F-F-I-C-E, HAVE PINK PICTURE

<u>(gaze at 'picture')pursed lips</u> <u>(gaze rt   )</u>
(2h)1$_\text{outline}$-CL'small square' L:-CL@*rt*'on wall'

Struc   'Lee, her office, it has a pink picture that is small and square located on the wall on the right.'

Trans   'Lee's office has a pink picture card on the right wall.'

Although both the '5' and 'B' handshapes can be used to describe the shape of a referent, they often communicate different information about the texture of the referent. For example, when the texture is 'rough' or 'uneven', the Signer will tend to use the '5' or 'bent 5' handshape. When the texture is 'smooth' or 'even', the Signer will tend to use the 'B' handshape. Thus, the Signer might describe a 'cart overflowing with apples' with the '5' handshape or describe 'rocky or jagged mountain peaks' with the 'bent 5' handshape. But a 'smooth-surfaced mountain' or 'cart full of sand' would probably be described with the 'B' handshape. (This difference between the two classifiers is illustrated in the next section.)

Like the 'B' handshape, the 'bent B' handshape is used to describe things that are 'smooth'. However, the 'bent B' handshape can also indicate that the surface is 'continuous' (continues on for a long distance). For example, the state of Kansas, as seen from an airplane, would be described with a 'bent B' (B:) handshape. However, a smooth surface that has specific boundaries (e.g. a football field or playground) would be described with a 'B' handshape. In the example below, both hands move outward with 'B:' handshapes to describe the 'corn fields in Iowa'. Notice the Signer's eye squint and pursed lips in the illustration which also indicate the continuous and smooth (to the eye) surface.

(2h)B:$_t$-CL'smooth, continuous surface'

Context   The Signer and a group of friends are discussing various places they've each visited.

(24)

$$\overline{\text{FINISH \quad TOUCH \quad I-O-W-A,}}^{\text{q}} \quad \text{WOW,} \quad \overline{\text{C-O-R-N \quad PLANT,}}^{\text{t}}$$

$$\overline{\text{(2h)B:}_t\text{-CL-}cntr\text{,move,out in repeated wavy motion'fields and fields'}}^{\text{pursed lips}}$$

> *Struc*   'Have you been to Iowa? Wow! The corn plants, there are smooth fields and fields of them.'
>
> *Trans*   'Have you ever been to Iowa? Man! There are corn fields out there as far as the eye can see.'

E. Signer *Perspective*: Selecting the Appropriate Classifier

Several times during the preceding discussion, we have talked about how the Signer's "perspective" influences his/her selection of an appropriate classifier to represent something. For example, if the Signer focuses on the feature of movement, the Signer might use the (2h)5↓-CL to illustrate throngs of people moving across the rows of benches in a stadium to find their seats. However, if the Signer wants to talk about the same throng of people but only wants to focus on the fact that there are 'people everywhere' (a large mass of people), s/he might use the (2h)5:↓-CL. In these cases, the Signer can 'see' both the fact that there are many people and that they are moving. The selection of the classifier depends on what the Signer wants to 'focus on'.

However, the distance between the Signer and the thing s/he wants to describe can also determine the choice of classifier. Naturally, the closer the Signer is to the thing, the larger it appears and the more 'detail' s/he can see. For example, suppose the Signer sees a 'bin' far away that has something green inside it. From a distance, the green surface (top) appears to be 'smooth'. So the Signer describes this referent with 'B' handshapes to represent the 'bin' and outline the surface of the contents in the bin.

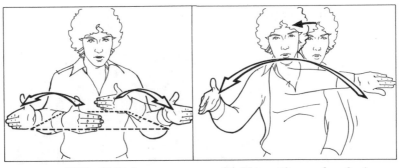

(2h)B$_t$-CL'bin'   B↓-CL'smooth curved surface'

Now suppose the Signer is standing close enough to see that the green stuff is not one solid mass but is composed of many different things of the same kind all thrown together. The surface now appears more 'uneven'; the Signer uses a '**5**' handshape to describe this surface.

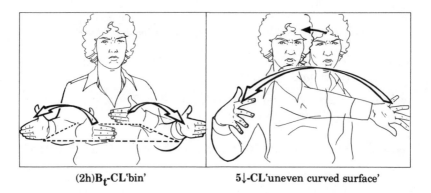

(2h)B$_t$-CL'bin'   5↓-CL'uneven curved surface'

Now suppose the Signer is standing a little closer and sees that the green things are ears of corn all thrown together in the bin. Now the Signer uses the (2h)alt.1→CL to represent this unorderly arrangement.

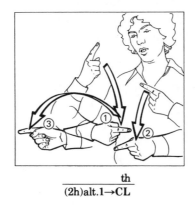

$\overline{\text{th}}$
(2h)alt.1→CL

Or, suppose the corn is neatly arranged in ascending rows.

(2h)1→CL-*upward*"*sweep in a row*"

If the Signer then moves even closer to the bin so that the corn becomes 'larger' visually, s/he may choose to use the C-CL to describe the 'corn'. These ascending rows of corn could then be indicated in either of the ways illustrated below.

(2h)C-CL-*upward"sweep in rows"*   (2h)C$_t$-CL-*upward"sweep in rows"*

Thus, through these examples, we see that the Signer's selection of various classifiers to describe and represent a referent may depend upon his/her *visual perception* of that referent. However, the selection of a classifier also depends upon the Signer's *focus* —what the Signer wants to draw attention to. For example, the Signer could be standing right next to the bin of corn and still only describe it as a 'bin' with a 'pile of' corn inside, rather than specify exactly how the corn is arranged. Thus, what the Signer sees and what the Signer chooses to focus on will influence which classifiers s/he chooses to use.

Let's look at another example. Suppose a Signer was asked to briefly describe the Capitol Building in Washington, D.C.—both from a distance far away and from a close-up perspective. From very far away, the Signer might use a '1' handshape (both hands) to outline the building and to indicate the columns (which would simply appear as straight parallel lines). As the Signer moved a little closer, the columns would begin to have some width (which could be indicated by using a 'G' handshape, facing outward, with downward movement). Or, the Signer might see that they are circular (which could be indicated by using an 'F' handshape with upward movement).

'Columns seen from a distance'

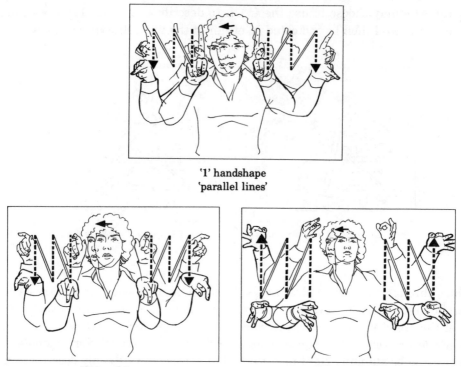

'1' handshape
'parallel lines'

'G' handshape
'parallel lines with some width'

'F' handshape
'narrow parallel columns'

However, if the Signer were standing closer to the Capitol Building, the columns would appear larger and have more depth. Then the 'C' handshape could be used, either following the pattern illustrated above (palms facing outward, hands moving upward), or by using the non-dominant hand as a 'base' while the dominant hand moves upward (i.e. the hands work together to 'create' each column, but do not work in tandem, as illustrated below). If the Signer stands very close to the building, then the columns would look enormous and could be described by using both hands in tandem together, as illustrated below.

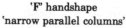

'Columns seen from close-up'

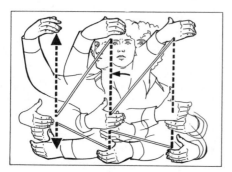

'C' handshape
'large parallel columns'

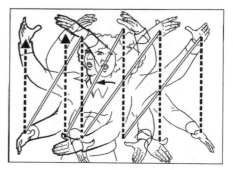

'C' handshape
'huge parallel columns'

Thus, in these examples, we see that the choice of classifier may be determined by the size and shape of the thing being described—but again, is mediated by the Signer's perception of that size and shape. From afar, things appear small and to have fewer dimensions. As the Signer moves closer, things appear larger and more three-dimensional (having height, width, and depth). However, as stated earlier, how something is described also depends on what the Signer wants to focus on. The Signer may choose to describe the columns of the Capitol building as 'huge parallel columns' or simply remark that there are 'parallel columns' in front of the building. Thus, the actual features of the referent (e.g. size, shape, texture), the Signer's perception of those features, and the Signer's choice of what to focus on all influence the appropriate choice of classifier handshapes.

F. Conventional Uses of Classifiers in Regular Signs

As this chapter has shown, classifiers are basically handshapes that are used in particular ways to represent the location and/or movement of a person or thing, or to describe certain characteristics of a person or thing, such as its shape, size, and texture. The palm orientation and movement of classifiers often vary to represent different things or to describe certain actions or characteristics of the referent.

However, classifiers are also seen in many ASL signs that have a more conventional (standard) movement and orientation. For example, using the non-dominant 1-CL to represent a 'person' is seen in many conventional signs, such as those often glossed as MEET, HIT, SLAP, NAG, FLATTER, POPULAR, GANG-UP-ON, CONVINCE (older form), and GRAB. Similarly, the V-CL and its variant V:-CL are often used to represent the 'legs' of a person—seen in signs like STAND, DANCE, DIVE, FALL, FROM-____-WALK-TO-____, GET-UP, KICK-LEG-UP, SIT, JUMP, RIDE-CAR, WEAK-KNEES, ROLL-ON-FLOOR-WITH-LAUGHTER, RESTLESS, and KNEEL.

Many conventional signs also use the '4' and '5' handshape classifiers. For example, signs like FENCE, CAGE, RAINBOW, JAIL, LIQUID-FLOW-FROM-*nose*, and EYELASHES use the '4' handshape. The signs meaning 'blood' and 'sweat' use its 'wiggly' variant. Notice how each of these signs include some notion of plurality—which is consistent with our earlier discussion of this classifier (e.g. a 'fence' has several rails; a 'rainbow' has several lines of different colors; 'sweat' is composed of drops of perspiration). Similarly, the '5' handshape classifiers are used in signs like FIRE, WAVES, ASSEMBLE-TO-____, TRAFFIC, and WAR (as well as POPULAR and GANG-UP-ON).

Because these classifier handshapes have a certain meaning associated with them apart from their use in any particular sign (e.g. 1-CL represents a 'person'; V-CL represents the 'legs' of a person; '4' and '5' handshape classifiers represent plural 'people' or 'things'), they can be used productively and creatively in ASL to show a wide variety of meanings. For example, the V-CL can illustrate someone standing, taking two steps backward and one step forward, stepping over something, stepping on the other foot, crossing one leg over the other leg, etc. Or, with the 1-CL, the Signer can illustrate walking up to someone, almost meeting, but then walking away, turning around as if with "second thoughts", and then walking back up to the person—(all of this, of course, with the appropriate non-manual behaviors). Or someone can keep nagging, slapping, or beating a person (1-CL on non-dominant hand) while that person moves around and tries to escape.

As such, classifiers, with their frequent use in conventional signs as well as their great potential for iconic variation to show a wide variety of meanings, are an especially fascinating part of ASL — and a part that needs much more study!

G. Summary

In this chapter, we have described the basic functions of a special set of 'signs' (actually handshapes) that are called *classifiers*. We have seen that some classifiers function as pronouns; some move as verbs; some show the spatial location of a person or thing; some indicate the 'manner' of an action; and some describe certain characteristics of a person or thing, such as its size, shape, depth, or texture. Classifiers can be singular or plural. Singular classifiers can be made plural in a variety of ways and can then indicate, for example, if people or things are 'lined up in rows' or 'scattered all over the place'. Classifier handshapes are used in many conventional signs and can be used creatively to express a wide variety of meanings.

Bibliography: Classifiers

Bellugi, U. & D. Newkirk (in press). Formal devices for creating new signs in ASL. To appear in *National Symposium on Sign Language Research and Teaching: 1977 Proceedings*. Silver Spring, Md.: National Association of the Deaf.

Klima, E. & U. Bellugi. 1979. *The Signs of Language*. Cambridge, Mass.: Harvard University Press.

Supalla, T. (in press). Morphology of verbs of motion and location in American Sign Language. To appear in *National Symposium on Sign Language Research and Teaching: 1978 Proceedings*. Silver Spring, Md.: National Association of the Deaf.

Dialogues
and
Cultural Information

Classifiers

The following three dialogues have been developed to illustrate various uses of the grammatical features described in this chapter. Each of these dialogues also appears in one of the three corresponding Student Texts. In the Student Texts, the transcription of each dialogue is less detailed than what is provided here for the teacher of ASL. Following the dialogues, in the sections called "Cultural Information", are brief discussions of the topic of each dialogue.

The following dialogues and cultural information correspond to:

Student Text: Unit 5
Unit 14
Unit 23

Dialogue: Classifiers
(Student Text - Unit 5)

First Signer (Pat)

Pat₁:
```
        co                    t
       ‾‾‾‾‾    ‾‾‾‾‾‾‾‾‾‾‾‾‾‾‾‾‾‾‾‾‾
       ONE-WEEK-PAST,  AWFUL  HAPPEN
"HEY",
```

Pat₂:
```
 t
‾‾‾‾‾
CAR,  ACCIDENT
```

Pat₃:
```
         t                                         t
        ‾‾‾‾‾            ‾‾‾‾‾‾‾‾‾‾‾‾‾‾‾‾‾‾‾‾‾‾‾‾‾‾‾‾‾‾‾
        ME+,   3→CL@rt'car',─────────────────────────→   ME   3→CL'stop for light',
"WELL"                      RED BURST-OF-light, ──────────────────────────→

                th                    (gaze lf, 'surprised'        )                  pow
              ‾‾‾‾‾‾                                                    ‾‾‾‾‾‾‾‾‾‾‾‾‾‾‾‾‾
ME   MULL-OVER++,   UNEXPECTEDLY        3→CL ─────────────────────────────────────────→
                                       3→CL'car come from lf and smash into first car'
```

Pat₄:
```
         nodding
       ‾‾‾‾‾‾‾‾‾‾‾                              th
       (2h)alt.DIZZY,  FEEL   ‾‾‾‾‾‾‾‾‾‾‾‾‾‾‾‾‾‾‾‾‾‾‾‾
                             (2h)alt.F-CL'eyes rolling around',

       t         nodding      t   puff.cheeks  (gaze at left side       )
     ‾‾‾‾‾     ‾‾‾‾‾‾‾‾‾‾     ‾‾‾‾‾ ‾‾‾‾‾‾‾‾‾‾‾
     LATER,   DISSOLVE,    CAR,    AWFUL      (2h)left rear-SMASHED-IN
```

Pat₅:
```
                 rhet.q    (gaze down        )   t      (gaze rt)
               ‾‾‾‾‾‾‾‾   ‾‾‾‾‾‾‾‾‾‾‾‾‾‾‾‾‾‾‾‾‾‾‾
     NOT-KNOW,  "WHY",   MONEY  RECT-CL'check',  NOT-YET   ME   me-SEND-TO-rt
```

Pat₆:
```
                  nodding          (gaze at 'bill'    )br.raise (look of 'dismay'    )
              ‾‾‾‾‾‾‾‾‾‾‾‾‾       ‾‾‾‾‾‾‾‾‾‾‾‾‾‾‾‾‾‾‾‾‾‾
     ONE-DAY-PAST  FINISH,   #BILL   B-CL'give me bill from rt' ──────────────────→
                                                                EIGHT   HUNDRED
```

Dialogue: Classifiers
(Student Text - Unit 5)

Second Signer (Lee)

Lee₁:
$$\overline{\text{(2h)\#WHAT \quad (2h)"WHAT"}}^{\text{wh-q}}$$

Lee₂:
$$\overline{\text{HOW \quad HAPPEN \quad HOWwg}}^{\text{wh-q}}$$

Lee₃:
$$\overline{\text{\#HURT \quad YOU}}^{\text{q}}$$

Lee₄:
$$\overline{\text{INSURANCE \quad PAY-TO-\textit{you} \quad RIGHT}}^{\text{q}}$$

Lee₅:
$$\overset{\text{(gaze lf \quad)}}{\overline{\text{CAR \quad SEND-TO-\textit{lf} \quad \#FIX \quad FINISH \quad YOU}}^{\text{q}}}$$

Lee₆: WOW

Dialogue: Classifiers
(Student Text - Unit 14)

First Signer (Pat)

Pat₁:
```
         co                           t              neg            wh-q
      _____  _____  _____  _____
      "HEY"        PAST NIGHT #CLUB,  NOT  GO-TO-rt,  WHAT'S-UP
                                                       YOU
```

Pat₂:
```
                                                            wh-q
      _____  _____
      BROTHER  brother-MAKE-CONTACT-WITH-you  FOR-FOR
```

Pat₃:
```
                      _____ t
      me-PITY-you,   PAST  NIGHT  #CLUB  THUMB-INDEX-back rt,

      (gaze rt    )puff.cheeks          (gaze rt)puff.cheeks    nodding
      _____          _____  _____
      (2h)alt.MOVE-things-rt,  PAINT-rt-arc    CHANGE-rt-arc    FINEwg
```

Pat₄:
```
                               br
                   ____  _____
      _____   KNOW  INDEX-lf thumb  "UMMM"
      "PSHAW"

      (gaze rt)  t                                              (nodding)t
      _____  _____
         WALL-rt,  PICTURE  STATE-SCHOOL  OLD  AWHILE-AGO  (2h)alt.C-CL-rt'pictures on the wall',

                              pursed lips      t
                           _____  _____
      (2h)alt.TAKE-DOWN-pictures  (2h)BARE-wall,  WHITE,  PAINT-wall
```

Pat₅:
```
                                                     (gaze rt;    nodding)t
                   ____  _____
      _____   KNOW  INDEX-lf index  YOU  TROPHY  BOWLING  (2h)A-CL-rt''in rows'',
      "PSHAW"

      (gaze down)  (gaze rt,down                        )  nodding
                                                           _____
          BOX     (2h)alt.PUT-trophies-IN-box  THROW-OUT-rt
```

Dialogue: Classifiers
(Student Text - Unit 14)

Second Signer (Lee)

Lee₁: (2h)"WELL" STUCK ME, $\overline{\text{ONE-DAY-PAST TIME THREE,}}^{\text{t}}$ BROKER $^{\text{(gaze rt   )}}$ *brother(rt)*-**MEET**-*me*

$^{\text{(gaze rt) nod}}_{\text{V:-CL@rt,out}}$ } 'sit facing each other', $^{\text{(gaze rt)}}_{\text{CHAT}}$"*long time*"
V:-CL@rt,in

Lee₂: $^{\text{(gaze rt)}}$ **INDEX**-*rt* $\overline{\text{NEXT SUMMER,}}^{\text{t}}$ **WANT** **FAMILY** $\overline{\text{FROM-}rt\text{-GROUP-GO-TO-}here,}^{\text{puff.cheeks}}$

ME $\overline{\text{NOT-WANT++,}}^{\text{neg}}$ **US-TWO**-*rt* $\overline{\text{STRUGGLE}}^{\text{sta}}$"regularly" **ALL-NIGHT**

Lee₃: $\overline{\text{"WHAT" CHANGE #DO-DO}}^{\text{wh-q}}$

Lee₄: **WHITE YECCH**-*rt,* **BETTER GREEN BETTER**

Lee₅: $\overline{\text{#CLUB CHANGE, IMPROVE TRUE "HMMM"}}^{\text{nodding}}$

Dialogue: Classifiers
(Student Text - Unit 23)

First Signer (Pat)

Pat₁:
<pre>
          co
"HEY", ME PEA-BRAIN*, TRUE+ MAKE-ME-SICK*
</pre>

Pat₂:
<pre>
                          cs   br (gaze down)   (gaze down   )   t
HAPPEN FEW-DAY-PAST, ME WORK, TABLE   PAPER   (2h)alt.B↓-CL'papers on table',
</pre>

<pre>
(gaze down,rt   )t   (nodding)qt
TIME   A-CL-rt'clock', BURST-OF-light-rt++ KNOW YOU
</pre>

Pat₃:
<pre>
                     (head,gaze lf   )
ME+ CARELESS,   "move arm to right suddenly"
</pre>

<pre>
(gaze down,rt   )   wh-q
A-CL'clock on table,fall off' (2h)SHATTER/SPLATTER-rt "SHUCKS", ME (2h)#DO-DO
B↓-CL'table'
</pre>

Pat₄:
<pre>
neg   (gaze down,rt   )   wh-q
    CHERISH, MOTHER rt-GIVE-TO-me, CHERISH*, WANT-rt (2h)#FIX-rt, HOWwg
</pre>

Pat₅:
<pre>
                  wh-q
STORE WHERE "WHAT"
</pre>

Pat₆:
<pre>
                              nodding
TOMORROW #WILL ME GO-TO-store #WILL
</pre>

Dialogue: Classifiers
(Student Text - Unit 23)

Second Signer (Lee)

Lee₁:
$$\overline{\text{wh-q}}\qquad\overline{\qquad\qquad\qquad\text{neg}}$$
#WHAT, NOT UNDERSTAND

Lee₂:
$$\qquad\qquad\overline{\qquad\qquad\qquad\qquad\qquad\text{nodding}}$$
RIGHT+, *you-*__SAME-AS__*-me* **MY+** *you-*__SAME-AS__*-me*

Lee₃:
$$\qquad\qquad\qquad\qquad\qquad\qquad\overline{\text{nodding}}$$
"SO-WHAT", (2h)IT'S-NOTHING, BUY-TO-*lf* **NEW+**

Lee₄:
$$\overline{\text{t}}\quad\overline{\text{neg}}\qquad\qquad\qquad\overline{\text{neg}}\qquad\qquad\overline{\text{neg+q}}$$
ME, INEPT, WHY‿NOT ASK-TO-*rt* ⚠ **, KNOW T-I-N-A**

$$\overline{\text{nodding}}\qquad\overline{\text{puff.cheeks}}\quad\overline{\qquad\text{nod}\qquad}\quad\overline{\qquad\text{t}}$$
INDEX-*rt+* **SKILL* FIX++-***arc* **THUMB-INDEX-***rt,* **POSS-***rt* **STORE,**

$$\overline{\text{nod}}\qquad\qquad\qquad\overline{\text{puff.cheeks}}$$
HAVE+ TIME (2h)C-CL'clock' A-CL"*in rows",* **REALLY-ADEPT INDEX-***rt*

Lee₅:
$$\qquad\qquad\qquad\qquad\qquad\qquad\qquad\overline{\text{(gaze at'street'}\qquad\qquad\qquad\qquad)\text{t}}$$
(2h)"WELL" KNOW+ FANCY HOME 5:↓-CL@*rt*'fancy home' $\longrightarrow$
B-CL'street running next to fancy home',

$$\overline{\qquad\text{t}}\quad\text{(gaze lf,cntr)}\qquad\qquad\text{(gaze at 'home'\&'store')}$$
$\longrightarrow$
STORE, INDEX-lf,cntr **NOT-MUCH** *INDEX-home & store↔*

Student Text: Unit 5

Cultural Information: Insurance and Deaf Drivers

A very common myth about deaf people is that they must be bad drivers because they can't hear. However, statistics and anecdotal data compiled by the National Association of the Deaf, the Department of Health, Education and Welfare, the U.S. Department of Transportation, and various state departments of motor vehicles show that this is not the case. In fact, these statistics show that, in general, deaf drivers tend to be better drivers than hearing drivers. According to the Department of Transportation, almost all driving decisions are made on the basis of sight, not sound (especially if the windows are up, the heater or air conditioner is on, and the radio is on). Thus, a deaf driver is functionally no different than a hearing driver in terms of making driving-related decisions. (In fact, automobile advertising frequently emphasizes the "quiet ride" and the ability of certain cars to eliminate outside noise).

The myth that deaf drivers are bad drivers made it somewhat difficult in the past for deaf drivers to obtain automobile insurance. In the past, most insurance companies felt that deaf drivers constituted a high-risk group. However, now there are approximately twenty-five major companies which provide deaf drivers with auto insurance. Thus, the "deaf-driver-bad-driver" myth is changing, and deaf drivers are now able to obtain reasonable insurance rates from reputable companies.

Student Text: Unit 14

Cultural Information: Deaf Clubs

The National Association of the Deaf (NAD) currently has listings of well over 175 different Deaf Clubs in the United States. Many of these Clubs have been established to serve specific functions or to serve the needs of special sub-groups of the Deaf Community. Names such as the Maryland Senior Citizens Deaf Club, Fresno Athletic Club of the Deaf, Ebony Social Club of the Deaf, 47 Alumni Association, Utah Sportsmen Club of the Deaf, Angel West Catholic Club provide some indication as to the wide range of social, political, religious, and recreational functions which Deaf Clubs serve.

Historically, the Deaf Club fulfilled a vital need in the lives of members of the Deaf Community—it provided a place where members of the Community could meet to share their ideas, interests, and language. Before captioned films (Unit 11) became available and before the increasing national sensitivity toward Deaf people, the Deaf Club often provided the only form of social life for its members. In addition, Club members would often share valuable information with each other, like which of the doctors, lawyers, and dentists were sensitive and understanding, where certain services could be obtained from people who could be trusted, etc. In short, the Club often functioned as a place where Deaf people could seek and give advice on how to best deal with the hearing world.

At the present time, however, because of the increased availability of interpreters and the increased number of hearing people who are learning Sign, this function of the Deaf Club seems to be declining. In addition, because a wider range of social activities are now accessible to Deaf people, the Deaf Club is no longer the only social outlet for many Deaf people. Consequently, the role and function of the Deaf Club in the lives of many Deaf people is changing.

Most Clubs are open at specific times. However, these times range from, for example, "every Thursday, Friday and Saturday evening" to "every third Friday of the month". Very often Clubs arrange for captioned films, social evenings, athletic events, etc., for their members. Many Clubs sponsor basketball and softball teams which compete with each other under the auspices of the American Athletic Association of the Deaf, Inc. (AAAD). In addition, many Deaf Clubs publish monthly newsletters to keep their members informed of local and national events.

Student Text: Unit 23

Cultural Information: Alarms/Signaling Devices for Deaf People

It should not be surprising that many of the alarms and signaling devices that are used by hearing people are not effective for many deaf people since these alarms and devices generally rely on sound. As a result, special alarms and signaling devices are now commercially available which rely on vision or vibration to signal the user. Some of these signaling devices are listed below. This list is not intended to be complete, but merely represents the range of the kinds of devices that are now available to deaf people.

Vibrating Alarm Timer: a heavy-duty bed vibrator that is plugged into an electric timer which can be pre-set to vibrate the bed at a specific time.

Electro-Alarm Clock: a standard clock with a large lighted clock face which is attached to a small pillow vibrator that vibrates at any pre-set time.

Flash Alarm: a clock with an attached light which flashes on and off at any pre-set time.

Whisper Lights: specially built lamps (or attachments to lamps) which are sound-activated and can be used to detect a baby crying, a knock on the door, etc.

Telephone/Doorbell Signaler: lights which are attached to the doorbell and/or telephone so that they flash if someone pushes the doorbell or if the phone rings.

Smoke Detectors: these devices are also connected to lights or bed vibrators which are activated in case of a fire.

For more information about specific products, see advertisements in the *Deaf American,* the monthly magazine published by the National Association of the Deaf, 814 Thayer Avenue, Silver Spring, Md. 20910.

Chapter XI

Locatives

A. Introduction

All languages have ways of describing the spatial relationship between two or more things. We refer to these descriptions as *locatives* since they indicate the spatial *location* of something in relation to something else.

Consider the following diagram which illustrates a variety of spatial relationships between a 'car' and a 'boy':

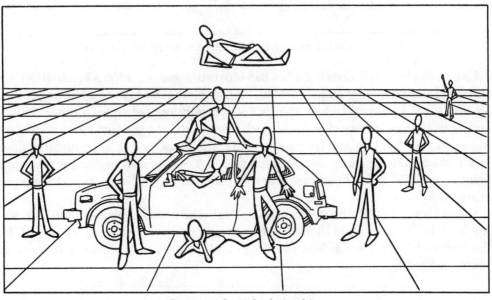

Fig. 11.1 Spatial relationships

To describe these relationships, English speakers use prepositional phrases like 'The boy is *under the car*' or 'The boy is *in the car*'. English has a large number of words called "prepositions" which are used in these locative expressions. Some of these are: in, inside, on, on top of, at, outside, by, with, alongside, next to, close to, near, far from, in front of, in back of, behind, against, above, below, beneath, under, around, between, and among. Using these English prepositions, we can identify all of the diagrammed relationships between the 'boy' and the 'car'.

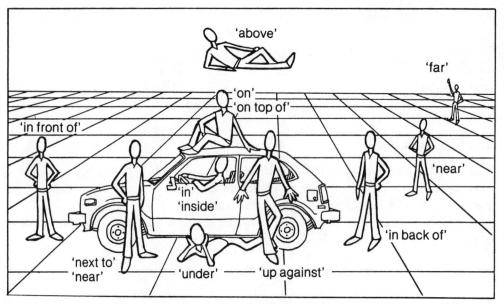

Fig. 11.2   English prepositions that describe spatial relationships

Unlike English, ASL does not often use separate signs (e.g. **ON, AT, AROUND**) to describe locative relationships. Instead, ASL Signers tend to take advantage of the signing space to illustrate how things are spatially related to each other. This is accomplished in a variety of ways—which include making the sign for each referent in a certain spatial location (frequently using classifiers) and/or by using directional verbs which indicate *where* something happens. Looking at a particular place and pointing with the index finger are also very common ways of indicating the location of something.

For example, to describe the various spatial relationships between the 'car' and the 'boy', the Signer would likely use the classifier for each referent (i.e. **3→CL** for the 'car' and **V-CL** for the 'boy standing') and position them in various ways, as illustrated below.

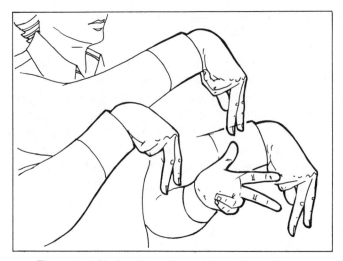

Fig. 11.3   ASL classifiers: three spatial relationships

Thus, in the following example, specific information about the spatial or locative relationship between the 'boy' and the 'car' is communicated by positioning the classifiers in certain locations in space—i.e. the V-CL is positioned behind the 3→CL.

Context   The Signer has been asked to describe a sketch of a boy and a car.

(1)

	t	(gaze at 'car')nod		(gaze at 'boy' and 'car')
	#CAR,		BOY	V↓-CL*@lf,cntr*'boy behind car'
		3→CL *@lf,cntr*'car'		⟶

Struc   'The car, it's here. The boy is standing behind the car.'

Trans   'The boy is standing *behind the car*.'

Because the positioning of the hands always indicates a particular spatial relationship, ASL tends to automatically give more specific information about such relationships than English normally does. For example, in English, one might say 'The boy is standing next to the car'. But in ASL, the location of the V-CL automatically gives more specific information than what is communicated in English with the phrase 'next to'. That is, depending on where the V-CL is placed, the boy would be standing 'next to the front bumper on the passenger's side of the car', 'next to the middle of the car on the passenger's side', 'next to the back bumper on the passenger's side of the car', or several other possible specific locations.

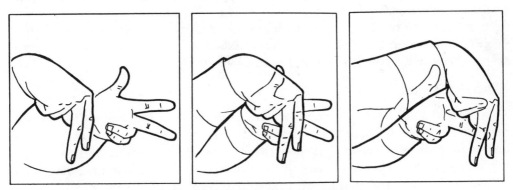

Fig. 11.4   Three spatial relationships:
precise information communicated with ASL classifiers

Similarly, the relative location of the V-CL behind the 3→CL would indicate if the boy is 'right behind the car', 'behind and near the car', or 'behind and far from the car'.

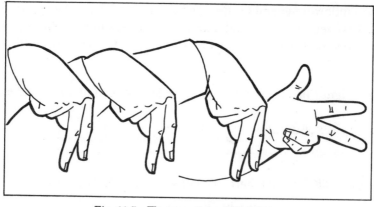

Fig. 11.5   Three spatial relationships:
information communicated by relative location

With these general differences between ASL and English in mind, now let's look more closely at the various ways that ASL expresses locative relationships.

B. Ways to Express Locative Relationships in ASL

In the following sections, we will discuss a range of examples which illustrate the several ways that ASL indicates locative (spatial) relationships. Note that all of these ways can and often do occur together in a sentence. In all of the examples, directional eye gaze is also an important indicator of the locative relationship between the referents.

As you read the transcriptions of each example and its English translation, notice how ASL communicates the locative information that English communicates with a prepositional phrase (which is in italics in each translation).

(B.1) Classifiers

As described in Chapter X, classifiers are frequently used to indicate the spatial relationship between two or more referents since many of them can be easily moved around in space. Many classifiers can either be 'placed' in a certain location (meaning 'is there') or can be moved as a verb toward a certain location (meaning 'goes there') or moved in a certain location (meaning 'does something there').[1]

For example, notice how the classifiers in the following narrative use the signing space to communicate continuous information about where things are located and what happens in those locations. Suppose the Signer recently went skiing and is telling a friend about a "misadventure". She begins by describing the location where it happened: 'there was a lake on the left' and 'there was a hill next to the lake on the right'—so 'the lake was at the bottom of the hill'.

---

[1]Actually, in each case, the classifier is used as a verb—either a *stative verb* (meaning 'is located there'), or an *active verb* which indicates an action in or toward a particular location.

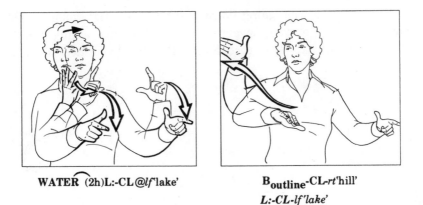

WATER (2h)L:-CL@*lf*'lake'

B~outline~-CL-*rt*'hill'
L:-CL-lf 'lake'

Now the Signer's perspective changes: from atop the hill, she recreates the 'hill' and 'stands on top of the hill'.

(2h)B~outline~-CL-*cntr*'hill'

V-CL-*cntr*'stand atop hill'
B↓-CL-cntr'hill'

From this position, she sees that 'there was a fence on the left side of the hill' and 'there was a row of trees on the right side of the hill'.

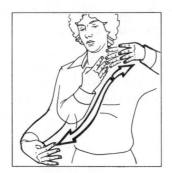

(2h)4→CL-*lf* 'fence on side of hill'

TREE-*lf,upward-arc*'trees on side of hill'

Now it happens: she was 'going down the hill' (on skis) when a rabbit came hopping out of the trees and she 'swerved to the left' to miss skiing into the rabbit. But alas! What's to the left? The fence. So she 'falls head over heels over the fence'.

1-CL-*cntr*'go down hill'   V:-CL-*rt*'rabbit'   V-CL'fall over fence'
                                   1-CL'swerve to lf'   *4→CL'fence'*

The result? She 'hurt her left shoulder'.

#HURT-*lf shoulder*

Notice how almost all of the locative information in this narrative was conveyed by using classifiers in specific locations in the signing space. The following six examples also illustrate how classifiers are used to describe the spatial relationship between various people, things, and places.

In example (2), the 1-CL moves as a verb in a specific location (i.e. 'under the tree'). In example (3), the 3→CL represents the 'bus' which does not move. However, the palm orientation of the classifier indicates that the bus is positioned 'across the road'. The 3→CL which represents the Signer's vehicle moves toward the 'bus' and ends up stuck 'behind the bus'.

Context   A gang of kids have dared each other to do several things. The Signer saw
Pat do one of those things and tells the other kids.

(2)
| (gaze at 'tree';   th)t   (gaze 'under tree') |
| KNOW   , P-A-T   1-CL-*lf* 'walk under tree' |
| *TREE-lf   TREE-lf* 'tilt forward', ———————————————→ |

Struc   'You know that tree that's leaning over, Pat walked under it.'

Trans   'You know the tree that's leaning over, Pat walked *under it.*'

Note: In this example, the V-CL could have been used in place of the
1-CL.

Context   The Signer lives in North Dakota and was supposed to fly to Texas yesterday but missed his plane. Now in Texas, he tells his friend why he missed
the plane.

(3)
| t   (look of 'concentration') |
| ONE-DAY-PAST, SNOW* AWFUL, ME   DRIVE+ |

| (eye squint   )   (look of 'surprise'   ) |
| 3→CL 'slowly move forward', —————————————————————————————→ |
| "hold steering wheel"————————→   *#BUS*   3→CL @*cntr* 'parked across the road' |

| (gaze at 'bus'   ) |
| ME   LATE   3→CL 'almost hit bus, but stop suddenly',   STUCK |
| *(hold 3→CL)* ——————————————————————————————→ |

Struc   'Yesterday, it really snowed hard and was awful! I was driving
along with great concentration and moving along slowly when
suddenly I was surprised to see a bus in front of me parked across
the road. It was too late and I almost hit the bus, but stopped
suddenly. I was stuck behind the bus.'

Trans   'Yesterday it was snowing like crazy. I was driving along real
carefully when *up ahead* there was this bus just parked *across the
road.* I saw it too late and had to jam on the brakes, and there I
was—stuck *behind the bus.*'

In example (4), the ⊤-CL is used to represent the action of a 'jet'. By moving this
classifier above and very close to the non-dominant hand 'tree', the Signer communicates that the jet flew *over* the tree and that it flew *very close to* the tree.

Context   The Signer and a friend are at a daredevil air show. The friend looked
down to pick up her program and missed one of the events. So the Signer
tells her what happened.

(4)
| (gaze lf)t   (gaze rt→lf; brow squint   )pursed lips |
| "WOW",   J-E-T   ⊤-CL-*rt→lf* 'fly over tree, barely missing treetop' |
| *TREE @lf* ——————————————————————————————→ |

Struc   'Wow! The tree there, a jet flew right over it, barely missing the
top.'

Trans   'It was terrific! A jet flew *right over the very top of the tree.*'

The next example again illustrates how classifiers in ASL can convey a great deal of information about locative relationships in a very efficient and concise way. Here the classifiers illustrate the former position of two pictures and then the present position of the pictures, showing how their relative location has changed.

Context   The Signer is telling a friend about how he re-decorated his apartment.

(5)

```
                    _____(nod)t          (gaze at 'pictures'                    )
          MY   PICTURE   TWO,   AWHILE-AGO   L:-CL @rt,cntr ⎫
                                            L:CL @lf,cntr  ⎬ 'on wall,side-by-side',
                                                           ⎭
```

```
          (headshake)  (gaze at 'pictures'                        )
          NOW   CHANGE,   L:-CL @rt,cntr 'on wall below other picture'
                         L:-CL @lf,cntr 'on wall above other picture'
```

Struc   'My pictures, the two of them, awhile ago they hung side by side at the same height on the wall. Now their position has changed. (It's not the same.) The one on the left is now hanging higher than the one on the right.'

Trans   'The two pictures I have used to be hanging *right next to each other on the wall.* But now I've changed them so that *the one on the left is higher than the other one.*'

Note: In this example, the C-CL or B-CL (palm facing outward) could have been used instead of the L:-CL.

In the next example, the relative positions of three people who are 'seated' at a party are indicated by using the V:-CL in three different locations. First the dominant-hand classifier is placed to the right (to represent 'Pat') and then moves to a position that is left of, but still close to, the first position (to represent 'Lee'). Then the Signer holds that hand in Lee's position while placing the non-dominant hand outward and opposite Lee's position (to represent the 'mother'). The orientation of the hands also shows that 'Pat' and 'Lee' are facing outward and the 'mother' is facing them. Thus, the placement and orientation of the classifiers indicates the spatial relationship between these three people at the party—which includes their relative distance from each other and their orientations toward each other, as illustrated below.

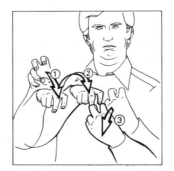

'a seating arrangement of three people'

Context The Signer is beginning to describe what happened at a party for a friend who was not at the party.

(6)

	t	(gaze rt,body lean rt)nod
ONE-WEEK-PAST PARTY, P-A-T		V:-CL@*rt*

	t (gaze rt,cntr)nod		t		nod
L-E-E,	V:-CL@*cntr*'next to Pat' ——————————————————————→				
			MOTHER,	V:-CL@*outward,cntr*'facing Lee'	

   Struc 'Last week at the party, Pat was seated on the right. Lee, he was seated next to Pat on Pat's left. Mother, she was seated across from them, opposite Lee.'

   Trans 'At the party last week, Pat and Lee were sitting *next to each other* and Mother was sitting *across from them, opposite Lee.*'

In example (7), the location of the 2-CL indicates that the 'boys' are 'under the table'. This fact is also shown on the verb **FIGHT** by holding the head and shoulders in a crouched position as if in a cramped position and by looking down while making the sign. Another classifier that appears in this example is the **B$_{forearm}$-CL** which represents the 'table' with the non-dominant hand. This classifier (involving the whole forearm and hand) is used to represent the surface of things like a 'counter, ledge, airport runway, mountain, ramp, or side of a building'. The orientation of the classifier varies, depending on its meaning. For example, it might be held at an angle to represent the 'side of a mountain', but be held parallel to the ground to represent a 'table'.[2]

Context The Signer is at a picnic with some friends and their families. Two of the young boys are always getting into trouble and are at it again. The Signer sees them and says:

(7)

	co		t
"HEY",	KNOW+ BOY TWO,		

(gaze lf	) (gaze down,lf	) (look under 'table')	
INDEX-*lf* TABLE-*lf*		**2-CL**-*lf*'go under table' **FIGHT***-*lf*	
	(hold)B$_{forearm}$-CL'table top'———————————————→		

   Struc 'Hey! You know those two boys—over there at the table, the two of them have gone under it and are fighting hard.'

   Trans 'Hey! You know those two boys—they're *over there* fighting like crazy *under the table.*'

(B.2) Directional Verbs

In the preceding section we saw how classifiers can be used to illustrate the locative relationship between two or more referents as well as indicate where an

---

[2]When the forearm classifier is held upright with a fist hand, it can represent things like a 'pillar, a large column, a post, or a building'.

action takes place. Similarly, directional verbs can indicate the location of an action or event by moving the verb from one spatial location to another spatial location. This function of directional verbs is illustrated in the following five examples.

In example (8), the verb moves from the Signer toward the location of the 'restaurant', indicating *where* the Signer goes frequently. Similarly, in example (9), the verb moves from the spatial location of the 'girl' to the place where the event occurred—i.e. 'on the Signer's nose'.

Context   The Signer is riding with some friends and notices a favorite restaurant.

(8)
```
           co   (gaze lf)                      (nod)t   (gaze lf)         puff.cheeks+mm
      "HEY",          RESTAURANT  JAPANESE,  ME  (2h)GO-TO-restaurant"regularly"
            INDEX-lf ──────────────────────→
```

   Struc   'Hey! There the Japanese restaurant? I go there regularly (a lot).'

   Trans   'Hey! You see that Japanese restaurant? I go *there* regularly.'

Context   The Signer and a friend are at a party. The Signer tells his friend what just happened.

(9)
```
            (gaze rt  )t   (gaze rt              "lips smack"      ) ('quizzical' look)
      GIRL  INDEX-rt,   1-CL-rt'walk up to me'   girl-KISS-me-ON-nose
```

   Struc   'The girl there, she walked up to me and kissed me on the nose. Huh?'

   Trans   'That girl walked right up to me and kissed me on the nose! I don't get it.'

Notice that the verb *girl*-KISS-*me*-ON-*nose* in example (9) is directional because it can be changed to mean 'I kiss you', 'you kiss me', 'I kiss him/her', etc. However, when the Signer is the object (the one who gets kissed), the verb can also show *where* the action takes place. In this case, the action occurred 'on the nose'. Other verbs like this were described and listed in Chapter IX—for example, BANG-ON-____, BLEED-FROM-____, BRUISE-ON-____, #HURT-(AT)-____, and SHAVE-(AT)-____. Notice how each of these verbs indicates *where* an action takes place.

The next example illustrates a very common occurrence in ASL (already seen in several previous examples) which involves locations that represent actual places. In most cases, the place (e.g. city, state, country) is automatically assigned a spatial location, and then all future references to that place make use of its spatial location. That is, future references 'agree with' that spatial location. For example, in (10), the cities 'New York' and 'Chicago' are given spatial locations via eye gaze and by actually signing their names in those locations. Then the verb FROM-____-FLY-TO-____ 'incorporates' their locations by moving from one location to the other location, and expresses the action of flying 'from New York to Chicago'.

Context   The Signer has just returned from a trip and is discussing flying time between cities.

(10a)   <u>   (gaze rt;body lean rt)(gaze lf)   t   </u>
       KNOW+   **NEW-YORK**-*rt*   **CHICAGO**-*lf,*

       <u>(gaze rt   )</u>
       FROM-*new york*-**FLY-TO**-*chicago* **TWO-HOUR,** **IT'S-NOTHING**

      Struc 'You know New York and Chicago, flying from New York to Chicago takes two hours. That's not much.'

      Trans 'You know you can fly *from New York to Chicago* in two hours. It's no big deal.'

Example (10b) illustrates an alternate way to express the same information as communicated in (10a). This time the right hand 'holds' the location of New York ('Y' handshape) while the left hand signs **CHICAGO**. Then the left hand 'holds the location of Chicago ('C' handshape) while the verb is signed.

(10b)   <u>   (gaze rt;body lean rt)(gaze lf)   (gaze rt)   t </u>
       KNOW+   **NEW-YORK**-*rt*————————→ **FROM**-*new york*-**FLY-TO**-*chicago,*
                             CHICAGO-*lf* ——————————————→

      TWO-HOUR, **IT'S-NOTHING**

      Struc 'You know New York is here and Chicago is here—flying from New York to Chicago, it takes two hours. That's not much.'

      Trans 'You know you can fly *from New York to Chicago* in two hours. It's no big deal.'

The next colorful example uses a variety of classifiers and directional verbs to indicate the location of several events and the person and things involved in those events (i.e. 'Signer', 'bird', and 'bird droppings').

Context   The Signer jokingly says she is going to renounce her membership in the Audubon Society. Her friend asks "Why?" and she replies:[3]

---

[3] For readers who have the accompanying videotape: Notice that the verb glossed here as **SPLATTER-ON**-*rt temple* begins with a closed fist and then opens to an 'F' handshape on the temple. This is the **F-CL** that represents small, roundish things.

(11)
<pre>
                    t   mm
ONE-DAY-PAST, ME WALK   1-CL'walking along',
</pre>

<pre>
(gaze up,rt   ) ___rhet.q___   (gaze up,rt   )
me-LOOK-AT-up,rt, HAPPEN,   BIRD B-CL-up,rt'fly overhead'
</pre>

<pre>
(look of 'disgust'   )
SPLATTER-ON-rt temple   "turn head and wipe head"
</pre>

> *Struc*   'Yesterday, I was casually walking along and looked up to the right. What happened? A bird was flying overhead, and it dropped 'stuff' that splattered on my right temple. I turned my head in disgust and wiped it off.'
>
> *Trans*   'Yesterday I was just walking *along,* and I happened to look *up.* Just as I did, this bird was flying *overhead* got me right *above the eye.* I wiped it off—Yecch!'

In example (12), the spatial location assigned to the 'table' is remembered, rather than held by the non-dominant hand (probably because the sign **BOOK** requires both hands), and the verb then moves to that location to indicate where the 'book' is placed.

> *Context*   A friend borrowed the Signer's book and is now returning it. He asks the Signer where he should put it and the Signer replies:

(12)
<pre>
          (gaze lf)t
TABLE INDEX-lf, you-PUT-ON-table
</pre>

> *Struc*   'The table over there on the left, put it on the table.'
>
> *Trans*   'Put it *on the table over there.*'

(B.3) Indexing

As seen in the preceding example, pointing with the index finger (*indexing*) is frequently used by ASL Signers to indicate the location of something. This location can be a 'real-life' location (as seen in examples 12 and 13). Or, its location may be understood in relation to other things that have been given locations in the signing space (as seen in examples 14 and 15).

In ASL, if the locative relationship between two things is obvious (i.e. clearly understood from the context), then it is usually unnecessary to specify that relationship. For example, in (13), the 'coat' is located *on* the 'chair' (the usual place for a coat to be in relation to a chair), so it is not necessary to explicitly sign that it is "on" the chair. Signing **CHAIR** and pointing to it is quite sufficient. However, if there were many different coats lying on, next to, and under the chair, then the Signer might need to be more specific—either by setting up the chair in space and then referencing a particular point around it, or by using a separate locative sign like **ON** or **NEXT-TO-ON-THE-RIGHT** (see Section B.4).

Context   The Signer is the host at a party. A woman asks him where she can find her coat. He replies:

(13)
            _____t___ (gaze rt)
            YOUR   COAT,   INDEX-*rt*   CHAIR   INDEX-*rt*

     Struc   'Your coat, over there at the chair there.'

     Trans   'Your coat, it's *over there on the chair*.'

In example (14), the Signer gives 'New York' a specific location and then indexes the space right next to (on the left) and slightly below that location. Here the Signer is calling attention to the spatial relationship between New York and New Jersey and is indicating that they are 'right next to each other' and that New Jersey is 'below' New York.

Context   The Signer is explaining the location of various states to a foreigner.

(14)
                                    nodding+q
            YOU   KNOW   #U.S.   THEREABOUTS,

               (gaze rt   )br   (gaze at 'place'   rhet.q   nodding
            NEW-YORK   INDEX-*rt*,————————————————————————————————→
                       INDEX-rt↔'next to & below New York'   *"WHAT"*,   #N.J.

     Struc   'You know the United States generally, right? New York is here, and right next to and below it is what? New Jersey.'

     Trans   'You know what the U.S. looks like, right? New York is *here* and New Jersey is *right below it*.'

'the relative locations of New York and New Jersey'

In the next example, the Signer sets up a 'house' to the right and a 'house' to the left. Then by gazing at and indexing several spaces between those two locations, the Signer indicates that she and a friend are trying to decide exactly where to put the 'tree' that will be placed somewhere between the two houses.

Context   The Signer wants to ask her mother for help in deciding where to plant a tree near her home. She tells her mother:

(15)

<pre>
              _____(body lean rt)___(gaze lf)_____t
              YOU   KNOW   MY   HOUSE-rt,   FRIEND-lf   HOUSE-lf,   A-CL@rt'my house'
                                                                   A-CL@lf'friend's house',
</pre>

<pre>
              (gaze lf   )
              US-TWO-lf   we-DISCUSS-WITH-"each other"
</pre>

<pre>
                  (gaze cntr   )   (gaze lf,cntr   )   (gaze rt,cntr   )
              TREE   PUT-TO-cntr   INDEX-lf,cntr   INDEX-rt,cntr
</pre>

<pre>
              (gaze lf,cntr,forward   )   (gaze lf,cntr,forward   )   (headshake)wh-q
              INDEX-lf,cntr,forward   INDEX-rt,cntr,forward   "WHAT"
</pre>

Struc   'You know my house and my friend's house are here next to each other. The two of us have been discussing—should the tree be put in the middle between our houses, or closer to his house, or closer to my house, or closer to his house and forward, or closer to my house and forward—where should it go? (We don't know.)'

Trans   'You know my house and my friend's house are *next to each other.* The two of us have been talking about where to put a tree—*in the middle between the houses,* or *closer to one of the houses* or *further forward on one side* or what? (We can't decide.)'

Also notice in the example above how the Signer indicates that the houses are 'next to each other'—by giving them spatial locations that are next to each other. This same use of actual sign location was seen in Chapter X (example 6) where **SCHOOL** and **HOUSE** were signed close to each other to convey the meaning 'the house and the school are *close to each other'.*

Pointing with the index finger is also used in certain standard locative expressions (where the position of the Signer is the place of reference.) For example, pointing upward can mean 'up there'; pointing downward can mean 'down there' or 'right here' (often with the *'cs'* signal); pointing to the right can mean 'to my right'; pointing to the left can mean 'to my left'; pointing outward and slightly upward can mean 'far away'. In each case, the relative distance from the Signer (or another spatial location) is indicated by the Signer's facial expression, head position, angle of the point, and actual movement of the index finger (including how far the arm is extended). For example, in (16), the index finger points outward and to the right with a wide angle between the arm and the ground. The actual movement of the **INDEX** is slow and tense and the Signer's facial behavior emphasizes the great distance (*'intense'*). Thus, the angle of the point, the movement of the point, and the facial signal indicate that the referent (Ocean City) is 'really far away'.

Context   The Signer and another man work at Gallaudet and are discussing where several of their co-workers live.

(16)
$$\overline{}^{t}$$ $$\overline{}^{small\ brow\ raise}$$

<u>   t   </u>   <u>   small brow raise   </u>
P-A-T,   PEA-BRAIN*,   **WORK   HERE   GALLAUDET,**

<u>   rhet.q   </u>   <u>   intense   </u>
LIVE   "WHAT",   INDEX*-*far rt*   O-C

> *Struc*   'Pat, he's really dumb! He works here at Gallaudet, but lives where? Far away, in Ocean City.'

> *Trans*   'Pat is nuts! He works here at Gallaudet but lives *way out in* Ocean City.'

(B.4) Separate Locative Signs

As discussed and illustrated in the preceding sections, ASL tends *not* to use separate signs to express locative relationships in the way that English uses prepositions. Instead, ASL usually takes advantage of the signing space to illustrate those relationships between two or more people, things, places, or events. As such, ASL rarely needs to use separate locative signs.

However, ASL does have several separate locative signs (e.g. **IN, OUTSIDE, ON, OPPOSITE-FROM, UNDER, FAR, NEAR, NEXT-TO-ON-THE-RIGHT, BE-TWEEN**) which are used in certain contexts. In general, these signs seem to be used when the Signer wants to focus on or *emphasize* the locative relationship.

For example, suppose I am looking for my friend, John, and Mary knows that he is in the car waiting for me. When I ask Mary 'Where's John?', she will probably respond '**INDEX**-*car* **CAR**' or '**CAR INDEX**-*car*'. There is no need to focus on the fact that John is *in* the car. However, suppose that I'm driving with John and he gets sick and starts throwing up *in* my car rather than sticking his head out the window or telling me to stop so he can get out of the car. When I tell someone what happened I will want to focus on the fact that John got sick *in* my car. This 'emphatic' use of the locative sign **IN** is illustrated in example (17).

Context   The Signer is describing what happened after a party yesterday.

(17)
```
              (gaze rt)t                              (gaze rt)
YESTERDAY   L-E-E,   (2h)BECOME-DRUNK,              me-TAKE-lee   HOME,
```

```
    mm         t    (gaze rt)nod
DRIVE   L-E-E-rt,    V:-CL-rt,
              "hold steering wheel" ——————→
```

```
              mm   (gaze rt; sudden 'disgust'      )   (head,gaze rt        )
DRIVE"regularly"——————————————————→ DISGUST,   VOMIT-rt"over time"
              "hold steering wheel" ——————————→
```

```
              (head,gaze rt      )
IN   #CAR   VOMIT-rt"over time",    IMAGINE   IN+   #CAR
```

```
(head,gaze rt      )                        (head turn away 'in disgust')
VOMIT-rt"over time"   "hold steering wheel"   DISGUST
              "hold steering wheel" ——————→
```

Struc   'Yesterday Lee, he got drunk. So I took him home. I was driving along and Lee, he was sitting next to me on the right. I was driving along as usual when I looked over at Lee and was suddenly disgusted. He was vomiting continuously—in the car vomiting non-stop. Imagine! Inside the car—vomiting continuously! As I held the wheel, I was disgusted!'

Trans   'Lee got drunk yesterday so I drove him home. He was sitting *next to me in the front seat.* As I was just driving along, I happened to look over at him and "Yecch!" He was throwing up *in* the car. Can you imagine that! Throwing up non-stop *inside* the car! Disgusting!'

The Signer may also want to emphasize an exact location with a separate locative sign when, in context, there are several possible spatial relationships and the Signer needs to specify which one is appropriate or accurate. For example, suppose there are books all around, under, and on several tables. You ask "Where are my books?" The response would need to specify the exact location, as seen in example (18). When something is emphasized in this kind of context where several possibilities exist, we call that emphasis *contrastive stress*.

Context   The Signer's friend is looking for her books in a room with several tables. There are books all around, under, and on the tables. The Signer tells the friend:

(18)
```
              t    (gaze lf        )   _____ nodding
YOUR   BOOK+,   TABLE   INDEX-lf   ON-lf   INDEX-lf
```

Struc   'Your books, the table over there—they're on it.'

Trans   'Your books are sitting *on that table over there.*'

However, when separate locative signs are used, they do not *always* emphasize the spatial relationship. Sometimes a separate locative sign is used when there is no classifier or directional verb in the sentence which could be used to identify that relationship. For example, there is no classifier in ASL that means 'person living', and the verb **LIVE** is not directional; so the locative sign **OPPOSITE-FROM-___** is used in example (19). However, a separate locative sign is not needed in example (20) because the Signer can use the classifier for 'person sitting' to show that same locative relationship.

Context   While eating lunch at Gallaudet College, someone asks the Signer where he lives. The Signer responds:

(19)
<pre>
        _____(gaze down   )t _____nod   (gaze down,cntr   )
        KNOW   GALLAUDET,   INDEX-down,   F-L-A   INDEX-down, lf & rt↔

        (gaze at 'place' where live)   nodding
        ME   LIVE   OPPOSITE-FROM-gallaudet
</pre>

> *Struc*   'You know Gallaudet, it's here. Florida Avenue runs along in front of the college. I live across from Gallaudet on the other side of Florida Avenue.'
>
> *Trans*   'I live across the street from Gallaudet on Florida Avenue.'

In the next example, the classifier (V-CL) is used to illustrate the same locative relationship that is expressed with a separate locative sign in example (19). In this example, 'Gallaudet' is located to the right, the 'boy' is to the left, and 'Florida Avenue' runs along between them.

Context   Someone has heard that a boy in the neighborhood is selling lemonade and asks the Signer where. The Signer responds:

(20)
<pre>
           _____(gaze down)t
           KNOW   GALLAUDET,

        _____nod (gaze down,lf cntr)   t   (body lean lf   )nod
        INDEX-down,rt cntr, ───→
                   F-L-A   B-CL-lf,cntr↔'street',   BOY,   V:-CL-lf'across from Gallaudet'
</pre>

> *Struc*   'You know Gallaudet College, it's here, and Florida Avenue runs along one side of the college. The boy, he's sitting across from and facing Gallaudet on the other side of the street.'
>
> *Trans*   'You know how Florida runs along one side of Gallaudet. Well, the boy is sitting *on Florida across from the college.*'

Notice that the sign often *mislabeled* as **ACROSS** in sign vocabulary books was not used in these examples. This is because that sign is *not* a separate locative sign. It is actually a verb that means 'go across' and, thus, cannot be used in examples like (19) and (20). However, as a verb, it can be used in an example like (21).

Context   The Signer and a friend are hiking in the woods and the Signer spots a
river up ahead to his left.

(21)   co   (gaze lf   )
    "HEY", INDEX-*lf* WATER (2h)5↓wg-CL-*lf'river'*,

    WHY͜NOT US-TWO GO-ACROSS-*river*

   Struc   'Hey! There's a river over there. Why don't we go across it.'

   Trans   'Hey! There's a river over there. Let's go across it.'

Unfortunately, many sign vocabulary books mislabel and misuse signs like **GO-ACROSS** or **GO-INTO/ENTER** (often glossed as **INTO**) and give the false impression that these signs function like English prepositions. However, by observing native Deaf Signers who use ASL, linguists have noticed that either: (1) these signs are rarely, if ever, used (such as the signs labeled as **AT, AMONG, AROUND**), or (2) these signs are not used as separate locative signs (such as the signs labeled as **TO, IN-FRONT-OF, BEHIND, INTO, ACROSS**). Instead, they have other functions in the language.

C. Summary

Linguists are just beginning to study how ASL expresses locative relationships. However, for now the teacher and student of ASL should remember that whenever possible (which is most of the time!), ASL tends to use the signing space (via classifiers, directional verbs, indexing, etc.) to illustrate the locative relationships between referents and the locations of various actions and events.

Bibliography: Locatives

McIntire, M. (In preparation), Locatives in American Sign Language. Ph.D. dissertation, University of California, Los Angeles.

Dialogues
and
Cultural Information

LOCATIVES

The following three dialogues have been developed to illustrate various uses of the grammatical features described in this chapter. Each of these dialogues also appears in one of the three corresponding Student Texts. In the Student Texts, the transcription of each dialogue is less detailed than what is provided here for the teacher of ASL. Following the dialogues, in the sections called "Cultural Information", are brief discussions of the topic of each dialogue.

The following dialogues and cultural information correspond to:

Student Text: Unit 6
                Unit 15
                Unit 24

Dialogue: Locatives
(Student Text - Unit 6)

First Signer (Pat)

Pat₁: <u>   co   </u>   ME   HEAR+   <u>   wh-q </u>
       "HEY"   (2h)WHAT'S-UP   (2h)"WHAT"

Pat₂: <u>nodding</u>   <u>(gaze rt   )</u>   <u>(nod)q</u>
       THAT-ONE-*rt*   INDEX-*rt*   A-A-A-D   HOUSTON   INDEX-*rt*   THAT-ONE

Pat₃: "OH-MY",   <u>   wh-q </u>
                   (2h)"WHAT"   HOW   HAPPEN   HOWwg

Pat₄: <u>   q </u>
       ROOMMATE   BORROW-FROM-*you*

Pat₅: <u>   (gaze lf   )   q </u>
       FEEL+   SOMEONE   1-CL-*rt*'person walk by'   NOTICE-TO-*lf*   GO-INTO-*lf*   SWIPE-*lf*

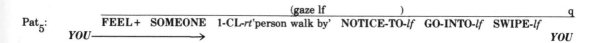

YOU————————————————▶   *YOU*

Dialogue: Locatives
(Student Text - Unit 6)

Second Signer (Lee)

Lee₁:
<u>nodding</u>   q
REMEMBER ONE-YEAR-PAST BASKETBALL TOURNAMENT,

                 (gaze lf   )   <u>nodding</u>   q
EXCITE WIN, (2h)*lf*-GIVE-TO-*me* TROPHY, REMEMBER

Lee₂:
<u>nod</u>
    SOMEONE STEAL

Lee₃:
          <u>neg</u>   <u>t</u>   <u>mm</u> (gaze rt) <u>nodding</u>
NOT-KNOW, PAST NIGHT, ME READ-*paper+*, INDEX-*rt* TABLE,

        (gaze rt)   (gaze rt,cntr)
TROPHY A-CL@*rt* ⎯⎯⎯⎯⎯⎯⎯⎯⎯⎯⎯⎯⎯⎯⎯⟶
                     C-U-P   ***C-CL**@rt,cntr'cup behind trophy'*

        <u>t</u> (gaze rt)   th
MORNING,   **SNATCHED-UP-*trophy*** ***C-CL-rt*** ⎫ 'cup on table is turned on its side' **"HUH"**
                                            B↑-CL-rt ⎭

Lee₄:
                     <u>neg</u>
NOT-POSSIBLE, NOT HERE FLY-TO-*lf* CHICAGO ONE-WEEK-PAST

Lee₅:
          <u>neg</u>   <u>nodding</u>
NOT-KNOW, SEEM+++

Dialogue: Locatives
(Student Text - Unit 15)

First Signer (Pat)

                                              (br.squint   )   q

Pat₁: REMEMBER ONE-DAY-PAST US-TWO TALK GIRL, REMEMBER YOU

Pat₁:

(br.squint) / **q**

REMEMBER ONE-DAY-PAST US-TWO TALK GIRL, REMEMBER YOU

---

nodding _____ **cs** _____ **t**

Pat₂: THAT-ONE-*rt* INDEX-*rt,* SELF-*rt* HEARING, INDEX-*rt* MOTHER FATHER, DEAF

                (gaze rt   )   (gaze rt)nodding

INDEX-*rt* LIVE INDEX-*rt,outward* STATE-SCHOOL THEREABOUTS-*rt*

                 (gaze rt)   (gaze rt to 'road'   )t

Pat₃: "UMMM", KNOW+ STATE-SCHOOL-*rt* 5:↓-CL@*rt*'school'————————→

                                          B-CL'road near school'

              (gaze rt to 'home'   )   (gaze rt   )

(hold 5:↓-CL)————————————————————————→

     LIVE INDEX-rt'next to school' NOT-MUCH INDEX-school & home↔

     _____ **neg**

Pat₄: NOT-KNOW, "THAT'S-RIGHT" INDEX-*rt* GO-*lf* CHICAGO, SEARCH #JOB

     _____ **neg**

Pat₅: NOT-KNOW, FEEL AGE-TWENTY THEREABOUTS

Dialogue: Locatives
(Student Text - Unit 15)

Second Signer (Lee)

                                                                                                    q

Lee₁: ‾‾

Lee$_1$: SMALL   GIRL   (2h)FRECKLES-ON-*face*   THAT-ONE   INDEX-*lf*

                                  wh-q

Lee$_2$:   ‾‾‾‾‾‾‾‾‾‾‾‾‾‾‾‾‾‾‾‾‾‾‾‾‾‾‾‾‾‾‾‾‾‾‾‾‾‾

                      EXACT   WHERE   "WHAT"   EXACT

OH-I-SEE

       (gaze lf)   wh-q

Lee$_3$: GIRL   #DO-DO   INDEX-*lf*

                                   "WHAT"

                            wh-q

Lee$_4$:   ‾‾‾‾‾‾‾‾‾‾‾‾‾‾‾‾‾‾‾‾‾‾‾

              AGE+   INDEX-*lf*

OH-I-SEE

Lee$_5$: YOUNG   "WOW"

Dialogue: Locatives
(Student Text - Unit 24)

First Signer (Pat)

<pre>
                                                  (puff.cheeks)wh-q
Pat₁: (2h)"WHAT" HAPPEN INDEX-Lee's rt cheek   PURPLE 5:-CL'bruise on cheek' YOU

                                  wh-q
Pat₂: (2h)"WHAT" (2h)#DO-DO (2h)"WHAT"

       nodding (gaze rt   )   (gaze rt   )   q
Pat₃: THAT-ONE-rt FARM   THEREABOUTS-rt ─────────→THAT-ONE-rt YOU
                                                B-CL-lf'hillside'──────────────→

Pat₄: WOW REALLY-ADEPT YOU

                           nodding   q
Pat₅: "WOW"+, #HURT INDEX-cheek   OTHER+ (2h)"WHAT"
</pre>

Dialogue: Locatives
(Student Text - Unit 24)

Second Signer (Lee)

Lee₁: FEW-DAY-PAST ME SKI BAD HAPPEN INDEX-*lf cheek*

<pre>
                    (gaze down,lf   ) (gaze at 'hill'   )   q
Lee₂: YOU KNOW   WATER⌒(2h)L:-CL@<i>lf</i>'lake' B-CL-<i>rt</i>'hillside next to lake', KNOW YOU
                    (hold lf hand L:-CL) ──→
</pre>

<pre>
        nodding (gaze down,cntr   )   br
Lee₃: RIGHT+, B-CL-<i>cntr</i>'front face of hill', ME V-CL@<i>cntr</i>'stand on hilltop'
                 B-CL-cntr'hilltop' ───────────────────────────────→

        (gaze lf at 'fence'   ) (gaze rt)   br
        (2h)4-CL-<i>lf</i>'fence on side of hill', TREE-<i>rt,upward-arc</i>'trees on side of hill',

             (gaze down,cntr; look of'concentration';body moving from side to side)
        ME   SKI 1-CL-<i>cntr</i>'ski down hillside,weaving side to side'
</pre>

<pre>
                                                      t
Lee₄: "PSHAW", 1-CL-<i>cntr</i>'ski down hillside', RABBIT,

                                        (look of 'fright'   )
        V:-CL++-<i>rt</i>'hop from trees in front of me'   ME 1-CL'swerve to lf to miss rabbit'

        (gaze lf, 'shocked'   )
             (2h)4-CL-<i>lf</i>'fence' V-CL-<i>lf</i>'fall over fence'
                 (hold lf 4-CL) ─────────────→
</pre>

<pre>
        (gaze at lf shoulder   )
Lee₅: INDEX-<i>lf shoulder</i> #HURT-<i>lf shoulder</i> INDEX-<i>lf shoulder</i>, "WOW"+
</pre>

Student Text: Unit 6

Cultural Information: American Athletic Association of the Deaf

The American Athletic Association of the Deaf, Inc. (AAAD) is a national organization devoted to fostering and regulating athletic competition among member clubs. There are approximately 160 member clubs and approximately 20,000 individual members. There are seven regional divisions within the AAAD: Eastern Athletic Association of the Deaf (EAAD), Central Athletic Association of the Deaf (CAAD), Midwest Athletic Association of the Deaf (MAAD), Far West Athletic Association of the Deaf (FWAAD), Southwest Athletic Association of the Deaf (SWAAD), Southeastern Athletic Association of the Deaf (SEAAD), and Northwest Athletic Association of the Deaf (NWAAD).

The AAAD works to develop standard rules for inter-club competition and to provide adequate inter-club competition for its members. Toward this end, the AAAD sponsors an annual national basketball tournament and an annual softball tournament. The AAAD also gives an annual award to the Deaf Athlete of the Year and has a Hall of Fame which honors deaf (as well as hearing) players, leaders, and coaches. Finally, the AAAD participates in selecting and sponsoring deaf and hard-of-hearing athletes to participate in the Summer and Winter World Games for the Deaf. For further information about the AAAD, write: Secretary/Treasurer, American Athletic Association of the Deaf, 3916 Latern Drive, Silver Spring, Md. 20902.

Student Text: Unit 15

Cultural Information: Hearing Children of Deaf Parents

It should not be surprising that the vast majority of deaf adults (85–90%) marry other deaf adults, rather than hearing adults. This type of intermarriage helps to provide a high degree of cohesiveness and continuity to the Deaf Community. What may seem surprising is that the vast majority of the children born to deaf parents have normal hearing. Although there has been very little study of these hearing children of deaf parents, there do seem to be some common experiences which many of them share. For example, many hearing children of deaf parents:

  —acquire signing skills before speaking skills. The type of signing skills they acquire depends on the type of signing that is used by the parents
  —are given the role of interpreter/transliterator for their parents at an extremely young age (often as young as five or six)
  —experience the pressures of participating in adult decisions (telephone calls, salespeople, etc.) at a very young age because of the interpreting or transliterating demands
  —go through a period of embarrassment because their parents are different and sign—which sometimes leads the child or adolescent to reject his/her parents and even refuse to sign in public
  —co-exist in two communities (the Deaf and the Hearing) and feel the need to become more deeply involved in each one

In 1979, the Registry of Interpreters for the Deaf (RID) published a small monograph entitled *Deaf Parents—Hearing Children*. This seems to be the only work currently available on this topic. The monograph describes the results of a survey of 300 hearing children of deaf parents and is available from the RID (814 Thayer Avenue, Silver Spring, Md. 20910).

Student Text: Unit 24

Cultural Information: World Games for the Deaf

In 1924, representatives from nine European countries met in Paris, France and established the International Committee of Silent Sports (CISS—"Comite International des Sports Silencieux"). This committee was developed to establish a union of all sports federations for deaf people and to institute and manage quadrennial World Games for the Deaf. The United States joined the CISS in 1935 as its first non-European nation. Until 1948, only Summer Games were held. Then in 1949, the first Winter Games were held in Seefeld, Austria. In 1955, the CISS was acknowledged by the International Olympic Committee as an international federation with Olympic standing. Currently, Jerald M. Jordan of the United States is President of the CISS and has served in that capacity since 1971.

The World Games for the Deaf are held exclusively for persons with a certain level of hearing loss, and each national federation is required to verify that its competitors do, in fact, have a hearing loss at or below this level. Those athletes with very mild losses are not permitted to compete. In fact, pretending to be deaf is considered as serious an offense as taking drugs in the "hearing Olympics".

The World Games features competition in such events as track and field, cycling, soccer, gymnastics, handball, wrestling, swimming, diving, ping-pong, skiing, tennis, shooting and volleyball.

Chapter XII

Pluralization

A. Introduction

The term *pluralization* refers to the ways in which a language indicates that there is more than one of something. For example, to indicate that there is more than one 'ship' in a harbor, the English language uses the process of adding an *'s'* to the noun - 'ships'. English speakers can also indicate degrees of plurality (i.e. how much more than one) by using words like *'several* ships', a *'fleet* of ships', a *'great number* of ships', or a *'hundred* ships'.

There are several ways in ASL to indicate that there is more than one of something. To show that something is plural, the Signer may: (1) add a plural modulation to a singular classifier, or use a plural classifier, (2) add a plural modulation to a pronoun, or (3) use a definite number sign (e.g. **TWO, FIVE**) or an indefinite number sign (e.g. **SEVERAL, MANY**). In some cases, the Signer may repeat a noun in different spatial locations to indicate that the referent is plural. In addition, verbs are often made to 'agree' with the plurality of the subject or object in the sentence (see following section).

Several of these ways of indicating that something is plural may occur in the same sentence. How plurality is indicated in a sentence depends on which signs occur and the form of those signs. In this chapter, we will first describe a useful concept called *number agreement* and then examine how ASL Signers indicate that something is plural with classifiers, pronouns, number signs, nouns, and verbs.

B. Number Agreement Rules[1]

ASL has several *number agreement rules* which, depending on the form of the sign, require that the noun, pronoun, classifier, adjective, and/or verb in a sentence must 'agree' with the fact that something in the sentence is plural. To illustrate the concept of *agreement rules,* it may be useful to look at some agreement rules in other languages. Let's look first at French and English.

(1)   French: Le<u>s</u> petit<u>s</u> garçon<u>s</u> <u>sont</u> triste<u>s</u>.
             English: The small   boy<u>s</u>   <u>are</u> sad.

Both of the sentences above show that more than one 'boy' is being talked about (i.e. that the subject of the sentence is plural). In the written French sentence, this fact is 'marked' (i.e. indicated) by adding an *'-s'* on the article ('le'), on the adjectives ('petit' and 'triste'), and on the noun ('garçon'), and by using the plural form of the

---

[1]The study of Linguistics uses the term *number* to refer to both singular (e.g. 'one goat') and plural (e.g. 'ten goats') forms in a language.

verb ('être'). In the English sentence, plurality is marked by adding an '-s' on the noun ('boy') and by using the plural form of the verb ('to be'). Thus, the article, adjectives, noun, and verb 'agree' (i.e. all of them reflect the fact that the subject is plural) in the French sentence, whereas only the noun and verb 'agree' in the English sentence.

Other languages like German and Latin also have number agreement rules. However, unlike French and German, these languages do not add an '-s' to show plurality but use a different plural marker.[2]

(2)   German: Die kleinen Knaben sind traurig.
                 Latin: Ø Breves   pueri   sunt maesti.
English translation: 'The small   boys   are   sad.'

As you can see, the forms used to indicate plurality are different in these languages. In the German sentence, the article, first adjective, noun, and verb 'agree' with the fact that the subject is plural. In the Latin sentence, the noun, verb, and both adjectives 'agree'. (Note that Latin does not have articles like 'a' and 'the'.)

Another type of agreement rule usually occurs in languages where the nouns have different "genders" (masculine, feminine, neuter). In these languages (e.g. Greek, German, Latin, French), the articles, demonstratives, and/or adjectives often 'agree' with the gender of the noun. For example, in the Latin sentence above, the noun that means 'boy' has a *masculine* gender, so the adjectives that mean 'small' and 'sad' are also masculine (as well as plural). The *feminine* plural form of 'sad' would be 'maestae'.[3]

As we saw in Chapter IX, the grammatical process called *verb directionality* also involves a type of agreement rule. In this case, the direction of the verb's movement 'agrees' with the spatial location of the subject and object in the sentence. This type of subject-object agreement also occurs on verbs in Swahili.

Returning to the subject of number agreement rules, we will be presenting examples of these rules in ASL and describing what is known about them so far while we review the various ways that ASL Signers indicate plurality.

In this chapter, the "structural equivalents" (*Struc*) are handled a little differently. Here they are written to show where the information that something is plural occurs in each example of ASL. Thus, since ASL and English often communicate this information in different places, some of the "structural equivalents" (which are written with English words) look strange. For example, whereas English generally shows that a referent is plural by adding an '-s' to the noun, ASL usually does not pluralize the noun itself. So in the "structural equivalent" of an ASL sentence, the noun usually will not have an '-s'. This is to draw your attention to the ways in which the structure of ASL is different than the structure of English concerning how information about plurality is communicated.

---

[2]Actually, both French and English have other ways to show plurality. For example, the English nouns 'children', 'sheep', 'men' and 'people' are plural forms. In French, the plural forms of the nouns 'animal' and 'cheval' ('horse') are 'animaux' and 'chevaux'. In example (2), the null symbol 'Ø' is used to indicate that Latin does not have a definite article that means 'the'.

[3]Latin also has agreement rules for 'case' (e.g. indicative, accusative, dative). Actually, the adjectives in the example above 'agree' with the number, gender, and case of the noun. And 'maestae' is actually the *plural, feminine, indicative* form of the word that means 'sad'.

C. Ways to Indicate Plurality with Different Types of Signs

(C.1) Classifiers

As described in Chapter X, many classifiers in ASL are singular—they represent one thing. If the Signer wants to represent more than one thing with a classifier, s/he will either pluralize the singular classifier (generally by adding repetition or a 'sweeping' movement to the classifier) or will use a plural classifier. These processes are described again in this section, with more attention to how singular classifiers are made plural.

Singular Classifiers

Classifiers like A-CL, 1→CL, C-CL, 3→CL, V:-CL, B↑-CL, B↓-CL, F-CL, L:-CL, Ψ-CL, and X-CL are singular—each is used to represent one thing. One way to pluralize a singular classifier is to repeat it. When the classifier is repeated once (i.e. articulated or produced twice), it indicates that there are two things. When the classifier is repeated twice (i.e. articulated three times), it indicates either that there are *three* things or that there are *some* things, depending on how each repetition is produced. If produced more slowly and deliberately (as if actually representing the location of each thing), then the meaning is 'three' things. If the meaning is 'some', then the articulations (usually three or four) are faster with less attention to actual placement.

Notice that each articulation (production) of the classifier must be made in a different location, reflecting to some degree the actual position or orientation of the things being described. Thus, we saw in Chapter X how the plural modulations of singular classifiers generally indicate whether the referents are lined up in a row (or rows) or if they are in a disorderly arrangement, as illustrated below.

(2h)A-CL*"in a row"*   (2h)alt.A-CL'scattered all around'

As stated above, if the Signer repeats the classifier slowly while giving each repetition a specific location, s/he can indicate a specific, small number of referents (approximately 2–4). In this case, the Signer is not focusing on the specific number (or else s/he would use a specific number sign), but the Addressee still knows how many things the Signer is talking about.

If the Signer wants to focus on the exact number of referents, then s/he can use a number sign followed by the repeated classifier (which 'agrees' with the number sign), as illustrated below. In this example, the Signer uses the number sign **FIVE** to indicate the exact number of 'pencils' and then repeats the classifier to show that they are 'in a row'. However, notice that 'agreement' does not mean the classifier must be articulated 'five' times, but that it is articulated three or more times to agree with the fact that the referent ('pencils') is *plural*.

Context   The Signer is asked to describe what she sees on the floor as she enters a room.

(3)   t   (gaze down)puff.cheeks
           FLOOR,   PENCIL   FIVE   1→CL"*in a row*"

     Struc   'On the floor, there are pencil five of them lying next to each other in a row.'

     Trans   'Five pencils in a row on the floor.'

(2h)1→CL"*in a row*"

As described in Chapter X, the modulations which indicate that 'some', 'several', or 'many' things are lined up 'in a row' or 'in rows' tend to use both hands. The non-dominant hand generally 'holds' the start of each row while the dominant hand makes each repetition of the classifier.[4] In general, the speed of the repetitions indicates the relative number of referents. To indicate a very large number of things, Signers usually repeat the classifier at a faster pace.

---

[4]However, there are several possible variations of these plural modulations in ASL. For example, in some contexts, they may be made with one hand. Or, both hands may act independently to indicate that two groups of things are lined up in separate rows.

For example, notice what happens if you sign the *"in a row"* modulation on a classifier very fast—it begins to look more and more like the *"sweep in a row"* modulation! And the *"sweep in a row"* modulation indicates a greater number of things than the basic *"in a row"* modulation.

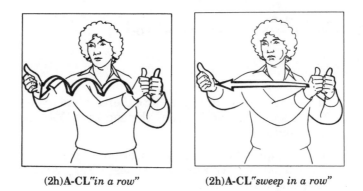

(2h)A-CL*"in a row"*   (2h)A-CL*"sweep in a row"*

In the same way, the *"sweep in rows"* modulation indicates that there is a greater number of things in each row than the *"in rows"* modulation. These two modulations show that the number of referents in each row is plural *and* that the number of rows is plural.

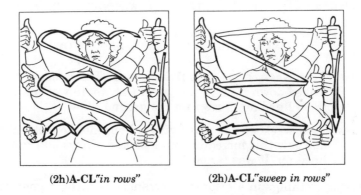

(2h)A-CL*"in rows"*   (2h)A-CL*"sweep in rows"*

Sometimes the plural modulation of the classifier is the only indication that a particular referent is plural. This is seen in examples (4) and (5) where the *"sweep in rows"* modulation indicates that the referent of **STATUE** and **#CAR** is plural. (Notice how the facial signal *'pursed lips'* in example (4) 'agrees' with the small size of the wooden statues.)

Context   The Signer is an art student who just recently returned from a trip to
            Germany. She tells a classmate:

(4)   ____co____   ____(gaze rt)____   _____t_____
            FINEwg,   GERMANY   INDEX-*rt*,   STORE   INDEX-*rt*,

                 ___(gaze at 'statue')___   ____q___ (Friend:'yes') _nod_
            HAVE   STATUE'small'   WOOD,   KNOW   YOU

            _(gaze rt   )____pursed lips_
            (2h)A-CL-*rt"sweep in rows"*

        Struc   'It was neat! In Germany, a store there, it had little wooden statue.
                  You know the kind I mean? (Friend says 'Yes') And there were
                  rows and rows of them.'

        Trans   'It was super! At this store in Germany, they had all these little
                  wooden statues. You know the ones? ('Yes') Well, there were just
                  rows and rows of them.'

Context   Last week while on a business trip, the Signer flew over Detroit. Now,
            during a coffee break, he tells a colleague:[5]

(5)   _____t_____   (body 'rocking')mm   _____t__ (gaze down,rt   )
            ONE-WEEK-PAST,   ME   Ч-CL-*rt*'flying'   WINDOW-*rt*,   ME   *me*-LOOK-AT-*down,rt*,

            (look of 'surprise')   ___t___   (gaze down,rt   )
                     #CAR,   (2h)3→CL-*rt"sweep in rows"*,   WOW

            Struc   'Last week, I was just flying along. The window on my right, I
                      looked down from it, and wow! Car, there was a huge number of
                      them lined up in rows on the ground. Wow!'

            Trans   'Last week while I was flying, I happened to look out the window
                      and saw this incredible mass of cars—rows and rows of them all
                      lined up. It was far out!'

When referring to things in a disorderly arrangement, the Signer can use slow
repetition with either one or two hands. However, when the repetitions are faster
and indicate a larger number of things, the Signer will generally use the 'two hands
alternating' form of repetition. This alternating form is illustrated in examples
(6)–(8). Notice that the facial adverb, written as *'th'*, also signals that the arrangement of things is unorganized.

---

[5]For readers who have the accompanying videotape: Notice how the Signer's body slightly rocks back
and forth while holding the Ч-CL in place to give the idea of 'flying along'. Also notice how the Signer's
left hand holds the location of the 'window' while signing **ME** *me*-**LOOK-AT**-*down,cntr* and how the sign
ME is not made with the index finger, but is 'assimilated' to the sign that follows it. As you may have
already noticed, this assimilation of handshape with the sign **ME** happens frequently in the examples on
this tape.

Context   The Signer is asked to describe what he sees on the floor as he enters a room.

(6)

t	(gaze down)th
FLOOR, PENCIL	(2h)alt.1→CL

    Struc   'On the floor, pencil are strewn all over.'

    Trans   'Pencils strewn all over the floor.'

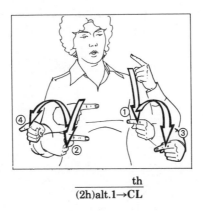

th
(2h)alt.1→CL

In the next example, the noun **PEOPLE** is plural and the plural modulation of the singular classifier **V:-CL** 'agrees' with the plural noun. It would be ungrammatical to use this classifier here without a plural modulation. (Also notice how the Signer changes her "perspective". First she points to the right to refer to the 'bar'. Then she 'moves' the bar to "center stage" (*me*-**GO-INTO**-*cntr*) to begin describing what happened at the bar.)

Context   A friend has been encouraging the Signer to visit a particular bar. So the Signer finally went, but had an unpleasant experience. The Signer is just beginning to tell her friend about what happened.

(7)

(gaze rt)t
BAR   INDEX-*rt,*   **ME**   *me*-**GO-INTO**-*cntr,*

t
PEOPLE,   (2h)alt.V:-CL'people seated'

    Struc   'The bar over there, I went into it. The people, they were seated all over the place.'

    Trans   'I went into that bar over there and saw that the people were sitting all over the place.'

Context   The Signer and a group of tourists are walking through an old house that will soon be restored and become a museum. Upon entering one of the rooms the Signer (who is the tour guide) says:

(8)

			(gaze at each 'picture'; mm)t
INDEX-*down*	ROOM,	PICTURE	(2h)alt.C-CL'pictures on walls',

pursed lips		nod	(gaze at each 'painting') pursed lips
FEW	MUST	AGAIN	PAINT-*pictures"each"*

Struc   'This room, the picture many of them placed all over the walls, a very few of them need to be painted again—each of them a little bit.'

Trans   'A few of the pictures on the walls in this room need some touch-up work.'

(2h)alt.C-CL'pictures on walls'   **PAINT**-*pictures"each"*

Notice that the verb **PAINT**-*pictures"each"* is repeated in an arc. This shows that the Signer is talking about painting several objects. As such, the verb 'agrees' with its plural object—the 'pictures'.

The illustrations below also show the 'two hands alternating', plural modulation—which indicates that the referents are positioned in an unorderly manner.[6] The modulation with the V-CL could be used to indicate that there are 'many people lying all over the floor'; the modulation with the B↓-CL could be used to express the meaning 'many papers strewn all over the desk'.

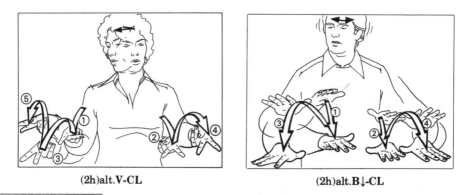

(2h)alt.V-CL   (2h)alt.B↓-CL

[6] This plural modulation is very similar to the plural modulation of verbs that we call *"unspec"* (see in Chapter XIV).

In this section, we have seen that, in general, singular classifiers are made plural via repetition. This repetition can be slow and deliberate to suggest a specific, small number of referents, or it can be at faster speeds to indicate increasingly larger numbers of referents. The type of repetition that the Signer uses will also provide information around the arrangement (locations) of the referents.

Plural Classifiers

As discussed in Chapter X, several classifiers in ASL are already (inherently) plural. Some refer to a specific number of people (e.g. 2-CL, 3-CL, 4-CL); others refer to a larger, unspecified number of people or things (e.g. (2h)4-CL, (2h)4:-CL, 5:-CL). Thus, the use of any of these plural classifiers will indicate that the referent is plural.

In the case of the specific-number plural classifiers, the classifier alone can indicate the number of referents (e.g. 2-CL). Or, a number sign may occur separately before the classifier. When both a number sign and a specific-number classifier occur in a sentence, the result is an increased emphasis on the actual number of referents, as illustrated in examples (9) and (10). (Compare the translations of the two examples.)

Context   In response to a friend's question about something that happened to the Signer yesterday, the Signer begins to describe that event.

(9)
$$\overline{\quad\quad t\quad\quad}\qquad \overline{\quad\quad mm\quad\quad}$$
YESTERDAY, ME WALK*"regularly"*,

$$\overline{\quad t\quad}\qquad \text{(gaze rt}\qquad\qquad\qquad)$$
BOY,   2-CL'come up to me from rt'

    Struc   'Yesterday, I was just walking along as usual. Boy, two of them came up to me from the right.'

    Trans   'Yesterday I was just walking along when these two boys came up to me.'

Context   (same as example 9, but later the Signer will describe how the boys ganged up on him and he didn't have a chance because it was "two on one". So the number 'two' is important in this context.)

(10)
$$\overline{\quad\quad t\quad\quad}\qquad \overline{\quad\quad mm\quad\quad}$$
YESTERDAY, ME WALK*"regularly"*,

$$\overline{\quad\quad t\quad\quad}\qquad \text{(gaze rt}\qquad\qquad)$$
BOY TWO,   2-CL'come up to me from rt'

    Struc   'Yesterday, I was just walking along as usual. Boy two of them, they came up to me from the right.'

    Trans   'Yesterday I was just walking along when these boys—two of 'em—came up to me.'

The plural classifiers which do not indicate a specific number have already been described and illustrated in Chapter X (see Section C.2). Another example of a plural classifier is given below. This example illustrates an interesting use of the 5:-CL, which indicates 'a relatively large mass of things'. Notice that the classifier after the sign **WOMAN** moves relatively far out to the right and is accompanied by the *'puffed cheeks'* signal. However, after the sign **MAN**, the same classifier moves only a very short distance to the left and is accompanied by the *'pursed lips'* signal.

Context   The Signer is trying to encourage two of her male friends to become interested in the field of interpreting. She tells them:

(11)

<pre>
                               t   (gaze rt)   puff.cheeks
   TRUE+ SAD, INTERPRET FIELD, WOMAN (2h)5:↓-CL-rt'large group',

     t   (gaze lf   )pursed lips
   MAN, NOT-MUCH   (2h)5:↓-CL-lf'small group'
</pre>

Struc   'It's really sad. In the interpreting field, woman there is a very large number of them, but man, there is an insignificant, small number of them.'

Trans   'It's really sad. In the field of interpreting, there are scores of females but only a small number of men.'

This example shows us that the 'distance traveled' by the 5:↓-CL also indicates the relative number of referents, and that the Signer's facial behavior can also communicate information about the number or size of the referents. Notice how each of these two features 'agree' with each other when referring to the females as opposed to the males. In addition, we know that using two hands with a (non-specific number) plural classifier will indicate an even larger group of things than that indicated with a similar, one-handed plural classifier. However, in this example, the one-handed variant was not used to represent the 'men' because, according to the Signer, that additional difference would have been "too much; overdone". Obviously, we have much to learn about how the different ways of indicating plurality interact with each other—which ones can occur together and which ones can't occur together. (For more information about plural classifiers, you may wish to re-read Section C.2 in Chapter X.)

(C.2) Pronouns

As discussed in Chapter VIII on Pronominalization, ASL has several plural pronouns (e.g. *dual, trial, quadruple*) as well as several ways to pluralize singular pronouns. These pronouns can then be used to indicate that a referent is plural.

Like the specific-number plural classifiers, the *dual, trial, quadruple* and *quintuple* pronouns will indicate the exact number of referents. For example, in (12), the pronoun **US-THREE**-*rt* indicates that there are 'three' linguists.

Context   The teacher of a course on "Teaching ASL as a Second Language" has asked the students why they are taking this course. The teacher points to three students who are sitting next to each other and one of them responds:[7]

(12)

	t			t	(		nod)t

TEACH-*lf* A-S-L-*lf,*   "WELL" US-THREE-*rt,*   LINGUISTICS‿AGENT-*rt,*

(gaze lf   )
WANT-*lf* LEARN+-*lf* MORE+-*lf* "WELL" HOW-*lf* POSS+-*lf,*

(gaze lf   nodding
"WELL" (2h)"WHAT" POSS+-*lf* (2h)"WHAT"

> *Struc*   'Teaching ASL, well, the three of us—we're linguist, want to learn more about, well, how—it's characteristics, well, what's involved in it, what it's all about.'

> *Trans*   'Concerning the teaching of ASL, the three of us—we're linguists—want to learn more about how it's done, what's involved, just what it's all about.'

Just as there are ways to pluralize singular classifiers, there are also ways to pluralize a singular pronoun. For example, the pronoun made by pointing with the index finger can be repeated in different locations to show that the referent is plural. This is seen in example (13) where the repeated **INDEX** shows that the referent of **HORSE WHITE** is plural. Notice that since the Signer points to four different locations on the right, we know that there are at least four white horses. If the speed of the pointing were slow and deliberate, then we would think there are probably exactly 'four' white horses.

Context   The Signer and a friend are at a ranch, looking at a huge herd of different colored horses.

(13)

	co			(gaze rt)t		q

"HEY",   HORSE   WHITE   INDEX+++-*rt,*   SEE   YOU

> *Struc*   'Hey! White horse there, there, there, and there on the right, do you see them?'

> *Trans*   'Hey! Do you see those white horses over there?'

As described in Chapter VIII, the "arc-point" modulation on a singular pronoun will also indicate that the referent is plural. This arc-point is like the *"sweep in a row"* modulation that we saw with singular classifiers. (It is also like the *"all"* modulation that occurs with verbs and that will be described in Section C.5 and in

---

[7]At present, there is no standard sign for the meaning 'linguist'. Some Signers use the compound LANGUAGE‿AGENT; others use LANGUAGE SCIENCE‿AGENT. The Signer in this example uses a compound sign made with a new sign for 'linguistics' ('L' to 'S' handshape, based on the sign LANGUAGE) that is used by some Signers, but is not commonly recognized.

Chapter XIV.) The arc-point can be used with all of the pronominal handshapes and refers to 'all' the members of a group (or some portion of a group, depending on where the arc begins and ends). For example, in (14), the arc-point on the left refers to 'all' of the 'moderates' and shows that the referent of the sign **WOMAN** is plural.

Context   The Signer is a minister and is lecturing to a group of women and men about the evils of alcohol. The men are seated to the minister's right; the women are to the left. The minister accusingly asks the women:

(14)   (gaze lf)br   (gaze lf   )q
         WOMAN,   INDEX-*arc-lf* **ALLOW   HUSBAND   (2h)alt.DRINK-WHISKEY   (2h)DRUNK**

    Struc   'Woman, do you permit your husband to drink to excess and be-
              come really drunk?'

    Trans   'Women, do you permit your husbands to drink and get drunk?'

In the next example, the arc-point is used three times. The first time, it moves from left to right and refers to all of the students. Then it only moves across the right side of the signing space to refer to all the students on that side and indicates that the referent of the sign **GIRL** is plural. The arc-point to the left side indicates that the referent of the sign **BOY** is also plural and refers to all the members of that group. Notice that the noun **RULE** is also plural because it is repeated.

Context   The Signer is a teacher and has just explained the rules of a new game to a group of girls and a group of boys.

(15)   (gaze down, lf & rt↔   )q
          NOW,   INDEX-*arc* **UNDERSTAND   RULE +,**

          (gaze down,rt   )br
          INDEX-*arc-rt* **GIRL   FIRST,   FINISH,**

          (gaze down,lf   )   (gaze lf & rt↔   )q
          lf-**TAKE-TURN-AFTER**-*girls* **BOY   INDEX**-*arc-lf,* *me-**SAY-#OK-TO**-girls*
                                                        *me-**SAY-#OK-TO**-boys*

    Struc   'Now, you all understand the rules? You all girl on the right are
              first; after you're done, then boy you all on the left will take a turn.
              OK with each group?'

    Trans   'Now you get the rules? First it's the girls' turn and then the boys'
              turn. OK?'

As stated earlier, this use of the arc-point to indicate plurality can also be used with other pronouns. And it can be used when the referents are not present in the communication area, as illustrated in example (16). In this example, the Signer uses the possessive pronoun (**POSS**) in an arc to show that the referent of **TEACH⌢AGENT** is plural.

Context Some of the teachers at a school are talking about going on strike because they are "overworked and underpaid". The administration is, of course, upset at the idea and has been trying to make the teachers feel guilty about their proposed action. The Signer is a teacher and sarcastically mimics the administration's position.

(16)
```
       (gaze rt)              t  (gaze rt   )                      rhet.q
        TEACH AGENT-rt,   POSS-arc-rt  DUTY  (2h)"WHAT",
```

```
                                        t   ('smirk' )
        TEACH*,  REBEL-rt,  (2h)alt.COMPLAIN-rt,  WRONG*
```

> *Struc* 'Teacher, their duty is what? To teach! To rebel and complain, that's wrong!'

> *Trans* 'Teachers are supposed to teach! It's wrong for them to rebel and complain.'

However, suppose the members of a group are *not* present in the communication area and they have been established in space as a *group*. In this case, a singular pronoun may be used to refer to the group as a single unit, as seen in example (17). Here the Signer uses a singular form of the possessive pronoun to refer to each group.

Context The Signer is a teacher and is talking about what she's been learning about her students with another teacher.

(17)
```
                           t  (gaze lf  )  (lean lf )  (gaze rt;body lean rt  )
        YOU  KNOW+  #SEX,  GROUP-lf   GIRL-lf,   GROUP-rt  BOY-rt,
```

```
        (gaze rt        ) (gaze lf       ) (gaze rt        ) (gaze lf          )
        POSS-boy group                    POSS-boy group
                      POSS-girl group                        POSS-girl group
```

```
        (2h)alt.IDEA,  (2h)alt.THOUGHT,  FEELING,  DIFFERENT*
```

> *Struc* 'You know, concerning sex, the group of girl and the group of boy, the boys' and the girls' feelings, ideas, and thoughts are really different.'

> *Trans* 'You know girls and boys have really different feelings and ways of thinking about sex.'

> *Note:* In this example, **INDEX**-*boy group* and **INDEX**-*girl group* could have been used instead of **POSS**-*boy group* and **POSS**-*girl group*.

(C.3) Number Signs

Another way that ASL can indicate plurality is by using a specific number sign (e.g. **TWO, FIVE**) or a non-specific number sign (e.g. **FEW, SEVERAL, SOME/PART, MANY**). In general (especially among young Signers), the specific number sign will occur *before* the noun, as illustrated in examples (18) and (19).

Context Someone asks the Signer why a boy named Lee had no classes yesterday. The Signer responds:

(18)
```
                        t    (gaze rt                         )t            nodding
YESTERDAY  L-E-E,  POSS-rt  FOUR  TEACH AGENT,  BECOME-SICK
```

    Struc 'Yesterday Lee, his four teacher, they became sick.'

    Trans 'Yesterday, Lee's four teachers were sick.'

Notice that the noun **PEOPLE** in example (19) is already plural. However, there are very few nouns in ASL like this. Also notice that the verb **ASSEMBLE-TO-***lf* (made with '5:↓-CL' handshapes) and the *'puffed cheeks'* signal 'agree' with the large number of people.

Context The Signer and a friend have been discussing past NAD conventions and how many people have attended. The Signer predicts:

(19)
```
                              t
ONE-YEAR-FUTURE-lf   N-A-D-lf,
                                        puff.cheeks
FEEL+  THREE  THOUSAND*  PEOPLE  ASSEMBLE-TO-lf
```

    Struc 'Next year at the NAD (meeting), I feel three thousand people will flock to the meeting.'

    Trans 'I think there's gonna be about three thousand people at the NAD convention next year.'

As illustrated in the examples above, number signs generally occur before the noun. However, when the number has special significance, then it is often signed *after* the noun and is stressed. For example, the sign **TEN**** occurs after the noun in example (20) because the Signer is focusing on the surprisingly large number of pencils that Pat bought.

Context The Signer works in a bookstore and is telling a friend about the people who came into the store today.

(20)
```
          t                          rhet.q
P-A-T-lf,  BUY  PENCIL  TEN*,  REASON,  TOMORROW  EXAM
```

    Struc 'Pat, he bought pencil—*ten* of them. Why? Because of the exam tomorrow.'

    Trans 'Pat bought *ten* pencils for the exam tomorrow.'

However, sometimes the number sign occurs both *before and after* the noun when the number has special significance. This is illustrated in the next example where the arrival of twins, two babies rather than one, was totally unexpected.

Context   The Signer bursts into the room and excitedly announces to a group of
friends that Pat has just given birth to *two* boys instead of just one.

(21)   co
          ‾‾‾‾‾‾‾
          "HEY", P-A-T BORN TWO BOY TWO*

     Struc   'Hey! Pat gave birth to two boys—*two* of them!'

     Trans   'Hey! Pat just had *two* boys—*two* of 'em!'

When both a number sign and a classifier refer to the same noun in a sentence,
generally the number sign will occur after the noun and the classifier will be last. So
the order is 'what', then 'how many', and then the 'location' and/or 'action', as seen in
examples (22) and (23).

Context   The Signer is describing a picture. This is a portion of that description.

(22)   t   (gaze at each 'cup'   )
          ‾‾‾‾‾‾‾‾‾‾‾
          CUP   FOUR, A-CL*"in a row"*-on surface
                       $B\downarrow_{forearm}$-CL*'surface'*

     Struc   'Cup—four of them, they are lined up in a row on a surface.'

     Trans   'Four cups standing in a row on top of something.'

     Note: In this example, it would have been possible to use just the $B\downarrow$-*CL*
instead of the whole forearm. In this case, the $B\downarrow$-*CL* would also
move with each repetition of the A-CL.

Notice that the classifier in example (22) must 'agree with' the number sign. That
is, it must be made at least three times (the fourth time is optional), but cannot be
made more than four times since the number sign indicates there are 'four' cups.

Context   The Signer has just returned from a beautiful drive in the country and is
telling a friend what he saw.

(23)   mm
          ‾‾‾‾‾‾‾‾‾‾‾‾‾‾‾‾‾‾‾‾‾‾‾‾‾‾‾
          ME   DRIVE   3→CL*'car moving forward'*,

          (gaze rt   )   (gaze rt   )puff.cheeks   nodding
          ‾‾‾‾‾‾‾‾‾‾‾‾   ‾‾‾‾‾‾‾‾‾‾‾‾‾‾‾‾‾‾‾‾‾‾‾‾‾‾
          NOTICE-TO-*rt* HORSE THREE   (2h)V:-CL-*rt'*horses galloping', COMPETE,

          (gaze rt   )intense
          ‾‾
          1→CL-*rt,outward*↔⎱
          1→CL-*rt,outward*↔⎰ 'horses competing'   (2h)V:-CL-*rt'*horses galloping'

     Struc   'I was just casually driving along, and I noticed to the right horse
three of them galloping along. They were competing, and each was
alternately racing ahead of the others, really galloping along.'

     Trans   'I was just driving along when I looked over and saw these three
horses galloping and racing with each other neck 'n neck.'

The non-specific (indefinite) number signs (**MANY, FEW, SEVERAL, SOME/ PART**) also tend to occur after the noun and follow the other patterns of the definite number signs. However, the indefinite number signs do not seem to be used as often in ASL as indefinite number words are used in a spoken language like English. Perhaps this is because ASL has so many other ways of showing an indefinite plural (e.g. with classifiers). When indefinite number signs do occur in ASL sentences, they often seem to be used to focus on the degree of plurality. For example, in (24), the repetition of the 'trees falling down' could mean either that 'the trees (meaning 'all') fell down' *or* that 'some trees fell down', depending on the context in which the sentence occurs. (We know that at least five trees fell because on the accompanying videotape, the verb is repeated four times.) However, by using the sign **SEVERAL** in example (25), the Signer indicates that a certain portion of the trees fell down, but not all of them. Similarly, the Signer could use the sign **MANY** in the same way to indicate that an even larger number of trees, but not all, fell down.

Context   The Signer has just returned from a walk in a nearby woods and tells a neighbor:

(24)
qt

REMEMBER   ONE-DAY-PAST NIGHT   AWFUL   WIND-BLOW*,

TREE   (2h)alt.TREE-FALL-DOWN

>   *Struc*   'Remember last night that awful strong wind? Trees (at least five) fell down.'

>   *Trans*   'Remember that awful wind last night? Some of the trees were blown over.'

Context   (same as example 24)

(25)
qt

REMEMBER   ONE-DAY-PAST NIGHT   AWFUL   WIND-BLOW*,

       <u>nodding</u>

TREE   SEVERAL   (2h)alt.TREE-FALL-DOWN

>   *Struc*   'Remember last night that awful strong wind? Tree—several of them—fell down.'

>   *Trans*   'Remember that awful wind last night? Several of the trees were blown over.'

The signs **SEVERAL** and **FEW** are similar in form except that more fingers are extended in the sign **SEVERAL** and it has a larger movement. In addition, the non-manual behaviors that accompany these two signs tend to be different. The sign **FEW** tends to occur with the *'pursed lips'* signal (indicating the 'smallness' of the number) and a squinting of the eyes. The illustrations below show two kinds of non-manual behaviors that may occur with the sign **SEVERAL**. Notice how the larger movement of the sign **SEVERAL** on the right and the *'puffed cheeks'* signal (which indicates a large number) 'agree' with each other.

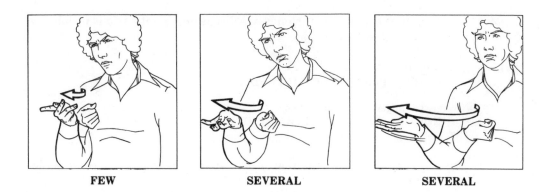

| FEW | SEVERAL | SEVERAL |

The sign **SOME/PART** seems to be infrequently used—although it occurs more often in English-influenced contexts. One context in which this sign may occur in ASL is when talking about dividing a large amount of money—'some' to one person and 'some' to another person.

(C.4) Nouns

Another way to indicate that a referent is plural is to repeat the noun itself (usually once). However, such repetition is only possible with a small number of nouns (such as **SENTENCE, LANGUAGE, RULE, MEANING, SPECIALTY-FIELD, AREA, ROOM/BOX, HOUSE, STREET/WAY,** and **STATUE**) and in a limited set of contexts. The two examples below illustrate one context where the noun would be repeated to indicate plurality and one context where the same noun would *not* be repeated to indicate plurality. We do not yet know the rules in ASL concerning where repetition of the noun is required *or* is not appropriate. However, it is generally true that repetition does *not* occur when a number sign modifies the noun (as seen in example 27)—unless the Signer wants to assign spatial locations to the things for later reference. As we saw in the examples of pluralized classifiers and pronouns, the separate articulations of nouns tend to have different spatial locations. (However, in rapid conversation, they are sometimes made in the same place.)

Context   The Signer has just learned about the new School of Communication at Gallaudet and asks for more information.

(26)

        t   wh-q

SCHOOL   COMMUNICATION,   SPECIALTY-FIELD+   HOW-MANY

Struc   'The School of Communication, how many majors are there?'

Trans   'How many majors are there in the School of Communication?'

Context   The Signer and a group of friends are discussing what various people are
            majoring in at school.

(27)   (body lean rt)t
                P-A-T-*rt,*   POSS-*rt*   SPECIALTY-FIELD

            (gaze at finger   )(lean lf)nod   (lean rt)nod
                INDEX-*lf index finger*   DRAMA,   INDEX-*lf middle finger*   HISTORY
            TWO ⸻⸻⸻⸻⸻⸻⸻⸻⸻⸻⸻⸻⟶

            Struc   'Pat, her major (there are) two—one is drama, the second is his-
                      tory.'

            Trans   'Pat has two majors—drama and history.'

(C.5) Verbs

Verbs are often repeated to 'agree' with the plurality of nouns. In general, when a
verb is repeated, it indicates that the *action* occurred more than once or occurred
over a certain period of time. (See Chapter XIII on Temporal Aspect.) By itself, such
repetition does not indicate if any noun in the sentence is plural. However, when the
repetition of the verb (a) is made in an arc, or (b) involves the alternation of both
hands, or (c) involves the simultaneous movement of both hands from/to different
locations in space, then the verb also shows that a noun in the sentence (subject or
object) is plural.[8] In the following three sections, we will describe each of these types
of verb repetition.

(a) Verb repetition in an arc will show that a noun is plural. For example, in (28),
the first sign, **BOOK**, is singular. But by repeating the verb *me-***READ**-*book* in an
arc, the Signer indicates that he means he enjoys reading books in general, rather
than a particular book.

Context   A friend is visiting the Signer and remarks that he has a lot of books in
            his apartment. The Signer responds:

(28)   t   puff.cheeks+mm   nodding
            BOOK,   (2h)ENJOY   *me*-READ-*book*+ +-*arc*

            Struc   'Book, I really enjoy reading through different books.'

            Trans   'I really enjoy reading different books.'

Similarly, in example (29) the Signer indicates that she met many friends in New
York by repeating the verb in an arc. Thus, this repetition in an arc shows that the
referent of the noun **FRIEND** is plural.

_____

[8]In point (c), we use the term "repetition" loosely. Here it does not actually mean that the sign is
repeated. But it refers to the fact that the sign is actually made twice because it is articulated on *both*
hands.

Context   A friend sees the Signer and tells her that she looks a lot better than before—happier and more relaxed. The Signer says she feels much better and explains:

(29)

<table>
<tr><td></td><td>_____t</td><td>(gaze rt)</td><td></td><td></td><td>_____mm</td><td>('smile')nodding</td></tr>
<tr><td>ONE-WEEK-PAST</td><td>GO-rt</td><td>NEW-YORK</td><td>FINEwg,</td><td>me-MEET+++-arc</td><td>FRIEND</td></tr>
</table>

> *Struc*   'Last week, I went to New York. It was really nice. I met many people who are friends of mine.'
>
> *Trans*   'My trip to New York was super. I ran into a lot of friends.'

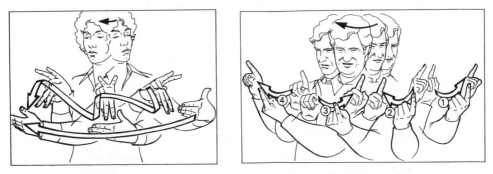

READ++-*arc*   MEET+++-*arc*

When we write '+++-*arc*' after a gloss, we are *describing* what the sign does. It means the sign is 'repeated that many times in an arc'. However, as you will see in Chapter XIV (Distributional Aspect), this type of verb repetition in an arc also gives information about how the action occurs over time, and it is glossed there as the modulation *"each"*. When we write *"each"* after a gloss, we are giving a *name* to the modulation that we describe as '+++-*arc*'. However, both refer to the same thing.[9]

So, for example in (30), we have used the description '+++-*arc*' after the adjective DIFFERENT to describe what happens with that sign. We could do the same with the verb COLLECT-____ because it has the same modulation; or we could write this as COLLECT *"each"*. Notice that both the adjective and the verb indicate that the referent of the sign CHAIR is plural and 'agree' with each other.

---

[9] In linguistic research, we generally start by *describing* the modulation that occurs. Later, when we better understand the meaning of that modulation, we try to use a name that shows what it means.

Context The Signer and his wife are talking about their friends' hobbies and the interesting kinds of things that some of them collect.

(30)
$$\overline{}^{\ \ t}$$
KNOW   CHAIR   DIFFERENT+++-*arc*,

(gaze rt)nod _____ puff.cheeks
SELF-*rt* L-E-E   COLLECT++++-*arc*

Struc 'You know chair—various different ones, Lee himself collects those various ones.'

Trans 'You know Lee is a collector of different kinds of chairs.'

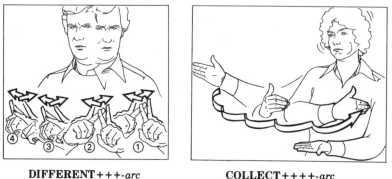

DIFFERENT+++-*arc*   COLLECT++++-*arc*
                           or COLLECT*"each"*

Notice in examples (28)–(30) how the repetition of the verb indicates that the action occurs repeatedly. That is, each of the books is read, so the action of 'reading' occurs repeatedly; each of the friends is met, so the action of 'meeting' occurs repeatedly; and each of the chairs is collected, so the action of 'collecting' occurs repeatedly. Thus, the *repetition of the verb* indicates that that action occurs repeatedly. It is the *different location of each repetition* which indicates that the number of things or people involved in the action is plural.

However, verbs can also be signed in an arc without repetition and still show that the object is plural. This modulation is described as '-*arc*' and is named *"all"*. It is also explained in Chapter XIV. The difference between the modulation in which the verb is *repeated in an arc* and the modulation which is made with a *'sweeping' motion in an arc* is that the first one indicates several repeated actions whereas the second one treats the action as a single event. This second modulation (called *"all"* in Chapter XIV) is illustrated in the next example.[10]

---

[10]The reader may notice some similarity between the two verb modulations described above and the plural modulations of classifiers that were described earlier (*"in a row"* and *"sweep in a row"*).

Context   A friend asks the Signer if she visited the Deaf club during the weekend. The Signer replies:

(31)   <u>nodding   t</u>   (gaze rt)
                YESTERDAY,   ME   GO-TO-*rt*   #CLUB,

                                     <u>qt</u>   <u>(gaze rt   )</u> puff.cheeks+nodding
                REMEMBER   OLD   TICKET,   ME   COLLECT-*rt-arc*   THROW-OUT-*rt*

         Struc   'Yeah. Yesterday, I went to the club. You remember old ticket? I collected them all and threw them out.'

         Trans   'Yeah, I went to the club yesterday. You know those old tickets? Well, I rounded them all up and threw 'em out.'

COLLECT-*rt-arc*
or **COLLECT-*rt*"*all*"**

Notice that in (31), the arc is made from right to center to 'agree' with the location of the 'chairs' at the club. Similarly, in example (32), the verb *me*-**SHOW-TO-*friend-arc*** is made from left to center to agree with the location of the 'friends' and indicate that the referent of **FRIEND** is plural.

Context   A few weeks ago, the Signer received a gift (a picture of Laurent Clerc) and explains to his aunt what he plans to do with it.

(32)   <u>   t</u>   <u>   q</u>
         KNOW+   PICTURE   CLERC   OLD*,   KNOW+   YOU,

                            <u>t</u>   (gaze lf   )
         TOMORROW   MY   FRIEND-*lf*,   WILL   *me*-SHOW-TO-*friend-arc*

         Struc   'You know the real old picture of Clerc, you know the one I mean? Tomorrow my friend, I will show it to a group of them.'

         Trans   'You know that old picture of Clerc? Tomorrow I'm gonna show it to a group of my friends.'

me-**SHOW-TO**-*friend-arc*
or *me*-**SHOW-TO**-*friend"all"*

Just as the *"sweep in a row"* modulation with classifiers can be repeated to show that there are several rows of things, the sweeping motion of the verb in an arc can be repeated. For example, in (33), the Signer uses the 'B' handshape classifier to indicate that there are 'rows and rows' of 'magazines'. She does this with the *"sweep in rows"* modulation. Then the verb *me*-**LOOK-AT-**___ follows the same pattern to indicate that the Signer looked through the magazines in each row until she found the right one. Thus, the plural modulation of the verb 'agrees' with the plural modulation of the classifier.

Context   The Signer and a classmate are discussing some class assignments, one of which involves reviewing a particular article in an issue of the 1969 *Deaf American*.

(33)
                                                                      t
KNOW+ DEAF AMERICA MAGAZINE 1969,

            cs   t
MORNING LIBRARY, ME SEARCH,

        t
MAGAZINE, (2h)B-CL*"sweep in rows"*-'rows of magazines',

                               tight lips ('sudden discovery')
ME *me*-**LOOK-AT**-*magazines in each row*

me-**PICK**-*magazine*-**FROM**-*shelf*

    Struc   'You know the 1969 *Deaf American* magazine? This morning at the library, I was looking for it. Magazine, there were shelves and shelves of them. I looked at all of the magazines on each shelf and finally found it and took it off the shelf.'

    Trans   'This morning I was at the library looking for the 1969 *Deaf American*. I looked through shelves and shelves of magazines until I finally found it.'

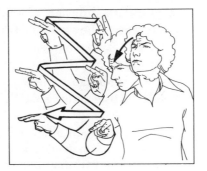

*me-**LOOK-AT**-magazines in each row*

Thus, we see in this section that signing a verb in an arc will indicate that the object is plural (i.e. it will show that there are at least three things). If the verb is repeated during the arc, then it also indicates that the action itself is plural.

(b) Alternating both hands while signing a verb will indicate that a noun is plural. This alternation also indicates that the action occurs repeatedly. There are two forms of this 'two hands alternating' movement and each of them has a slightly different meaning. Both of these forms and their meanings are described in the last chapter on Distributional Aspect. For now, we simply want to point out that this repeated, alternating movement of the verb will indicate that a noun is plural. This noun can be the subject or object, depending on the type of verb and its direction of movement.

In the first example, (34), this plural modulation of the verb **GO** indicates that the referent of the sign **SENIOR** is plural.

Context The Signer is a college professor and tells her husband what happens during "Senior Sneak Week".

(34)

	t		puff.cheeks
M-A-Y TWELVE BEFORE↔,		SENIOR	(2h)alt.GO

Struc 'May twelfth sometime before then, senior—many of them leave one after the other.'

Trans 'Some time before May twelfth, the seniors take off in all directions.'

(2h)alt.**GO**

In the next example, the plural modulation of the verb ____-TAP-*me*-ON-SHOULDER shows that the referent of the sign STUDY⌢AGENT is plural. Later in the example, the pronoun INDEX-*arc-rt* 'agrees' with the fact that the subject ('students') is plural and with the location of that noun. We know that the 'students' have been given a location to the right because the Signer shifted her body to that location and then looked to the left while signing BETTER QUIT #JOB, etc.

Context   Two years ago the Signer, a student advisor at a college, had a very bad experience with the college administration and the Signer almost quit his job. Now the Signer is talking with another teacher at the college.

(35)
```
                    _____t
        TWO-YEAR-PAST,   STUDY⌢AGENT   (2h)alt.TAP-me-ON-SHOULDER

        (body shift to rt,gaze lf                           )
        BETTER   QUIT   #JOB,   BETTER   QUIT   #JOB,

                  (gaze rt      )                  _____nodding
        NOW   FEEL+   INDEX-arc-rt   RIGHT   INDEX-arc-rt
```

Struc   'Two years ago, student—many of them kept coming up to me and telling me, "You better quit your job, you better quit your job." Now I feel they were right them.'

Trans   'Two years ago, many students kept telling me that I should quit my job and now I think they were right.'

From these two examples, we can see that, like the plural modulation where the verb is repeated in an arc, this 'two hands alternating' modulation indicates that the noun is plural and that the action occurs repeatedly (in fact, many times). This is described more fully in Chapter XIV.

(c) ASL can also take advantage of the fact that it has two "manual articulators" (i.e. two hands!) to indicate on a directional verb that there are either two subjects or two objects in a sentence. For example, in (36), both hands simultaneously sign the verb *me*-ASK-TO- ____ *toward* two separate locations, and later sign the verb ____-SAY-#NO-TO-*me from* those two spatial locations. In this example, one location represents 'the girls' and the other location represents 'the boys'. The fact that both hands sign the verb simultaneously generally means that there was only *one* action (not repeated actions) and that this action is performed simultaneously on both groups or by both groups. Notice that if these verbs had been signed twice—either with only one hand (like some of the examples in section *a*) or with both hands alternating (like the examples in section *b*), this would have indicated that there were two separate actions (e.g. 'asked the girls and then asked the boys').

Context   The Signer and a group of friends are discussing how children react to various subjects—love, marriage, etc. The Signer remembers an experience she had.

(36)
           <u>   t   </u>
PAST+,   ME   TEACH   SCHOOL,

           (gaze rt) (body lean rt)
HAVE   GROUP-*rt* GIRL,   GROUP-*lf* BOY

       (gaze down at each group↔   )q   (head jerk back; 'surprised'   )
ME   *me*-ASK-TO-*girl group*,   WILL   MARRY   WILL,   *girl group*-SAY-#NO-TO-*me**
      me-ASK-TO-*boy group*,   *boy group*-SAY-#NO-TO-*me**

   Struc   'Awhile ago, I taught school. I had a group of girl and a group of boy. I asked the two groups "Will you get married? Will you?" Both groups emphatically told me "No!".'

   Trans   'I used to teach school and had a group of girls and a group of boys. I asked them if they would ever get married and they both told me "No way!".'

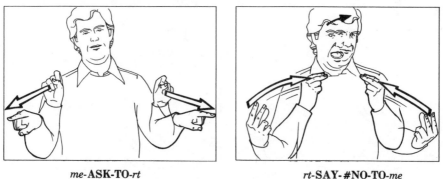

         me-ASK-TO-*rt*   *rt*-SAY-#NO-TO-*me*
         me-ASK-TO-*lf*   *lf*-SAY-#NO-TO-*me*

   Some verbs in ASL always imply that the subject is plural. These verbs seem to be composed of plural classifier handshapes—i.e. the '4' and '5' handshapes. For example, in (37), the verb glossed as ASSEMBLE-TO-___ (meaning 'many people coming together at a certain place') can only be used when the subject is plural. In this example, it indicates that the referent of the sign WOMAN is plural. Similarly, in (38), the sign glossed as GROUP-MARCH-___ (meaning 'many people marching') indicates that the referent of the sign SOLDIER is plural. The same is true for the verbs DISPERSE and MANY-LOOK-AT-*me* in examples (39) and (40). (These four verbs are illustrated below.)

Context The Signer and a friend are talking about different national conferences and how there are always more women at these meetings than men. The Signer cites another example:

(37)

<pre>
                                q   (gaze rt   )puff.cheeks
REMEMBER MEETING S-D-rt, WOMAN ASSEMBLE-TO-san diego
</pre>

  Struc 'Remember the conference in San Diego? Woman—many flocked to it.'

  Trans 'Remember the San Diego conference? Lots of women went there.'

Context The Signer and a group of friends have just returned from a parade. They meet another friend, and the Signer asks:

(38)

<pre>
                        (puff.cheek)q _____q
FINISH SEE SOLDIER (2h)GROUP-MARCH-rt, SEE FINISH YOU
</pre>

  Struc 'Did you see the soldier—many marching? Did you see them?'

  Trans 'Did you see the soldiers marching? Did you see 'em?'

    ASSEMBLE-TO-*rt*   (2h)GROUP-MARCH

Context The Signer lives near a state school. A friend is supposed to visit him tomorrow and the Signer tells his friend not to show up at the house any later than 2:55 PM. The friend asks why, and the Signer replies:

(39)

<pre>
                    t   pow
KNOW STATE-SCHOOL, THREE-O'CLOCK KID DISPERSE-FROM-school
</pre>

  Struc 'You know the state school, at three o'clock kid—many of them suddenly leave from there.'

  Trans 'At three o'clock, gobs of kids come tearing out of the state school.'

Context   The Signer, a male, is telling a companion about an embarrassing incident which occurred when he innocently entered a room reserved for women only.

(40)
                                          ('startled')   (head back   )
      HAPPEN ME GO-INTO-*cntr* ROOM-*cntr*,   WOMAN (2h)MANY-LOOK-AT-*me*

     Struc   'When I went into the room, "Huh?" Woman—many of them turned to look at me.'

     Trans   'When I happened into the room, I realized something was wrong. Many of the women turned and just looked at me.'

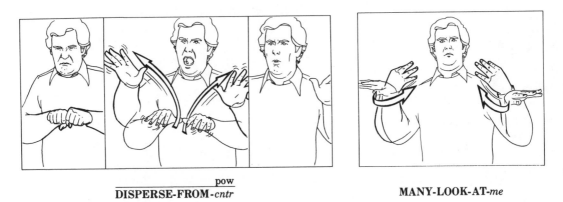

                                     pow
            DISPERSE-FROM-*cntr*   MANY-LOOK-AT-*me*

From these examples, we see that certain verbs imply that the subject is 'many' people (animals, or things). Thus, using them in a sentence provides another way of indicating that a noun is plural.

D. Summary

In this chapter, we have considered some of the ways that ASL Signers can indicate that there is more than one of something. Many different kinds of signs can provide this information—including classifiers, pronouns, number signs, nouns, verbs, and adjectives (remember **DIFFERENT+++-*arc*** ?). These signs often 'agree' with each other in showing that a referent is plural. A very small number of nouns are inherently plural (e.g. **PEOPLE**). A slightly larger number of nouns can be made plural by repeating them (e.g. **LANGUAGE, STATUE**). In general, the fact that a referent is plural is *not* marked on the noun, but instead is indicated with one or more other kinds of signs as well as certain facial signals.

We saw that there are several ways to pluralize classifiers, pronouns, and verbs. In general, all of these ways involve some kind of repetition or a 'sweeping' or 'arc-like' movement of the sign. Obviously, there are great similarities between the *"in a row"* modulation of classifiers, the repetition of pronouns in different locations, and the '+++-*arc*' or *"each"* modulation of verbs. There are also great similarities

between the "*in rows*" modulation of classifiers, the 'arc-point' modulation of pronouns, and the '*arc*' or "*all*" modulation of verbs. These recurring patterns strongly
suggest that there is a basic system for pluralizing signs in ASL which is based on
the feature of repetition. However, for the present, we do not yet understand this
system well enough to be able to "tie up the loose ends". Again, we recommend that
teachers of ASL stay in close touch with ongoing linguistic research.

Dialogues
and
Cultural Information

PLURALIZATION

The following three dialogues have been developed to illustrate various uses of the grammatical features described in this chapter. Each of these dialogues also appears in one of the three corresponding Student Texts. In the Student Texts, the transcription of each dialogue is less detailed than what is provided here for the teacher of ASL. Following the dialogues, in the sections called "Cultural Information", are brief discussions of the topic of each dialogue.

The following dialogues and cultural information correspond to:

Student Text: Unit 7
Unit 16
Unit 25

Dialogue: Pluralization
(Student Text - Unit 7)

First Signer (Pat)

<u>   co   </u>   <u>   wh-q</u>

Pat_1: "HEY", CURIOUS, (2h)CHILDREN HOW-MANY YOU

<u>   q</u> <u>   q</u>

Pat_2: OH-I-SEE, GIRL INDEX-*lf* DEAF, GO-TO-*rt* STATE-SCHOOL

<u>   q</u>

Pat_3: MANY DEAF INDEX-*lf*

<u>   (gaze lf   )   </u> <u>   q</u>

Pat_4: TEACH AGENT GROUP-*lf* GOOD+ INDEX-*lf*

<u>   (gaze lf   )   q</u>

Pat_5: FINISH (2h)GO-TO-*lf* OBSERVE-*lf*

Dialogue: Pluralization
(Student Text - Unit 7)

Second Signer (Lee)

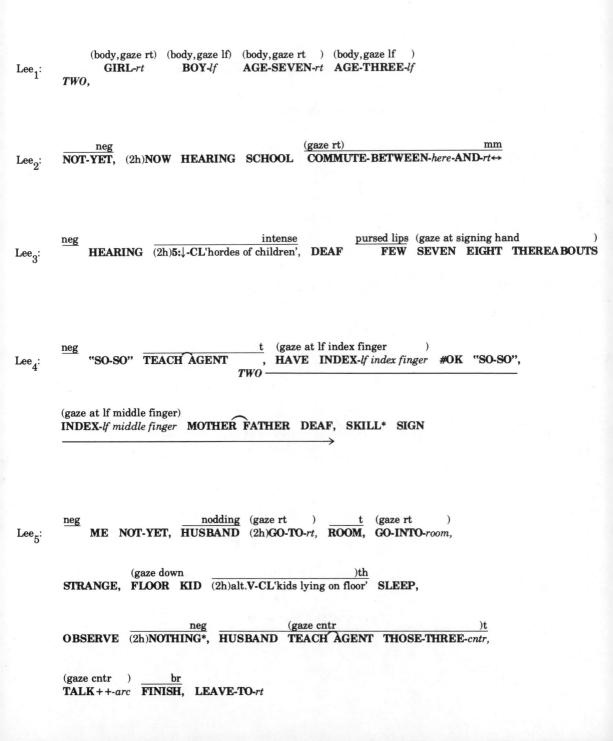

Lee₁:
    (body,gaze rt) (body,gaze lf) (body,gaze rt) (body,gaze lf)
    GIRL-*rt*   **BOY**-*lf*   **AGE-SEVEN**-*rt* **AGE-THREE**-*lf*
TWO,

Lee₂:
         neg   (gaze rt)   mm
    NOT-YET, (2h)**NOW** **HEARING** **SCHOOL** **COMMUTE-BETWEEN**-*here*-**AND**-*rt*↔

Lee₃:
  neg   intense   pursed lips (gaze at signing hand   )
    HEARING (2h)**5:↓-CL**'hordes of children', **DEAF**   **FEW** **SEVEN** **EIGHT** **THEREABOUTS**

Lee₄:
  neg   t (gaze at lf index finger   )
    "SO-SO" **TEACH⌢AGENT**   , **HAVE** **INDEX**-*lf index finger* **#OK** **"SO-SO"**,
                      TWO

(gaze at lf middle finger)
INDEX-*lf middle finger* **MOTHER⌢FATHER** **DEAF,** **SKILL*** **SIGN**
————————————————————————→

Lee₅:
  neg   nodding (gaze rt   )   t (gaze rt   )
    ME **NOT-YET,** **HUSBAND** (2h)**GO-TO**-*rt,* **ROOM,** **GO-INTO**-*room,*

              (gaze down   )th
  STRANGE, **FLOOR** **KID** (2h)**alt.V-CL**'kids lying on floor' **SLEEP,**

                neg   (gaze cntr   )t
  OBSERVE (2h)**NOTHING*,** **HUSBAND** **TEACH⌢AGENT** **THOSE-THREE**-*cntr,*

  (gaze cntr)   br
  TALK++-*arc* **FINISH,** **LEAVE-TO**-*rt*

Dialogue: Pluralization
(Student Text - Unit 16)

First Signer (Pat)

Pat₁:
<pre>
                    co   (gaze rt;   cs)   t   q
_____ _____ _____ _____
                          KNOW-THAT GIRL RECENT LEAVE-TO-rt INDEX-rt, KNOW+ YOU
"SHOULDER-TAP"
</pre>

Pat₂:
<pre>
(gaze rt   )   nod   t
_____   _____
THAT-ONE INDEX-rt, INDEX-rt NARRATE, SIGN LANGUAGE WORLD, (2h)SAME-ALL-OVER,

       (gaze rt) neg (gaze rt   )   (gaze rt)
ME _____ SIGN-rt LANGUAGE-rt DIFFERENT++-rt-arc
          "NO-NO"-rt

                                        (gaze lf→rt   ) (gaze rt   )
(2h)rt-SAME-AS-lf SPEAK LANGUAGE-lf DIFFERENT++-lf-arc (2h)rt-SAME-AS-lf (2h)"WELL"
</pre>

Pat₃:
<pre>
              t   (gaze rt   )
_____ _____
YES+, DEAF TWO, 2-CL'come up to me', INDEX-rt SIGN DIFFERENT*,

(gaze rt)_____neg
    ME NOT UNDERSTAND INDEX-rt
</pre>

Pat₄:
<pre>
                    _____q
FINEwg, OTHER REMEMBER YOU INTERPRET DIFFERENT++-rt-arc
</pre>

Pat₅:
<pre>
RIGHT YOU,

                            (gaze rt at 'each interpreter'   )
ME REMEMBER #FUN ME me-LOOK-AT-interpreter"each" DIFFERENT++-rt-arc
</pre>

Dialogue: Pluralization
(Student Text - Unit 16)

Second Signer (Lee)

Lee₁:
$\qquad$(gaze lf)$\qquad\qquad\qquad\qquad\qquad\qquad$q
GIRL (2h)GLASSES THAT-ONE INDEX-*lf*

Lee₂: GIRL KNOW-NOTHING,

$\qquad\qquad\qquad\qquad\qquad\qquad\qquad\qquad$(nodding) (gaze cntr $\qquad$)qt
REMEMBER W-F-D AWHILE-AGO NINETEEN SEVEN FIVE, DEAF ASSEMBLE-TO-*cntr*

(gaze cntr $\qquad$)tight lips
SIGN DIFFERENT+++-*arc*

Lee₃: $\qquad\qquad\qquad$(gaze lf $\qquad\qquad$)puff.cheeks
W-F-D FINEwg, DEAF (2h)4-CL'people mingle together',

$\qquad\qquad$(gaze lf & cntr↔ $\qquad$) $\qquad$br (gaze lf $\qquad$)
SHOULD #TV CAMERA-RECORD-*lf* & *cntr-arc*↔ FINISH, ANALYZE++-*lf*

Lee₄: $\qquad\qquad\qquad$(gaze up,lf)
YES+, INTERPRET (2h)4-CL-*up,lf*'interpreters in a line,facing Signer',

(gaze up,lf) (gaze up,lf) (gaze up,lf cntr)
$\qquad$SPAIN, $\qquad\qquad$RUSSIA, $\qquad\qquad\qquad$FRANCE,
INDEX-up,lf $\qquad$ *INDEX-up,lf* ⟶ *INDEX-up,lf cntr* ⟶

(gaze up,lf) (gaze down, 'thinking')
ALTOGETHER-*lf* TWELVE+ THIRTEEN

Lee₅: $\qquad\qquad\qquad\qquad\qquad\qquad$rhet.q
SIGN LANGUAGE (2h)SAME-ALL-OVER, NOT*,

GIRL PEA-BRAIN*

Dialogue: Pluralization
(Student Text - Unit 25)

First Signer (Pat)

Pat₁:
```
          co                              wh-q        q              q      wh-q
      "HEY",  ONE-YEAR-FUTURE  #DO-DO,  #JOB-rt,  COLLEGE-lf,  (2h)"WHAT"
```

Pat₂:
```
                                                    wh-q
      #DO-DO  INDEX-lf  N-T-I-D,  #DO-DO  (2h)"WHAT"
```

Pat₃:
```
                                          q
      LIKE  INDEX-lf  ROCHESTER,  LIKE  YOU
```

Pat₄:
```
                                t   (gaze lf                )
      RIGHT,  INDEX-lf  PAST  AUTUMN,  ME  (2h)GO-TO-rochester,

        t        neg
      COAT,  (2h)NONE,  KNOW-NOTHING,

      (gaze lf)                 br   (gaze lf)
              ARRIVE-rochester,         PEOPLE   (2h)4-CL'people look at me'*
```

Pat₅:
```
      neg       (gaze lf                )
          ME  SEARCH  STORE  SEARCH,

      (gaze cntr           )br              (gaze lf )
      NOTICE-TO-cntr,  ENTER-store,  COAT  HAVE  X-CL-lf ⎱ "sweep in rows"-'coats on racks',
                                             1→CL-lf ⎰

      (gaze lf                        )  (gaze down)mm
      ME  "flip through coats, take one out and try it on"   EXACT,

              br
      BUY  FINISH,  RELIEVED
```

Pat₆: (Facial signal that means 'Yeah, I know that')

Dialogue: Pluralization
(Student Text - Unit 25)

Second Signer (Lee)

Lee₁: (2h)"WELL",   NOT-YET   DECIDE   ME   <u>(gaze rt&lf↔</u>
  INDEX-*rt* ⟶ INDEX-*rt* ⟶)
INDEX-lf ⟶ *INDEX-lf*

<u>   (gaze rt)cond</u>
SUPPOSE   COLLEGE-*rt,*   (2h)GO-TO-*rt*   N-T-I-D   ME

Lee₂: (2h)"WELL"   SPECIALTY-FIELD   DIFFERENT++-*arc,*   INDEX-*lf thumb*   <u>nod</u>
PHOTOGRAPHY,

(gaze at lf index)   <u>nod</u>   (gaze at lf middle finger)   <u>nod</u>
           ART,   INDEX-*lf middle finger*   MATH,   LIST-OF-ITEMS   (2h)"WELL"

Lee₃: (2h)"WELL"   "SO-SO",   <u>(gaze rt)</u>   <u>(gaze rt)</u>   <u>mm</u>
INDEX-*rt*   HAVE   ROCK B-CL-*rt*'hill' ⟶ SEVERAL,
B-CL-lf'hill'

<u>   mm+nodding</u>   <u>rhet.q</u>
CAN   SKI,   WALK   VARIOUS-THINGS   "WELL",   PROBLEM   ONE,

INDEX-*rt*   COLD   "WOW"   COLD*   INDEX-*rt,*   (2h)"PSHAW"

Lee₄: "OH-MY",   PEOPLE   (2h)4-CL'people look at you',   <u>t</u>   <u>wh-q</u>   <u>q</u>   <u>wh-q</u>
#DO-DO,   (2h)IGNORE,   (2h)"WHAT"

Lee₅: LUCKY   YOU

Student Text: Unit 7

Cultural Information: Mainstreaming

In 1975, the government passed a public law (Education for All Handicapped Children Act) which was designed to make sure all handicapped children are placed in appropriate educational programs. This public law (PL 94-142) has resulted in an increased number of "mainstreamed" or "integrated" programs. *Mainstreaming* is a term used to describe an educational situation in which a deaf child spends all or part of the school day in classes with hearing children. This includes programs in which a deaf student is integrated into a couple of classes with hearing children but spends most of his/her time in classes with other deaf students. There are also many special programs for deaf students in schools for hearing students. In these programs, the deaf students do not attend classes with hearing students but stay in what are called "special education classes".

According to a 1977 report from the Office of Demographic Studies (ODS) at Gallaudet College, approximately 20% of all deaf students are "mainstreamed". Another 22% of them are enrolled in full-time special education classes located within schools for hearing students.

Full implementation of PL 94-142 occurred on September 1, 1978. Under this law, each state is responsible for a free, "appropriate" education for all handicapped children. The way schools decide what is or is not "appropriate" is by using an Individualized Educational Program (IEP). The IEP is supposed to consider the child's present level of performance, determine the child's needs, and state goals which must be met during the upcoming school year. IEPs are prepared each year for each child and must be approved or amended by the parent or guardian. For more information, contact: Coordinator, PL 94-142 Program, Pre-College Programs, Gallaudet College, Washington, D.C. 20002.

Student Text: Unit 16

Cultural Information: National Sign Languages and Gestuno

Contrary to what many people believe, Sign Language is not a universal language among Deaf people. This can be easily seen by examining books that illustrate signs from different countries like France, Australia, England, and Sweden; very often, different signs are used to represent the same thing. In addition, different signed languages often use different handshapes. For example, the handshape used in the ASL signs **FEEL** and **WHAT'S-UP** does not occur in Swedish signs; the handshape with the fourth finger extended is used in Taiwan signs (e.g. **SISTER**) but does not occur in any ASL signs. It is also reasonable to expect that there are differences in the grammar of different signed languages, but there has not yet been much research on this.

At international conferences and meetings, a common reaction of many hearing people is that because Deaf people from different countries seem to be able to communicate somewhat easily with each other, they must all be using the same Sign Language. However, several research studies have shown that this is not the case at all. In fact, according to Deaf people themselves, what happens is that they stop using their own Sign Language and instead use mime and gestures. This type of communication is generally slower than signing and involves much repetition and a constant give-and-take to figure out the meanings of various gestures. For more information on communication differences and difficulties with foreign Signers, there are two articles by Battison and Jordan in *Sign Language Studies 10* (1976). These articles report on some preliminary research done during the VII World Congress of the Deaf that was held in Washington, D.C. in 1975.

In 1975, the British Deaf Association (BDA) published a book entitled *Gestuno: International Sign Language of the Deaf* on behalf of the World Federation of the Deaf (WFD). This book contains photographs of approximately 1500 signs and represents an attempt at unifying the signed languages used by Deaf people. The signs shown in this book were selected by a committee that was set up by the WFD and that had one representative from each of the following countries: the United States, Great Britain, Russia, Denmark, and Italy. This committee relied on their own personal experience and knowledge as well as books of signs published in many countries. Their primary goal was to provide a quick and easy means of communication at international meetings of Deaf people.

In many ways, Gestuno is like Esperanto (an artificially devised spoken language intended to provide quick and easy communication among hearing people from different countries). However, Gestuno cannot be called a "language" for several reasons: first, it has no grammar (the book is simply a grouping of individual signs according to various topics); second, Gestuno has no native users (i.e. no children grow up using it as their first language); third, very few people are fluent in the use of Gestuno since there is little opportunity to practice or use it. Gestuno is not used by the Deaf people in any single country for daily, regular conversations; its use is restricted to international meetings.

It is highly unlikely that Gestuno will ever replace national signed languages even at international meetings. This is borne out by the fact that at the World Federation of the Deaf meeting in Bulgaria in 1979, each contingent of Deaf delegates and participants brought its own interpreters. In fact, many of the Deaf participants said that they felt cheated and only partially informed when they were forced to rely solely on Gestuno interpretation. Whether this was due to inadequate training and preparation of the Gestuno interpreters or the inadequacies and limitations of Gestuno itself, or both reasons, is not clear. In any case, just as Esperanto has not been widely accepted among hearing people, it is highly unlikely that Deaf people will replace their own Sign Language with Gestuno and that it will become universally accepted and used.

Student Text: Unit 25

Cultural Information: The National Technical Institute for the Deaf (NTID)

In 1965, a law was passed which created a National Technical Institute for the Deaf (NTID). The site chosen for this special institute was Rochester, New York, on the campus of the Rochester Institute of Technology (RIT). After several years of planning, the first group of 71 students enrolled in 1968. Now there are approximately 900 students enrolled at NTID. The primary purpose of the institute is to provide educational training opportunities for deaf students in technological areas.

The historical underemployment or unemployment of deaf people was a primary reason for the creation of NTID. In response to this need, NTID not only provides academic training for its students but also provides academic career counseling and job placement counseling. In fact, as of 1979, 95% of NTID graduates who had sought jobs had found employment; 94% had been hired at a level appropriate for their training, and 84% had been hired in business and industry.

Because NTID is located on the campus of RIT (and, in fact, is one of the nine colleges of RIT), the deaf students there frequently have the option of being "integrated" with the hearing students at RIT. To deal with this situation, NTID provides a number of support services for its students. Some of these services are: providing interpreters for NTID students, and providing note-takers in classes.

For further information, contact: NTID, RIT, Public Information Office, One Lomb Memorial Drive, Rochester, New York 14623.

Chapter XIII

Temporal Aspect

A. Introduction

In Chapter VII, we discussed how ASL uses the time line and time adverbs (like RECENTLY and ONE-WEEK-PAST) to indicate *when* something happens. For example, we saw that in a sentence like the one written below, the sign TWO-MONTH-PAST indicates that the action or event of 'joining the NAD' occurred in the past—specifically, 'two months ago'.

Context   A friend is surprised to see a copy of the *Deaf American* on the Signer's desk and asks where she got it. The Signer replies:

(1)   _____t   (gaze lf   )
         TWO-MONTH-PAST,   ME   *me*-JOIN-TO-*lf*   N-A-D

      Struc   'Two months ago, I joined the NAD.'

      Trans   'Two months ago, I join*ed* the NAD.'

References to the time of an event (e.g. present, future, distant future, past, distant past) are called *tense*. Whereas English often indicates tense via an affix on the verb (e.g. 'I join*ed* the NAD') or an auxiliary verb (e.g. 'I *will* join the NAD'), ASL usually indicates the time of an event with a time adverb. After the time has been indicated, each subsequent sentence is understood to refer to that time frame until a new time is established, as illustrated in example (2). In this example, the time adverb TWO-MONTH-PAST indicates that the following events ('joined', 'paid', 'went') occurred in the past. When a new time frame is established with the adverb TWO-YEAR-FUTURE, we know that all subsequent events (e.g. 'will go to') refer to that future time.

Context   (same as example 1)

(2)

                  t   (gaze lf   )
‾‾‾‾‾‾‾‾‾‾‾‾‾‾‾‾‾‾‾‾‾‾‾‾‾‾
TWO-MONTH-PAST,   ME   *me*-JOIN-TO-*lf*   N-A-D-*lf,*

                       t   (gaze lf)
‾‾‾‾‾‾‾‾‾‾‾‾‾‾‾‾‾‾‾‾‾‾‾‾‾‾
FIFTEEN-*lf*   DOLLAR-*lf,*   MAKE-PAYMENT-*lf,*

(gaze rt   )
me-GO-TO-*rt*   MEETING-*rt*   ROCHESTER-*rt,*

                     t (gaze cntr   )
‾‾‾‾‾‾‾‾‾‾‾‾‾‾‾‾‾‾‾‾‾‾‾‾‾‾
TWO-YEAR-FUTURE,   *me*-GO-TO-*cntr*   MEETING   C-I-N-N-*cntr*

> *Struc*   'Two months ago, I joined the NAD. The fifteen dollars, I paid it. I went to the meeting in Rochester. Two years from now, I'll go to the meeting in Cincinnati.'

> *Trans*   'Two months ago, I join*ed* the NAD. I *paid* the $15.00, and *went* to the meeting in Rochester. Two years from now, I *will go* to the meeting in Cincinnati.'

In this chapter, we are going to discuss how ASL gives information about time via verb modulations (inflections). This information concerns things like the 'duration' or 'frequency' of an event rather than the actual time of the event. Whereas reference to the actual time of an event is called *tense,* reference to things like the duration of an event (e.g. 'for a long time') or the frequency of an event (e.g. 'often') is called *aspect.* Thus, this chapter is entitled "Temporal Aspect" since we will be discussing some of the aspectual distinctions in ASL that give information about time. However, there are many other types of aspectual distinctions, such as those which give information about 'distribution'—which will be discussed in the following chapter.

The distinction between *tense* and *aspect* is complex, especially for English speakers since English does not clearly separate the two. We feel the use of such terminology may be unnecessary for students of ASL, but we do think teachers should be aware of the theoretical distinction between tense and aspect and know something about the different dimensions of time.

Notice, for example, that although we included some explanation of the signs FINISH and NOT-YET in the chapter on Time, these signs actually focus on the *aspect* of *completion* —they refer to the 'completion' of an event, rather than specifically the 'time' of an event, as seen in examples (3) and (4).

Context   Someone asks the Signer if he has finished a particular assignment, which included writing a paper and reading an article.

(3)

                t   nodding
‾‾‾‾‾‾‾‾‾‾‾‾‾‾‾‾ ‾‾‾‾‾‾‾‾‾
WRITE   PAPER,   FINISH   ME

> *Struc*   'As for writing the paper, Yeah, I finished it.'

> *Trans*   'I finished writing the paper.' (or 'I've already written the paper.')

Context   (same as example 3)

(4)
$$\frac{\hspace{2cm}\text{t}\hspace{2cm}}{\text{WRITE \quad PAPER,}}\quad\frac{\hspace{1.5cm}\text{neg}\hspace{1cm}}{\text{NOT-YET \quad ME}}$$

     Struc   'As for writing the paper, I haven't done it yet.'

     Trans   'I haven't written the paper yet.'

Thus, these two signs (**FINISH** and **NOT-YET**) can be used to indicate the temporal aspect of 'completion' (or non-completion). ASL also has a large set of verb inflections that indicate other temporal aspects—such as those which refer to the 'duration' and 'frequency' of an event. There are not yet standard names that linguists who study ASL have agreed to use to identify each inflection for temporal aspect in ASL. However, such terminology is not really necessary for students anyway, since it is more important for them to understand the *meaning* of these inflections and how to *use* them appropriately than what they are called.

Like the inflections for subject and object (see Chapter IX), inflections for a specific temporal aspect are often required in certain contexts. However, since this area of ASL is so complex and since research on this area is still very new and needs more testing, we are presently unable to provide explicit rules for their use. Instead, we will try to describe the meaning of each inflection and then provide examples of their use in context.

B. Some Inflections for Temporal Aspect in ASL

In this section, we list several English words or phrases which approximate the meaning(s) of each inflection for temporal aspect. From this list, we have somewhat arbitrarily chosen a particular word or phrase to use as a standard way of referring to each particular inflection. (Of course, there are many possible English translations for each inflection depending on the context in which they are used.)

Again, please note that linguistic research on this area of ASL is still in the beginning stages, and that this present discussion will undoubtedly need to be modified and much expanded in the future when more information is available. For the purpose of this text, we have considerably simplified what is actually a very complex area of ASL. For example, we describe four inflections for temporal aspect, but we know there are many more similar inflections that have not yet been adequately studied, and even the ones we describe are not completely understood. However, we know that Sign Language teachers need to be aware of what information *is* available from research and to begin thinking about these issues and begin trying to incorporate this new knowledge in their teaching.

To best understand the information provided below, the reader should note the approximate meaning(s), physical description, and illustration of each inflection for temporal aspect and then refer to the sentences in which that inflection occurs, carefully examining each structural equivalent and translation.[1]

(a) *"over time" (continually; regularly; for awhile)*
   This inflection is made with a repeated, circular movement.

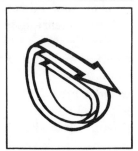

(b) *"regularly" (frequently; repeatedly; a lot; with active focus)*
   This inflection is made with a repeated, small (non-tense) straight-line movement.[2]

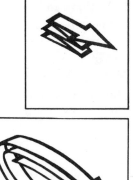

(c) *"long time" (for a prolonged period of time)*
   This inflection is made with a slower, repeated, elliptical movement—composed of a rounded 'thrust' and 'return'.

(d) *"over and over again" (prolonged, repeated focus)*
   This inflection is made with (a) a repeated cycle— composed of a tense straight-line movement (short 'hold' at end of 'thrust', followed by an arc-like transitional movement back to the starting place) and (b) a forward rocking motion of the body and/or head with each 'thrust'.

---

[1]Both of the first two inflections (a & b) include the meaning 'regularly' in some contexts. Note, however, that the English word 'regularly' is ambiguous: it can refer to the 'steady repetition' of an event or indicate that its occurrence is 'normal' or 'routine'. Both of these senses (meanings) seem to fit both inflections in some contexts.

[2]Another inflection that has a meaning like 'to do something so often that it seems like it never stops; incessantly' is similar to the inflection described in (b). However, the movement of this inflection is very tense, small, and rapid.

The choice concerning which verb inflection the Signer will use is very much dependent upon the *Signer's perception of the event*. That is, the same event can often be described in several different ways. For example, suppose that a man and a woman have been going to a particular restaurant about twice a month during the past year. The man likes that restaurant and says "We go there frequently" or "We go there regularly". In ASL, he might sign *we*-GO-TO-*restaurant"regularly"*, using the temporal aspect described in (b). However, the woman feels like they go there too often and would prefer to try out other restaurants. So she says "I'm tired of that place. We go there over and over again". In ASL, she might sign *we*-GO-TO-*restaurant"over & over again"*, using the temporal aspect described in (d).

Similarly, suppose a little boy's pet turtle died yesterday, and when he found the dead turtle, the boy cried for about an hour. When describing what happened yesterday, the boy's sister might say that her brother "cried for awhile". In ASL, she might use the temporal aspect described in (a): CRY*"over time"*. However, she might, instead, think that an hour is a long time for anyone to cry over a turtle and say that her brother "cried for a long time". In ASL, she might use the temporal aspect described in (c): CRY*"long time"*. These two inflections are illustrated below.

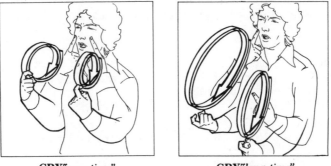

CRY*"over time"*   CRY*"long time"*

Native Signers feel that the inflections for temporal aspect described in (a) and (b) are more like a simple reporting of an event (e.g. going somewhere, crying, working)—with the first one (a) focusing on the *duration* of the event, and the second one (b) focusing on the *frequency* of the event. However, the third and fourth inflections for temporal aspect, described in (c) and (d), indicate that the duration or frequency is more unusual. Signers use the inflection described in (c) to show their feeling that the event lasted for a long time. Signers use the inflection described in (d) to show their feeling that the event occurred unusually often, with a 'break' (period of time) between each repetition of the event. This fourth inflection is often used when the Signer has a negative feeling about the event—like having to do something again and again that is hard to do.

Not all verbs in ASL can be inflected in each of these four ways. Some verbs which can be inflected in each of these four ways are:

____-GO-TO-____	____-ASK-TO-____	____-FORCE-____
____-RUN-TO-____	____-HIT-____	____-BLAME-____
____-THROW-AT-____	____-GIVE-TO-____	____-BAWL-OUT-____
____-INSULT-____	____-INFORM-____	____-BOTHER-____
____-SEND-TO-____	____-LOOK-AT-____	TELL-LIE
____-PREACH-TO-____	____-TEACH-____	PLAY
____-PICK-ON-____	____-TEASE-____	WRITE
____-MAKE-FUN-OF-____	____-TTY-CALL-TO-____	ANALYZE
____-BLAME-____	____-TELL-TO-____	STUDY
		MEETING

In the first set of examples below (5a–5d), the same basic sentence is given four times, each time with a different inflection on the verb. In these sentences, only the verb inflection is different. However, in natural contexts, other parts of the sentence often vary—especially the Signer's facial behavior, as illustrated in the second and third set of examples. The Signer's facial behavior during the signing of the verb in examples (5a)–(5d) gives the meaning 'intently'. (See the illustrations.) It is very common for a non-manual adverb to occur with a verb that is inflected for temporal aspect.

Context   An officemate asks the Signer if he has noticed the abstract painting on the wall in the lobby of their office building. The Signer says "Yes" and adds:

(5a)   (brow squint   )   (gaze up,rt)t
          M-A-Y UP-TILL-NOW, THAT-ONE* PICTURE   C-CL-*up,rt*,

          (gaze up,rt   )'intently'
          ME   *me*-LOOK-AT-*picture"over time"*

   Struc 'Since May, the picture on the wall up on the right, I have been intently looking at it continually.'

   Trans 'Since May, I've been continually studying that picture.'

Context   (same as 5a)

(5b)   (brow squint   )   (gaze up,rt)t
          M-A-Y UP-TILL-NOW, (THAT-ONE*) PICTURE   C-CL-*up,rt*,

             (gaze up,rt   )'intently'
          ME   *me*-LOOK-AT-*picture"regularly"*

   Struc 'Since May, the picture on the wall up on the right, I have been intently looking at it regularly.'

   Trans 'Since May, I've been regularly studying that picture.'

*me-***LOOK-AT**-*picture"over time"*   *me-***LOOK-AT**-*picture"regularly"*

Context   (same as 5a)[3]

(5c)   (brow squint   )   (gaze up,rt)   t
M-A-Y   UP-TILL-NOW,   THAT-ONE*   PICTURE   C-CL-*up,rt,*

(gaze up,rt   )'intently'
ME   *me-***LOOK-AT**-*picture"long time"*

Struc   'Since May, that picture on the wall up on the right, I have been intently looking at it for a long time.'

Trans   'For a long time now, since May, I have been studying that picture.'

Context   (same as 5a)

(5d)   (brow squint   )   (gaze up,rt)t
M-A-Y   UP-TILL-NOW,   THAT-ONE*   PICTURE   C-CL-*up,rt,*

(gaze up,rt   )'intently'
ME   *me-***LOOK-AT**-*picture"over & over again"*

Struc   'Since May, that picture on the wall up on the right, I have been intently looking at it over and over again.'

Trans   'Ever since May, I have been wrestling with that picture, looking at it over and over.'

---

[3]For readers who have the videotaped examples: The movement of the verb (with this inflection) is normally slower than shown on the videotape.

*me-***LOOK-AT**-*picture"long time"*   *me-***LOOK-AT**-*picture"over & over again"*

In the next set of examples, (6a)–(6d), the Signer's non-manual behaviors are different with each inflection. The reader should be aware that some facial signals only occur with certain inflections and not with others. For example, in the context of 'working', the *'pursed lips'* signal would add the meaning of working 'fast' or 'breezing through' the work. But this signal would not make sense if the verb had the inflection *"over and over again"* —since, logically, if the person 'breezes through' the work, then it doesn't have to be focused on again and again.

In these next examples, the fingerspelled loan sign **#BUSY** is stressed (which also involves a tight closing of the Signer's eyes). In each example, a different non-manual adverb is used with the verb. The meanings of these adverbs are reflected in the structural equivalents and the translations; what they look like is shown in the illustrations below.

Context Someone asks the Signer, "Where is Pat? I haven't seen her recently". The Signer replies:

(6a)   _____t   (eyes tightly closed)   (br squint)tight lips
           P-A-T,   **#BUSY***   **WORK**"*over time*"

       Struc 'Pat, she's really busy continually working with great concentration.'

       Trans 'Pat's been awfully busy, really concentrating on her work.'

In the next example, the verb is moved back and forth in an arc while it is repeated. Remember that repetition of a verb in an arc indicates a plural object (also indicated by moving the eyes in an arc with the verb). Thus, in (6b), the Signer is also indicating that Pat is working on 'many different tasks'.

Context   (same as 6a)

                                     (head forward,gaze follow hands)

(6b)   <u>   t   </u> (eyes tightly closed) (teeth bared,br squint   )

       P-A-T,   **#BUSY***   **WORK-***arc*↔*"regularly"*

     Struc 'Pat, she's really busy working a lot with great effort on many different tasks.'

     Trans 'Pat's been awfully busy, having a hard time working her way through a bunch of things she has to do.'

          WORK*"over time"*   **WORK-***arc*↔*"regularly"*

Context   (same as 6a)

(6c)   <u>   t   </u> (eyes tightly closed) <u>(br squint)puff.cheeks</u>

       P-A-T,   **#BUSY***   **WORK***"long time"*

     Struc 'Pat, she's really busy doing a lot of work for a long time.'

     Trans 'Pat's been awfully busy working on a ton of stuff for a long time.'

Context   (same as 6a)

(6d)   <u>   t   </u> (eyes tightly closed) <u>(brow squint   )sta</u>

       P-A-T,   **#BUSY***   **WORK***"over & over again"*

     Struc 'Pat, she's really busy working hard, struggling with the same thing over and over again.'

     Trans 'Pat's been awfully busy, slaving away at the same darn thing over and over.'

WORK*"long time"*   WORK*"over & over again"*

Recent research has found that many of these inflections (as well as other types of modulations) can occur with some signs that usually are thought of as "adjectives"—such as SICK, FRUSTRATED, WRONG, and SILLY.[4] Notice that in a sentence like $\overline{\text{P-A-T}}^{\,t}$, FRUSTRATED—the adjective gives the meaning *'is* frustrated'. Thus, the adjective also includes the meaning of the verb 'to be'. Adjectives like these are called "predicate adjectives" and perhaps should be glossed as BE/BECOME-SICK, BE/BECOME-FRUSTRATED, BE/BECOME-WRONG, BE/BECOME-SILLY, and so on.

For example, the sign SICK can be inflected in each of the four ways described above. In fact, in the grammatical context established by an adverb like ALL-*his*-LIFE (e.g. ALL-*his*-LIFE, P-A-T SICK"____"), it would be ungrammatical in ASL to use an uninflected form of the predicate adjective SICK. Below are illustrations of the four inflections for temporal aspect with the sign SICK. Under the gloss for each inflection, note the approximate meaning in English—which includes the meaning of the different non-manual adverbs that occur in the illustrations with these different inflections.

$\overline{\qquad\qquad\text{mm}}$
BE-SICK*"over time"*

'be continually sick
as a regular matter of course'

$\overline{\qquad\qquad\text{puff.cheeks}}$
BECOME-SICK*"regularly"*

'become sick very frequently'

---

[4]Klima & Bellugi (1979), Chapter 11.

 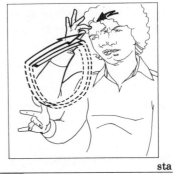

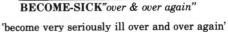

th	sta
BE-SICK"*long time*"	**BECOME-SICK**"*over & again*"
'be sick for long periods of time and really incapacitated'	'become very seriously ill over and over again'

C. More Examples

This section is intended to demonstrate other contexts in which these temporal inflections may occur and to show how these inflections change the meaning of the verb. Also notice how the non-manual adverbs affect the meaning of each sentence.

Context   The Signer is talking with a friend about a younger brother, Lee, who is always being a pest.

(7)

_____(body lean rt; nod)t_
KNOW   LEE,   BROTHER-*rt,*

(gaze rt   )   sta
EVERY-DAY   *lee*-**TEASE**-*me*"*over time*"

Struc   'You know Lee, my brother—every day he continually teases me over and over.'

Trans   'You know my brother, Lee, he's always teasing me, again and again and again.'

sta
lee-**TEASE**-*me*"*over time*"

In the next example, the verb ____-**GO-TO**-____ occurs with the inflection "*regularly*". ASL also has a verb meaning 'go to (generally, a place) somewhat exclusively'—which is always made with this repeated, straight-line movement, indicating the 'regularity' of the event. Both verbs are illustrated below.

Context   The Signer is in a car with some friends and notices a favorite restaurant.[5]

(8)

       <u>co</u>   <u>(gaze lf)</u>   <u>t</u>
      "HEY",   RESTAURANT   JAPANESE,
                   INDEX-lf —————————————→

                             <u>pursed lips</u>
      ME   *me*-GO-TO-*restaurant"regularly"*

     Struc   'Hey! That Japanese restaurant—I go there really frequently.'

     Trans   'Hey! You see that Japanese restaurant? I go there a lot.'

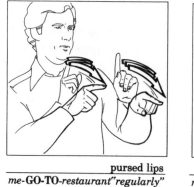 

                <u>pursed lips</u>   <u>pursed lips</u>
    me-GO-TO-*restaurant"regularly"*   *me*-GO-TO-*lf*-EXCLUSIVELY

The next two examples have more than one verb which is inflected for temporal aspect. Both examples illustrate the use of the inflections *"over time"* and *"regularly"*.

Context   The Signer has just returned from lunch and is telling a co-worker about a regular occurrence at lunchtime.

(9)

       <u>co</u>   <u>(gaze rt   )</u>   <u>(th)qt</u>
      AWFUL*,   KNOW+   CORNER-*rt*   INDEX-*rt*   MAN   BEG-MONEY*"over time"*,

                                <u>(gaze rt   )</u>
      EVERY-DAY   ME   25-CENTS   *me*-GIVE-*quarter*-TO-*man"regularly"*

     Struc   'It's awful! You know that corner over there with the man that's continually begging money? Every day I regularly give him twenty-five cents.'

     Trans   'Man, it's awful! You know that guy who's always begging for money on the corner? I end up giving him a quarter every day.'

---

[5]For readers who have the videotaped examples: The *'mm'* and *'puff.cheeks'* adverbs occur with the verb on the videotape instead of the *'pursed lips'* signal.

Context   The Signer is describing what happened after a party yesterday.

(10)

        <u>   (gaze rt)t   </u>   (gaze rt)
  YESTERDAY L-E-E, (2h)BECOME-DRUNK,   *me*-TAKE-*lee* HOME,

  <u> mm </u>   <u> t </u> <u>(gaze rt)nod</u>
  DRIVE L-E-E-*rt*,   V:-CL-*rt*,
          "hold steering wheel"

               <u> mm (gaze rt,sudden'disgust'</u>   ) (head,gaze rt   )
  DRIVE*"regularly"* ————————————→ DISGUST, VOMIT-*rt"over time"*
          "hold steering wheel" ————————→

             (head,gaze rt   )
  IN #C-A-R VOMIT-*rt"over time"*, IMAGINE IN+ #CAR

  (head,gaze rt   )   (head turn away 'in disgust')
  VOMIT-*rt"over time"* *"hold steering wheel"* DISGUST
          "hold steering wheel" ————————→

Struc   'Yesterday Lee, he got drunk. So I took him home. I was driving along and Lee, he was sitting next to me on the right. I was driving along as usual when I looked over at Lee and was suddenly disgusted. He was vomiting continuously—in the car vomiting nonstop. Imagine! Inside the car—vomiting continuously! As I held the wheel, I was disgusted!'

Trans   'Lee got drunk yesterday so I drove him home. He was sitting next to me in the front seat. As I was just driving along, I happened to look over at him and "Yecch!" He was throwing up in the car. Can you imagine that! Throwing up non-stop inside the car! Disgusting!'

In the next example, the verb ____-DISAGREE-WITH-____ has two inflections—the inflection for reciprocity (*"each other"*) and an inflection for temporal aspect (*"long time"*).

Context   After a very lengthy discussion, the Signer and her sister finally agree to see a particular movie together. The Signer exclaims to a friend who has watched the discussion:

(11)   (grimace   )
     UP-TILL-NOW* US-TWO-*rt* *we*-DISAGREE-WITH*"each other"+"long time"*

     <u>(look of 'surprise')pow</u> (gaze rt   )
         SUCCESS   *we*-AGREE-WITH*"each other"*

Struc   'For a long time now, the two of us have disagreed with each other for a long time and at last! Finally we agree!'

Trans   'For a long time now, we've continually disagreed with each other, but finally we agree on something!'

Notice how the verbs in each of the examples so far have had inflections that indicate the subject and/or object as well as a particular temporal aspect. For example, in (7), the verb indicates that Lee is the subject, the Signer is the object, and the event occurs 'continually'. Similarly, in (8), the verb indicates that the Signer is the subject, the restaurant is the object, and the event occurs 'frequently'. Again in example (12), the verb indicates that the Signer is the subject, that some unmentioned recipient(s) on the right is the object, and that the event occurs 'over and over again'.

Context   Someone asks the Signer if he enjoyed Halloween and all the children with their costumes. The Signer replies:

(12)   **HALLOWEEN   BORE*,**

<u>   sta</u>
FOUR-HOUR*   CANDY   *me-***DROP**-candy-**IN**-rt"over & over again"*

    Struc   'Halloween was really boring! For four whole hours, I was laboriously dropping candy (in bags) over and over again.'

    Trans   'Halloween—what a bore! I had to keep handing out candy over and over again for four solid hours.'

<u>   sta</u>
*me-***DROP**-candy-**IN**-rt"over & over again"*

As discussed earlier in this chapter, the inflection *"over & over again"* is often used when the Signer has a negative feeling about the event. This type of 'affective (emotional) context' was seen in example (12) and is also illustrated in the next example. In this example, the Signer also shows his feeling that the event ('writing') is taking an overly long time by stressing the first two adverbs **UP-TILL-NOW*** and **TWO-YEAR***.

Context   The Signer and a friend have been working on a project for a long time. Someone asks them when they will finish. The Signer replies:

(13)
<pre>
                              (gaze rt) _____ sta
       UP-TILL-NOW* TWO-YEAR* US-TWO-rt WRITE"over & over again",

              _____ rhet.q (frown   )
       FINISH #WHEN, (2h)NOT-KNOW
</pre>

> *Struc*   'For a long time now—two full years—the two of us have been laboriously writing and writing and writing and writing. When will we finish? I don't know.'

> *Trans*   'For two whole years, we've been writing our fingers to the bone and I have no idea when we'll finish.'

D. Summary

This chapter has described the movements and meanings of four verb inflections for temporal aspect. These inflections provide information about the duration and/or the frequency of an event. The choice of which inflection a Signer will use is dependent upon his/her perception of that event. For example, the event of 'working for eight hours' may seem like a very long time to one person, but a regular amount of time to another person. So the first person might describe that event with the *"long time"* inflection, whereas the second person might describe it with the *"over time"* inflection. There are other inflections for temporal aspect which occur in ASL, but are not described in this chapter due to insufficient information about them. As always, teachers will need to stay abreast of current research findings as well as rely on their own intuitions and the intuitions of Deaf native Signers to "fill in the gaps" and expand on this information.

Bibliography: Temporal Aspect

Fischer, S. & B. Gough. 1978. Verbs in American Sign Language. *Sign Language Studies 18*, 17–48.

Klima, E. & U. Bellugi. 1979. *The Signs of Language*. Cambridge, Mass.: Harvard University Press.

Pedersen, C. 1977. Verb modulations in American Sign Language. Paper presented at the First National Symposium on Sign Language Research and Teaching, Chicago, May.

Poisner, H., D. Newkirk, U. Bellugi & E. Klima. 1978. Short-term encoding of inflected signs from American Sign Language. Paper presented at the Second National Symposium on Sign Language Research and Teaching, San Diego, October.

Dialogues
and
Cultural Information

TEMPORAL ASPECT

The following three dialogues have been developed to illustrate various uses of the grammatical features described in this chapter. Each of these dialogues also appears in one of the three corresponding Student Texts. In the Student Texts, the transcription of each dialogue is less detailed than what is provided here for the teacher of ASL. Following the dialogues, in the sections called "Cultural Information", are brief discussions of the topic of each dialogue.

The following dialogues and cultural information correspond to:

Student Text: Unit 8
Unit 17
Unit 26

Dialogue: Temporal Aspect
(Student Text - Unit 8)

First Signer (Pat)

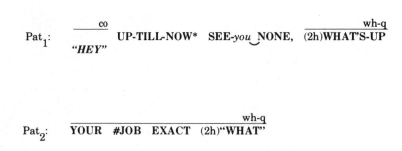

Pat₁:
$$\overline{\quad\text{co}\quad}$$ UP-TILL-NOW*   SEE-*you* NONE, $$\overline{\text{(2h)WHAT'S-UP}}^{\text{wh-q}}$$
"HEY"

Pat₂:
$$\overline{\text{YOUR   \#JOB   EXACT   (2h)"WHAT"}}^{\text{wh-q}}$$

Pat₃:
$$\overline{\text{MEETING   FOR-FOR}}^{\text{wh-q}}$$
                "WHAT"

Pat₄: *OH-I-SEE* +

Pat₅:
$$\overline{\text{WHY NOT   QUIT}}^{\text{wh-q}}$$
          "WHAT"

Pat₆:
$$\overline{\text{HEAR NONE,}}^{\text{br}} \quad \overline{\text{OH-I-SEE}}^{\text{nodding}}$$

Dialogue: Temporal Aspect
(Student Text - Unit 8)

Second Signer (Lee)

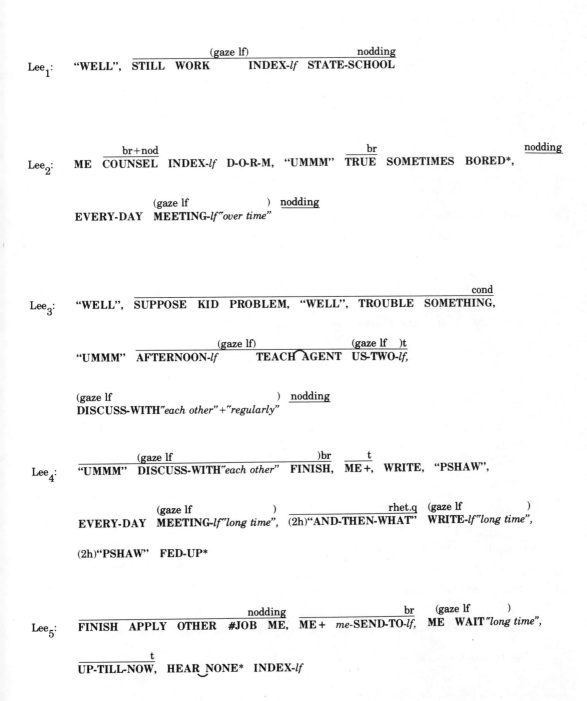

```
                          _____(gaze lf)_____nodding_____
Lee₁:   "WELL",   STILL   WORK            INDEX-lf   STATE-SCHOOL


              ____br+nod____                               _____br_____               ____nodding____
Lee₂:   ME   COUNSEL   INDEX-lf   D-O-R-M,   "UMMM"   TRUE   SOMETIMES   BORED*,

                  _____(gaze lf_____)  nodding___
        EVERY-DAY   MEETING-lf"over time"


        _____cond____
Lee₃:   "WELL",   SUPPOSE   KID   PROBLEM,   "WELL",   TROUBLE   SOMETHING,

                  _____(gaze lf)_____  ___(gaze lf___)t
        "UMMM"   AFTERNOON-lf        TEACH AGENT   US-TWO-lf,

        (gaze lf_____)  nodding___
        DISCUSS-WITH"each other"+"regularly"


        _____(gaze lf_____)br  __t__
Lee₄:   "UMMM"   DISCUSS-WITH"each other"   FINISH,   ME+,   WRITE,   "PSHAW",

                  _____(gaze lf_____)  _____rhet.q  ___(gaze lf_____)
        EVERY-DAY   MEETING-lf"long time",   (2h)"AND-THEN-WHAT"   WRITE-lf"long time",

        (2h)"PSHAW"   FED-UP*


        _____nodding_____  _____br  __(gaze lf_____)
Lee₅:   FINISH   APPLY   OTHER   #JOB   ME,   ME+   me-SEND-TO-lf,   ME   WAIT"long time",

        _____t__
        UP-TILL-NOW,   HEAR NONE*   INDEX-lf
```

Dialogue: Temporal Aspect
(Student Text - Unit 17)

First Signer (Pat)

Pat_1: $\overline{\text{"HEY",}}^{\text{co}}$ $\overline{\text{WHAT'S-UP}}^{\text{wh-q}}$

Pat_2: *me*-SAME-AS-*you*+, SATURDAY $\overline{\text{WHY⌣NOT US-TWO}\;\;\overline{\text{GO-TO-}rt}^{\text{(gaze rt)}}\;\;\text{MOVIE}}^{\text{wh-q}}$

Pat_3: $\overline{\text{AGE+ INDEX-}brother}^{\text{wh-q}}$

Pat_4: $\overline{\text{BROTHER NOT-LIKE LOOK-AT-}cntr\;\;\text{\#TV}}^{\text{neg+q}}$

Pat_5: $\overline{\text{FINISHwg,}}^{\text{nodding}}$ $\overline{\text{\#TV NAME,}}^{\text{t}}$ R-A-I-N-B-O-W-'S E-N-D,

    SEEM #ALL-*arc* PEOPLE DEAF, $\overline{\text{SEEM+,}}^{\text{nodding}}$

    SIGN CONVERSE-IN-ASL, $\overset{\text{(gaze down,cntr)}}{\text{ME } me\text{-LOOK-AT-}tv}$ BELLY-LAUGH"*over & over again*",

    GOOD INDEX-*tv* WOW

Dialogue: Temporal Aspect
(Student Text - Unit 17)

Second Signer (Lee)

                                      <u>   nodding   </u>

Lee₁: (2h)NOTHING SAME-OLD-THING

Lee$_1$: (2h)NOTHING $\overline{\text{SAME-OLD-THING}}^{\text{nodding}}$

Lee$_2$: $\overline{\text{CAN'T}\quad\text{STUCK,}}^{\text{neg}}$ MOTHER FATHER, $\overline{\text{GO-}lf}^{\text{t}}$

(gaze lf   )
(2h)SATURDAY⌣SUNDAY *parents*-TELL-TO-*me* TAKE-CARE-OF BROTHER INDEX-*rt*

Lee$_3$: (2h)"WELL" AGE EIGHT,   INDEX-*rt* $\overline{\text{EVERY-DAY,}}^{\text{t}}$
                              "WELL"

brother-BOTHER-*me*"*regularly*" ME SICK-OF. INDEX-*rt*

Lee$_4$: (2h)"WELL", $\overline{\text{SATURDAY}\quad\text{ALL-MORNING,}\quad\text{INDEX-}brother}^{\text{t}}$ $\overline{\text{(2h)LOOK-AT-}tv\text{(lf)"}over\ time\text{",}}^{\text{(gaze down,lf\qquad\qquad)mm}}$

$\overline{\text{PROBLEM,}\quad\text{INDEX-}brother}^{\text{rhet.q\quad(gaze rt\quad)}}$ $\overline{\text{NOT}\quad\text{UNDERSTAND}\quad\text{INDEX-}lf}^{\text{(gaze lf)}}$ $\overline{\text{SPEAK,}}^{\text{neg}}$

(2h)"WELL", INDEX-*brother* ALWAYS *brother*-ASK-TO-*me*

(body shift rt,gaze up lf   )
    INDEX-*tv* SAY #TV SAY INDEX-*tv*, ME "PSHAW",

$\overline{\text{WISH}\quad\text{#TV}}^{\text{br}}$ $\text{INDEX-}tv$ $\overline{\quad\text{SIGN,}\quad\text{INTERPRET,}\quad\text{SOMETHING}}^{\text{(gaze lf\quad puff.cheeks\qquad)}}$ $\overline{\text{WISH*}}^{\text{nod}}$

Lee$_5$: FINEwg, $\overline{\text{ME}\quad\text{NOT-YET}\quad\text{SEE}\quad\text{INDEX-}tv\text{,}}^{\text{neg}}$ SHOULD+ $\overline{\text{ME}}^{\text{rapid nodding}}$

Dialogue: Temporal Aspect
(Student Text - Unit 26)

First Signer (Pat)

Pat₁: $\overline{\text{"UMMM"}}^{\text{co}}$+   KNOW-THAT   YOU $\overset{\text{t}}{\triangle}$,   BECOME-SICK, $\overline{\text{KNOW-THAT} \quad \text{YOU}}^{\text{q}}$

Pat₂: $\overline{\text{"NO-NO"}}^{\text{neg}}$ WORSE,   SICK $\overline{\text{BECOME-SERIOUSLY-ILL}}^{\text{nodding}}$

Pat₃: $\overline{\text{YOU} \quad \text{KNOW} \quad \text{INDEX-}rt \quad \text{WORK} \quad \text{\#VR} \quad \text{INDEX-}rt,}^{\text{qt}} \; \overline{}^{\text{nod}}$

ONE-WEEK-PAST   SOMETHING   IMPORTANT,

INDEX-*rt* $\triangle$ INDEX-*rt* $\overline{\text{WORK"over time"}}^{\text{'intently'}}$ ALL-WEEK,

ALL-DAY‿ALL-NIGHT   ALL-DAY‿ALL-NIGHT $\overline{\text{WORK"over \& over again",}}^{\text{sta}}$

$\overline{\text{FEW-DAY-PAST,}}^{\text{t}}$ BECOME-SERIOUSLY-ILL   THROW-*rt*   HOSPITAL

Pat₄: (2h)"WELL",   DOCTOR $\overline{\text{(2h)SEARCH-}body(lf)\text{"over time"}}^{\text{(gaze lf, lean lf} \qquad) \text{ 'intently'}}$

$\triangle$ $\overset{\text{(body shift rt,gaze lf 'anxiously')}}{\text{WAIT-}lf\text{"long time",}}$ $\overline{\text{NOT-YET} \quad doctor(lf)\text{-INFORM-}john(rt)}^{\text{neg}}$

Pat₅: "WELL"   UP-TILL-NOW $\overline{\text{THREE-DAY,}}^{\text{br}}$ WIFE $\overline{\text{(2h)CRY"long time",}}^{\text{sta}}$

ME   FEEL   BREAK-DOWN $\overline{\text{FEEL} \quad \text{ME}}^{\text{nodding}}$

Pat₆: $\overset{\text{puff.cheeks+nodding}}{\text{YES++}}$

Dialogue: Temporal Aspect
(Student Text - Unit 26)

Second Signer (Lee)

Lee₁: INDEX-*lf* TEND-TO BE-SICK*"over time"*

$$\overline{\text{wh-q}}$$
Lee₂: HOWwg

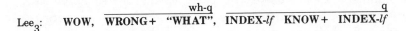
Lee₃: WOW, WRONG+ "WHAT", INDEX-*lf* KNOW+ INDEX-*lf*

$$\overline{\text{q}}$$
Lee₄: WIFE #OK

Lee₅: WHY NOT US-TWO FROM-*here*-GO-TO-*lf* HOSPITAL (2h)NOW, WANTwg

Note: In Lee₁, the modulation of the sign **BE-SICK** gives the meaning 'characteristically sick'.

Student Text: Unit 8

Cultural Information: Deaf Dorm Counselors and Houseparents

In each residential school for Deaf students, there is a group of adults who deal with the students "after hours", when the students are not attending classes. Various titles have been given to these adults, including "houseparents", "dorm supervisors", and "dorm counselors". In many cases, these dorm counselors are required to live at the school. Quite often, such positions are advertised at relatively low salaries because room and board are included.

In the past, a large number of dorm counselors were Deaf and many of them worked at the same school they graduated from. For many students, these dorm counselors were their first sustained contact with Deaf adults. Thus, for these students, the dorm counselors often functioned as adult Deaf role models, disciplinarians, "alter" parents, tutors, and language models. As language models, these adults often helped the students learn ASL. Many deaf people who attended residential programs recall one or more Deaf dorm supervisors who would tell stories or explain the day's lessons in a way that the students could understand and enjoy them.

For some Deaf houseparents, the job was simply 'something to do' while they waited for a better opportunity to come along—like a teaching position or job outside the field of education. For others, the school became their home. They worked as dorm supervisors during the school year (and often as coaches or sponsors of various school organizations) and during the summer, they worked on the grounds or maintenance crews.

Now, however, the number of Deaf houseparents is decreasing. Housing problems, pay scales, and limited summer employment are some of the reasons why there are fewer and fewer Deaf dorm counselors. In addition, more jobs and better jobs are now being made available to Deaf people, so there is less incentive to accept and remain in the position of dorm counselor.

Student Text: Unit 17

Cultural Information: Rainbow's End

In January, 1979, a five-part television series entitled "Rainbow's End" was aired nationally on PBS. This creative new series is like Sesame Street—except that it is designed for Deaf children, their families, and their teachers. The series focuses on the amusing antics of a special group of characters (almost all of whom are Deaf) who work in a TV studio. The program was funded by the Bureau of Education for the Handicapped and was produced by D.E.A.F. Media, Inc., a non-profit California-based organization.

The overall goals of this series are: to provide positive role models—adult and peer—for Deaf children; to facilitate the development of English and reading; to foster family and classroom interaction; and to develop an awareness of the language and culture of Deaf people. To accomplish these goals, there are regular segments in each show: for example, "Famous Deaf Adults" from the past and present; dramatized stories and humorous situations; visits by "Supersign" who provides opportunities for learning helpful signs; and Deaf Awareness segments which provide some cultural information about the Deaf Community.

In general, the five-part series is presented in American Sign Language with voice-over narration. In addition, because of the educational goals of the program, each show is captioned. Future shows in the "Rainbow's End" series are planned and, hopefully, will soon be available. For more information write: D.E.A.F. Media, Inc., 401 E. 21st Street, Oakland, Ca. 94606.

Student Text: Unit 26

Cultural Information: Deaf Patients in Hospitals

In the past, Deaf individuals have had and often still have a somewhat difficult time obtaining adequate and appropriate medical services in hospitals. While this situation is changing in many hospitals, it continues to be an unnecessary cause of anxiety and fear for many Deaf people. Some of the difficulties encountered are due to a lack of sensitivity and awareness on the part of the hospital staff. Consider, for example, the following situations:

—a Deaf person who is right-handed is given an intravenous infusion in the right arm and, thus, can neither sign nor write.

—a Deaf person is prepared for surgery and, after sedation is administered, the doctor explains the upcoming procedure. The sedative, however, affects the patient's eyesight and s/he does not understand what is happening.

—a Deaf person rings for the nurse, but the nurse answers via an intercom system which the Deaf person cannot hear.

These examples illustrate some of the difficulties encountered by Deaf patients in hospitals. There are some obvious solutions to these problems such as training members of the hospital staff to use Sign Language or employing qualified interpreters. One of the best ways of dealing with such problems would be to hire qualified Deaf personnel. And, in fact, an increasing number of programs are making available to Deaf individuals the training and background needed to become nurses, nurse's aides, and medical technicians or to work in other health-related areas.

Chapter XIV

Distributional Aspect

A. Introduction

In the previous chapter, we focused on four verb inflections that give information about the frequency and/or duration of an action. These were called inflections for *temporal aspect* since they indicate something about the timing or temporal nature of an action—e.g. work 'for a long time'.

In this chapter, we will focus on four verb inflections that give information about the 'distribution' of an action—e.g. 'to each individual in a group', 'to specific individuals, but not all', etc. These inflections indicate what is called *distributional aspect*. The use of these inflections often seems to be a matter of the Signer's choice and focus. For example, the Signer can choose to focus on the fact that the action involved 'sending letters to *each* individual in a particular group' (e.g. 'I sent each of them a letter'), or simply say 'I sent them a letter'. This type of distinction concerns the 'distribution' of a particular action and should become clearer as you read through the description of each inflection and see how each inflection changes the meaning of various verbs in sentences.

B. Some Inflections for Distributional Aspect in ASL

In this section, we will use English phrases to approximate the meanings of each inflection as a way of referring to that inflection. (Of course, there are many possible English translations for each inflection depending on the context in which it is used.) We have chosen to describe the four verb inflections which seem to be the best understood in the research literature on ASL. However, several other inflections for distributional aspect have been studied and the reader may wish to consult other sources.[1]

To best understand the information presented below, the reader should note the approximate meaning and physical description of each inflection and then refer to the illustrations and sentences in which each inflection occurs, carefully examining the approximate structural equivalents and English translations.

(a) *'to all in a group'*: This inflection is made with a 'sweep' of the hand in an arc along a horizontal plane. The Signer's eyes/head tend to follow the 'sweep'. When this inflection is used, the action is viewed as a single event.[2] (We call this inflection *"all"*.)

---

[1] See Klima & Bellugi (1979), Chapter 12.

[2] In Klima & Bellugi (1979), this inflection is not described as indicating a "distributional aspect", but rather, as indicating "number" (a type of general plural inflection). However, we have decided to include it here for pedagogical purposes so that we can compare and contrast its form and meaning with the inflection described in (b).

(b) *'to or from each in a group'*: This inflection is made with repeated, separate articulations of the verb in an arc along a horizontal plane. The Signer's eyes/head tend to follow each articulation along the arc. When this inflection is used, the action is viewed as repeated events of the same type. (We call this inflection *"each"*.)

(c) *'to or from specified individuals (some/many, usually not all)'*: This inflection is made with repeated articulations of the verb, with both hands alternating and moving toward or from several different points in space (not in serial order). The Signer's eyes/head tend to move back and forth with each articulation, and there is frequently some kind of repeated opening and closing of the mouth (often releasing air from the mouth with each articulation). When this inflection is used, the action is viewed as repeated events of the same type. (We call this inflection *"spec"*.)

(d) *'to or from un-specified individuals (some/many, but not all)'*: This inflection is made with repeated articulations of the verb, with both hands alternating with a somewhat circular movement. The Signer's eyes/head tend not to focus on any specific point, but the head often 'bobs' with each articulation of the verb. Sometimes the head is bent forward with the eyes partially or fully closed, showing a lack of attention to any specific individuals. Sometimes the Signer's cheeks are 'puffed', releasing air. When this inflection is used, the action is viewed as repeated events of the same type. (We call this inflection *"unspec"*.)

Illustrated below are these four inflections for distributional aspect with the verbs ____-GIVE-TO-____ and ____-ASK-TO-____ .

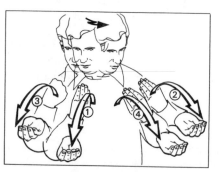

me-**GIVE-TO**-*"all"*

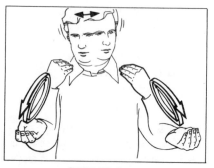

me-**GIVE-TO**-*"each"*

me-**GIVE-TO**-*"spec"*

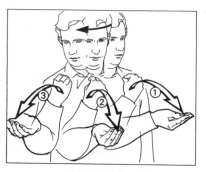

me-**GIVE-TO**-*"unspec"*

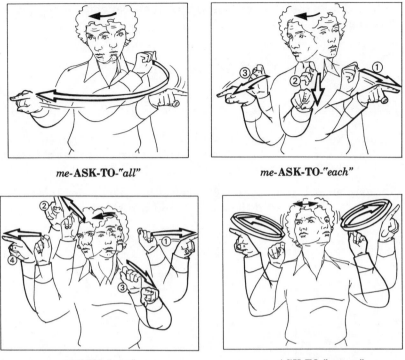

me-**ASK-TO**-*"all"*   *me*-**ASK-TO**-*"each"*

me-**ASK-TO**-*"spec"*   *me*-**ASK-TO**-*"unspec"*

C. Examples

In this section, two examples are given of each inflection in the context of sentences. The first two examples illustrate uses of the inflection *"all"*. Notice that this inflection does not specify exactly *how* the distribution occurs. For example, the teacher mentioned in example (1) could have actually handed out the test papers one-by-one to each student, but the Signer does not give us that information with the *"all"* inflection. The Signer simply says that the test papers were passed out to the students. Similarly, the Signer in example (2) could have actually collected all the blue tickets together, then the green tickets, then the yellow tickets, etc. But with the plural inflection *"all"*, the Signer does not specify *how* the tickets were collected, but simply says that she gathered them all together.

Context   A student is just beginning to describe what happened in class during a weekly test.

(1)   t
      ‾‾‾‾‾
TEST, TEACH͡ AGENT   (2h)*teacher*-**GIVE-TO**-*"all"*

    Struc   'The test, the teacher gave it out to all those in the group.'

    Trans   'The teacher passed out the test.'

Context   A friend asks the Signer if she visited the Deaf club during the weekend. The Signer replies:[3]

(2)   <u>nodding   t</u>   (gaze rt)
      ONE-DAY-PAST,   ME   GO-TO-*rt*   **#CLUB,**

      <u>   qt</u>   <u>   (gaze rt   )</u>   <u>puff.cheek+nodding</u>
      REMEMBER   OLD   TICKET,   ME   *me*-**COLLECT**-*rt"all"*   *me*-**THROW-OUT**-*rt*

> *Struc*   'Yeah. Yesterday, I went to the club. You remember those old tickets? Well, I gathered all of that large number of them together and threw them out.'

> *Trans*   'Yeah, I went to the club yesterday. You know those old tickets? Well, I rounded them all up and threw 'em out.'

<u>   puff.cheeks</u>
me-**COLLECT**-*rt"all"*

In contrast with the *"all"* inflection, the inflection that we write as *"each"* does give us information about how the action is 'distributed'. The *"each"* inflection tells us that the same type of action occurs again and again, each time with a different thing or a different individual (or group), and in an orderly manner. For example, in (3), the Signer indicates that each child in the line gives the teacher his/her homework and that this action is done one-by-one, consecutively down the line.

Context   A teacher at a military school is explaining to another teacher the procedure he uses for collecting his students' homework.

(3)   <u>   t</u>   (gaze down   )   (gaze at 'line of children'   )
      HOME WORK,   (2h)CHILDREN   **(2h)4-CL**'in a line facing me'

      (gaze at each 'child' as gives in homework)
      "each"children-**GIVE-TO**-*me*

> *Struc*   'The homework, the children stand in a line facing me and each in turn down the line gives it to me.'

> *Trans*   'The children stand in a line and we go right down the row and they each give me their homework.'

---

[3]For readers who have the accompanying videotape: The *'puff.cheeks'* signal is less visible on the videotape in comparison with the **drawing.**

Notice that in example (4), the sign **FEW** indicates the relative number of pictures that need to be re-painted. The inflection *"each"* on the verb **PAINT-____** then refers to 'each' of those 'few' pictures, rather than all of the pictures in the room.

Context   The Signer and a group of tourists are walking through an old house that will soon be restored and become a museum. Upon entering one of the rooms, the Signer (who is the tour guide) says:

(4)
                                               (gaze at each 'picture';   mm)t
         INDEX-*down*   **ROOM**   **PICTURE**   (2h)alt.C-CL'pictures on walls',

         pursed lips   nod (gaze at each 'painting')pursed lips
            FEW   **MUST** **AGAIN** **PAINT**-*pictures"each"*

         Struc   'This room—the pictures placed all over the walls as usual, a very few of them need to again be painted—each of them a little bit.'

         Trans   'A few of the pictures in this room need a little re-painting.'

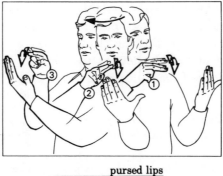

pursed lips
PAINT-pictures"*each*"

The inflection that we write as *"spec"* also tells us that the same type of action occurs again and again, each time with a different thing or a different individual (or group). However, the *"spec"* inflection indicates that the action does *not* occur in serial order with those specific things or individuals. Instead, the action occurs with 'this one here' and then 'that one over there', etc. Another way the *"spec"* inflection is different from the *"each"* inflection is that the *"each"* inflection implies that the action occurs with all of the things or individuals in the group.[4] But the *"spec"* inflection does not tell us this. To the contrary, the *"spec"* inflection usually indicates that the action occurred with some or many of the individuals/things in the group, but not all of them. This is clearly shown in example (5)—not all of the people asked the Signer for money, but several individuals did.

---

[4]Notice how the inflection *"each"* on the verbs in example (4) indicated that every one (or all) of the pictures of the small group designated by the sign **FEW** need repainting.

Context   It's close to Christmas and many of the poorer families in the neighborhood have been having a hard time getting loans to buy presents for
their children. The Signer (who is very wealthy, but apathetic to their
needs) is telling a friend about his own response to these people's requests
for loans.

(5)
```
                              t              (head back, gaze at each 'person')
     MONEY   BORROW-FROM-me,   PEOPLE   "spec"people-ASK-TO-me
```

```
      t  (head back              )neg
     ME,  me-SAY-#NO-TO-people"spec"
```

> *Struc*   'As for borrowing money from me, people, various specific ones
> have asked me for it at different times. But me, I have said "No" to
> each of those individuals, respectively.'

> *Trans*   'Several different people have asked me to lend them money, but
> I've told each of them "No".'

In example (6), the inflection *"spec"* tells us that the action occurs in a random
fashion, one-by-one. The inflection itself does not tell us that all of the children hand
their homework to the teacher. But the nature of the event—the fact that it involves children turning in their homework (which they are all supposed to do)—
leads us to believe that all of the children do this.

Context   Another teacher at the military school follows a slightly different procedure for collecting her students' homework. She explains:

(6)
```
                     t   (gaze down      ) (gaze at 'line of children'    )
     HOME WORK,   (2h)CHILDREN   (2h)4-CL'in a line facing me'
```

```
     (gaze at each 'child' as gives in homework)
     "spec"children-GIVE-TO-me
```

> *Struc*   'The homework, the children stand in a line facing me and ran-
> domly take turns giving it to me.'

> *Trans*   'The children stand in a line and randomly take turns giving me
> their homework.'

Below are three illustrations of different verbs with the *"spec"* inflection that mean 'I say "yes" to specific individuals, one after the other', 'I select specific individuals, one after the other', and 'I eliminate specific individuals, one after the other', respectively.

me-**SAY**-**#YES**-**TO**-*"spec"*   *me*-**SELECT**-*"spec"*   *me*-**ELIMINATE**-*"spec"*

The inflection that we write as *"unspec"* also tells us that the same type of action occurs again and again, each time with a different thing or a different individual. However, this inflection does not focus on specific individuals or things, and the Signer does not look at any specific locations in space while signing a verb with the *"unspec"* inflection. Instead, the focus seems to be on the idea that there are a lot of people or things involved in the action. By increasing the speed of the (alternating) circular repetitions, the Signer can show that an even greater number of people or things are involved in the action. The *"unspec"* inflection on the verb in example (7) indicates that the police arrest many of the protesters and implies that the action happens so much that the protesters are no longer viewed as individuals. Instead, the meaning is more like 'mass arrests'.

Context   A friend is visiting Washington, D.C. and remarks to the Signer that he often sees reports on TV about protesters in the city. The Signer replies "Yes, you're right"...

(7)

<pre>
                          t   (gaze rt   )   puff.cheeks
HERE   WASHINGTON D-C, PEOPLE FROM-rt-ASSEMBLE-TO-here (2h)alt.COMPLAIN,
</pre>

<pre>
        t   (head back   )puff.cheeks
POLICE,   police-ARREST-people"unspec"
</pre>

Struc   'Here in Washington, D.C., people —many of them flock here and protest a lot. The police, they arrest lots of them.'

Trans   'Many people come to Washington, D.C. to protest and the police arrest a lot of them.'

Context An accountant is talking with the Signer (who works in the Public Relations Division of the U.S. Government). The accountant asks why the Division's monthly bill for mailing is so high. The Signer replies:

(8)

                                 (head forward)qt
KNOW PRESIDENT PICTURE SIGNED, KNOW YOU,

        mm   puff.cheeks
EVERY-MONTH (ME) *me*-SEND-TO-*"unspec"*

> *Struc* 'You know the president's picture that's autographed, you know the one? Regularly every month, I send out a lot of them.'

> *Trans* 'You know that autographed picture of the president? I sent out a whole boatload of 'em every month.'

police-**ARREST**-*people"unspec"*

              puff.cheeks
me-**SEND-TO**-*"unspec"*

D. Summary

As we said in the beginning of this chapter, Signers may choose to use an inflection when they want to give more detailed information about the 'distribution' of an action. They can simply state that the action happened to all the members of a group *or* say that it involved each individual or thing in serial order, various specific individuals or things in a non-serial order, or many un-specified individuals or things in a non-serial order.

For more advanced classes in ASL, teachers may also want to examine how both an inflection for temporal aspect and an inflection for distributional aspect can occur together on the same verb—to express complex meanings like 'to continuously give things to each of the members of a group' (e.g. *me*-**GIVE-TO**-*people"each"*+*"over time"*) or 'to ask various specific individuals again and again' (e.g. *me*-**ASK-TO**-*people"spec"*+*"over and over again"*). This is another area of ASL that linguistic research is just beginning to explore.

Bibliography: Distributional Aspect

Klima, E. & U. Bellugi. 1979. *The Signs of Language*. Cambridge, Mass.: Harvard University Press.

Dialogues
and
Cultural Information

DISTRIBUTIONAL ASPECT

The following three dialogues have been developed to illustrate various uses of the grammatical features described in this chapter. Each of these dialogues also appears in one of the three corresponding Student Texts. In the Student Texts, the transcription of each dialogue is less detailed than what is provided here for the teacher of ASL. Following the dialogues, in the sections called "Cultural Information", are brief discussions of the topic of each dialogue.

The following dialogues and cultural information correspond to:

Student Text: Unit 9
Unit 18
Unit 27

Dialogue: Distributional Aspect
(Student Text - Unit 9)

First Signer (Pat)

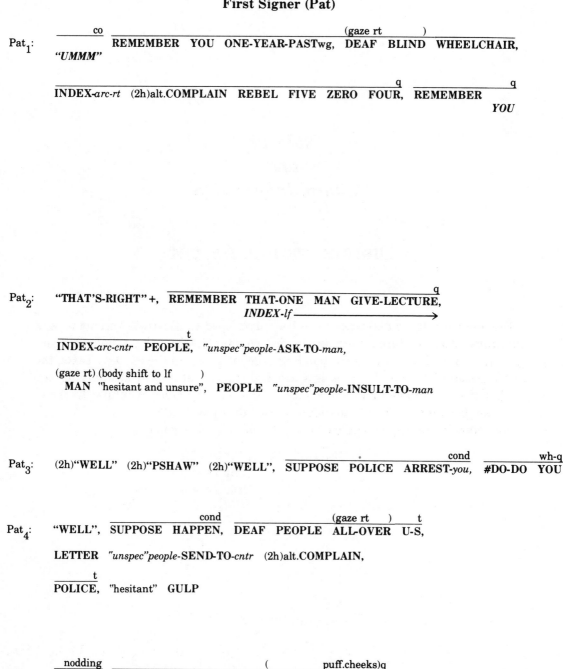

Pat₁:
```
                 co                                              (gaze rt        )
             ‾‾‾‾‾‾‾‾‾‾   ‾‾‾‾‾‾‾‾‾‾‾‾‾‾‾‾‾‾‾‾‾‾‾‾‾‾‾‾‾‾‾‾‾‾‾‾‾‾‾‾‾‾‾‾‾‾‾‾‾‾‾‾‾‾‾‾
             REMEMBER   YOU   ONE-YEAR-PASTwg,   DEAF   BLIND   WHEELCHAIR,
"UMMM"
```

```
                                                                q                    q
                                                          ‾‾‾‾‾‾‾‾‾‾‾‾‾‾‾‾    ‾‾‾‾‾‾‾‾‾‾
INDEX-arc-rt  (2h)alt.COMPLAIN  REBEL  FIVE  ZERO  FOUR,  REMEMBER
                                                                            YOU
```

Pat₂:
```
                                ‾‾‾‾‾‾‾‾‾‾‾‾‾‾‾‾‾‾‾‾‾‾‾‾‾‾‾‾‾‾‾‾‾‾‾‾‾‾‾‾‾‾‾‾‾q
    "THAT'S-RIGHT" +,  REMEMBER  THAT-ONE  MAN  GIVE-LECTURE,
                                 INDEX-lf ‾‾‾‾‾‾‾‾‾‾‾‾‾‾‾‾‾‾‾‾‾‾‾‾‾‾‾‾⟶
```

```
                          t
    ‾‾‾‾‾‾‾‾‾‾‾‾‾‾‾‾‾‾‾‾‾‾‾‾‾‾
    INDEX-arc-cntr  PEOPLE,  "unspec"people-ASK-TO-man,
```

```
    (gaze rt) (body shift to lf      )
        MAN  "hesitant and unsure",  PEOPLE  "unspec"people-INSULT-TO-man
```

Pat₃:
```
                                                             ·           cond            wh-q
                                                     ‾‾‾‾‾‾‾‾‾‾‾‾‾‾‾‾‾‾‾‾‾‾‾‾‾‾‾    ‾‾‾‾‾‾‾‾‾‾‾‾‾‾
    (2h)"WELL"  (2h)"PSHAW"  (2h)"WELL",  SUPPOSE  POLICE  ARREST-you,  #DO-DO  YOU
```

Pat₄:
```
                          cond               (gaze rt    )   t
                  ‾‾‾‾‾‾‾‾‾‾‾‾‾‾‾‾‾    ‾‾‾‾‾‾‾‾‾‾‾‾‾‾‾‾‾‾‾‾‾‾‾‾‾‾‾
    "WELL",  SUPPOSE  HAPPEN,  DEAF  PEOPLE  ALL-OVER  U-S,
```

```
    LETTER  "unspec"people-SEND-TO-cntr  (2h)alt.COMPLAIN,
```

```
           t
    ‾‾‾‾‾‾‾‾‾
    POLICE,  "hesitant"  GULP
```

Pat₅:
```
       nodding                         (          puff.cheeks)q
    ‾‾‾‾‾‾‾‾‾   ‾‾‾‾‾‾‾‾‾‾‾‾‾‾‾‾‾‾‾‾‾‾‾‾‾‾‾‾‾‾‾‾‾‾‾‾‾‾‾‾‾‾‾‾‾‾‾‾
    TRUE++  REMEMBER  YOU  #TV+  CAMERA-RECORD-arc,  CAMERA-RECORD-arc↔
```

Dialogue: Distributional Aspect
(Student Text - Unit 9)

Second Signer (Lee)

Lee₁: **RIGHT YOU RIGHT YOU,**

                   (gaze up,rt   ) (gaze lf,outward   )
  REMEMBER MAN   V-CL*@up,rt*'stand on platform'   **GIVE-LECTURE***"regularly",*

    _____t   (gaze lf   ) (gaze lf   )
  PAPER,   WOMAN   GIVE-TO*-people"all"*   **PEOPLE**   *"all"people*-**SIGN-NAME,**

            (gaze lf   )
  WOMAN   COLLECT*-papers"all"*   **C-CL** } 'thick stack of papers'
                                  B↑-CL }

  (gaze up,rt   )
  GIVE*-stack of papers*-**TO***-man*

Lee₂: **RIGHT*,   THAT-ONE*   PERIOD-OF-TIME,**   (gaze lf   )
                                          ME   FEEL+

                                                              neg
  POLICE   FROM*-lf*-**ASSEMBLE-TO***-cntr*   *police*-**ARREST***-people"unspec"*

Lee₃: _____q   _____neg   _____neg
  ARREST*-me,*   **NOT-KNOW,   SAY-NOTHING   TAKE***-me*-**AWAY***-rt,*   **NOT-KNOW**

Lee₄: t
  PEOPLE   MEETING   INDEX*-rt*   **DEAF,   BLIND,   VARIOUS-THINGS,**

                                          q   neg
  TRUE WORK   POLICE   *police*-**ARREST***-people"unspec",*   **DISBELIEVE   ME   DISBELIEVE**wg

Lee₅: **RIGHT   YOU,**   t
  RIGHT   YOU,   ONE-DAY-FUTURE MORNING   NEWSPAPER,

                                     pow (gaze rt) (gaze lf   )
  L:-CL } 'newspaper headline'   **INDEX***-rt*   **(2h)BECOME-EMBARRASSED**
  B↑-CL }

Dialogue: Distributional Aspect
(Student Text - Unit 18)

First Signer (Pat)

$$\overline{\text{wh-q}}$$

Pat₁: **FUTURE SATURDAY #DO-DO**

(gaze rt   )   t

Pat₂: **INDEX-*rt* #CLUB HAVE MOVIE, ONE DRAMA AGENT, SIGN**

                                       (gaze rt   )

Pat₃: **NOT-KNOW, SATURDAY ME (2h)alt.ASK-TO-*rt"spec"* SEE-SEE**

                                    ('trying to remember'   )puff.cheeks nodding

Pat₄: **RIGHT*, #CO   SOMETHING BUY TICKET (2h)GIVE-TO-*"all"* FREE,**

                    INDEX-rt $\longrightarrow$

(gaze lf & rt 'guiltily')

      GIVE-TO-*"each"*

           (gaze rt   )   brow raise

Pat₅: **MAYBE SATURDAY NIGHT MOVIE DRAMA AGENT DEAF INDEX-*rt***

Pat₆: **"HAND-IT-OVER"**

Dialogue: Distributional Aspect
(Student Text - Unit 18)

Second Signer (Lee)

Lee_1: "DON'T-KNOW" $\overline{\text{(2h)NOT-KNOW (2h)NOT-YET DECIDE,}}^{\text{neg}}$ $\overline{\text{(2h)WHY (2h)WHAT'S-UP (2h)"WHAT"}}^{\text{wh-q}}$

Lee_2: OH-I-SEE, $\overline{\text{DEAF INDEX-}lf}^{\text{q}}$

Lee_3: "THAT'S-RIGHT" $\overline{\text{REMEMBER AWHILE-AGO MOVIE, NAME ME FORGET, DOESN'T-MATTER}}^{\text{qt}}$

$\overline{\text{THAT-ONE}\underline{}\text{INDEX-}lf,}^{\text{t}}$ DRAMA TWO DRAMA⌢AGENT INDEX-rt $\overline{\text{SIGN}}^{\text{nodding}}$ $\overline{\text{THOSE-TWO-}rt,}^{\text{t}}$ HEARING

Lee_4: $\overline{\text{DEAF ALL-OVER,}}^{\text{t}}$ $\overline{\text{(2h)BECOME-ANGRY,}}^{\text{pow}}$ $\overline{\text{LETTER,}}^{\text{t}}$

(2h)alt."*unspec*"-SEND-TO-*cntr* (2h)alt.COMPLAIN,

$\overline{\text{#CO,}}^{\text{t}}$ (body lean back) (2h)alt."*unspec*"-SEND-TO-*me* "STAY-BACK" ENOUGH,

DECIDE FROM-NOW-ON $\overline{\text{#IF MOVIE HAVE SIGN-}rt,}^{\text{(lean rt)}}$ $\overline{\text{DEAF,}}^{\text{(lean lf)}}$ $\overline{\text{"WELL",}}^{\text{cond}}$

WILL (2h)alt.ASK-TO-"*spec*" HIRE DEAF

Lee_5: ME DISBELIEVE ME, $\overline{\text{SUPPOSE DEAF,}}^{\text{cond}}$

ME ONE-DOLLAR DOLLAR *me*-PAY-OUT-TO-"*each*" $\overline{\text{ME}}^{\text{rapid nodding}}$

Dialogue: Distributional Aspect
(Student Text - Unit 27)

First Signer (Pat)

Pat$_1$: "HI" (2h)"WELL" ONE-WEEK-PAST $\overline{\text{NOT HERE}}$ $\overline{\text{WORK,}}^{\text{neg}}$ $\overline{\text{YOU SICK YOU}}^{\text{q}}$

Pat$_2$: $\overset{\text{neg('not understand')}}{\overline{\text{#DO-DO}}}$ $\overline{\text{YOU,}}^{\text{wh-q}}$ $\overline{\text{J-U-R-Y}}^{\text{q}}$

Pat$_3$: $\overline{\text{YOU HAVE INTERPRET AGENT YOU}}^{\text{q}}$

Pat$_4$: $\overline{\text{FOR-FOR ASK-TO-}\textit{people"each"} \text{"WHAT"}}^{\text{wh-q}}$

Pat$_5$: $\overline{\text{ELIMINATE YOU}}^{\text{q}}$

Pat$_6$: $\overset{\text{nodding}}{\overline{\text{OH-I-SEE}}}$

Dialogue: Distributional Aspect
(Student Text - Unit 27)

Second Signer (Lee)

Lee₁:
```
        neg                (gaze lf            )
        ME  STUCK,         lf-SUMMON-me  (2h)GO-TO-lf  COURT,  "WOW"
```

Lee₂:
```
          nod              (gaze lf
        RIGHT  J-U-R-Y,    (2h)alt.SELECT-people(lf)"spec"   C-CL⎰ -lf'group'  THEREABOUTS-lf  FIFTY++,
                                                             C-CL⎱ ──────────────────────────────────────→

        (lean,gaze lf)  (lean rt,gaze lf)  (lean,gaze lf)  (lean rt,gaze lf )
        MAN-lf,          WOMAN,             BLACK,          WHITE-FACED,    ONLY-ONE-me  DEAF
```

Lee₃:
```
          nod  (gaze lf        )  puff.cheeks                              t
        YES++  FASCINATINGwg "WOW"++,  INDEX-lf thumb+  LAW  AGENT,

        (gaze lf                    )
        lawyer-GIVE-TO-people(lf)"each"  (2h)1outline-CL'rectangular paper',

        (gaze lf              )                      nod              t  (gaze down,lf                    )
        NAME  ADDRESS  VARIOUS-THINGS,  INDEX-lf index+,  (2h)alt.lawyer-ASK-TO-people(lf)"spec"

        (gaze down,lf                                              )  (        puff.cheeks)q
        FINISH-lf  READ-paper-lf  NEWSPAPER-lf,  LOOK-AT+-lf  #TV+-lf,  VARIOUS-THINGS
```

Lee₄:
```
            (    nod)br                              (gaze lf            )
        SUPPOSE  FINISH*-lf  READ-paper-lf  NEWSPAPER-lf,   LOOK-AT-lf  #TV+,

                                                  neg
        KNOW+  PROBLEM  SITUATION,  CAN'T  J-U-R-Y  CAN'T,  DOESN'T-MATTER,

        (gaze down,lf                )      t  (body lean lf;gaze up,lf)puff.cheeks+nodding
        (2h)alt.lawyer-ASK-TO-people"spec",  PEOPLE,  (2h)alt."spec"people-SAY-#YES-TO-lawyer,

        (gaze lf,down                                      )
        (2h)alt.lawyer-INDEX-people"spec"  (2h)alt.lawyer-ELIMINATE-people"spec"
```

Lee₅:
```
          neg                          t
        ME,  READ-paper  NEWSPAPER,  BEHIND*  "WOW"+,

        (gaze lf                )t  (gaze lf                )      rhet.q
        C-CL⎰ 'relatively large group',  L:-CL⎰ 'class dwindle in size',  LEAVE-IT-lf,  FIFTEEN+
        C-CL⎱                            L:-CL⎱
```

Student Text: Unit 9

Cultural Information: Section 504 and the American Coalition of Citizens with Disabilities

The Rehabilitation Act of 1973 was a milestone for millions of disabled Americans. This Act contained one particular section—Section 504—which said that no program receiving federal funding could discriminate against a person solely on the basis of his or her disability. Prior to Section 504, disabled persons were often denied admission to the college of their choice, discriminated against in the job market, denied services by clinics, were often unable to take advantage of public housing and, in general, were unable to take advantage of thousands of federally-supported programs. Section 504 was designed to put an end to such discrimination and to make all such programs accessible to disabled persons.

Although the law was passed in 1973, no real action was taken to implement it until 1977 when the rules and regulations were signed. This signing would not have happened, however, without some pressure from disabled citizens. When the American Coalition of Citizens with Disabilities (ACCD) learned that the government was considering rewriting and substantially weakening the regulations, it called for nationwide demonstrations of protest. On April 5, 1977, thousands of disabled Americans all over the nation staged protests and sit-ins. The regulations were signed on April 28, 1977.

The American Coalition of Citizens with Disabilities (ACCD) is a national association of more than 75 national, state, and local organizations of and for almost every category of disabled people. More than seven million of the nation's 36 million disabled citizens are represented by the organizations that belong to the ACCD. For more information about Section 504 and the ACCD, write: American Coalition of Citizens with Disabilities, 1200 15th Street, N.W., Suite 201, Washington, D.C. 20005.

Student Text: Unit 18

Cultural Information: Deaf Actors and Actresses

In March, 1979, a special preview of the MGM film "Voices" was held in San Francisco. The film portrays a love story about a Deaf woman who aspires to be a dancer and who falls in love with a hearing man. The role of the Deaf woman was portrayed by a hearing actress. For many Deaf actors and actresses in California, this brought to focus many years of frustration and anger at being denied roles in movies and on television. Consequently, a "Coalition Against Voices" was formed to protest such discrimination. On April 6, 1979, a demonstration was held at the San Francisco premier of the film. This demonstration was one more attempt to sensitize those in the television and film industry toward the type of discrimination that Deaf artists have been enduring for so many years.

Ironically, while the film "Voices" demonstrates that a Deaf person *can* be a dancer, the film and television industry have felt that a Deaf person *cannot* be an actor and have consistently chosen hearing actors to portray Deaf roles—for example, "Dummy", "The Miracle Worker", "Airport '79", "Mom and Dad Can't Hear Me", etc. A notable exception was the recent film "And Your Name is Jonah" which cast a Deaf child in the leading role.

As a result of the demonstration in San Francisco (which closed the theatre showing "Voices"), MGM agreed to make every effort to use Deaf actors to fill Deaf roles in future productions. MGM also agreed to use the National Association of the Deaf as a referral agency for this purpose as well as for technical assistance in films relating to deafness.

Student Text: Unit 27

Cultural Information: Deaf People and Jury Duty

It is generally true that Deaf people rarely, if ever, receive notices to report for jury duty. In fact, most states have laws which specifically prohibit the names of Deaf people from being included in the "jury pool". (The jury pool is a list of people's names who can be called for jury duty if the need arises.) The rationale that is most often used to exclude Deaf individuals is that the inability to *hear* testimony prevents them from being competent jurors.

However, with the signing of Section 504 of the Rehabilitation Act of 1973, Deaf people are demanding their right to participate more fully and equally in all aspects of American society. During the past few years, individuals and groups have begun to organize efforts to change state laws which prohibit Deaf people from being called for jury duty. The focus of these efforts is simply to allow Deaf individuals to be included in the jury pool. Since any potential juror can be challenged and not chosen for jury duty, being included in the jury pool does not mean that a person will be selected to serve on a jury. However, at least Deaf people would not be automatically excluded simply because they cannot hear.

During the past few years, a few Deaf individuals have served on juries. These individuals live in states which do not automatically exclude Deaf people from jury duty. In the state of Washington, a Deaf man served on a jury in a criminal case and, reportedly, was the first Deaf juror to serve on a criminal trial in this country. Experiences and precedents such as this one help support and motivate efforts to change state laws which deny Deaf people the right to serve on juries. Apart from the increasing awareness that Deaf people can be effective jurors, there is the recognition that automatically excluding any group from jury duty prevents a fair cross-section of the community from being represented. For further information about legal action being taken to assure that the rights of Deaf people are not violated, contact: The National Center for Law and the Deaf, Gallaudet College, 7th Street and Florida Avenue, N.E., Washington, D.C. 20002.

SIGN LANGUAGE BIBLIOGRAPHY

GLOSSARY

INDEX

445

SIGN LANGUAGE BIBLIOGRAPHY

The following bibliography on Sign Language is an adapted and updated version of the one originally prepared and distributed by Lawrence Fleischer at the 1978 National Symposium on Sign Language Research and Teaching. We thank him for permission to adapt and include this bibliography. We have removed from Dr. Fleischer's original bibliography any entry which we felt the reader could not easily locate (e.g. working papers, unpublished manuscripts). Thus, the reader should be able to locate any of the entries in the following bibliography. Inclusion of an entry does not constitute an endorsement of the contents of that entry.

A. History of Sign Language

Akerly, S. 1824. Observations on the language of signs. *Journal of Science and Arts,8,* No. 2, 348–358.

Cochrane, W. 1871. Methodical signs instead of colloquial. *American Annals of the Deaf,16,* No. 1, 11–17.

DuChamp, M. 1877. The National Institution for the Deaf and Dumb at Paris. *American Annals of the Deaf,22,* No. 1, 1–10.

Fay, G. 1882. The Sign Language: the basis of instruction for deaf-mutes. *American Annals of the Deaf,27,* No. 3, 208–211.

Frishberg, N. 1975. Arbitrariness and iconicity: historical change in American Sign Language. *Language,51,* 696–719.

Gallaudet, E. 1871. Is the Sign Language used to excess in teaching deaf-mutes. *American Annals of the Deaf,16,* No. 1, 26–33.

Gallaudet, E. 1887. The value of the Sign Language to the deaf. *American Annals of the Deaf,32,* No. 3, 141–147.

Jacobs, J. 1859. The relation of written words to signs, the same as their relation to spoken words. *American Annals of the Deaf and Dumb,11,* No. 2, 65–73.

Keep, J. 1871. Natural signs—shall they be abandoned. *American Annals of the Deaf,16,* No. 1, 17–25.

Keep, J. 1871. The Sign-Language. *American Annals of the Deaf,16,* No. 4, 221–234.

Lane, H. 1977. Notes for a psycho-history of American Sign Language. *The Deaf American,30,* No. 1, 3–7.

Markowicz, H. 1972. Some sociolinguistic considerations of American Sign Language. *Sign Language Studies,1,* 15–41.

Peet, H. 1859. Words not 'representatives' of signs, but of ideas. *American Annals of the Deaf,11,* 1–8.

Peet, I. 1861. Initial signs. *American Annals of the Deaf,13,* 171–184.

Siegel, J. 1969. The enlightenment and the evolution of a language of signs in France and England. *Journal of the History of Ideas,30,* 96–115.

Siger, L. 1968. Gestures, the language of sign, and human communication. *American Annals of the Deaf,113,* No. 1, 11–28.

Valentine, E. G. 1872. Shall we abandon the English order? *American Annals of the Deaf,17,* No. 1, 33–47.

Woodward, J. 1976. Signs of change: historical variation in American Sign Language. *Sign Language Studies,10,* 81–94.

Woodward, J. 1978. Historical bases of American Sign Language. In P. Siple (Ed.) *Understanding Language Through Sign Language Research.* New York: Academic Press, 333–348.

Woodward, J. & C. Erting, 1975. Synchronic variation and historical change in American Sign Language. *Language Sciences,37,* 9–12.

B. Educational Aspects of Sign Language

Baker, C. & R. Battison (Eds.) 1980. *Sign Language and the Deaf Community: Essays in Honor of William C. Stokoe.* Silver Spring, Md.: National Association of the Deaf.

Bellugi, U. & E. Klima. 1972. The roots of language in the sign talk of the deaf. *Psychology Today,* June, 61–64;76.

Bergman, E. 1972. Autonomous and unique features of American Sign Language. *American Annals of the Deaf,117,* No. 1, 20–24.

Bonvillian, J. & V. Charrow. 1972. *Psycholinguistic Implications of Deafness: A Review.* Technical Report, 188, Institute for Mathematical Studies in the Social Sciences, Stanford, Calif.

Bonvillian, J., K. Nelson & V. Charrow. 1976. Language & language-related skills in deaf & hearing children. *Sign Language Studies,12,* 211–250.

Caccamise, F., C. Bradley, R. Battison, R. Blasdell, K. Warren & T. Hurwitz. 1977. A project for the standardization and development of technical signs. *American Annals of the Deaf,122,* No. 1, 44–49.

Cicourel, A. & R. Boese. 1972. Sign Language acquisition and the teaching of deaf children. *American Annals of the Deaf,117,* No. 1, 27–33 (part 1); *117,* No. 3, 403–411 (part 2).

Coats, G. 1950. Characteristics of communication methods. *American Annals of the Deaf,95,* No. 5, 489–490.

Cokely, D. 1979. *Pre-College Programs: Guidelines for Manual Communication.* Gallaudet College, Washington, D.C.

Cokely, D. 1980. Sign Language: teaching, interpreting, and educational policy. In C. Baker & R. Battison (Eds.), 137–158.

Cokely, D. & C. Baker. 1980. *American Sign Language: a teacher's resource text on curriculum, methods, and evaluation.* Silver Spring, Md.: T.J. Publishers, Inc.

Cokely, D. & R. Gawlik. 1973. Options: a position paper on the relationship between Manual English and Sign. *The Deaf American,25,* No. 9, May, 7–11.

Cokely, D. & R. Gawlik. 1974. Options II: Childrenese as pidgin. *The Deaf American,26,* No. 8, April, 5–6.

Collins-Ahlgren, M. 1974. Teaching English as a second language to young deaf children: a case study. *Journal of Speech and Hearing Disorders,39,* No. 4, 486–495.

Collins-Ahlgren, M. 1975. Language Development of two deaf children. *American Annals of the Deaf,120,* No. 6, 524–539.

Conrad, R. 1979. *The Deaf Schoolchild.* London: Harper & Row.

Cross, J. 1977. Sign Language and second language teaching. *Sign Language Studies,16,* 269–282.

De L'Epee, A. 1860. The true method of educating the deaf and dumb: confirmed by long experience. *American Annals of the Deaf,12,* No. 2, 61–132.

Ellenberger, R. & M. Steyaert. 1978. A child's representation of action in American Sign Language. In P. Siple (Ed.), 261–270.

Erting, C. 1980. Sign Language and communication between adults and children. In C. Baker & R. Battison (Eds.), 159–176.

Fleischer, L. & M. Cottrell. 1976. Sign Language interpretation under four interpreting conditions. In H. Murphy (Ed.) *Selected Readings in the Integration of Post-Secondary Deaf Students at CSUN: Center on Deafness Publication Series (No. 1)*. Northridge, California: California State University, Northridge.

Furth, H. 1971. Linguistic deficiency and thinking: research with deaf subjects, 1964–69. *Psycholinguistics Bulletin,76,* No. 1, 58–72.

Furth, H. 1973. *Deafness and Learning: A Psychosocial Approach*. Belmont, Calif.: Wadsworth Publishing Co., Inc.

Fusfeld, I. 1953. How the deaf communicate—manual language. *American Annals of the Deaf,103,* No. 2, 264–282.

Gallaudet, T. 1848. On the natural language of signs and its value and uses in the instruction of the deaf and dumb. *American Annals of the Deaf,1,* No. 1, 55–60 (part 1); *1,* No. 2, 79–93 (part 2).

Goldin-Meadow, S. & H. Feldman. 1975. The creation of a communication system: a study of deaf children of hearing parents. *Sign Language Studies,8,* 225–234.

Hester, M. 1963. Manual communication. *Proceedings of the International Congress on Education of the Deaf and of the 41st Meeting of the Convention of American Instructors of the Deaf.* Washington, D.C.: Gallaudet College, 211–321.

Higgins, E. 1973. An analysis of the comprehensibility of three communication methods used with hearing impaired students. *American Annals of the Deaf,118,* No. 1, 46–49.

Hoemann, H. & R. Tweney. 1973. Is the Sign Language of the deaf an adequate communication channel? *Proceedings of the 81st Convention American Psychological Association,11,* 801–802.

Hoffmeister, R., D. Moores & R. Ellenberger. 1975. *The Parameters of Sign Language Defined: Translation and Definition Rules*. Research Report, 83, University of Minnesota, January.

Hoffmeister, R., D. Moores & R. Ellenberger. 1975. Some procedural guidelines for the study of the acquisition of Sign Language. *Sign Language Studies,7,* 121–137.

Howse, J. & J. Fitch. 1972. Effects of parent orientation in Sign Language on communication skills of preschool children. *American Annals of the Deaf,117,* No. 4, 459–462.

Klopping, H. 1972. Language understanding of deaf students under three auditory-visual conditions. *American Annals of the Deaf,117,* No. 3, 389–392.

Kohl, H. 1966. *Language and Education of the Deaf*. New York: Center for Urban Education.

Lane, H. 1976. *The Wild Boy of Aveyron*. Cambridge, Mass.: Harvard University Press.

Markowicz, H. 1973. What language do deaf children acquire? a review article. *Sign Language Studies,3,* 72–78.

Marmor, G. & L. Petitto. 1979. Simultaneous Communication in the classroom: how well is English grammar represented? *Sign Language Studies,23,* 99–136.

Mayberry, R. Manual communication. In H. Davis & R. Silverman (Eds.) *Hearing and Deafness*. 4th edition. New York: Holt, Rinehart & Winston, in press.

Meadow, K. 1968. Early manual communication in relation to the deaf child's intellectual, social, and communicative functioning. *American Annals of the Deaf,113,* No. 1, 29–41.

Mills, C. & I. K. Jordan. 1980. Timing sensitivity and age as predictors of Sign Language learning. *Sign Language Studies,26,* 15–28.

Mindel, E. & M. Vernon. 1971. *They Grow in Silence*. Silver Spring, Md.: The National Association of the Deaf.

Moores, D. 1970. Psycholinguistics and deafness. *American Annals of the Deaf,115,* No. 1, 37–48.

Moores, J. 1980. Early linguistic environment: interactions of deaf parents with their infants. *Sign Language Studies,26,* 1–13.

Murphy, H. & L. Fleischer. 1977. The effects of Ameslan versus Siglish upon test scores. *Journal of Rehabilitation of the Deaf,11,* No. 2, 15–18.

Olson, J. 1972. A case for the use of Sign Language to stimulate language development during the critical period for learning in a congenitally deaf child. *American Annals of the Deaf,117,* No. 3, 397–400.

O'Rourke, T. (Ed.) 1972. *Psycholinguistics and Total Communication: The State of the Art.* Silver Spring, Md.: American Annals of the Deaf.

Ovrid, H. 1971. Studies in manual communication with hearing impaired children. *The Volta Review,73,* No. 7, 428–438.

Penna, J. & F. Caccamise. 1978. Communication instruction with hearing-impaired college students within the Manual/Simultaneous Communication Department, NTID. *American Annals of the Deaf,123,* No. 5, 572–579.

Prinz, P. & E. Prinz. 1979. Simultaneous acquisition of ASL and spoken English (in a hearing child of a deaf mother and hearing father). *Sign Language Studies,25,* 283–296.

Sallop, M. 1973. Language acquisition: pantomime and gesture to Signed English. *Sign Language Studies,3,* 29–38.

Schlesinger, H. & K. Meadow. 1972. Development of maturity in deaf children. *Exceptional Children,* Vol. 38, No. 6, 461–467.

Schlesinger, H. 1972. Language acquisition in four deaf children. *Hearing and Speech News,* December, 4–7, 22–28.

Schlesinger, H. 1972. Meaning and enjoyment: language acquisition of deaf children. In T. O'Rourke (Ed.), 92–102.

Schlesinger, H. & K. Meadow. 1972. *Sound and Sign: Childhood Deafness and Mental Health.* Berkeley, Calif.: University of California Press.

Siple, P. (Ed.) 1978. *Understanding Language Through Sign Language Research.* New York: Academic Press.

Stevens, R. 1976. Children's language should be learned and not taught. *Sign Language Studies 11,* 97–108.

Stevens, R. 1980. Education in schools for deaf children. In C. Baker & R. Battison (Eds.), 177–191.

Stokoe, W. 1972. A classroom experiment in two languages. In T. O'Rourke (Ed.), 85–91.

Stokoe, W. 1975. The use of Sign Language in teaching English. *American Annals of the Deaf,120,* No. 4, 417–421.

Stuckless, E. & J. Birch. 1966. The influence of early manual communication on the linguistic development of deaf children. *American Annals of the Deaf,111,* No. 2, 452–460 (part 1); *111,* No. 3, 499–504 (part 2).

Tervoort, B. 1961. Esoteric symbolism in the communication behavior of young deaf children. *American Annals of the Deaf,106,* No. 5, 436–480.

Tomlinson-Keasey, C. & R. Kelly, 1974. The development of thought processes in deaf children. *American Annals of the Deaf,119,* No. 6, 693–700.

Tomlinsen-Keasey, C. & R. Kelly. 1978. The deaf child's symbolic world. *American Annals of the Deaf,123,* No. 4, 452–459.

Tweney, R., H. Hoemann & C. Andrews. 1975. Semantic organization in deaf and hearing subjects. *Journal of Psycholinguistic Research,4,* No. 1, 61–73.

Vernon, M. & S. Koh. 1970. Early manual communication and deaf children's achievement. *American Annals of the Deaf,115,* No. 5, 527–535.

Vernon, M. & S. Koh. 1971. Effects of oral preschool compared to early manual communication on education and communication in deaf children. *American Annals of the Deaf,115,* No. 6, 569–574.

Williams, J. 1976. Bilingual experiences of a deaf child. *Sign Language Studies,10,* 37–41.

Woodward, J. 1973. Linguistics and language teaching. *Teaching English to the Deaf,1,* 2.

C. Attitudes Toward Sign Language

Anderson, T. 1938. What of the Sign Language? *American Annals of the Deaf,83,* No. 2, 120–130.

Baker, C. & R. Battison (Eds.) 1980. *Sign Language and the Deaf Community: Essays in Honor of William C. Stokoe.* Silver Spring, Md.: National Association of the Deaf.

Bellugi, U. 1975. Interview for the Deaf American. *The Deaf American,27,* No. 9, 12–14.

Bellugi, U. 1976. Attitudes toward Sign Language. In A. Crammatte & F. Crammatte (Eds.) *Proceedings of the Seventh World Congress of the World Federation of the Deaf.* Silver Spring, Md.: National Association of the Deaf.

Bragg, B. 1973. Ameslish: our national heritage. *American Annals of the Deaf,118,* No. 6, 672–674.

Eastman, G. 1974. *Sign Me Alice.* Washington, D.C.: Gallaudet College.

Erting, C. 1978. Language policy & deaf ethnicity in the United States. *Sign Language Studies,19,* 139–152.

Greenberg, J. 1970. *In This Sign.* New York: Holt, Rinehart & Winston.

Gustason, G. 1973. The language of communication. *Journal of Rehabilitation of the Deaf,* Annual Volume III, 83–93.

James, W. 1892. Thought before language: a deaf-mute's recollections. *Philosophical Review,1,* 613–624.

Kannapell, B. 1974. Bilingualism: a new direction in the education of the deaf. *The Deaf American,26,* No. 10, 9–15.

Kannapell, B. 1980. Personal awareness and advocacy in the Deaf Community. In C. Baker & R. Battison (Eds.) *Sign Language and the Deaf Community: Essays in Honor of William C. Stokoe.* Silver Spring, Md.: National Association of the Deaf, 105–116.

Markowicz, H. 1977. *American Sign Language: Fact and Fancy.* Washington, D.C.: Gallaudet College.

Meadow, K. 1972. Sociolinguistics, Sign Language and the deaf sub-culture. In T. O'Rourke (Ed.) *Psycholinguistics and Total Communication: The State of the Art.* Silver Spring, Md.: American Annals of the Deaf, 19–33.

Meadow, K. 1977. Name signs as identity symbols in the Deaf Community. *Sign Language Studies,17,* 237–246.

Moores, D. 1972. Communication—some unanswered questions and some unquestioned answers. In T. O'Rourke (Ed.), 1–10.

Newman, L. 1972. Cherry blossoms come to bloom. *The Deaf American,24,* No. 11, 25–27.

Padden, C. 1980. The Deaf Community and the culture of deaf people. In C. Baker & R. Battison (Eds.), 89–103.

Padden, C. & H. Markowicz. 1976. Cultural conflicts between hearing and deaf communities. In A. Crammatte & F. Crammatte (Eds.) *Proceedings of the Seventh World Congress of the World Federation of the Deaf.* Silver Spring, Md.: National Association of the Deaf.

Schein, J. 1973. Sign Language: coming of age. *Sign Language Studies,3,* 113–115.

Schowe, B. 1975. What is the true Sign Language? *The Deaf American,28,* No. 1, 3–4.

Stevens, R. 1976. Children's language should be learned and not taught. *Sign Language Studies,11,* 97–108.

Stokoe, W. 1969–1970. Sign Language diglossia. *Studies in Linguistics,21,* 27–41.

Stokoe, W. & R. Battison. Sign Language, mental health, and satisfying interaction. In E. Mindel & L. Stein (Eds.) *Proceedings of the First National Symposium on Mental Health Needs of Deaf Adults and Youth.* New York: Grune, Grune & Stratton, in press.

Trybus, R. 1980. Sign Language, power, and mental health. In C. Baker & R. Battison (Eds.), 201–217.

Vernon, M. & B. Makowsky. 1969. Deafness and minority group dynamics. *The Deaf American,21,* No. 11, 3–6.

Woodward, J. 1972. Implications for sociolinguistic research among the deaf. *Sign Language Studies,1,* 107.

Woodward, J. 1973. Language continuum, a different point of view. *Sign Language Studies,2,* 81–83.

Woodward, J. 1973. Deaf awareness. *Sign Language Studies,3,* 57–60.

Woodward, J. 1973. Some observations on sociolinguistic variation and American Sign Language. *Kansas Journal of Sociology,9,* No. 2, 191–200.

D. Sign Language Research

Abbott, C. 1975. Encodedness and Sign Language. *Sign Language Studies,7,* 109–120.

Baker, C. 1976. Eye-openers in ASL. *Sixth California Linguistics Association Conference: Proceedings,* 1–13.

Baker, C. 1976. What's not on the other hand in American Sign Language. In S. Hufwene, C. Walker & S. Streeven (Eds.) *Papers from the 12th Regional Meeting of the Chicago Linguistic Society.* Chicago, Illinois.

Baker, C. 1977. Regulators and turn-taking in American Sign Language discourse. In L. Friedman (Ed.) *On the Other Hand: New Perspectives on American Sign Language.* New York: Academic Press, 215–236.

Baker, C. 1980. Sentences in American Sign Language. In C. Baker & R. Battison (Eds.) *Sign Language and the Deaf Community: Essays in Honor of William C. Stokoe.* Silver Spring, Md.: National Association of the Deaf, 75–86.

Baker, C. & R. Battison (Eds.) 1980. *Sign Language and the Deaf Community: Essays in Honor of William C. Stokoe.* Silver Spring, Md.: National Association of the Deaf.

Baker, C. & C. Padden. 1978. *American Sign Language: A look at its history, structure, and community.* Silver Spring, Md.: T.J. Publishers, Inc.

Baker, C. & C. Padden. 1978. Focusing on the nonmanual components of American Sign Language. In P. Siple (Ed.) *Understanding Language Through Sign Language Research.* New York: Academic Press, 59–90.

Battison, R. 1974. Phonological deletion in American Sign Language. *Sign Language Studies,5,* 1–19.

Battison, R. 1978. *Lexical borrowing in American Sign Language.* Silver Spring, Md.: Linstok Press.

Battison, R. 1980. Signs have parts: a simple idea. In C. Baker & R. Battison (Eds.), 35–51.

Battison, R., H. Markowicz & J. Woodward. 1976. A good rule of thumb: variable phonology in American Sign Language. In R. Shuy & R. Fasold (Eds.) *New Ways of Analyzing Variation in English,2,* Washington, D.C.: Georgetown University Press.

Bellugi, U. 1972. Studies in Sign Language. In T. O'Rourke (Ed.) *Psycholinguistics and Total Communication: The State of the Art.* Silver Spring, Md.: American Annals of the Deaf, 68–83.

Bellugi, U. 1980. How signs express complex meanings. In C. Baker & R. Battison (Eds.), 53–74.

Bellugi, U. & S. Fischer. 1972. A comparison of Sign Language and spoken language: rate and grammatical mechanisms. *Cognition: International Journal of Cognitive Psychology,1,* 173–200.

Bellugi, U. & E. Klima. 1975. Aspects of Sign Language and its structure. In J. F. Kavanagh and J. E. Cutting (Eds.) *The Role of Speech in Language*. Cambridge: M.I.T. Press, 171–203.

Bellugi, U. & E. Klima. 1975. Remembering in signs. *Cognition: International Journal of Cognitive Psychology,3,* No. 2, 93–125.

Bellugi, U. & E. Klima. 1975. Two faces of Sign: iconic and abstract. In S. Harnad (Ed.) *Origins and Evolution of Language and Speech*. New York: New York Academy of Sciences.

Bellugi, U. & P. Siple. 1974. Remembering with and without words. In F. Bresson (Ed.) *Current Problems in Psycholinguistics*. Paris: Centre National de la Recherche Scientifique, 215–236.

Cicourel, A. 1974. Gestural Sign Language and the study of nonverbal communication. *Sign Language Studies,4,* 35–76.

Cicourel, A. 1978. Sociolinguistic aspects of the use of Sign Language. In I. M. Schlesinger & L. Namir (Eds.) *Sign Language of the Deaf: Psychological, Linguistic, and Sociological Perspectives*. New York: Academic Press, 271–313.

Cogen, C. 1977. On three aspects of time expression in American Sign Language. In L. Friedman (Ed.) *On the Other Hand: New Perspectives on American Sign Language*. New York: Academic Press, 197–214.

Covington, V. 1973. Juncture in American Sign Language. *Sign Language Studies,2,* 29–38.

Covington, V. 1973. Features of stress in American Sign Language. *Sign Language Studies,2,* 39–50.

De Matteo, A. 1977. Visual imagery and visual analogues in American Sign Language. In L. Friedman (Ed.), 109–136.

Edge, V. & L. Hermann. 1977. Verbs and the determination of subject in American Sign Language. In L. Friedman (Ed.), 137–179.

Ellenberger, R., D. Moores & R. Hoffmeister. 1975. *Early Stages in the Acquisition of negation by a Deaf Child of Deaf Parents*. Research Report, 94, University of Minnesota, August.

Fischer, S. 1973. Two processes of reduplication in the American Sign Language. *Foundations of Language,9,* 469–480.

Fischer, S. 1974. Sign Language and linguistic universals. In T. Rohrer & N. Ruwet (Eds.) *Actes de Colloque Franco-Allemand de Grammarie Transformationelle, Band II: Etudes de Semantique et Autres*. Tubingen: Max Neimeyer Verland, 187–204.

Fischer, S. 1975. Influences on word order change in American Sign Language. In C. N. Li (Ed.) *Word Order and Word Order Change*. Austin, Texas: University Press.

Fischer, S. 1975. The ontogenetic development of language. In E. Strauss (Ed.) *Language and Language Disturbances: Fifth Lexington Conference on Phenomenology*. Pittsburgh, Penn.: Duquesne University Press, 22–43.

Fischer, S. 1978. Sign Language and creoles. In P. Siple (Ed.), 309–332.

Fischer, S. & B. Gough. 1978. Verbs in American Sign Language. *Sign Language Studies,18,* 17–48.

Friedman, L. 1975. Space, time, and person reference in American Sign Language. *Language,51,* 940–961.

Friedman, L. 1975. Phonological processes in the American Sign Language. *Proceedings of the First Annual Meeting of the Berkeley Linguistics Society,* University of California, Berkeley, 147–154.

Friedman, L. 1976. The manifestation of subject, object, and topic in ASL. In C. N. Li (Ed.) *Subject and Topic*. New York: Academic Press.

Friedman, L. 1977. Formational Properties of American Sign Language. In L. Friedman (Ed.), 13–56.

Grosjean, F. 1979. The production of Sign Language: psycholinguistic perspectives. *Sign Language Studies,25,* 317–329.

Hoemann, H. 1978. Categorical coding of Sign and English in short-term memory by deaf and hearing subjects. In P. Siple (Ed.), 289–305.

Hoemann, H. & R. Tweney. 1973. Back Translation: a method for the analysis of manual languages. *Sign Language Studies,2,* 51–80.

Hoemann, H. 1975. The transparency of meaning of Sign Language gestures. *Sign Language Studies,7,* 151–161.

Hoemann, H. & V. Florian. 1976. Order constraints in American Sign Language. *Sign Language Studies,11,* 121–132.

Hoffmeister, R. & D. Moores. 1974. *The Acquisition of Specific Reference in the Linguistic System of a Deaf Child of Deaf Parents.* Research Report, 65, University of Minnesota, June.

Hoffmeister, R., B. Best & D. Moores. 1974. *The Acquisition of Sign Language in Deaf Children of Deaf Parents: Progress Report.* Research Report, 65, University of Minnesota, June.

Julesz, B. & I. Hirsch. 1972. Visual and Auditory perception: an essay of comparison. In E. E. David & P. B. Denes (Eds.) *Human Communication: A Unified View.* New York: McGraw-Hill, 283–340.

Kegl, J. & H. Chinchor. 1975. A frame analysis of American Sign Language. In T. Diller (Ed.) *Proceedings of the 13th Annual Meeting, Association for Computational Linguistics.* St. Paul, Minn.: Sperry-Univac.

Kegl, J. & R. Wilbur. 1976. When does structure stop and style begin? Syntax, morphology, and phonology vs. stylistic variation in American Sign Language. In S. Hufwene, C. Walker & S. Streeven (Eds.) *Papers from the 12th Regional Meeting of the Chicago Linguistics Society.* Chicago, Illinois.

Klima, E. 1975. Sound and its absence in the linguistic symbol. In J. Kavanagh & J. Cutting (Eds.) *The Role of Speech in Language.* Cambridge, Mass.: M.I.T. Press, 249–270.

Klima, E. & U. Bellugi. 1974. Language in another mode. In E. Lenneberg (Ed.) *Language and the Brain, Developmental Aspects. Neurosciences Research Program Bulletin,12,* 539–550.

Klima, E. & U. Bellugi. 1975. Wit and poetry in American Sign Language. *Sign Language Studies,8,* 203–224.

Klima, E. & U. Bellugi. 1975. Perception and production in visually based language. In D. Aaronson & R. W. Rieber (Eds.) *Developmental Psycholinguistics and Communication Disorders.* New York: New York Academy of Sciences, 225–235.

Klima, E. & U. Bellugi. 1976. Poetry and song in a language without sound. *Cognition: International Journal of Cognitive Psychology,4,* 45–97.

Klima, E. & U. Bellugi. 1979. *The Signs of Language.* Cambridge, Mass.: Harvard University Press.

Lane, H., P. Boyes-Braem & U. Bellugi. 1976. Preliminaries to distinctive features analysis of handshapes in American Sign Language. *Cognitive Psychology,8,* 263–289.

Liddell, S. 1978. Nonmanual signals and relative clauses in American Sign Language. In P. Siple (Ed.), 59–90.

Mandel, M. 1976. Dimensions of iconicity in American Sign Language. *Proceedings of the Second Annual Meeting of the Berkeley Linguistics Society,* Berkeley, California.

Mandel, M. 1979. Natural constraints in Sign Language phonology: data from anatomy. *Sign Language Studies,23,* 99–136.

Marmor, G. & L. Petitto. 1979. Simultaneous Communication in the classroom: how well is English grammar represented? *Sign Language Studies,23,* 99–136.

Mayberry, R. 1978. French Canadian Sign Language: a study of inter-Sign Language comprehension. In P. Siple (Ed.), 349–372.

McKeever, W., H. Hoemann, V. Florian & A. Van Deventer. Evidence of minimal cerebral asymmetries for the processing of English words and American Sign Language in the congenitally deaf. *Neuropsychologics,* in press.

Newport, E. & U. Bellugi. Linguistic expression of category levels in a visual-gestural language. In E. Rosch (Ed.) *Cognition and Categorization.* Hillsdale, N.J.: Lawrence Erlbaum Associate, in press.

Poisner, H. & H. Lane. 1978. Discrimination of location in American Sign Language. In P. Siple (Ed.), 271–288.

Robinson, J. & P. Griffith. 1979. On the scientific status of iconicity. *Sign Language Studies,25,* 297–315.

Siple, P. (Ed.), 1978. *Understanding Language Through Sign Language Research.* New York: Academic Press.

Siple, P. 1978. Visual constraints for Sign Language communication. *Sign Language Studies,19,* 95–110.

Stokoe, W. 1966. Linguistic description of Sign Language. In F. P. Dinneen (Ed.) *Monograph Series on Language and Linguistics.* Georgetown University, Washington, D.C., 243–250.

Stokoe, W. 1971. *The Study of Sign Language.* Silver Spring, Md.: The National Association of the Deaf.

Stokoe, W. 1972. Classification and description of Sign Language. In T. Sebeok (Ed.) *Current Trends in Linguistics,12,* The Hague, Netherlands: Mouton.

Stokoe, W. 1972. *Semiotics and Human Sign Languages.* The Hague, Netherlands: Mouton.

Stokoe, W. 1976. The study and use of Sign Language. *Sign Language Studies,10,* 1–36.

Stokoe, W. 1978. Sign Language versus spoken language. *Sign Language Studies,18,* 69–90.

Stokoe, W. 1978. *Sign Language Structure.* (Revised edition of 1960 monograph). Silver Spring, Md.: Linstok Press.

Stokoe, W. 1980. *Sign and Culture: A Reader for Students of ASL.* Silver Spring, Md.: Linstok Press.

Stokoe, W., H. Bernard & C. Padden. 1976. An elite group in deaf society. *Sign Language Studies,12,* 189–210.

Stokoe, W. & R. Kushchel. 1979. *A Field Guide for Sign Language Research.* Silver Spring, Md.: Linstok Press.

Supalla, T. & E. Newport. 1978. How many seats in a chair? The derivation of nouns and verbs in American Sign Language. In P. Siple (Ed.), 91–132.

Tweney, R., G. Heiman & H. Hoemann. Psychological processing of Sign Language: The effects of visual disruption on sign intelligibility. *Journal of Experimental Psychology,* in press.

Wilbur, R. 1979. *American Sign Language and Sign Systems.* Baltimore, Md.: University Park Press.

Woodward, J. 1973. Some characteristics of Pidgin Sign English. *Sign Language Studies,3,* 39–46.

Woodward, J. 1973. Inter-rule implication in American Sign Language. *Sign Language Studies,3,* 47–56.

Woodward, J. 1974. Implicational variation in ASL: negative incorporation. *Sign Language Studies,5,* 20–30.

Woodward, J. 1980. Sociolinguistic research on American Sign Language: An historical perspective. In C. Baker & R. Battison (Eds.), 117–134.

Woodward, J. 1977. Sex is definitely a problem: interpreters' knowledge of signs for sexual behavior. *Sign Language Studies,14,* 73–88.

Woodward, J. & S. De Santis. 1977. Two to one it happens: dynamic phonology in two sign languages. *Sign Language Studies,17,* 329–346.

Woodward, J., C. Erting & S. Oliver. 1976. Facing and hand(l)ing variation in American Sign Language phonology. *Sign Language Studies,10,* 43–51.

GLOSSARY

ACTIVE HAND—The hand that moves when making a sign (as opposed to the *passive* hand). For example, with a right-handed Signer, the right hand is *active* when making the sign **MONEY**. However, both hands are *active* in the sign **EXCITED.**

ADDRESSEE—The person that the Signer is communicating with and who is at the moment watching, not signing.

AFFIX—In spoken languages, a letter, syllable, or syllables that is placed before (prefix), after (suffix) or within (infix) a word with the result that the meaning of the new unit (word + affix) is different than the meaning of the base word.

AGREEMENT—In relation to grammar, the correspondence or accord of a word or sign with another word(s) or sign(s) as to the grammatical categories of *number, person, case,* or *gender*. For example, in the English phrase 'two cups', the '-s' on the noun 'cups' is in agreement with the adjective 'two'. In this example, the correspondence concerns the grammatical category of *number*.

AMERICAN SIGN LANGUAGE (ASL)—A visual-gestural language that is indigenous to the American Deaf Community and that is often acquired as a first language by deaf children who have Deaf parents.

ARBITRARY—A type of relationship between a symbol and its referent in which the symbol does not resemble the thing it stands for. For example, the English symbol 'house' does not resemble the thing it stands for, so that symbol is *arbitrary*.

ASPECT—Referring to verbs, a category which indicates whether the action or state denoted by the verb is viewed as completed or in progress, momentary or habitual, extending to all members of a group or to specific individuals, etc. In spoken languages, this information is often conveyed with affixes on the verb, or phonetic changes in the root of the verb, or by using auxiliary verbs, etc. In ASL, this information is conveyed by varying the size, shape, rate, rhythm, etc., of the verb as well as the number of times its movement is repeated.

ASSIMILATION—In spoken languages, a phonetic process by which two phonemes which are near each other in a word or a phrase will change to become more alike or identical. In signed languages, a process by which one or more primes in a sign will change to become more alike or identical to primes in another sign that occurs before or after that sign.

ATTITUDINAL DEAFNESS—Refers to the values and behaviors of individuals who identify themselves with the Deaf Community and are accepted by other members of that Community. Generally, this implies that a person has a positive, accepting attitude toward the Deaf Community as a cultural group with its own language and values.

AUDIOLOGICAL (AUDIOMETRIC) DEAFNESS—Refers to the physical condition of having a hearing loss.

BILINGUAL COMMUNITY—A community in which two languages are used. Generally one language is preferred for interactions within the community and the other is used for interactions with people who are not members of the community. Members of the community may have different levels of skill in the two languages.

BODY-ANCHORED SIGN—A sign that contacts the body as it is being made (e.g. **FEEL, GIRL**).

BODY SHIFT—In this text, a movement of the Signer's torso, generally to the right or to the left, to represent one or more characters in a narrative. Usually the direction of the Signer's eye gaze and the Signer's facial expression will also change with the *body shift*.

BORROWING—A process in which a word or a sign from one language is incorporated into the vocabulary of another language. Generally the pronunciation or production of the word or sign is changed somewhat to fit the rules of the language doing the borrowing. This term is also used to refer to the word or sign which has been borrowed.

CENTRALIZATION—A pattern of historical change (also called *Displacement*) in which the location of a sign changes and moves closer to the center of the signing space (see Figure 4.1).

CITATION FORM—The form of a word or sign when it is produced in isolation or in response to the question "How do you say ___?" or "What is the sign for ___?".

CLASSIFIER—A prefix, word, or sign that is used in some languages to indicate certain semantic or grammatical categories.

CODE—A system of signals (written, spoken, gestural, electronic, etc.) which are arbitrarily used to represent the words, phrases, or sentences of a language.

COGNATES—Words or signs from different languages which have the same root, i.e. which are historically related.

COMPOUND—A single word or sign which is made from two or more words or signs. This single word/sign usually has a meaning which is different from the meaning of the two words/signs when they occur as a phrase. For example, the ASL compound EAT NOON means 'lunch'; the English compound *butterball* means 'a chubby person'.

CONTEXT—In this text, a brief description of the situation immediately preceding the utterance of the ASL example. In general, the personal and environmental factors present during a particular event (e.g. the participants, the place, the time of day, the purpose of the event) which influence the linguistic and non-linguistic behaviors of the participants in that event. Also, *context* can refer to the words or signs in a sentence which surround other words or signs and, thus, help to give them their particular meaning in that sentence.

CONTRACTION—A shortened form of a word or sign or word/sign group. For example, 'don't' (from 'do not') in English; WHY NOT and NOT HERE in ASL. The meaning of the contraction is the same as the meaning of the unshortened form, but the contraction is stylistically more colloquial.

CONVERSATION REGULATORS—A set of linguistic and non-linguistic behaviors which differ from culture to culture and which members of a culture use in conversations to help them take turns effectively, to provide feedback to the speaker/signer, and to "hold the floor", etc.

CONVERSATIONAL CHANGES—Changes which occur in the production of a word or a sign in the context of a conversation. These changes result in producing words or signs which are different than their citation form.

CULTURE—The beliefs, values, patterns of behavior, language, expectations, and achievements of a group of people which are passed on from generation to generation.

DEAF COMMUNITY—A cultural group comprised of persons who share similar attitudes toward deafness. The "core Deaf Community" is comprised of those individuals who have a hearing loss and who share a common language, values, and experiences and a common way of interacting with each other, with non-core members of the Deaf Community, and with the Hearing Community. The wider Deaf Community is comprised of individuals (both deaf and hearing) who have positive, accepting attitudes toward deafness which can be seen in their linguistic, social, and political behaviors.

DIRECT ADDRESS—In ASL, the use of body shifting, eye gaze direction, and facial behaviors to indicate that the Signer is directly quoting someone and what it is that s/he said or signed.

DIRECT OBJECT—The person or thing directly affected by the action expressed in a sentence.

DIRECTIONAL VERB—A verb that indicates its subject and/or object via its direction of movement and/or its palm orientation and location. For example, the directional verb ___-HELP-___ moves from the subject toward the object (e.g. from the Addressee toward the Signer to express the meaning 'you help me').

DISPLACEMENT—A pattern of historical change in which the location of a sign changes. Generally, the new location is closer to center of the signing space. (See *Centralization*)

DOMINANCE CONDITION—In ASL, a general rule concerning signs made with both hands. The rule states that if the two hands have different handshapes, then the dominant hand will do the movement and the other hand usually will not move (e.g. **ENOUGH, WORD, AMONG**). Another part of this rule says that the passive hand will usually have an unmarked handshape.

DOMINANT HAND—In a right-handed Signer, the right hand is the *dominant hand*. When only one hand is "active" when making a sign, that hand will usually be the *dominant hand*.

FINGERSPELLED LOAN SIGNS—Fingerspelled words from a spoken language which have undergone certain changes in the way they are formed and which have been borrowed into the signed language of a Deaf community.

FINGERSPELLING—A way of manually representing words and sentences from a spoken language (that has a written form) by using a separate handshape for each letter of the alphabet in that spoken language (e.g. **P-A-T, B-O-O-K**). Fingerspelling has also been called *dactylology*.

FLUIDITY—A pattern of historical change in which the parts of a compound sign become more like each other and the transition between them becomes more "smooth" or "fluid".

GESTURE—A movement of the body which occurs for the purpose of communication. Some *gestures* are universally understood; however, many *gestures* are culture-specific.

GLOSS—An English word or words used to represent a particular ASL sign. This "name" for the sign attempts to show the most common meaning of that sign.

GRAMMATICAL—Referring to the structure, rules, and principles of a language.

ICONIC—A type of relationship between a symbol and its referent in which the symbol resembles the thing it stands for. For example, the English symbol 'bow-wow' resembles the sound it stands for, so that symbol is *iconic*. The ASL symbol **HOUSE** resembles the thing it stands for, so that symbol is also *iconic*.

IDIOM—A set phrase consisting of two or more words or signs; the meaning of the phrase cannot be determined or understood just by knowing the meaning of the individual words or signs in the phrase.

INDEX—A pointing to someone, something, or a particular location with the index finger.

INDIRECT OBJECT—The person or thing *to, toward,* or *for* whom the action expressed in a sentence takes place. For example, in the sentences 'I gave the cup *to* Pat' and 'I wrote the book *for* Pat', 'Pat' is the *indirect object*.

INFLECTION—A modulation of a sign that changes or adds to the meaning of that sign. In ASL, inflections usually involve changes in the movement of a sign and can indicate such things as the subject and object of the verb and the frequency or duration of an event.

INITIALIZATION—A process in which a particular handshape from the manual alphabet is used in a sign because that handshape corresponds to a letter (usually the first letter) in a word from a spoken language which may have a similar meaning. For example, the ASL sign **SEARCH** has a 'C' handshape which comes from the *initialized* French sign **CHERCHER**. Manual codes for English often change the handshape of ASL signs so that they become *initialized* signs which correspond to English words (e.g. <u>C</u>AR, <u>B</u>US, <u>T</u>RUCK, <u>W</u>AGON).

LANGUAGE—A system of relatively arbitrary symbols and grammatical signals that change across time and that members of a community share and use for several purposes: to interact with each other, to communicate their ideas, emotions, and intentions and to transmit their culture from generation to generation.

LES SIGNES METHODIQUES—The set of signs invented by Abbé Charles-Michel de l'Epée to represent certain grammatical signals of spoken French and intended to supplement the signs in French Sign Language.

LINGUISTICS—The scientific study of language: its elements and structure, how people use it, and the way it changes. For example, linguists study the grammatical rules found in different languages, how children acquire those languages, how people use a language differently in different contexts, and how elements of a language change across time.

LINGUISTICS OF VISUAL ENGLISH (L.O.V.E.)—A manual code for English originated by Dennis Wampler which tries to achieve a one-to-one correspondence between English, syllables, and affixes and a single sign for each word, syllable, or affix. For example, the English word 'behind' is signed as **BE + HIND**. The word 'today' is signed as **TO + DAY**.

MANUALLY CODED ENGLISH (MCE)—A general term which refers to any of the artificially developed manual codes for representing English.

MARKED—Refers to language units that occur infrequently. These units are also learned later by children. For example,

the 'E' handshape and 'waist' location are *marked* in signed languages since they occur infrequently in signs.

MODULATION—A general term that refers to a change in the form of a sign that changes or adds to the meaning of that sign.

NATIVE SIGNER—In reference to ASL, a deaf or hearing person who has one or two Deaf parents (usually two) that used ASL with that person from infancy. Thus, the person grew up acquiring ASL as his/her first language in the same way that a hearing child acquires English from hearing parents. In some cases, the child may grow up with two "first" languages—ASL and English—if the parents or other caretakers interacted with the child in both languages.

NEGATIVE INCORPORATION—In ASL, the use of an outward, twisting movement with a small group of verbs to indicate negation (e.g. **NOT-KNOW, NOT-WANT**).

NEUTRAL SPACE—The area in front of the Signer's upper chest, neck, and lower face where the greatest number of signs are made (in comparison with other locations).

NON-DOMINANT HAND—In a right-handed Signer, the left hand is the *non-dominant hand*. (The right hand would be the "dominant hand".)

NON-MANUAL—Refers to behaviors that do not involve the hands, such as eye and head movements, facial expressions, and body posture.

NUMBER INCORPORATION—In ASL, the use of a number handshape in a sign to indicate, for example, a specific quantity of time (e.g. **TWO-DAY, THREE-HOUR**).

PARAMETER—A part of a sign. Signs have been described as having three parts or *parameters*: a handshape, location, and movement. Some researchers also include palm orientation as a fourth parameter.

PASSIVE HAND—The hand that does not move when making a sign (as opposed to the *active hand*). For example, with a right-handed Signer, the left hand is *passive* when making the sign **MONEY**. The *passive hand* is also sometimes called the *base hand*.

PIDGIN—A language variety which develops naturally between two or more groups of people who do not share a common language but wish to communicate with each other. In general, the *pidgin* is a combination of certain words or signs and certain grammatical structures from the native languages of the different groups. Often, one language supplies most of the vocabulary while the other supplies most of the grammatical structures.

PIDGIN SIGN ENGLISH (PSE)—Varieties of signing used by deaf and hearing people which combine certain elements of both ASL and English. The varieties of PSE found in deaf people's signing often include more of the features of ASL, whereas the varieties of PSE found in hearing people's signing often include more English-like structures.

PLURAL—More than one.

PLURALITY—The state of being plural.

PREDICATE—The word/sign or group of words/signs which states or negates something about the subject of the sentence.

PREDICATE ADJECTIVE—An adjective or adjective phrase which modifies a noun and which functions as the predicate of the sentence.

PRIME—The smallest unit that does not have meaning in a signed language but which indicates or signals a change in the meaning of a larger language unit. For example, the handshapes '1' and 'X' are primes in ASL. If a Signer keeps the same location, movement, and palm orientation as found in the sign **CHINA**, but changes the handshape prime from '1' to 'X', the meaning is changed (creating the sign ONION). The term *prime* is like the term *phoneme* in the study of spoken languages.

PRONOMINAL REFERENCE—The act of re-

ferring to someone or something by using a pronoun.

PRONOUN—A word or sign used to replace a noun, or to refer to the person, thing, idea, etc., designated by a noun.

REFERENCE—The act of referring to or mentioning someone or something.

REFERENT—The person, place, thing, idea, or event that a symbol (e.g. a word or sign) is used to represent. For example, the sign **PENCIL** refers to a wooden writing instrument; that wooden thing is the *referent* of the sign **PENCIL**.

ROCHESTER METHOD—Also called *Visible English*; a means of communication in which English words are fingerspelled and spoken at the same time. In general, proponents of this method discourage or prohibit the use of signs. This method is used in a small number of schools and programs for deaf students.

SEEING ESSENTIAL ENGLISH (SEE I)—A manual code for English originated by David Anthony which tries to achieve a one-to-one correspondence between English words, syllables, and affixes and a single sign for each word, syllable, or affix. For example, the English word 'secretary' is signed as **SECRET + ER + Y**. The word 'appendectomy' is signed as **AP +PEN +DEC +TOM +Y**.

SEMANTIC—Relating to the meaning of something.

SIGNED ENGLISH—A manual code for English developed under the direction of Harry Bornstein which is intended to be used with young deaf students; in general, a "one sign for one word" approach is used and the number of signed English affixes is limited.

SIGNER—The person who is using Sign Language.

SIGNING EXACT ENGLISH (SEE II)—A manual code for English originated by Gustason, Pfetzing, and Zawalkow which tries to achieve a one-to-one correspondence between English words or syllables and a single sign for each word or syllable. For example, the English word for 'beautifully' is signed as **BEAUTY +FUL +LY**.

STRESS—Special emphasis on a sound (or group of sounds) or on a sign.

STRUCTURAL EQUIVALENT—In this text, an English sentence or sentences which attempts to show the grammatical structure and amount of information contained in an ASL example.

SYMBOL—Something that stands for or represents something else. Words and signs are *symbols*.

SYMMETRY—A pattern of historical change in which signs made below the neck tend, through time, to become two-handed signs with the same handshape for both hands.

SYMMETRY CONDITION—In ASL, a general rule concerning signs made with both hands. The rule states that if both hands move, they will usually have the same handshape, location, and type of movement (e.g. EXCITED, MAYBE, PLAY).

SYNTACTIC RULES—Rules that concern how phrases or sentences are formed. (Also *grammatical rules*)

TENSE—A grammatical category which concerns the time of an action.

TIME LINE—In ASL and at least several other signed languages, an imaginary line that runs through the Signer's body and out into the areas in front of and in back of the body. Locations on this imaginary line correspond to past, present, and future time.

TRANSCRIPTION—A written copy or a written representation of a spoken or signed language. *Transcriptions* (transcripts) can be prepared using the written form of the language (if it has one) or by using a set of transcription symbols.

TRANSCRIPTION SYMBOLS—In this text, a set of conventions for writing down signs and sentences from ASL. A complete explanation of these *transcription symbols* can be found on pages 1–29.

TRANSLATION—In this text, one of several possible ways that native speakers of English might express the meaning and intent conveyed by the ASL example.

UNMARKED—Refers to language units that occur frequently or commonly. These units are also learned earlier by children. For example, the '5' handshape and 'chest' location are *unmarked* in signed languages since they occur frequently in signs.

VARIATION—Refers to differences in the pronunciation/production, vocabulary, and grammar of the people who use a particular language. *Variation* is often due to such factors as age, sex, racial or ethnic background, geographic area, education, context, etc.

Index